JOSSEY-BASS™
A Wiley Brand

Do Good Well

Your Guide to Leadership, Action, and Social Innovation

Nina Vasan and Jennifer Przybylo

WILEY

Published by Jossey-Bass
A Wiley Imprint
One Montgomery Street, Suite 1200, San Francisco, CA 94104-4594—www.josseybass.com

Jossey-Bass books and products are available through most bookstores. To contact Jossey-Bass directly call our Customer Care Department within the U.S. at 800-956-7739, outside the U.S. at 317-572-3986, or fax 317-572-4002.

Wiley publishes in a variety of print and electronic formats and by print-on-demand. Some material included with standard print versions of this book may not be included in e-books or in print-on-demand. If this book refers to media such as a CD or DVD that is not included in the version you purchased, you may download this material at http://booksupport.wiley.com. For more information about Wiley products, visit www.wiley.com.

Cover design: Michael Cook
Illustrations: Richard Sheppard/Richard Sheppard Illustration (www.artstudios.com)
Interior design: Paula Goldstein/Blue Bungalow Design (www.bluebungalowdesign.com)

Library of Congress Cataloging-in-Publication Data
Vasan, Nina, 1984–
Do good well : your guide to leadership, action, and social innovation / Nina Vasan and Jennifer Przybylo.
pages cm — (The Jossey-Bass higher and adult education series)
Includes bibliographical references and index.
ISBN 978-1-118-38294-3 (pbk.); 978-1-118-41738-6 (ebk); 978-1-118-42071-3 (ebk); 978-1-118-43422-2 (ebk)
1. Social movements. 2. Social action. I. Przybylo, Jennifer, 1984–II. Title.
HM881.V37 2013
303.48′4—dc23

2012049087

Printed in the United States of America

FIRST EDITION

PB Printing 10 9 8 7 6 5 4 3 2 1

Contents

Preface: The Spirit of Community *vii*
Thank-Yous *xiii*
About the Authors *xv*

Introduction **1**

PART 1 The Vision 11

1 **Know Yourself** 13
2 **Know Your World** 28
3 **Identify a Problem** 46
4 **Understand the Problem** 57
5 **Brainstorm Solutions** 67

PART 2 The Method 81

Step 1: DO WHAT WORKS **83**

6 **Design a Systemic Solution** 85
7 **Build on What Works** 94
8 **Measure, Evaluate, Improve, Repeat** 101
9 **Challenge What Works, Innovate, Keep What Works** 110

Step 2: WORK TOGETHER **119**

10 **Balance Strengthening and Starting** 121
11 **Cultivate Community Ownership** 128
12 **Foster Team Unity** 135
13 **Forge Partnerships** 140

Step 3: MAKE IT LAST 147

14 Start Small, Then Scale What Works 149
15 Engineer Self-Sustainable Solutions 156
16 Integrate Social Entrepreneurship 165
17 Share What Works 173

18 The Method in Action 179

PART 3 The Tools 197

Step 1: DO WHAT WORKS: Proven Strategies to Increase Your Impact 199

19 What Works in Choosing a Name 200
20 What Works in Writing a Mission Statement 208
21 What Works in Goals and Planning 219
22 What Works in Fundraising 231
23 What Works in Media and Marketing 261
24 What Works in Activism 280
25 What Works in Educational Curricula 299
26 What Works When Running for Office 317
27 Do What's Right 326

Step 2: WORK TOGETHER: Start and Strengthen Meaningful Relationships 335

28 Find Mentors 336
29 Build a Team 350
30 Optimize Communication 373
31 Create Partnerships 386
32 Organize a Conference 406
33 Serve on a Board 418
34 Develop Community Ownership 429

Step 3: MAKE IT LAST: Add Value and Sustain Success 442

35 Apply Social Entrepreneurship 443
36 Revitalize Your Efforts 456
37 Transition Leadership 469
38 Incorporate as a Business 479
39 Incorporate as a Nonprofit 488
40 Incorporate Reflection 497
41 Make Social Responsibility a Career 506
42 Make Social Responsibility a Lifestyle 520

Notes *531*
Index *541*

For my family, who instilled in me a love of community.
And for my community, who has loved me like family.
–Nina Vasan

For my mother and father—the most loving, supportive, and selfless parents anyone could ever ask for.
–Jennifer Przybylo

Preface: The Spirit of Community

How This Book Got Started

We met in May 2002 at the Prudential Spirit of Community Awards in Washington, DC, where we were honored to be included among America's Top Youth Volunteers. Nina, from Vienna, West Virginia, was lauded for launching American Cancer Society Teens, a nationwide network that empowered student volunteers of the American Cancer Society to recognize their potential as leaders and work together to develop creative solutions to improve health in their communities. Jennifer, from Lincolnwood, Illinois, was recognized for her innovative work to help shelter residents on their journey to secure employment and financial independence.

We found ourselves surrounded by inspiring students from around the country who had founded groundbreaking nonprofits, socially conscious businesses, activist movements, or had initiated other forms of lasting change in their communities. The diversity of backgrounds, interests, and experiences that could be found within this single group of students was impressive, and the potential for collaboration was evident. Though we brainstormed ideas to bring together these young leaders, no idea seemed quite right at the time.

Fast forward to 2004. Nina, now a sophomore in college, was invited by Jim and Pam Toole of the University of Minnesota's School of Social Work and College of Education and Human Development to speak at the National Service Learning Conference about her experiences as a young social entrepreneur. While there, she was asked by a publisher to develop the ideas from her talk into a how-to book on leadership for kids.

Nina loved the idea. Over the years, she'd received numerous e-mails from students, parents, schools, and organizations—all looking to make an impact but needing the guidance to do so. From the volume of these requests, it was clear no good resource was available despite the pressing need. She felt that Jennifer, then a college freshman, would feel similarly passionate about such a project, so Nina approached Jennifer with the idea.

As we talked over the potential of such a book, it became clear that the need extended well beyond the original demographic proposed; many of our classmates and friends also wanted to take meaningful, directed action but didn't know where or how to dive in. Convinced that a practical, fun, and honest guidebook to social change was needed for today's generation of students and young professionals, we set out to tackle this challenge.

So we started writing.

How This Book Got Finished

This book is a true labor of love many years in the making. Though it has taken many different shapes and gone through numerous revisions and edits, the vision has always remained the same: to design a practical, guide to help anyone with a desire to do good in this world not only do good, but do good *well.* We wanted a tool to answer the questions we had when we started, and address those we continue to ask today as we try to solve community problems. In our own work, we stumbled frequently, and often success was only found through trial and error. We realized an actual framework was a critical missing component of the equation to do good well, which led us to create a simple three-step method for social innovation that is grounded in both personal experience and academic research on innovation in business, nonprofits, community action, and leadership. Aware of our own need for engagement while learning, we aimed to make the style fun and interactive, like getting advice from a peer or mentor in real time, a book that not only inspires but also gives practical and even step-by-step instructions for turning idealistic aspirations into tangible, real-world solutions. The school supplies lover in us advocated for a book you could highlight, write notes in and personalize. Finally, understanding the need for versatility and a range of learning styles, we aimed for a resource you could use anywhere—in bed by yourself, in school with a class, or in the field with your team.

Tip The people you work with make all the difference. When you find great people, keep them close. We're glad we did!

Just as the spirit of community helped launch this book, it was also the driving force to finish it. We feel extremely fortunate to have recruited to our team an exceptional community of young leaders, and it has been nothing short of an honor to collaborate with them. They are the peers we most respect and admire, stellar visionaries and fearless trailblazers who truly embody what it is to do good well in their work and lifestyle. They've been our partners throughout this journey and continue to inspire us each day, testaments to the tremendous potential for good in this world. For their commitment, generosity, and unwavering support, we are humbled by the following contributors: Nathaniel Whittemore, Jonathan Marino, Katherine Klem, Mackenzie Lowry, Alia Whitney-Johnson, Daniel Zoughbie, William Hwang, Lyric Chen, Sarah Kleinman, Ernestine Fu, Meg Sullivan, Lexie Tabachnick, Mona Jones-Romansic, Ravneet Kaur, Trent Weaver, Phebe Meyers, Om Lala, Kelly Cotter, Yuriy Bronshteyn, Jennifer Kasten, Amy Dinh, Sheba Mathew, Max Novendstern, Annie Ryu, Shin Daimyo, Sejal Hathi, Sean Genis, Alex Mittal, Vinod Nambudiri, Christina Adams, Eunice Buhler, Divya Srinivasan, Richard Lonsdorf, Daniel Pike, Chas Taylor, Tova Reichel, Sujay Tyle, Janet Fischburg, Dalya Massachi, Alison Cohen, Scott Warren, Sheel Tyle, Yasmin Mandviwala, Shalini Palmal, Leila Makarechi, Kelydra Welcker, and Anna Offit.

We are also forever indebted to our editor, Erin Null. Erin has been our biggest champion and advisor. Without her support and belief in us, we could never have made this dream a reality. We are grateful to the entire Jossey-Bass/Wiley team for welcoming us into their family: Paul Foster, Cathy Mallon, Aneesa Davenport, Alison Knowles, Michael Cook, Samantha Rubenstein, Beverly Miller, Paula Goldstein and Richard Sheppard. We would also like to thank Susan Cohen at Writers House Literary Agency for seeing this book's potential in its very earliest stages and encouraging us to pursue it, Elizabeth Przybylo (aka Jennie's lovely mom) whose copyediting talents still seem to be the result of magic, Danny Moldovan for generously sharing the domain DoGoodWell.org with us, and Lyric Chen, our dear friend who played a unique role, weighing in on the strategy of this book while coordinating with us to develop a sister book on leadership for young women.

We would also like to acknowledge the contributions of our special friends: Microsoft Word's Track Changes, Google Docs, and Skype's Share Screen.

When we started this book nearly 10 years ago, it was our little passion project, driven solely by our own enthusiasm for the fields of leadership and social change. Back then, we could never have anticipated the revolution of the past few years and the dawn of a new era of social responsibility. We are incredibly lucky to live at a time when creativity, innovation, and entrepreneurship are celebrated and encouraged, and particularly so when applied to solving the problems of the local and global community. We are blessed to have in our lives Muhammad Yunus, Bill Drayton, Alan Khazei, Sonal Shah, Nancy Lublin, Christopher Winship, Jessica Jackley, and Lauren Bush—revolutionaries who inspired us with their innovative work and who encouraged our own with their generous endorsements.

The spirit of community inspired, sustained, and finished this book and will be the force driving it forward. So now we thank you, for valuing and building your own community, and celebrating this spirit in your future action and leadership.

Nina's Thank-Yous

First to my family, whose value for community and social responsibility has been the driving force behind this book. To Mommy, the most loving and selfless person I know. Everything good in our family is because of you. To Daddy, whose reverence for art, history, and the Renaissance advanced our creativity at home, and whose generosity established the Vasan Family Center for Philanthropy, a loving legacy to our community. To Neil, who taught me everything from how to color to how to apply for college, who is the voice of reason and honesty, and who pushes me when I least want it but most need it. My family let me continue to work on this book for years, even as the rejection letters piled up; their dedication to my dreams is beyond what I deserve. For a lifetime of support, thank you to my extended family of aunts, uncles, and cousins; and to the Gawandes, Reddys, Vilasagars, Hensleys, Khalils, Modis, Sekars, Shahs, Phillips, and Carters—the friends who have become family.

The best gift my parents gave me was making West Virginia our home. To my community, your impact on my life has been so profound that even today, when I think of who I am, the first words that come to mind are "a West Virginian." While I have yet to find the right way to thank you, I dedicate this book to you with hope that these pages are used by our young neighbors to bring out the best in themselves and lead progress in our community.

The educators in my community are a blessing—my deepest appreciation to Wood County Schools and all the teachers and staff at Greenmont, TREK, Jackson, and PHS, for inspiring your students to learn not only in the classroom, but also on the court, on the stage, at the buzzer, and of course, in the community. And for their own commitment to "challenge what works" and innovate—Katie Hardin, Val Hoover, Victor Tweel, Cathy Mildren, Larry Hattman, Fredrick Doak, Carolyn McCune, and Teresa Law, whose demand for excellence created a culture of continuous improvement.

An architect of the spirit of community, the American Cancer Society (ACS) cultivated me into a budding social entrepreneur. Sally Davis warmly welcomed me as an elementary school volunteer and uncovered my inner saleswoman, having me dress up in a handmade daffodil costume—complete with a green felt skirt and yellow petal headdress—and sell flowers in the mall during the ACS's Daffodil Days. Linda Goodwin was the first to see the potential of a dedicated group to engage students in community action, and extending involvement beyond fundraising to include education, advocacy, and service. Moreover, she pushed tirelessly for what was then a novel model for the organization: a group of youth, for youth, *led by youth.* The Wood County ACS Teen Board's early success launched the opportunity that built the foundation for this book: ACS Teens, a nationwide network of student volunteers, started thanks to the innovative vision of ACS leaders Linelle Blais, Beth Stevenson, Diana Harrison, Hersha Arnold, and John Seffrin. Encouraging entrepreneurship and celebrating service, the ACS empowered my fellow youth volunteers and me with proof that our actions could breed hope, progress, and answers

Institutions have a unique power to develop leaders. These organizations and their executives have given remarkable opportunities to me (as well as generations of students and young leaders), not only by championing leadership and community, but perhaps more importantly by building a family of alumni to "work together" and "make it last": the Girl Scouts of America (Susan Thompson and Cathy Adams), Center for Excellence in Education (Maite Ballestero and Joanne DiGennero),

Coca-Cola Scholars Foundation (Carolyn Norton and Mark Davis), America's Junior Miss/Distinguished Young Women (Rick and Joanna Mathena), Gloria Barron Foundation (Barbara Ann Richman), Caring Institute (Val Halamandaris), Glamour Magazine (Katie Sanders), and DoSomething.org (Nancy Lublin and Ellie Zeitlin).

Reflecting on the significance of my own mentors is what led to dedicating a full chapter to this influential position. For investing in me and demonstrating by example what good leadership is, I am indebted to Drs. Jeremy Wolfe, Arthur Pardee, William Li, Vincent Li, Margaret Chan, Ian Smith, Rahul Rajkumar, Eugene Beresin, John Matthews, RP Rajarethinam, and Nancy Oriol.

Henry Ford said, "My best friend is the one who brings out the best in me." I'm fortunate to have a team of best friends who inspire me to "do good better", and who are as loving as they are admirable. To Jen, Aaron, Yuriy, Shin, Lisa, and Om—the first ones to reply to my e-mails/texts/voicemails and able to solve any problem with reason and reassurance—and to Amara, Randy, Athi, Manisha, Aisha, Jayme, Connie, Richard, Anda, Natalie, Vivek, Jason, Liz, Matt, Harrison, Aya, Sheena, Chetan, Sheel, Rachele, Vijay, Andrew, Linda, and Lyric. <3 And to Jennie, for being my friend, family, editor, illustrator, coauthor, mentor … my person.

For the very special role they played in getting this book into your hands, I am grateful for the Prudential Spirit of Community Awards, Jim and Pam Toole, the National Service Learning Conference, Bill Damon, and especially Christopher Winship, whose course at Harvard College was the first to connect the classroom with the community; his applause was the catalyst for moving forward with this book. To our extraordinary contributors and to our editor Erin Null, I will continue to thank you for years to come.

Finally, thanks to you. You will determine the impact this book has on you, your community, and our world. Do good well, it's in your hands …

Jennifer's Thank-Yous

So very many acknowledgements are due! I've been fortunate enough to have no shortage of caring, inspiring people in my life.

To the teachers who encouraged my curiosity and instilled within me a lifelong love of learning: the late Arlene Bozek, Betsy D'Angelo, Margaret Wade, Helga Coyne, Wenche Haverkamp, Mark Anderson, Lynn Patterson, Dale Ziegler, Jody Stawicki, Shirley Fowler, Katie Baal, Kathy Giunta, John Baliban, David Schmittgens, Timothy Mitchell, Holly Kennedy, Richard Blackwell, Donald Nekrosius, Jim Spalding, Dr. William Carroll, Martin Kelley, and Sister Therese DeCanio. I'm so lucky to have had so many exceptional teachers.

To my research supervisors and mentors, for their patience, friendship, and unwavering support, even when my projects and experiments didn't always pan out: Dr. Jeffrey Field, Dr. Samuel Gorovitz, Dr. Scott Swenson, Dr. Philip Maini, Dr. Michael Snyder, Dr. Michael Cherry, Dr. Lisa Shieh, and Dr. Ian Tong. Particularly big thank-yous are due to Dr. Derek Radisky, for taking me under his wing and nurturing my love of science, as well as his continued friendship over the years, and Dr. Kenneth Offit, for his fierce support, keen insights, and much-valued advice.

To my enormously understanding and loving family, for putting up with my crazy schedules and believing in me through thick and thin. I owe especially large debts of gratitude to my grandparents: Chester L. Przybylo, for always challenging me intellectually and encouraging me to consider all sides of a problem, Josephine Przybylo, for inspiring me with her resourcefulness and indomitable spirit, Joseph Rogoz, for teaching me the value of family and tradition, and Lillian Rogoz, for her joyful spirit and kindness toward all. I also thank my amazing and talented cousins, who inspire me daily: Frances, Philip, and Ellen Rogoz, and Stephen and Lucia Kubiatowski. A great big "thank you" is also due to the rest of my fantastic family: the Rogoz, Kubiatowski, Pawlicki, Kolpak, Pindras, Przybylo, Kroger, Kealy, and Sliwa families, as well as the extended Latocha clan. And to the friends I consider family: Anna Offit, Ryan Patap, Xiao-Hu Yan, Amy Yuan, Corey Rennell, and of course, Nina Vasan.

And last but not least, to my parents: Chester and Elizabeth Przybylo. There are no words to describe my gratitude for their endless reserves of love and support. I just couldn't wish for better parents.

About the Authors

Nina Vasan's road of writing *Do Good Well* began at home in Vienna, West Virginia, where she grew up watching her family and community champion a shared value: social responsibility. As a teenager, she observed that fellow students had passion and promising ideas for addressing social problems, but there was no system to channel, engage, and sustain their efforts. Inspired to create this opportunity, she worked with the American Cancer Society to launch ACS Teens; through an online network, ACS Teens served as an incubator for social change: it trained, mobilized, mentored, and united student volunteers, empowering them to recognize their potential as leaders and work together to find creative solutions for improving health in their communities. For her leadership as a young social entrepreneur, Nina was recognized as one of America's top 10 youth volunteers by the Prudential Spirit of Community Awards, a Young Adult Winner of the National Caring Award, and a Girl Scouts National Young Woman of Distinction.

Winner of the $50,000 top Grand Award at the Intel International Science and Engineering Fair, Nina presented her research during the Nobel Prize ceremonies at the Stockholm International Youth Science Seminar. She studied government at Harvard College, graduating as one of *Glamour* magazine's Top 10 College Women. During the 2008 presidential election, she served as co-leader of Battleground State Outreach for Barack Obama's Health Policy Advisory Committee. Internationally, she worked at the World Health Organization in the office of the director-general, Dr. Margaret Chan.

Currently completing an MD at Harvard Medical School, Nina has been honored as one of our country's most promising young scholars by a number of corporate foundations including Coca-Cola, Toyota, Tylenol, and Target, and publications including *Cosmogirl,* Time Inc./*Teen People,* and *USA Today.* An Olympic torchbearer, she represented her home state as West Virginia's Junior Miss at America's Junior Miss, where she won the top national prizes for Scholastics and Community Service, as well as the Spirit of Junior Miss, an award voted on by the 50 contestants. Compelled by her own personal struggles, Nina is now working to apply the methods of social innovation and entrepreneurship to mental health. She will pursue a residency in psychiatry, where she hopes to contribute to developing tools and technologies that empower patients with mental illness by improving health, building community, and advancing opportunity.

Jennifer Przybylo's dedication to social responsibility evolved in an unusual way. During a particularly difficult period in her adolescence, she sought out activities that would allow her to channel her teenage angst into productive, positive causes. When she began volunteering with a group that prepared meals for a local soup kitchen, she discovered the intense joy that could come from helping others and the satisfaction of knowing she'd made a difference, however small. She then organized a group to collect toiletries and makeup for a Chicago women's shelter that provided a safe haven for homeless women and their children, many of whom had fled from violent homes. The shelter encouraged and helped its residents seek employment as a next step toward securing new lives and greater stability for themselves and their families. By collecting sample-sized toiletries and makeup that would otherwise be discarded or collect dust in closets, Jennifer's group provided these women with items they could use when preparing for job interviews. For this innovative service work, Jennifer was named Illinois's top high school volunteer by the Prudential Spirit of Community Awards. For her community leadership, she was honored as a United States Senate Youth Program Delegate and a Toyota Community Scholar.

As an undergraduate at Yale, Jennifer combined her love of service with a long-standing passion for health promotion and medicine as co-president of a campus health education group. It was through her experience with Peer Health Educators that she realized the power of health education to make a difference in the lives of those in her community and that long-term, sustainable change was best achieved through education and the advancement of knowledge. During this time, Jennifer gained additional leadership experience as chair of Yale's Undergraduate Organizations Funding Committee, the body responsible for distribution of university funds to the more than 300 student groups. In this capacity, she also served as a member of the executive board of the Yale College Council, and an appointed member of the Dean's Office Committee on Undergraduate Organizations. After graduation, she earned an M.Phil. in computational biology at Cambridge University. There she promoted partnerships between business leaders and students with innovative technological or biomedical ideas as a member of the executive board of Cambridge University Entrepreneurs.

In college, Jennifer discovered that she loved scientific research and the thrill of advancing the collective body of knowledge, albeit ever so incrementally. Encouraged by her research supervisors, Jennifer went on to pursue cancer research at world-renowned institutions: the University of Pennsylvania School of Medicine, Mayo Clinic, Oxford University, and Memorial Sloan-Kettering. Upon graduating from Yale, she received the prestigious Boell Prize for excellence in the senior research she had undertaken at the Yale School of Medicine. Her work has also been published in numerous journals. Currently a student at Stanford University School of Medicine, she continues to be actively engaged in both research and her community. Jennifer hopes that this book will help students and young adults not only discover their own passion for community action and sustainable change, but also provide them with the tools to make their dreams for this world a reality.

Introduction

We are in the midst of a revolution unlike any other. Without guns or swords, without dictatorial edicts or government campaigns, without even any semblance of opposition, a cultural transformation has taken root as we've ever-so-quietly but ever-so-surely embraced the value that will come to define our generation: social responsibility.

Like most great revolutions, the era of social responsibility had its catalysts—trailblazers who empowered us to go green, eat local, and teach for America. It also has its popular heroes: Bill and Melinda, Barack and Michelle, Angelina and Brad. But unlike most revolutions, the era of social responsibility isn't propelled forward by big money, political leaders, or even the cult of celebrity. Its power lies in us, the everyday people who embrace the movement and live by it, who lead quietly by the socially conscious choices we make and the actions we take. And now that the movement has gained momentum, its next generation of leaders will be people like you, people who will be called to lead more vocally, to organize collective action, to answer Gandhi's challenge to "be the change you wish to see in the world." *You* are needed to carry the movement forward.

To answer this call to action, you'll need a coach—someone to show you not just what to do, but *how* to do it, and how to do it *well.*

Meet *Do Good Well*, a book that champions the simple yet powerful notion of grounded idealism. At the core of this book is a new paradigm for progress—a readily adaptable method for social innovation, an action plan for making a difference and changing the world that is as practical as it is idealistic. It's easy to understand and flexible enough to apply to any idea and any community, helping you take purposeful action in three simple steps:

1. Do What Works.
2. Work Together.
3. Make It Last.

These steps are accompanied by specific how-to advice, a toolbox of best practices, personal anecdotes, and illustrative examples to help you mobilize your action plan. Distilled from the shared experiences of our generation's top innovators, entrepreneurs, humanitarians, activists, and public servants, this extensive primer of practical tools—from how to fundraise or launch a media campaign, to incorporating as a 501(c)(3) or nonprofit organization—will help you build and strengthen the communities around you. This book is your partner in realizing your potential as a leader and driver of progress. It is your guide as you embark on your own journey toward positive change.

What follows is a more detailed explanation of the current era of social responsibility, as well as a description of the important concepts and ideas you'll find within this book.

The Timing: Welcome to the Era of Social Responsibility

The current era of social responsibility began quietly. At first, the change was almost imperceptible: a few green products popped up on the shelves of your local grocery store, a classmate joined Teach For America, your favorite gossip blog published photos of celebrities speaking at the United Nations. But in the beginning, it was all the work of a handful of idealists, the social justice titans like Muhammad Yunus (Grameen Bank), Alan Khazei (CityYear), Bill Drayton (Ashoka), Jim Kim and Paul Farmer (Partners In Health), innovators who developed groundbreaking solutions for uniting communities, increasing opportunities, and saving lives.

Before long, you looked down at your shopping cart and realized it was filled with biodegradable detergent, grass-fed beef, and free-range eggs. When you learned that a former classmate was leaving a cushy job to work in a developing country, your reaction wasn't "Wow! That's unbelievable!" but rather "I should introduce her to my friend running a microfinance project with that NGO in Brazil." Your favorite public figures—athletes, actors, musicians, politicians, and CEOs—weren't just lending their names to good causes or posing for photo-ops at charity dinners, but were instead rolling up their sleeves to work with organizations dedicated to building low-income housing or campaigning for human rights. "Doing good" quickly shifted from the admired exception to the expected norm.

You got excited by the creative work of Nancy Lublin (DoSomething .org), Sonal Shah (White House Office of Social Innovation and Civic Participation), Sheryl WuDunn and Nick Kristof (*Half the Sky*). You soon realized that doing good was the passion of your generation, led by rock stars like Ben Rattray, founder of Change.org, the world's fastest growing platform for social change; Lauren Bush, model and designer of the iconic FEED bag, which feeds one hungry school child for a year; and Jessica Jackley and Matt Flannery, who as twenty-somethings started Kiva.org, which has facilitated over $100 million in microcredit loans. You were humbled by the voices of your peers who led revolutions in countries across the world, toppling corrupt regimes and ushering in a new era of human rights, equality, and community. These visionaries turned social responsibility from a fad into a value, and issued to you a powerful call to action.

What started small has mushroomed into a cultural revolution: a true era of social responsibility. But why? And why now? The answer is in the convergence of three important cultural undercurrents that are environmental, economic, and political in nature.

The first is the green movement, an increasing awareness of the social, economic, and environmental impact of everyday choices. We've learned that by taking personal responsibility for our actions and by voting with our wallets, we can enforce environmental sustainability as well as demand corporate responsibility. We can decrease our carbon footprint and support small farmers by buying local, we can choose to shop with reusable cloth bags instead of disposable paper or plastic, and we can purchase cars from companies that invest in the production of hybrid or fuel-efficient models. The green movement has taught us that while government regulation of business plays an important role in safeguarding the environment, individual voices can indeed be heard, and they have the power to effect large-scale change.

The second cultural undercurrent contributing to the current era of social responsibility is the world economic downturn that began in the late 2000s. In the midst of high unemployment, widespread bankruptcies and foreclosures, and a tanking stock market, Americans tightened their belts and pinched their pennies. They also dove headlong into community service, and the ranks of volunteers swelled to record numbers.[1] Many of the unemployed have turned to community service work not only to help others, but also to fill their free time productively, learning new skills that might ultimately help them find employment. Even among groups not seeking employment (the employed, for example), volunteering has increased.[2] This is likely the result of several factors: gratitude for relative prosperity and a desire to help those less fortunate, increased sensitivity to the plight of others during difficult times, and a natural inclination to band together to overcome adversity. The economic downturn has heightened societal awareness of unmet needs and has mobilized the population to respond to those needs. And it isn't just individuals who are transformed; companies have ushered in a wave of initiatives to promote corporate social responsibility, committing to creating products and services that have marketable functions and promote shared values.

The third element critical to the genesis of this era of social responsibility is political in nature, stemming in large part from the 2008 presidential election. The Obama campaign galvanized the population, and especially young adults, not only to expect and demand change but also to become active participants in bringing about that change. Service and community action came to the forefront of national dialogue. The Obama administration reinforced the importance of civic service, helping to pass landmark legislation and create new institutions to promote and facilitate social responsibility, including the Edward M. Kennedy Serve America Act, which created four new service corps and the White House Office of Social Innovation and Civic Participation, committed to "promoting service as a solution."[3] And what made this even more powerful was that it wasn't limited to one candidate or party. Former Presidents George W. Bush, Bill Clinton, George H. W. Bush, and Jimmy Carter all dedicated themselves to foundations and initiatives championing social responsibility.

The green movement's success taught us that we as individuals can make a meaningful difference, the economic downturn sensitized us to the problems around us and showed us that sustainability is integral to progress, and the positive reinforcement from both the Oval Office and Hollywood has helped make do-gooding cool. What in the past may have been limited to so-called "bleeding hearts" is now well beyond the fad stage. It has become a deeply ingrained part of our culture.

Recognizing the educational value of social responsibility, schools have instituted leadership and service requirements and are increasingly trying to integrate social change into the curriculum. Colleges and universities are now offering courses, majors, and even entire degrees in innovation, social entrepreneurship, activism, community development, leadership, and human rights. Times have changed, and the world is responding.

Do Good Well is the authors' response to this exciting and unprecedented era. It is our hope that by fanning the flames of idealism with a practical, readily adaptable method for social change, this book will help bridge the gap between good intention and effective action. We feel fortunate to be able to help you not only dive into the powerful movement unfolding all around us, but also participate meaningfully in its evolution and future leadership.

The Destination: Social Progress

In this new era of social responsibility, the goal is progress, not perfection. As a global community, we've come to realize that while world peace may be on everyone's wish list, it's not something we're likely to find tied up with a bow anytime soon. Even Superman never managed to rid Metropolis of poverty or prevent global warming.

So rather than fixate on an unachievable utopia, we as a society have refocused our sights on smaller, tangible goals that in aggregate, produce substantive change. This is the same, pragmatic mind-set you'll find in *Do Good Well.* It's chipping away at a problem day by day, bit by bit, that drives real social progress. And all that's needed to get started is for concerned citizens to pick up a chisel and take action. This action can be as involved as starting a company to bring clean drinking water to villages in developing countries, or as simple as choosing to buy local sustainably produced foods. Through collective efforts, individual actions are magnified, and thus through collaboration, we can reach more people, effect more change, and dream even bigger. Leadership and united action advance social progress, driving freedom, equality, and opportunity a little bit closer to the ideal.

The Vehicle: Social Innovation

One of the key vehicles for progress is social innovation—novel ideas, behaviors, methods, products, services, and organizations that either alter the way we think about the process of change-making, or themselves fulfill unmet societal needs. Best of all, social innovation can come from anyone, anywhere, at any time. All that's required is some out-of-the-box thinking and a healthy dose of determination.

Students and young adults are a primary driving force for social innovation, particularly today. We are the innovation generation. For us, the new currency is impact, and the terms of sale have changed entirely. We are not afraid to challenge norms, to ask why things are the way they are, and then dare to dream of more efficient or more equitable possibilities. Moreover, today's brand of social innovation comes in many forms, from repurposing an existing technology or finding a new application for a classic methodology, to creating a new product or process from scratch to help right social ills. Far from relying on traditional organizational structures like charities or nongovernmental organizations (NGOs) to incubate and deliver these social innovations, we've found creative ways to partner with governments or establish businesses devoted to furthering our social aims. Along the way, we've incorporated important lessons from the business world in general (and startups in particular), engineering accountability, maximizing efficiency, and emphasizing sustainability in our social ventures to better safeguard their long-term health and productivity.

Do Good Well celebrates social innovation and the entrepreneurial spirit of our time, emphasizing creativity and divergent thought. It will walk you through how to thoroughly research a given problem, and how to critically examine existing solutions to that problem. It will challenge you to think big, think differently, and think fearlessly when brainstorming new solutions. You'll also be introduced to the key business principles and tenets underlying the culture of social innovation, and how you can harness their power to bring about lasting social change.

The Fuel: You

Make no mistake about it—*you* are the most important part of the social progress equation. You—your inspirations, your motivations, and your convictions—are the fuel propelling your efforts toward lasting change in your community, whether that community is local or global. Thus it's essential to have a thorough understanding of yourself, to possess a self-awareness that includes your inner drives, greatest strengths, personal pitfalls, and highest-held values. Once you have a keen understanding of yourself, you'll be best equipped to identify the problems (and opportunities) around you that would provide you with a great sense of fulfillment to work toward solving, and be well-matched to your unique talents and personality. The importance of identifying the right problem to tackle cannot be understated, as the more satisfying the task is to you and the better suited you are to the task, the greater your chance of success.

Part 1 of *Do Good Well* helps facilitate this critical pairing with chapters designed to help you better define who you are and what matters most to you, as well as the types of causes and issues you're most naturally drawn to. Numerous exercises designed to structure your thinking highlight key insights as you wind along this road of self-discovery. Part 1 also prepares you to see the possibilities in the problems you encounter, helping you adopt a mind-set that will ensure you recognize the right cause for you when it crosses your path, if it hasn't already. Finally, you'll learn how to thoroughly research all aspects of the problem you've identified and apply this research to brainstorming a comprehensive set of potential solutions.

The Journey: The Do Good Well Method

Of course, it would be fantastic if there was a single set of step-by-step instructions that could be applied to solve all the world's problems. Imagine: "Just follow steps 1–10 and you too can end world hunger, raise money for Girl Scout Troop 1062, and fix Detroit's unemployment woes ... " Unfortunately, no such universal prescription exists because real-world problems are messy and complicated and, of course, no two problems are alike. The steps necessary to solve a given problem are as unique as the problem itself.

To lead effectively and promote lasting change, you'll need to tailor your solutions to the specific challenges before you. And while a rigid set of directions won't be of much benefit, it's always good to have a general game plan, a flexible strategy that's readily applicable to a wide variety of scenarios. Part 2 of *Do Good Well* presents just such a methodology—a novel paradigm for social progress that can be applied to any issue, from protecting the environment to advancing human rights. And while it won't anticipate every bump in the road you'll encounter, the Do Good Well method highlights the critical components of successful social innovation, ensuring your ambitious efforts to do good are effective, collaborative, and sustainable—empowering you to do good well.

The method is simple: do what works, work together, and make it last. You'll learn to implement novel, evidence-based solutions that build on the experiences of others, to leverage the power of teamwork, community, and concerted action, and to engineer sustainability into your efforts to ensure your actions are self-perpetuating. We break down these basic ideas into their key components:

Step 1: Do What Works
Design a Systemic Solution
Build on What Works
Measure, Evaluate, Improve, Repeat
Challenge What Works, Innovate, Keep What Works

Step 2: Work Together
Balance Strengthening and Starting
Cultivate Community Ownership
Foster Team Unity
Forge Partnerships

Step 3: Make It Last
Start Small, Then Scale What Works
Engineer Self-Sustainable Solutions
Integrate Social Entrepreneurship
Share What Works

It's our hope that you'll use this book to guide your actions not only as you're starting out, but also as your efforts mature and prosper. Think of it as a hands-on, do-it-yourself manual. Refer back to it frequently, and as you work through its pages and exercises, don't be afraid to write in it and bookmark important pages (or highlight them, for you e-book readers). Use the space in the margins to take notes, brainstorm, pose and answer questions. This book is your personal guide to creating meaningful change in the world, so go ahead and make it your own.

The Road Map: The Toolbox

While the Do Good Well method outlines the strategy for the social change you hope to catalyze, you'll need the nuts and bolts advice found in Part 3 to help turn your vision into a reality. Brimming with practical, detailed advice on a host of essential topics, Part 3 walks you through the process of generating and executing your idea, from naming your organization and forming partnerships, to transitioning leadership and making social responsibility a career. Included are plenty of success stories to help inspire you, as well as useful tips, examples, and exercises to help organize your ideas.

And because we feel strongly that it's not just action, but *united* action that drives social progress, we chose to work together: each chapter in Part 3 features pearls of wisdom from one or more of the country's top young leaders—experts who can speak directly to the best practices and potential pitfalls of their respective topics. We are extraordinarily lucky to have assembled such an unprecedented team of student and young adult leaders to give you the benefits of their experience: Silicon Valley's youngest venture capitalist advises you on fundraising, a Peter Thiel 20 Under 20 Fellow explains how to find a mentor, the founder of the first national youth-led anti-tobacco organization gives you a crash course on activism, and more. This collective knowledge will equip you with the tools you need to realize your dreams for a better tomorrow.

The Network: dogoodwell.org

Do Good Well provides you with the inspiration (Part 1), framework (Part 2), and tools (Part 3) to take action and lead social innovation. But you'll need something else—a community to support you, sustain your efforts, and provide you with the opportunity to pay it forward. That's where the Do Good Well Network comes in. At dogoodwell.org, you'll find a home for leadership and social innovation on the Web, with tools to help you work together and share what works. So log on, unite with fellow leaders, and join us in celebrating social responsibility as a value, mission, and lifestyle.

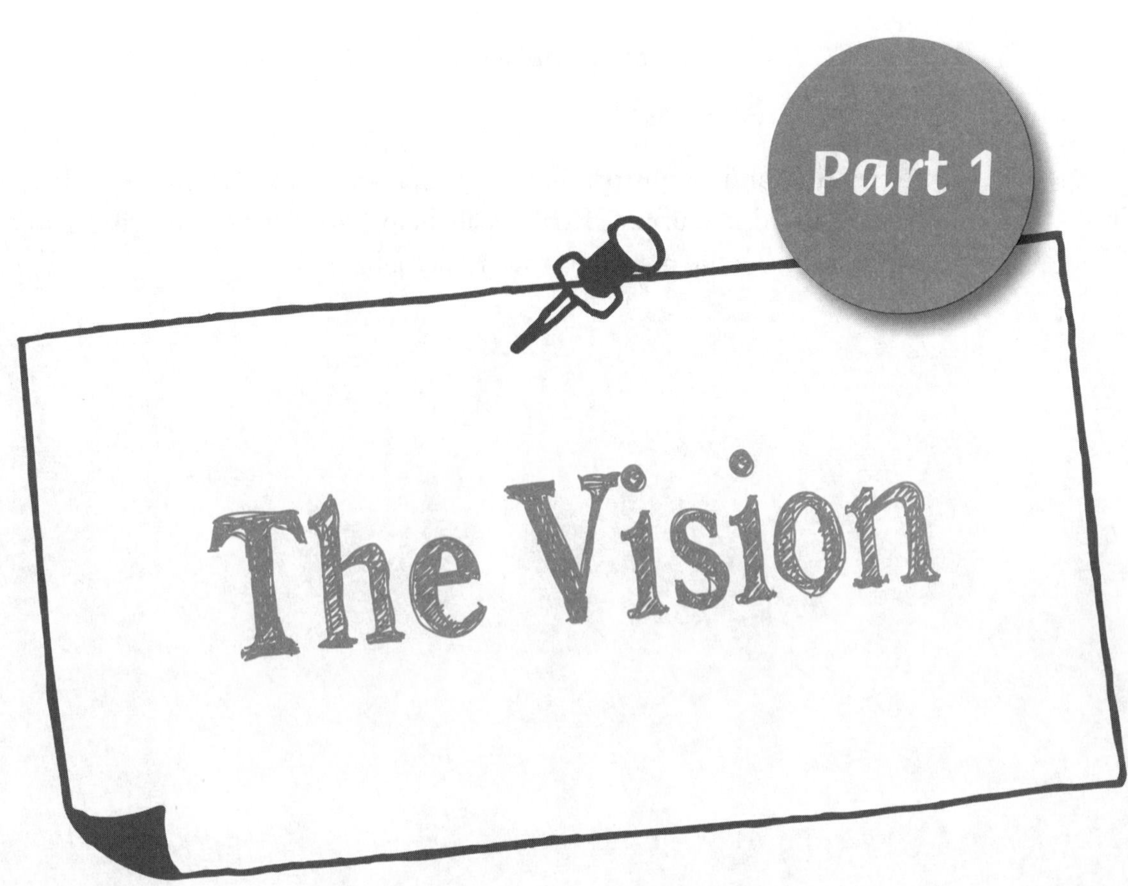

Welcome, and congratulations on taking the first step toward creating meaningful and lasting change in the world around you! This book will equip you with the tools and strategies you need to take your good intentions and energy to the beginning of what we hope will be a very fulfilling journey.

Part 1 begins at square one. If you're eager to begin making an impact on the world but haven't yet identified a specific issue of interest, Part 1 will prepare you to recognize the potential in the problems all around you. Through a series of self-reflection exercises designed to crystallize your values and highlight your strengths, you'll gain great personal insights and learn to home in on the issues you're most likely to find the most fulfilling. Alternatively, if you've already identified a problem you're passionate about working to solve, these chapters show you how to better define that issue, from distilling the essential components of the problem to envisioning the ultimate goals of an intervention and brainstorming potential solutions. No matter where you are on your journey, Part 1 will help you clarify your vision for change and take the first steps toward actualizing it.

Chapter 1

Know Yourself

To thine own self be true.

—*WILLIAM SHAKESPEARE,* HAMLET

You want to make an impact. You're motivated to make positive change, brimming with energy and eager to get started. But just what do you want to do? What cause do you want to advance? And what skills will help you along the way?

To answer these questions, you'll need to spend some time getting to know yourself. Who you are as a person—what you value, what you enjoy, and what you're good at—is critical to determining both how you fit into the world and how you might change it for the better. In particular, the more you know yourself, the easier it will be for you to identify the causes that really resonate with you, as well as the ways you might use your unique skills and talents to contribute in the most meaningful, effective ways. Moreover, the better the fit is between you and your cause, the more fulfilling you'll find the work, the more energy you'll devote to it, and the more change you'll be able to make.

Getting to know yourself isn't something that happens overnight. It isn't a to-do item you can scratch off in a weekend. It's a process—one that will continue throughout the course of your life. And while this chapter won't be able to chart your entire course of self-discovery (nor should it!), it will help you begin to think through the questions of greatest relevance to a life of meaning and purpose.

Note To be true to yourself, you must first know yourself.

Who Are You?

This is a pretty big question. In fact, you could argue that the entire chapter is devoted to answering this question. But for a moment, take a step back and do a quick assessment of how you see yourself and how others see you. Exercise 1.1 facilitates this self-reflection.

How Do You See Yourself?

If you had to choose just 10 words to describe yourself, what would they be? These words can be nouns (for example, roles you fill: *sister, lawyer, mentor*) or adjectives (for example, personal characteristics: *adventurous, intelligent, loyal*).

Above all, be honest! If something is an important part of who you are, don't be shy about writing it down, even if it seems silly or not quite as serious as some of your other descriptors.

Write down these 10 words in the first column of Exercise 1.1.

How Do Others See You?

Recruit a friend, family member, or anyone who knows you well to help with this task. Ask them to make a list of the ten words that best describe you.

Copy these 10 words into the last column of Exercise 1.1.

Exercise 1.1 Who Am I?

Make a list of 10 self-descriptors in the first column. For example, you might write something like: *innovator, daughter, mathematician, world-traveler, peace-maker, funny, intelligent, tutor, caring, entrepreneur*. Next, have a friend fill in 10 descriptors of you in the third column. Use the center column to mark any words that appear twice.

My Descriptors	Overlap?	My Friend's Descriptors of Me
Empathetic		Compassionate
Genuine		Trustworthy
Kind		Sweet
Silly		Generous
Intelligent	✓	Curious
Fun	✓	Enthusiastic
Passionate		Patient
Open-minded		Loyal
Creative		Understanding
Hardworking	✓	Hardworking

Once you've filled out Exercise 1.1 with your own descriptors and your friend's descriptors of you, compare the two sets of words. If one of your words also appears in your friend's list, put a checkmark in the "overlap" column. Place extra weight on these descriptors because they match both your own self-assessment and others' perceptions of you. Words that differ from your own can also be informative because they may hint at qualities or roles you've overlooked or underemphasized.

If you can get additional lists of 10 descriptors from more friends and family, all the better! Just replace the third column with a new list and repeat the exercise. Tally up the times each of your own descriptors is repeated in others' lists to get a sense of what words come up the most. You may also wish to compile a single list of all the words from your friends and family to determine what words come up most frequently among those who know you best. This will give you the best sense of how others see you. As you do so, your own list of descriptors may change to reflect the insights you've gained.

What Do You Care About?

Understanding what you care about is the key to knowing what motivates you. And the things that motivate you are ultimately the causes and ideas that will drive you to take action, happily sacrificing your weekends or piling more responsibility onto an already full plate. They're the things you want to do because you find them deeply fulfilling.

When you have a good grasp of what makes you tick, life gets a whole lot easier. That's because if you can find the courage to be true to what you love and find personally rewarding, you'll find that the choice of not only the cause you devote yourself to, but also your college major, career path, even life partner, isn't so much a calculated choice as it is a natural gravitation toward the attributes you value most, the features you find most enriching.

This section will help you begin to identify some of the ideas and qualities that matter to you and your leadership.

What Are You Grateful For?

Start by identifying the things and experiences that you're grateful for. These can be objects (like your home), people (like your family), or ideas (like freedom of speech). Use Exercise 1.2 to help you organize your thoughts.

Figure 1.1. Who Are You?

Exercise 1.2 What I'm Grateful For

List 10 things you feel lucky to have in your life. Then jot down a few specific reasons you're grateful for each of them, as well as what your life might be like if they disappeared tomorrow. An example has been provided for you.

I'm grateful for . . .	**Why?**	**Without it, I . . .**
my home	• I feel safe at night. • It keeps me warm and dry.	• I don't know who I'd stay with or where I'd stay. I might not feel (or actually be) safe. • I might get sick from the heat, cold, or rain.
Naya	• makes me feel so happy, loved, and secure	• would feel lost + without having grounding or a sense of purpose/future
my friends	• make me so happy • fun things to do	• would feel lonley + unsupported
Stanford	• opportunity to persue great future	• wouldn't value myself as much • would lose purpose
my family	• cares for me • helps me out • loves me unconditionally	• would struggle without having a safe place to call home

The things you're most grateful for are likely things that most other people would also feel grateful for, but might not have. Taking the time to reflect on why these parts of your life are important to you and what your life might be like without them will help you better appreciate what it's like for someone without the same good fortune. Perhaps you'll find that the thought of other people going without what you consider so essential (stable housing, for example) motivates you to help others achieve the same ends.

What Do You Value?

Think in the abstract on this one: What qualities, ideas, or perspectives do you hold most dear? Do you hold honesty in high esteem? The freedom to disagree with the government and publicly voice your dissent? What about racial and religious diversity? These may be things you've come to value because you've had a lot of experience with them, or that you value all the more because they've been in short supply in your life.

You'll probably find overlap between the things you're grateful for and the things you value. However, to include them in Exercise 1.3, you'll need to extract exactly what it is about them you find so valuable. For example, if "friends" and "family" appear on the list of things you're grateful for (see Exercise 1.2), the overarching thing you value might be "close, supportive relationships" or "feeling understood by people I trust."

Exercise 1.3 What I Value

List 10 things you value. Then identify why they're important to you and what your world might look like without them.

I Value …	Why?	Without It …
Diversity	• People of different faiths challenge me to explore my own beliefs.	• I might not challenge myself as much; I might not grow as much as a person.
Empathy	• understanding + relating to others is key	
Kindness		
Genuineness		

The things we value are the things we seek to preserve and protect, hope to magnify both within ourselves and others, and wish to spread far and wide throughout the world. Determining what you value is essential to understanding who you are as a person and what type of mark you hope to make on the world.

What Makes You Emotional?

Anything that moves you enough to stir up an emotion—any emotion—is a powerful experience that you shouldn't ignore. Pay attention to these experiences because they signal much deeper processes at work. An emotional reaction is just the tip of the iceberg; closely held convictions and our most basic human instincts lie well below the surface. This means that if you strike an emotion, you've also stumbled across all the underlying beliefs that make that emotional response possible. And if you can identify these beliefs, these core principles, you can harness your emotions in a productive way. What makes you angry will drive you to seek justice. What makes you happy will motivate you to bring that same joy to others.

Think about incidents that either bothered you or elated you when they happened. These might be the result of your own firsthand experiences or simply stories you heard on the news. What emotions did you feel? Were you sad? Angry? Disappointed? Or maybe you were proud? Overjoyed? Relieved? Consider what it was about the occasion that triggered this reaction. What specifically did you find upsetting or pleasing? Reflect on these instances in Exercise 1.4.

Exercise 1.4 What Affects Me Emotionally

Reflect on five occasions when you felt deeply moved by an experience, story, or situation. In the table, write down a brief description of the incident, the emotion you felt, and what specific aspects of the scenario triggered your response. If you can think of more than five instances, by all means, add additional lines.

The Incident	The Emotion	The Triggers
In a lecture about disparate pay in the workforce, my high school economics teacher revealed to the class that women in the US routinely receive less money than men for the same job.	Anger	• Equality and fairness are incredibly important to me. • This new knowledge was at complete odds with my naïve vision of the modern-day world. I was stunned that such an unfair practice could persist.
Spanish teacher + mental health unit	· triggered · worried/anxious · angry	

Bookmark the list of triggers you identified in Exercise 1.4 because these are key issues you care a great deal about. Examine your list of triggers for key commonalities. Is injustice the thread that runs through the things that upset you most? Does careless behavior make you disappointed? Do you find that when you see communities working together to enact change, that tends to make you the most hopeful, the most excited? When you're aware of the things that move you, you can more readily identify the causes you care about. For example, if you find that a lot of your emotional triggers center around equality and fairness, you might find great personal fulfillment working to eliminate socioeconomic, gender, or racial disparities.

Who Do You Admire?

The ancient Greeks had a saying, "Tell me who you admire and I'll tell you who you are." Our role models say a lot about who we are. We revere and seek to emulate them because their actions inspire us or they embody the qualities we seek to cultivate within ourselves. Exercise 1.5 will help you home in on these people.

Exercise 1.5 10 People I Admire

List 10 people you admire. They can be famous or familiar, living or dead, of any occupation or experience. Identify the qualities and actions that make them stand out to you.

Person	Qualities	Actions
My father My mother	• Supportive, strong, dependable, trustworthy • Generous, selfless, nurturing, caring	• Takes charge in a crisis; gives great advice • Thinks of others before herself; always lends a helping hand
Babcia	· Smart, caring, devoted	
Naya	· Genuine, extremly caring, wants to do good in word	

Now examine the lists of qualities and actions in Exercise 1.5. Do you find that certain qualities are repeated again and again? Do particular types of actions command your respect? Do you tend to admire tenacity in the face of adversity? Do people who dare to innovate inspire you? Identifying the qualities and types of actions you hold in high regard will help guide your personal development.

What Are Your Strengths and Weaknesses?

Another essential component of getting to know yourself is recognizing your strengths. Once you identify the things you're good at, you can make a special effort to continue to nurture those strengths and develop them further. You'll also be better equipped to recognize opportunities where your talents may be of particular use.

On the flip side, it's equally important to come to terms with your weaknesses because they're as much a part of you as your strengths. We all have flaws, and the sooner you can acknowledge yours, the sooner you can begin working to improve them.

Exercise 1.6 will help you identify your strengths and weaknesses.

Exercise 1.6 My Strengths and Weaknesses

List your 10 top strengths and weaknesses. These can be qualities, skills, or past experiences (or lack thereof). If you're having trouble getting to 10, ask others for some help.

Strengths	Weaknesses
Excellent relating to people of all backgrounds	Not much business experience
	Rushing to start things I'm passionate abt
	Getting overwhelmed

What can you learn from this careful accounting of your gifts and deficiencies? Your strengths are assets that you should keep in mind when thinking about how to solve problems you identify. If you have a unique talent or perspective, apply it; no one else may have examined the problem in that light. Things you're good at are also likely things you enjoy, as you've probably poured considerable time and energy into developing those talents. Keep an eye out for problems that would make use of your unique skill set and that you'd enjoy.

In addition, acknowledging areas that aren't your strong suit will simultaneously highlight the talents and strengths you should seek out in potential team members and partners. These individuals will help compensate for deficiencies in your own skill set and serve as teachers from whom you can learn much.

After completing these exercises, you should have a little more insight into who you are as a person, what you care about, and what your strengths and weaknesses are. Armed with this critical self-knowledge, you'll be better equipped to evaluate and impact the world around you.

Chapter 2

Know Your World

Before you can change the world, you need to have a good sense of how it works—or doesn't work, as the case may be. A solid understanding of current world issues is an important part of being an engaged global citizen because that knowledge gives context to everything from the stories you read in the paper to the problems you see within your own community. It also informs the way you think about these problems and their potential solutions.

This chapter is a simple overview of some of the major issues facing the world today. It's intended only as a jumping-off point for future self-directed research. We hope that reading this chapter will pique your interest in the world around you and that you'll seek to learn more about it by reading newspapers, blogs, and books, as well as by talking to the people affected by, and working to fix, these issues. The world is an incredibly complicated and fascinating place, so get informed and get engaged!

Animals

Animal Homelessness

In the US alone, millions of animals are homeless, and for many reasons. In some cases, pet owners may find themselves in a position in which they're no longer able to care for their pets. In others, pet owners

Figure 2.1. The World's Problems Are Interconnected

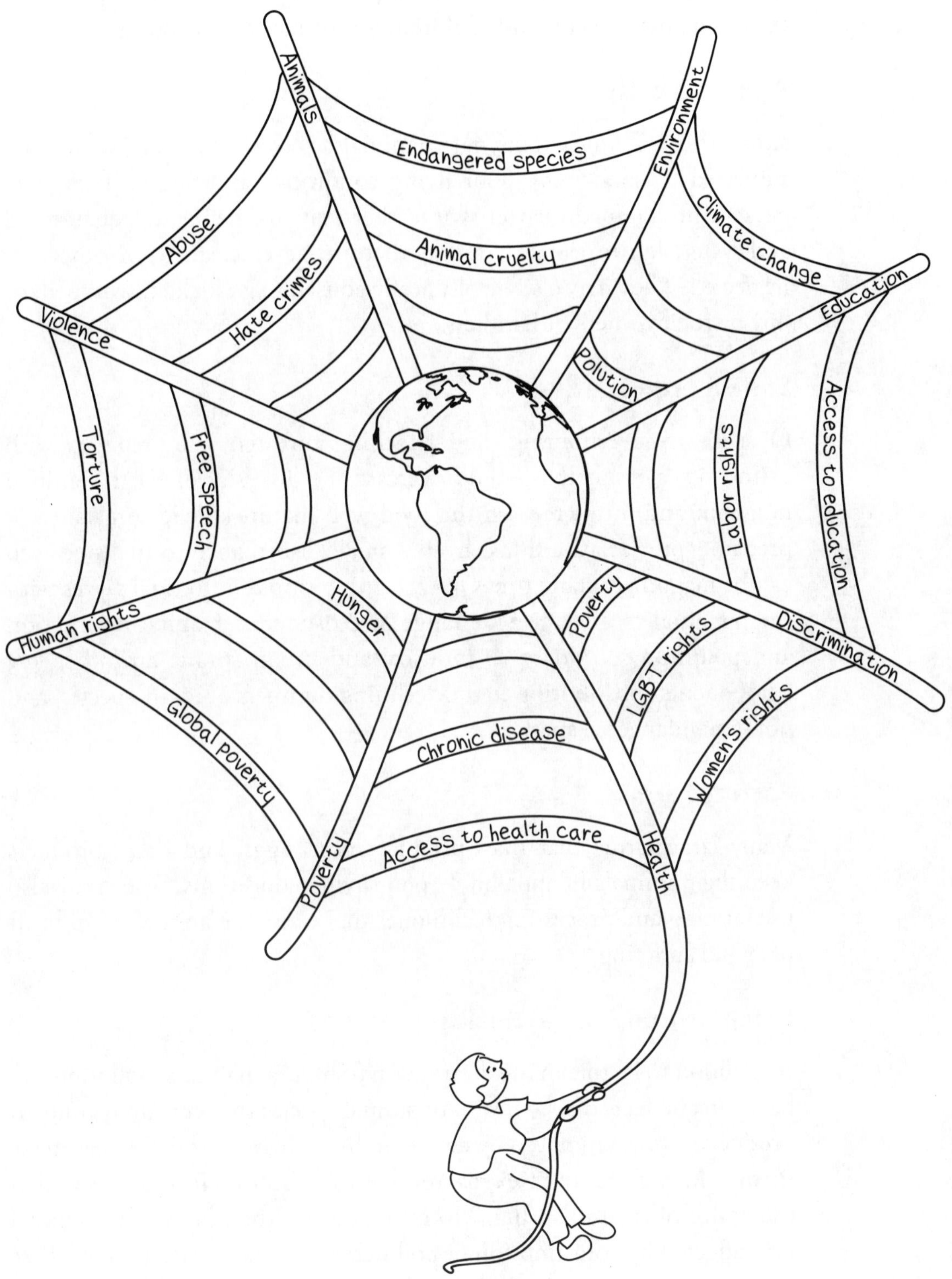

may be unable to find homes for the offspring of a pet that was not spayed or neutered. Animals that are picked up off the street or brought to shelters may be euthanized if homes for them aren't found.

Animal Cruelty

Animals of all kinds (pets, farm animals, zoo animals) are sometimes subjected to shockingly poor living conditions and abuse. They may be kept in cramped quarters with other animals, denied adequate food and water, left in cages or rooms that are never cleaned, or otherwise neglected. They may also be physically abused (e.g., kicked, whipped, or hit) by their owners or handlers.

Endangered Species

Overfishing, overhunting, and poaching threaten many species with extinction, a result that would decrease the diversity of Earth's animal kingdom and interfere with the food web, nature's delicate balance of predator–prey relationships. Even a small disturbance to the food web can be magnified many times over, turning ripples into tidal waves with the potential to affect a wide range of ecosystems. Habitat destruction and pollution secondary to industry and urban sprawl are other key components contributing to the declining numbers of many species, and not just endangered species.

Factory Farms

Many large farms that mass-produce meat, eggs, and dairy products keep their animals in appallingly poor living conditions. They may also use farming and processing techniques that cause the animals significant pain and suffering.

Pollution and Animal Health

In addition to its role in the destruction of natural habitats, pollution can have direct effects on the health of animal species that consume polluted products. These animals may choke on litter, ingest products that make them sick, or suffer toxic exposures that can affect their health as well as the health of their offspring. Moreover, even if the health of the animal is unaffected by consumption of polluted products, the buildup of these products within an animal's tissues (a process known as bioaccumulation) can have health effects on the animals (and humans) that consume it. And because we humans are at the top of the food chain, this should concern all of us.

Puppy Mills

Animal abuse is widespread among "puppy mills" and other businesses that breed dogs, cats, and other pets to provide a constant supply of baby animals for pet stores, even while millions (yes, millions!) of animals are put down each year because adoptive homes cannot be found for them.[1]

Discrimination

Age Discrimination

Age discrimination refers to practices that unfairly limit the opportunities of individuals on the basis of age. While individuals of any age (depending on the context) may experience age discrimination, most frequently young people and older adults experience it, with older adults the group most strongly associated with the term. Although laws exist in the US to prevent discrimination on the basis of age, older individuals may nevertheless find that in practice, they have more difficulty getting hired or promoted or are strongly encouraged to retire early. Age discrimination may extend to other fields such as health care and housing.

Disability Rights

According to the US Equal Employment Opportunity Commission, a disability is "a physical or mental condition that substantially limits a major life activity (such as walking, talking, seeing, hearing, or learning)."[2] Although the Americans with Disabilities Act and other legislation has made discrimination or harassment on the basis of disability illegal in the workforce, such discrimination (like age discrimination) can be difficult to prove. Discrimination may also be experienced in access to goods and services, health care, transportation, and education.

LGBT Rights

The rights of lesbian, gay, bisexual, and transgendered (LGBT) individuals vary enormously from country to country and even between states in the same country. In some nations, same-sex relations are punishable by imprisonment or even death. Within a handful of these places, only male-male sexual relations are illegal; that is, female-female sexual relations are legal. Still other countries don't specifically condemn same-sex orientation but maintain laws that make particular sexual practices illegal, thus implicitly discriminating against the LGBT community.[3]

In countries where same-sex relations are legal, the degree to which such relationships are recognized spans the spectrum from marriage (same rights as heterosexual couples) to civil unions (ranging from same rights to fewer rights) to domestic partnerships (fewer rights) to no recognition whatsoever.[4] These legal designations are important because they determine hospital visitation rights, power of attorney over medical decisions, insurance eligibility, adoption rights, taxation brackets, property and inheritance rights, and more.

Discrimination and intolerance affect LGBT individuals the world over, regardless of whether the government recognizes same-sex relationships. The LGBT community is still subject to violent hate crimes, abusive language, and childhood bullying so severe that some LGBT teens have taken their own lives. In many parts of the world, gays and lesbians are subject to job and housing discrimination, exclusion from military service, and exclusion from adoption.

Racial and Ethnic Discrimination

Globally, racism and discrimination on the basis of race or ethnicity continue to be major problems. These issues are especially evident in areas of the world in which changing patterns of immigration have brought different racial and ethnic groups into contact in short periods of time. Rapidly changing demographics and a lack of cross-cultural understanding have resulted in particularly pronounced cases of discrimination and racial strife. In other instances, long-standing racial and ethnic tensions continue to prove problematic.

In the US, though constitutional and legislative protections against racial discrimination exist and despite much societal progress over the past 50 years, racial discrimination remains an issue of great concern. Though illegal, discrimination in employment practices occurs and is reflected in unemployment rates. According to the Bureau of Labor Statistics, in August 2012, 14.1% of African Americans were unemployed compared with 7.2% of white Americans.[5] Racial minorities in the US also face discrimination in such areas as housing, education, health care, and the criminal justice system.

Religious Discrimination

Religious discrimination is the unequal treatment of an individual or group of individuals based on their religious beliefs. Individuals who do not subscribe to a particular religion (atheists and agnostics) may also experience discrimination. Religious discrimination may be manifest in unfair employment, education, health care, law enforcement, and housing practices. Though freedom of religion is guaranteed in the US by the First Amendment, religious intolerance and discrimination are realities. This was particularly evident after September 11, 2001, when many Muslim Americans experienced discrimination and even religious persecution though they were in no way affiliated with the 9/11 terrorists or the terrorists' extremist beliefs.[6]

Women's Rights

Much progress remains to be made in the area of women's rights. In some countries, laws prohibit women from owning property.[7] In other countries where women have had the right to vote for decades, the number of women holding public office is still much lower than 50%, which would be expected in proportional representation.[8]

Sexual and physical violence against women is a major issue in all countries but is so widespread in some areas of the world that it is far from the exception.[9] Gender inequality is evident in higher rates of illiteracy, job discrimination, longer hours worked for less pay, and higher rates of poverty. In some areas of the world, female genital mutilation, "honor" killings of female family members, and sex-selective abortions (with female fetuses aborted due to strong cultural preferences for males) are not uncommon. Young girls may be forced into prostitution, sold into slavery, or married off at a very early age.

Poor prenatal and perinatal care translates into high rates of maternal mortality in many regions of the world. Lack of health and family planning knowledge is also detrimental, leading to high rates of HIV infection and family sizes larger than the household income can support.

Education

Access to Education

Education is one of the fundamental human rights listed in the United Nations 1948 Universal Declaration of Human Rights. Specifically, the declaration states that all people are entitled to at least a free primary school education.[10] The extent to which countries fulfill this obligation to their citizens varies greatly, especially with regard to the education of girls. Some countries guarantee primary school education and secondary school education or even university-level education, while others struggle to provide even a few years of primary school education, if any at all. Many governments in developing countries have few funds to build schools, buy books, train teachers, and pay teacher salaries.

Even if educational opportunities exist, a number of roadblocks may prevent children from taking full advantage of them. In areas with few schools, students may travel long distances to get to school, some walking several hours each way. Once at school, students may struggle to learn because their parents can't afford to buy the paper, pencils, and books they need or because their hunger distracts them. In areas of the world where children can work for a wage or participate in the family business, parents may hold back their children from school in order to help the family earn additional income.

Curricular Cuts and Exclusions

In the US, music and visual arts programs in public schools have suffered serious setbacks in the wake of budget cuts. Proponents of arts education have argued that music and visual arts programs are an important component of a well-rounded education and contribute to children's creative development. Physical education and sports programs, so important to the development of healthy physical fitness behaviors in children, are also at risk from budget cuts at a time when childhood obesity is growing at an alarming rate.[11]

Another issue of note is that of sex education in public schools and the degree to which it varies in terms of availability and content. Many schools that have sex education programs do not discuss contraception options, emphasizing abstinence instead.[12] Around the world, attitudes toward sex education vary from progressive (mandatory sex education in Sweden, for example) to more conservative (no formal policy on sex education, deferring to parents). In some countries, including the US, states or regions dictate school sex education policy. American public schools are in large part divided into those that provide abstinence-only education (no discussion of contraceptives) and those that provide comprehensive education (full discussion of contraceptive options, with encouragement of abstinence).

While the content provided in sex education classes is often a topic of heated debate, there is no question as to whether comprehensive sex education is effective. Study after study has proven that comprehensive sex education decreases unplanned pregnancies and sexually transmitted infections without any effect on the likelihood that teens engage in sexual activity.[13] In countries where the rate of HIV infections is high, sex education (for both adults and adolescents) with emphasis on barrier methods of contraception is the best weapon in the battle against HIV/AIDS.

Educational Inequalities

Even when free education is provided by the government, all educational systems face their own unique set of problems. In the US, for example, the public school system is decentralized, so school curricular decisions are made at the state and local levels, resulting in significant differences among schools. Public schools are funded by a mix of federal, state, and local funds, the vast majority of which are state and local. In some cases, local property taxes are used to help fund area schools, a controversial practice that greatly increases the funds available to public schools in wealthy neighborhoods where property taxes are high. In other areas, relatively small funding cuts at federal, state, or local levels may result in the loss of entire departments or enrichment programs.

Education Reform

In the US, low salaries, difficult working conditions, and inadequate preparation and mentorship contribute to an alarmingly high turnover rate for teachers.[14] Another key issue in American education has been the quality of education provided, with many comparisons made to international educational systems that outperform American students in standardized tests. In the 2009 Performance of International Student Achievement study, American students ranked 25th in math, 17th in science, and 14th in reading among the 34 countries in the study.[15] However, if US test results are stratified by school poverty rates, a wide performance gap between the poorest and richest schools becomes apparent, with the richest schools in some cases (reading, for example) attaining higher scores than the most highly ranked country in the same category.[16] These results highlight the dramatic socioeconomic performance gap that plagues the American educational system, which is also struggling to address similar performance gaps by gender and race.

Environment

Climate Change

The burning of fossil fuels, for example, oil, coal, and natural gas, has led to a marked increase in atmospheric levels of carbon dioxide, and the mass production of animals for meat consumption has led to higher levels of atmospheric methane; both are greenhouse gases that contribute to global warming. Use of chlorofluorocarbons, a type of greenhouse gas commonly used in refrigerants and propellants, has contributed to depletion of the earth's ultraviolet-protective ozone layer. This has had many negative consequences, including increased rates of skin cancers in many parts of the world.[17]

Energy Conservation and Recycling

Although cleaner, more environmentally friendly sources of energy like wind and solar power are making great advances, they remain relatively expensive and less efficient alternatives. In recent years, proposals to pay consumers to use less energy have gained support. If consumers cut back on energy use, power companies can avoid building additional expensive generators for use during high-demand times of the year.

Recycling remains an important part of the energy conservation equation, as reclaimed materials cut manufacturing costs and decrease the amount of waste in overflowing landfills. Recycling of electronic waste (e.g., computers, cell phones, televisions) is of particular importance as processing speeds (and thus the number of discarded electronics) grow rapidly. These items have toxic components like lead and mercury, which can seep into the soil if they are not disposed of properly.

Pollution

The effects of pollution are widespread and are evidenced by smog, acid rain, eutrophication of lakes and rivers, acidification of oceans, and decreased ozone. Pollution disrupts ecosystems by destroying natural habitats and can result in direct harm to animals and their offspring, as well as animals that consume them. Various forms of pollution have also been linked to birth defects, cancer, and asthma in humans. Pollution is even found in space in the form of rings of human-generated space debris (e.g., spent rockets, old satellites, collision particles) in orbit around the earth. In the Pacific Ocean, a massive collection of garbage and degraded plastics known as the Great Pacific Garbage Patch continues to grow in size each year.[18]

Resource Depletion and Habitat Destruction

Coal mining and oil drilling are fast depleting the earth's natural resources and destroying many of its natural habitats. Oil spills and nuclear power accidents endanger the health of both animals and humans, causing damage to marine habitats and stretches of land that may take centuries to fully recover. Chemical waste from factories and pesticide runoff from farms result in eutrophication of rivers and lakes, disturbing the delicate balance of wildlife in and around these bodies of water. Deforestation (often as a result of urban and suburban sprawl) destroys natural habitats and contributes to the problem of increased atmospheric carbon dioxide, since fewer trees mean fewer natural carbon dioxide consumers. Increased carbon dioxide levels contribute to global warming and also seep into oceans, resulting in ocean acidification and suboptimal conditions for many aquatic species.

Health

Access to Care

Access to health care varies widely throughout the world. Some countries or regions have many doctors and hospitals, and others have few. Those who live far from a hospital may travel long distances over difficult terrain to seek medical attention. But even if a country has a large and well-developed health care network, this doesn't guarantee that everyone has the financial resources to access it. Medical care is expensive, and in countries without universal health care, those with jobs that don't provide health insurance and who can't afford private insurance pay for medical services out-of-pocket. Even those with insurance may have sky-high bills because their insurance policies may not cover the costs of many services. Health care system reform is a hot topic the world over, as all nations work to increase access, lower cost, and improve quality. Of particular note are ongoing debates about the way health systems should be financed, care delivered, and if and when care should be rationed given financial constraints.

Chronic Disease

Developed countries have long tended to have a higher burden of chronic diseases (such as diabetes, heart disease, and chronic obstructive pulmonary disease) than infectious diseases (such as malaria, tuberculosis, and cholera). In recent years, developing countries have seen a huge increase in chronic diseases over and above the high burden of infectious diseases they've historically struggled with.[19] High rates of smoking, the adoption of high-fat Western diets, soaring obesity rates, and, in many cases, the relative lack of public health resources have all contributed to the rise of chronic diseases in developing countries.

Mental Health

While progress has been made toward destigmatizing psychiatric disorders, much more openness and acceptance are needed. Barriers to treatment, including access to and affordability of mental health services, must also be better addressed. A 2005 study found that a staggering 26.2% of American adults had experienced a diagnosable mental disorder in the year preceding the study.[20] According to the Centers for Disease Control and Prevention, suicide was the 10th most common overall cause of death in the US in 2010, the third most common cause among youth ages 10 to 24, and the second most common cause among adults 25 to 34.[21]

Global Health

Global health focuses on worldwide patterns of health and disease and seeks to not only better understand the factors underpinning regional and international differences but also address any iniquities. Key issues of concern in a global health context include access to and quality of care, both of which vary widely among countries and even among hospitals and regions in the same country. This is due to a host of factors, including differential distribution of financial resources, health care workers, and access to advanced medical training, among other things. In some regions, a lack of infrastructure may make delivery of care particularly challenging. Even relatively inexpensive drugs (pennies per treatment) may be in short supply, resulting in easily preventable deaths. Moreover, public health systems, or networks of organizations that work together to promote health and prevent disease through education, surveillance, and promotion of healthy behaviors, are well established in some areas of the world and virtually absent in others.

Addictions

An individual who craves a substance and continues to use that substance despite experiencing detrimental effects as a result of that usage has an addiction to it. Common substances of abuse and addiction are illegal drugs (such as heroin and cocaine), prescription drugs (such as oxycontin and xanax), alcohol, and tobacco.

Addictions can and do frequently destroy lives. Their health effects range from death or incapacitation from overdoses to contraction of infections such as HIV or hepatitis C due to needle sharing or risky sexual behaviors. Addictions tear families apart, often fueling violence or exacerbating underlying psychiatric conditions. On a societal level, the economic costs of addiction are enormous, from missed workdays and lost productivity to health care expenditures for resultant outcomes like lung cancers and liver failure.

Tobacco addiction is particularly deadly in terms of sheer numbers. Lung cancers are the top cause of cancer deaths in the US,[22] and cancer is the second cause of death overall.[23] This is tragic because many of these deaths are preventable; it is estimated that 90% of all lung cancers are directly attributable to smoking.[24]

Poverty

Global Poverty

According to data released by the World Bank in February 2012, great strides have been made in reducing global poverty. Between 1981 and 2008, the percentage of individuals in developing countries living on less than $1.25 per day (the average poverty line of the 10 to 20 poorest countries) dropped from 52% to 22%. The World Bank also determined that the first United Nations Millennium Development Goal to halve the percentage of people living off less than a dollar a day by 2015 (relative to 1990 levels) was accomplished by 2008.[25] Nevertheless, much work remains to be done. Even if we maintain the same rate of poverty reduction, 1 billion people will still live on less than $1.25 per day in 2015.

There has also been far less growth in the number of people living above $2 per day (the poverty line in middle-income developing countries), indicating that gains are mostly being made by the very poorest.[26] In addition, the Gini index, a measure of income inequality, has been increasing for many countries, indicating that the income gap between rich and poor is increasing.[27] Wealth disparities can have a destabilizing effect on countries and may discourage further economic growth by making the very wealthy less likely to make investments that help drive growth. In the future, reductions in the absolute number of individuals living in poverty as well as decreases in income inequality will hinge on the success of other UN Millennium Development Goals such as universal primary school education and empowerment of women.

Homelessness

There are many reasons for housing insecurity—for example, the loss of a job, unexpected expenses (such as health care expenses) that result in bankruptcy, sudden disability, mental illness, exigent circumstances (such as leaving an abusive relationship or home environment), and eviction due to foreclosure. Other contributing factors include a lack of affordable housing, decreases in government welfare programs, and substance abuse.

Hunger

According to a 2010 report released by the Agriculture Organization of the United Nations, 16% of individuals living in developing countries are hungry, and 925 million people worldwide are undernourished. Forty percent of undernourished individuals live in China and India, and if those in Bangladesh, Ethiopia, Pakistan, Indonesia, and the Democratic Republic of the Congo are added, this accounts for two-thirds of the total.[28]

While 98% of the world's malnourished are located in developing countries, hunger is far from absent in developed countries.[29] The 2010 US Census revealed that 46.9 million Americans lived in poverty.[30] A 2011 report by the US Department of Agriculture's Economic Research Service reported that in 2010, 14.5% of US households experienced food insecurity at least once over a 12-month period.[31]

Unemployment

The bursting of the US housing bubble and the global financial crisis of the late 2000s upturned the world economy, leading to the tanking of global stock markets, the collapse of powerful banking institutions, government bailouts, and widespread foreclosures. Along with the turmoil came massive layoffs and higher unemployment rates the world over. The US unemployment rate increased from 4.4% in May 2007 to a high of 10% in October 2009, then decreased slowly to 8.1% as of August 2012.[32] High rates of unemployment are closely tied to housing and food insecurity.

Human Rights

Free Speech

Guaranteed by the First Amendment, freedom of speech and its closely related freedom of the press are often taken for granted in the US. This is not to say that there are never violations of the First Amendment or that all forms of speech are protected (for example, you can't yell "Fire!" in a crowded theater if there isn't a fire). On the whole, however, freedom of speech and the press are closely held tenets with layers of safeguards. In contrast, in many countries around the world, censorship is far more widespread, even among democratic developed countries, where individuals may be detained for insulting foreign dignitaries or imprisoned for speaking ill of a religion. Under authoritarian regimes, severe restrictions may be placed on freedom of speech and the press, with censorship of the Internet itself and imprisonment of reporters, among other actions.

Genocide

Genocide is the methodical destruction of a group or groups of people targeted because of their ethnicity, race, religion, or other identifying factors. Mass murder, forced sterilization, and other actions intended to result in the elimination of the group are all considered genocidal acts. The Holocaust was the most infamous example of genocide in the 20th century, but other examples abound. In just the past two decades, the Bosnian War, Rwandan genocide, and Darfur conflict, among others, reminded the world of the need to remain vigilant against such atrocities. Critics of international efforts to prevent genocide and bring its perpetrators to justice have called for swifter action on the part of international peacekeeping forces.

Human Trafficking

Human trafficking is essentially modern slavery. It is the exploitation of vulnerable or displaced populations such as homeless people, prostitutes, drug users, refugees, travelers, runaway teens, and children. Members of these groups are typically kidnapped, sold to traffickers by family, or tricked into situations from which they cannot extricate themselves. Once under the control of a trafficker, an individual may be forced into prostitution or other forms of coerced labor in order to generate income for the trafficker. In some forms of trafficking, individuals work to pay off debts but are compensated at rates that make it impossible for them to repay the debt. Though it is a problem that affects all countries, laws to prevent trafficking and punish traffickers vary considerably from country to country. Shockingly, some countries do not have specific legislation on human trafficking, or prohibit only certain forms.[33]

Labor Rights and Sweatshops

Labor rights are the minimum standards that workers may demand of their employers: fair wages, a safe work environment, and the freedom to organize into unions to exert collective bargaining power. Individuals may not be denied the opportunity to work or the ability to choose the nature of their work. They should also expect to be treated with respect, to be paid equal pay for equal work, and to be provided with reasonable time off as well as social protections from unemployment. Nevertheless, labor rights violations are fairly common. In some instances, individuals may even be subjected to hazardous conditions.

A critical labor issue in the US is the fact that women are routinely compensated less than a man for performing the same job at the same level of mastery.

Reproductive Rights

Reproductive rights refer to an individual's ability to exercise control over his or her fertility and sexual health, and to do so in an informed way that is free from coercion or force. In some countries, forced abortions or sterilizations, female and male genital mutilation, and denial of access to contraception or other sexual health services are commonplace.[34] The realization of full reproductive rights is a key component of the United Nations' Millennium Development Goal to improve maternal health.

Wrongful Imprisonment and Torture

Wrongful imprisonment spans the gamut from the forcible or coerced detainment of an individual against his will by an individual or state, to faulty convictions that result in the imprisonment of innocent individuals. In these cases, individuals may be detained or imprisoned without charge or for false charges, they may not be tried at all or tried unfairly, and they may be subject to torture or other coercive tactics in order to elicit false confessions.

According to a national registry of exonerations compiled by Northwestern University's Center on Wrongful Convictions and the University of Michigan Law School, over 2,000 individuals were wrongfully convicted of a crime in the United States between 1989 and 2012.[35] Torture is also an unfortunate reality the world over. Detainees at the US Guantanamo Bay facility have been subject to torture,[36] and despite vociferous protests by many Americans, condemnation of the camp by the United Nations, and repeated attempts by politicians to close the camp, the facility remains open and without a scheduled closing date as of October 2013.[37]

Violence

Abuse

Abuse is the intentional infliction of physical, psychological, or sexual harm. While anyone may be abused, there are several larger categories of abuse that are characterized either by the groups of people targeted by the abuse or the nature of the relationship between the target and the abuser. Child abuse is the mistreatment of a child, elder abuse is the mistreatment of older adults, and domestic abuse is the mistreatment of a spouse, partner, family member, or significant other. In addition to the immediate harms caused by acts of abuse, long-term consequences may also result in the form of psychological scars or learned abusive behaviors that perpetuate the cycle of abuse. Substance abuse is often associated with other forms of abuse, either as a factor contributing to, or a result of, the physical, psychological, or sexual abuse.

Bullying

Childhood bullying has long been a problem, and with the rise of social networking sites, it has taken on entirely new forms. While cruel words and even physical violence are just as prevalent as ever before in classrooms, hallways, and playgrounds, children and teens are now subject to verbal attacks online. In cyberbullying, bullies can coordinate malicious, repeated attacks that are publicly displayed as wall or photo postings, either on their own profiles or on the profiles of their targets.

In the US, a series of suicides of young adults bullied for their sexual orientations has spotlighted the severity and hateful nature of today's bullying. In 2010, the It Gets Better Project (www.itgetsbetter.org) was founded in an effort to combat the bullying that many LGBT teens experience.

Gang Violence

Violence is a central component of the gang lifestyle. Gangs amass money through drug trafficking, extortion, and other dangerous activities in which violence often plays a role. Turf wars with other gangs are another major source of violence, as are gang initiation rituals in which a potential gang member is required to perform a random or directed act of violence. Because a gang's control of a neighborhood is the result of the fear it is able to generate in the community, these violent acts can hold entire neighborhoods and even entire sections of cities hostage, stunting community development and solidarity.

Gun Control

In the US, the Second Amendment guarantees the right of private citizens to keep and bear arms. Gun control generally refers to regulations intended to limit the production, distribution, sale, or uses of guns. These regulations vary greatly by state, and there is fierce debate as to how rigorous these regulations should be, with some arguing for laxer laws to allow citizens to protect themselves more ably and others arguing for stricter laws to keep weapons out of the hands of criminals. Gun control becomes a part of national dialogue and debate each time a shooting occurs at a school or public arena; more often than not, these incidents also highlight gaps in the access to quality mental health care for the shooters, further complicating the issue.

Hate Crimes

A hate crime is any criminal act directed at an individual because of personal characteristics such as race, religion, national origin, sexual orientation, or gender identity. In the US, federal and state hate crime laws serve to increase the penalties associated with criminal acts motivated by hate. The range of groups protected and the severity of additional penalties imposed on offenders vary from state to state.

The various issues outlined here are intended only as very general overviews to help familiarize you with "the big picture." Think of them simply as a starting point for future research and exploration. To be a truly informed and engaged global citizen, you'll need to keep reading and observing to stay in tune with the problems all around you, to see how issues are interconnected. Always question why things are the way they are and challenge yourself to reflect on what can be done to make things better. In the course of reading this chapter, you've hopefully identified one or more issues that you find particularly interesting, or that trigger a strong emotional reaction. Keep these in mind as you read through Chapter 3.

Chapter 3

Identify a Problem

Chance favors the prepared mind.

—*LOUIS PASTEUR*

How do great leaders and activists find the causes they ultimately devote their lives to? Do they sit down with a list of global problems, scratching them off one by one until they're left with the issue of greatest interest to them, the cause that best suits their talents? Or do they sit back and wait for inspiration to strike?

The answer? Neither. No amount of reasoning, no amount of comparing your dreams, interests, and skills against a list of problems, is going to result in an answer that's anything more than a cold, optimized solution. You don't want to find something that just ticks all the right boxes. You want to find your calling—something you're passionate about, the thing you were meant to do. That spirit, that zeal for the cause, can't be arrived at by reason; it needs to be experienced. On the other hand, you can have lots of experiences in the course of your life without ever having that "Aha!" moment, that instance when a problem just sits up, grabs you by the lapels, and says, "Fix me!"

So how do you find the issue that will inspire you to greatness? The answer may surprise you. Unfortunately, there's no single action you can take that will guarantee you find your passion, no "if you do A, you will find B" prescription we can advocate. Rather, the answer isn't so much a methodology or strategy as it is a mind-set. For some people, this mind-set is natural; they see problems and opportunities everywhere that scream out to them. Others need to train themselves to think in this way. But if you have the right mind-set in place and an active involvement in the world around you, problems will find you. Or rather, you'll stumble across them without even looking. That's because with the right mind-set, you're both receptive to the world and keenly attuned to the possibilities for change.

If this mind-set comes naturally to you, you may already have a problem (and maybe even a solution) in mind. But once you've felt that natural draw to something, how do you make sure it's right for you? Although you can't reason your way into a cause to adopt or a problem to fix, you *should* apply a critical eye to opportunities as they pique your interest. This chapter walks you through this evaluative process.

So there are really two camps of people at this point:

1. You've already identified a problem you're passionate about and want to check to make sure it's right for you before proceeding. If this is the case, skip to the section "Once You Have a Problem in Mind" later in this chapter.
2. You haven't yet identified a problem that really inspires you. If this is the case, keep right on reading. The next section will prepare you to see the opportunities all around you!

Identify a Problem

Most people home in on a specific problem they feel strongly about long before realizing their interests actually extend to a larger cause, or broader set of issues, of which that problem is only one offshoot. We discuss the differences between problems and causes later in the chapter, but for now, let's focus on identifying problems that invigorate you and inspire you to work for change.

While finding these types of problems is largely a natural process, you can help things along a bit if you embrace the following three principles (explained in detail later): action, mind-set, and chance. The first two are things you can directly influence. Get these in order, and you've positioned yourself as best you can.

Action

Get up and get out there! You're never going to find your passion sitting around your room, no matter how hard you try. To be a conscientious

Figure 3.1. Identify a Problem

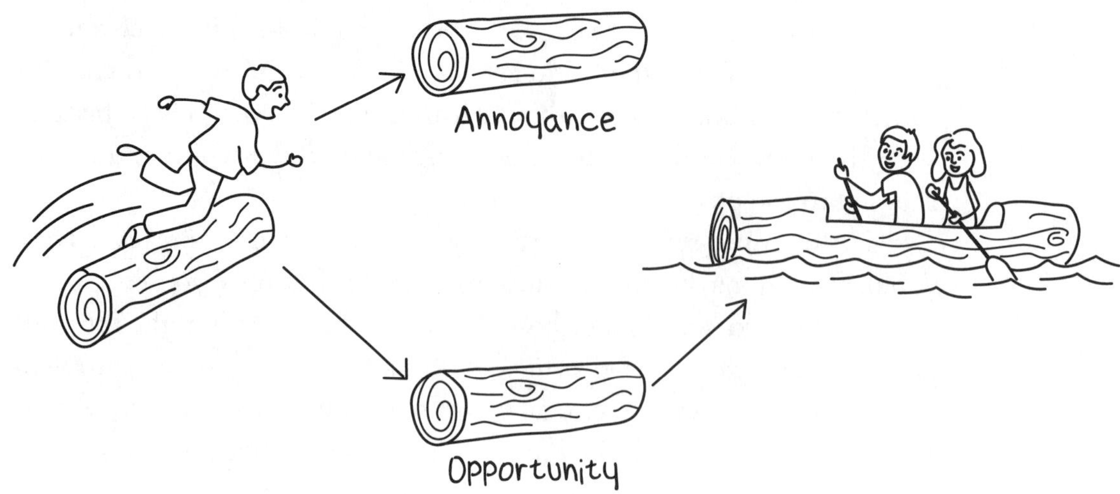

global citizen, you need to engage with the world around you. That means making a concerted effort to expose yourself to new environments, ideas, and people. Travel somewhere off the beaten path, try out new activities, and go out of your way to make new friends. Don't just think—do! You never know what locale, situation, or conversation will alert you to a problem that inspires you. In the great words of Jack London, "You can't wait for inspiration. You have to go after it with a club!"

Mind-set

The right mind-set is by far the most important part of the equation. Without it, you can have a million experiences but fail to recognize the potential in even one of them. With the right mind-set, you're mentally engaged in all your experiences. You're prepared to process what you encounter, and when you can do that, you can recognize new opportunities to make an impact.

To cultivate this frame of mind:

1. Do Your Homework

Nourish your brain with a nutritious mix of newspapers, books, and blogs. Strive to develop as broad a knowledge base as possible so you can better understand the context of the situations you encounter and make key connections to other fields that may provide insights essential to a solution.

2. Be Observant

Keep your eyes and ears open at all times so you don't miss a key detail or opportunity. Problems aren't always easy to recognize.

3. Indulge Your Curiosity

Question everything. Examine all situations with a critical eye to get a better idea of whether a problem even exists, and if it does, why that's the case. Moreover, why does it remain unresolved? In most cases, you will probably just uncover new, interesting bits of information. Sometimes, however, you'll uncover a problem that really captivates you.

4. Remain Open-Minded

You never know where your next great inspiration may come from, so keep an open mind about new experiences and challenges. Don't get too attached to a particular idea or notion of how you think you "should" get involved in the world around you. Stay receptive to whatever the universe throws your way; it may be something unexpected and wonderful!

5. Know Yourself

Knowing who you are, what you care about, and what you're good (and not so good) at are essential to finding a cause that's as good a match to you as you are to it. Ideally you want to find something that fits you and your interests well, and is something that you're also well suited to and can affect in a meaningful way. Chapter 1 features a series of exercises to help you better understand yourself and your motivations. If you haven't already completed these exercises, take a moment to revisit the chapter now. When you have a good sense of self, you'll naturally gravitate toward problems that are good matches.

Case Study: Global Village Fruits

Do Your Homework: Before setting off on a trip to India, college student Annie Ryu learned as much about the local culture as she could, as well as some of the problems facing the populations in the areas she planned to visit.

Be Observant: While in India, Annie noticed something that most tourists pass right by: piles and piles of unusual-looking fruit by the side of the road.

Indulge Your Curiosity: When Annie asked about the fruits, she found out they were jackfruits: large tropical fruits native to the region. She could have stopped there but was intrigued and probed further, asking why the fruits were by the side of the road. Annie learned that farmers in the region didn't have the resources to cart the large, heavy fruits long distances, and only a relatively small percentage actually made it to the side of the road for sale. The rest of the fruits were left to rot on or under the jackfruit trees.

Remain Open-Minded: Annie had traveled to India for work related to Remindavax, a social venture she cofounded to help improve patient compliance through mobile technology. She had no idea she'd stumble on an agricultural distribution problem. But instead of dismissing the problem as something outside her immediate interest in health care, Annie gave the issue some thought. She realized that if she could find a way to keep the fruit from going to waste, she might help the local populace generate more income, a result that could improve the health of the region. She discovered that jackfruit waste was a problem she was excited to tackle.

Know Yourself: Annie knew she was up for the innovative challenge posed by the jackfruits. From previous experience, she knew she was determined, resourceful, and creative, key qualities that would help her along the way. Through her work with Remindavax, she'd gained experience in social innovation, as well as some business know-how. For these reasons, Annie believed she'd not only enjoy working to solve the problem, but would also be able to contribute useful skills and knowledge. Ultimately Annie founded Global Village Fruits, a socially conscious for-profit company that supports the local economy by helping farmers export dried jackfruit for sale in the US.

To learn more from Annie Ryu about getting a socially conscious for-profit started, turn to Chapter 38.

Chance

As with all things, there's a random element of chance involved in finding the right problem for you to address. For example, if you had decided to go to the beach on Saturday rather than Sunday, you might not have seen the sea turtle entangled in trash on the beach that moved you to get involved with a local environmental group. Instead, you might have decided to go for a hike in the mountains, witnessing an accident on the drive over that made you realize the need for better traffic lights in your community. The point is that what ultimately captures your attention will at least in some part be due to chance decisions you make. Embrace this random component and revel in the excitement of never knowing exactly what's next.

So get up and get active in the world around you! Throw yourself into new experiences and activities. At the same time, work on the points outlined above to develop the right mind-set to recognize problems (or opportunities, depending on how you look at it). Finally, embrace the randomness of it all. With the right mind-set, you'll be equipped to turn a chance occurrence into a lifelong passion and force for good.

Once You Have a Problem in Mind

Once you've identified a challenge that piques your interest, pause to reflect for a moment. Although you can't use your powers of deduction to reason your way into a problem, you can reason your way out of a problem. It would be silly to jump headlong into an issue without stopping to consider if your first impression was valid, if your excitement holds true, and if the problem at hand is something you're passionate about and want to commit to. There's also the possibility you're torn between several very different problems. In either case, ask yourself the following questions when considering a problem you've identified:

1. Is It Something I'm Interested In?

This is an important question; you'd be surprised how many people get involved in particular problems or causes because doing so just seems like the "right" thing, or at least the popular thing, to do. And sure, these issues are worthy; they're areas we all tend to agree need attention. They set off our charitable instincts. But if you're not genuinely interested in the problem, you'll probably lose interest after awhile or lack the motivation to shake up the field with new, innovative solutions, which is what you should be aiming for.

Ideally, you should wait until your interest is sparked by a problem you want to learn more about. Maybe the reasons the problem exists are complicated and nuanced, and that challenge excites you. Maybe the cause or larger category of causes it falls under is related to a subject you enjoyed in high school or the major you chose in college. Or maybe it's just an area you've always wanted to know more about. The point here is that whatever you choose, make sure it's something you'd want to read more about for fun.

2. Is It Something I'm Passionate About?

Do you feel energized and excited when you think about solving the problem? Do you have strong opinions about the problem or the solution? Is it a topic you could talk about forever? If you feel as if you can't wait to roll up your sleeves and get to work, that's a great sign.

3. Do I Have a Strong Emotional Reaction to It?

When you think about the problem, do you experience an intense emotion? Are you sad to see such suffering, or destruction, or carelessness? Are you angry because no one has done anything about it or disappointed because nothing that has been tried has worked? Maybe you're frustrated and upset to see that the problem even exists, or hopeful that one day it will be a thing of the past. These are powerful emotions to harness: they'll drive you forward, motivating you to keep going even when the going gets tough (and it *will* get tough at some point!). Causes that affect you at a deep enough level to trigger an emotional reaction—any emotional reaction—are causes that are worth a second look.

4. Does It Reinforce My Personal Values?

Here's a great example of why self-knowledge is so important. (And if you still haven't completed the short exercises in Chapter 1, go back and do that now.) Knowing what you stand for is an important yet highly underrated type of self-awareness. If you have a good sense of self, a good sense of the values and principles you hold dear, this knowledge will help guide you in all avenues of life. The decisions you make, and especially the difficult decisions you make, can and should be based on your personal values.

When you're considering a problem, ask yourself whether the change you'd help bring about would improve the world in a way that aligns with your value set. Let's say that equality is one of the most important principles to you. You strongly believe that everyone, regardless of race, creed, gender, or sexual orientation, is equal and should be treated that way. Now let's say you're choosing between two admirable problems: protecting a forest near your home from destruction or securing a transparent equal pay for equal work compensation policy at your job. Both issues are worthwhile, but the one that would probably fit best with your guiding principle of equality is eliminating the gender pay gap. This result would help increase the level of equality in the world, and that's something that would greatly reinforce one of the personal values you've identified as important.

5. Can I Contribute Meaningfully?

Ask yourself if you have special skills or experiences that would be of value when working to solve the problem in question. If the answer is "yes," that's an extra point in favor of whatever problem you're considering. For example, if you're interested in helping refugees resettle in the US, having a law degree or connections to lawyers who specialize in international law would be an asset when helping refugees seek asylum here. Similarly, you or someone in your family might know a hotel owner who'd be willing to donate a few rooms in the off-season for temporary housing for transitioning families. Or maybe you were once a refugee yourself, and your own experiences would help you connect with those going through such a difficult and uncertain time.

Moreover, talents or knowledge that are a bit out of the ordinary may be of particular importance, especially if no one has ever applied them in the context of the cause you're thinking about. For this reason, it's a good idea to make a list of all your strong points. Don't leave anything out, even if it seems a bit disconnected to the problem at hand. If you've completed the exercises in Chapter 1, you can simply flip back to Exercise 1.6 where you identified your strengths and weaknesses. Turn to it frequently when thinking about your options.

These questions are intended to help direct your thinking as you consider whether to tackle a particular problem you've noticed.

There's no strict cut-off for whether you should or shouldn't pursue an issue. However, as a rough guide, if you answered yes to at least four of the five questions, then it's an issue you should strongly consider. If you answered yes to only one or two of these, you'd probably be happier waiting to find something you feel more excited about. The idea is to choose a problem you love—something you'll gladly get out of bed early on a Saturday to work on. You need to be dedicated to the problem so that when the going gets tough, you'll stick with it.

From Problem to Cause

Once you've identified a concrete problem to solve, a good next question to ask yourself is, "What is the larger cause I'm working to advance?" A cause is much broader and more general than a problem. Whereas a problem is a specific circumstance that requires a solution, a cause is a set of many issues or problems unified by a key commonality. The main point is that if you're enthusiastic about solving a particular problem, you might find that your real passion, what you really find fulfilling, is advancing the larger cause. And once you've figured out the cause you care about, you may find a host of related problems you'd like to work toward solving.

To work your way back from a specific problem to a cause, think about all the factors that contributed to the development of the problem. What are the forces at work that caused the problem to happen? How might it have been prevented?

To get a better idea of what this might look like, let's look at a few examples of various categories of problems and causes at the local, national, and international levels:

Category: Education

- Local level

  The problem: Budget cuts may force public school #118 to eliminate sports teams.

  Your cause: Increasing school funding
- National level

  The problem: In the US, 46% of teachers leave the profession within five years.

  Your cause: Lowering teacher attrition rates

- International level
  The problem: In areas of the world where educating women isn't seen as a priority, girls are kept home from school to help with housework or the family business.
  Your cause: Increasing gender equality in education

Category: LGBTQ Rights

- Local level
  The problem: Two teenage boys were prevented from attending their high school prom because they planned to go together as a couple.
  Your cause: Stopping LGBTQ discrimination
- National level
  The problem: Same-sex couples in the US may enter into civil unions, domestic partnerships, or marriages in certain states, but these relationships aren't officially recognized by the federal government. As a result, same-sex couples don't enjoy the same federal benefits and protections as heterosexual couples do .
  Your cause: Achieving marriage equality
- International level
  The problem: In 78 countries, homosexuality is considered a criminal offense and in five of these countries, it is punishable by death.[1]
  Your cause: Decriminalizing homosexuality

When thinking about the umbrella cause for the problem you've identified, examine the problem from as many different perspectives as possible. Because problems are often complex, a particular problem may fall under many different causes. For example, if you're concerned about high rates of teen pregnancy in your community, you might discover you're more interested in any number of overarching causes like reproductive rights or health education. Practice tracing problems to causes in Exercise 3.1.

Let's say you trace your interest back to the larger cause of increasing access to health education because you believe that sex education has the power to greatly reduce the teen pregnancy problem. Discovering your interest in health education could lead you to find you're passionate about a number of other problems that also fall under this health education umbrella: the need to educate children about healthy food choices, the lack of mental health services at your local community college, or the need to better educate those with diabetes about keeping their blood sugar levels under control.

Exercise 3.1 Problems and Causes Worksheet

Identify a few problems you're interested in then think of at least three causes that the given problem might fall under. An example is given in the table.

The Problem	Your cause	Your cause	Your cause
Homelessness in your community	Increasing the availability of affordable housing	Decreasing the unemployment rate	Increasing access to mental health services

Chapter 4

Understand the Problem

Now that you've found a problem that really gets your blood pumping and you can't wait to dive right in, the first thing you need to do is... restrain yourself! It'll be difficult, but the wisest thing to do before you get started, before you even consider solutions, is to pause.

You can't devise a solution until you have a good idea of the scope of the problem, the contributing and mitigating factors, and the historical and social context. And you can't devise a *good* solution unless you've learned what's been tried before, what's worked or failed, and what the people or groups affected by the problem think about how it might be solved. This means you'll need to do some research to better understand the problem before proceeding.

This chapter provides a broad overview of the research process, from clearly defining the problem you want to understand and the questions you'll need to ask, to identifying the right resources to address those questions. Once you have a good grasp of the problem and its larger context, you'll be ready to start thinking about potential solutions.

The Value of Research

You can learn a lot just by paying attention. Let's say you're on a basketball team. During the fourth quarter of a particularly close game, your coach decides to sub you in for another player. If you've been paying attention to the game up to this point, you know that number 22 on the opposing team plays dirty, one of your forwards has taken a lot of hits and is looking pretty tired, and your usual triangle offense just doesn't seem to be cutting it. Equipped with a knowledge of the game's history, its players, and what seems to be working or not, you step onto the court prepared to switch things up in an effective way. On the other hand, if you'd instead spent the game texting on your cell phone, you'd have no idea what was going on and would be doomed to repeat the same mistakes.

In a similar vein, when you've identified a problem you're passionate about solving, it's equally essential to familiarize yourself with the players already on the field, as well as the field itself. What are the demographics and history of the community you'll be working with? How did the problem arise, why is it still an issue, what has been tried to solve the problem in the past, etc.? This information will help you tailor your strategy when approaching the problem, maximizing your chances of success. Without this information, you'd likely miss key components of the problem or try solutions that had already been shown to fail.

The point here is that a little advance preparation helps you better address the problems you encounter on the court and off. When you do your research and arm yourself with as much knowledge as possible about the situation at hand, you're much better prepared to meet and overcome the challenges ahead of you.

Define the Problem and Identify Your Knowledge Gaps

Clearly and narrowly defining the problem is something that's frequently overlooked but incredibly vital. Well-meaning individuals and groups often take on too much too fast, and, as a result, they splinter their efforts and decrease their impact. Keep your scope narrow, especially when starting out, and stick to a specific problem. To whittle down the issue to its most basic components, ask yourself the following questions:

- Who is affected?
- What is happening?
- Where is the problem localized?
- When did it start or get worse?
- Why is the problem happening?
- How have others tried to address the problem before?

Any question you can't answer with your current knowledge of the problem is a question you'll need to research in order to answer. This is a good way of identifying weaknesses in your knowledge base that you can shore up with the research strategies and tools presented in the rest of the chapter. The more information you have, the better prepared you'll be and the better you'll be able to narrowly define the problem in such a way that it becomes a manageable and realistic goal.

Let's say that the problem you've identified is that sea turtles in your area are dwindling in number. With a little research into the who, what, where, when, why, and how, you can get a much better picture of the situation.

Who is affected?
- *Directly*: Sea turtles (specifically, the Kemp's Ridley species of sea turtle)
- *Indirectly*: People like you who enjoy the presence of the sea turtles; the local food chain that depends on the sea turtles to keep other species in check

What is happening?
- The number of sea turtles is dwindling.

Where is the problem localized?
- In your area, the problem's been noted at Lunar Bay and Gentle Tides Beach.

When did it start or get worse?
- Decreasing numbers of sea turtles were first noticed at Lunar Bay three years ago and at Gentle Tides Beach two years ago.

Why is the problem happening?
- Sea turtles are choking on plastic garbage in the waters.
- Sea turtles lay their eggs on dark, quiet beaches, and the bright lights from new condominiums near Lunar Bay and Gentle Tides prevent the turtles from laying their eggs there.

How have others tried to address the problem before?
- No one in your community has intervened yet.

You can see how researching the who, what, where, when, why, and how has finely tuned the scope of the problem. The focus narrowed from "sea turtle numbers are decreasing" to "Kemp's Ridley sea turtle numbers have been decreasing in Lunar Bay and Gentle Tides Beach over the last three years due to pollution and destruction of their natural habitat by new condominium developments." Now *that* is a well-defined problem that will help direct your efforts moving forward.

In addition to information specific to the problem in your community, cast your net a bit wider to learn about the broader history and context of the various topics, populations, and challenges related to your problem. These additional pieces of information can prove very helpful when brainstorming solutions to the problem. In the sea turtle example, after doing some additional research, you might learn …

Figure 4.1. Better Define the Problem

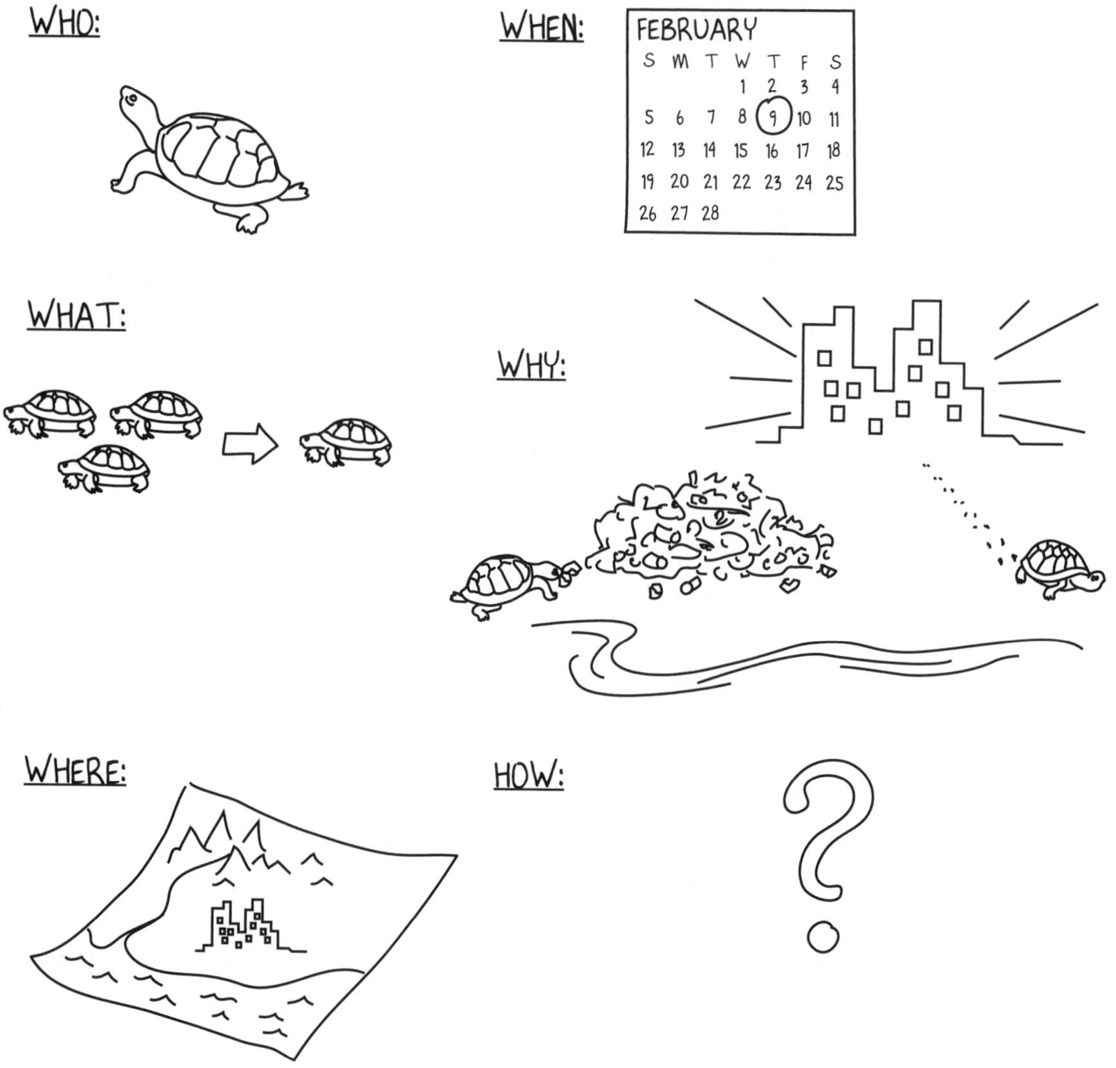

- that Kemp's Ridley sea turtles are an endangered species found primarily in the Gulf of Mexico.
- about the natural habitats, mating behaviors, and food sources of the Kemp's Ridley sea turtles.
- the types of pollution found in local waters and the source of the plastics the turtles are choking on.
- that the lights from the condominiums that reach the beaches at night are from outdoor tennis courts.

> **Tip** You can't evaluate your progress toward solving a problem if you can't measure it. And you can't measure it if it's not a well-delineated problem with clear goals.

Another key is to seek out information on the larger cause or causes your problem falls under to familiarize yourself with the history and progression of the field. Make a point to learn what others faced with a similar problem have tried. For example, have efforts been made elsewhere along the coast to save the Kemp's Ridley sea turtles? Don't be afraid to ask what worked and what didn't. You may draw inspiration from what others have done or take away a few best practices that others have learned from trial and error. Even a solution that worked in another field might prove equally effective if applied in your case. Again, all of these data will be great to have at your disposal when it comes time to start thinking about solutions (but not yet … hold off just a little bit longer until you get to Chapter 5).

Research the Problem

With these specific questions and research objectives in mind, how do you find and collect all the data you'll need? While there are almost limitless resources available to you, we've organized them by mode of access, because when you boil it all down, there are four general ways to research a problem—you can read, watch, do, and talk.

Read

Reading (and lots of it) is probably the first thing that comes to mind when you think of research. That's because the written word is one of the most efficient, organized ways of conveying ideas to an audience. With the increasing amount of online resources available, advanced indexing and search capabilities have made it easier than ever before to find exactly what you need when you need it. Consider the following sources of information.

Figure 4.2. Dig Deep to Understand the Root Causes of the Problem

Wikipedia

While you'll need to be careful to double-check information you get from Wikipedia, the online open source encyclopedia is a great place to get a broad overview of an issue. Scroll down to the bottom of an entry and you should find a lot of high-yield citations. The works cited may be books, peer-reviewed journal articles, movies, etc. that you can use as additional resources.

Search Engines

Use a search engine like Google or Bing as your launch pad to a variety of websites with helpful, targeted information. For example, if you're interested in finding out more about the sea turtles in your area, search for "sea turtle distribution," and your search engine will not only suggest websites to visit but also pull up sea turtle distribution maps under the images search function.

Search engines are particularly useful if you have no idea where to begin online. You never know what useful but unexpected results will be returned, and you'll likely get a mix of government, nonprofit, corporate, and personal websites and blogs—resources you might never have thought to consult otherwise.

A Warning on Sources

Although any source of information may unintentionally (or intentionally, in some cases) present false or misleading information, the Internet is particularly vulnerable in this regard. Because the Internet as a whole is unregulated, there's nothing to stop people from publishing whatever they please. This means that opinions may be presented as facts, "facts" may in reality be unproven, and actual facts may be misrepresented.

The Internet is essentially the wild, wild west because there's relatively no accountability. This means you have to be very careful when selecting online sources of information. You'll need to examine each website to determine who created it and why, when it was last updated, and whether the information seems biased in any way. This will help you separate the wheat from the chaff.

In contrast, books, newspapers, magazines, and peer-reviewed journals *generally* have some form of built-in accountability. If they don't present accurate information, their readers will turn elsewhere. An exception is self-published material, which the author or authors have paid to publish. Information in these types of publications should be viewed with a more critical eye. Newsletters or magazines published by any organization, public or private, should also be evaluated more critically, as they may present information in a way that presents the group in a more favorable light or is biased in some way due to the nature of the group.

Nevertheless, almost all sources of information, while factually correct, may contain biases in the way that information is presented. For example, the *New York Times* is generally considered more liberal politically, while the *Wall Street Journal* is considered more conservative.

Books

Books are a great resource for in-depth information on a topic, so make a trip to your local library, bookstore, or online bookstore. Consult encyclopedias for a definitive overview of a topic, biographies for inspiration from activists who share your cause, and nonfiction books for information and best practices on a countless array of subjects. If you prefer to read with an e-reader, more and more books (typically newer releases) are available in e-book format, so check an online bookseller for titles of interest.

Newspapers

Local newspapers are a great way to learn about the history of a problem in a particular community and any efforts that have been made to correct it. You can often check for archived articles online, but if your local paper doesn't have an online archive, head to the local library to examine digitized microfilm records. You can check with the paper itself to see if it has back issues or a database you can search. Large regional and national newspapers can also be useful for a broader picture of the problem or any associated issues. Search articles, editorials, and letters to the editor, which may contain valuable perspectives worth noting.

Newsletters and Magazines

Many nonprofits, companies, professional societies, and leisure groups publish regular newsletters or magazines to update their members or employees about developments in the field. Although these publications may be snail-mailed, they are increasingly e-mailed out in pdf form. They're typically free to members, though becoming a member may require a fee.

For groups that e-mail their periodic publications, you can often subscribe to the newsletter free of charge by submitting your e-mail address online. If you come across a group whose interests overlap with yours, it's worth checking to see if you can find copies of the newsletter or magazine on the group's website or sign up for future mailings. Depending on your area of interest, you may also find it worthwhile to subscribe to or look up back issues of independent magazines.

Peer-Reviewed Journal Articles

Searching through peer-reviewed journals for articles related to your problem or cause is a must. *Peer-reviewed* means that the articles have been evaluated for accuracy and approved by third-party experts in the field prior to publication. Peer review is the gold standard for publishing in academic disciplines. It means that you can trust to a reasonable degree that the information contained in the publication is correct: experiments hold up to rigorous scrutiny and employ sound experimental practices, and reviews and other articles cite credible sources and present accurate information and logical conclusions. Peer-reviewed journals are a particularly great place to look for articles about past solutions that have been implemented in an attempt to address your problem and whether they were efficacious.

Great places to start an online search for peer-reviewed articles include:

- *Scopus* has broad coverage of peer-reviewed journals that date back to 1885. However, it's subscription only, so check to see if your university or library is signed up so you can access it for free.
- *Web of Knowledge* provides access to older peer-reviewed journals than Scopus but has a narrower scope. It's also a subscription-only service.
- *Google Scholar* is free to search, but its results may not be as well curated as those on subscription sites.
- *PubMed* is a government site that's free to search. It should be your first site to check for health or medical topics.

Watch

A lot of informative content can be watched on television or a computer screen. In particular, you may want to look up news footage about a problem in your area, instructional videos, and documentaries. While you can always request copies of broadcasts or rent or buy videos, much of this content is now available (and more easily accessible) online. News footage and even entire news broadcasts can be found on news websites, short instructional how-to clips are a mainstay of sites like YouTube, and documentaries can be downloaded or streamed from online sources like Amazon Instant Video, iTunes, or Netflix.

Do

There's no replacement for experiencing something firsthand. This is a particularly useful strategy when you're trying to understand the roots of the problem you've identified. You can gain priceless insights by placing yourself in a position to experience or see the problem for yourself.

In the sea turtles example, let's say you're unsure what factors might be contributing to the decline in sea turtles. Your initial research into sea turtles (consulting Wikipedia, some sea turtle advocacy websites, and a book on amphibian habitats) suggests that bright lights can scare turtles away from breeding grounds. You realize the beachside condominiums were built about a year before the sea turtle numbers began declining. Could light from the condominiums be scaring away the sea turtles at night? There's only one way to find out: visit the beaches at night, perhaps even on a number of occasions at different times of night. When you do, you find that lights from two tennis court complexes associated with the condominiums shine directly onto large portions of the affected beaches.

Even if you can't directly see or experience a problem, you may find it useful to immerse yourself in the community in which the problem exists. This will give you a better idea of any attitudes, beliefs, or cultural practices that may potentially contribute to, or help solve, the problem.

Talk

While you're out there doing and experiencing, you should also be talking—a lot. Talk to the people in the community affected by the problem. Why do they think it's a problem, what do they think is causing it, how does it affect them, and how do they think it might be solved?

Engaging the community in which a problem exists is essential to understanding the problem and designing a sustainable, community-based solution. (For more on community ownership, see Chapters 11 and 34.) You should also seek out advice from people with more experience in your field. Approach leaders of local groups tackling similar problems; e-mail professors whose research interests match yours; and arrange to meet with politicians, journalists, or anyone else who may be able to provide additional historical or social context.

Whoever you speak to, be sure to ask what they think is contributing to the problem and whether they know of any past efforts to address it. If you can find others who have previously attempted to fix the problem, put these people high on your list of those to talk to. Ask them about what they tried, as well as what did or didn't work.

Take your time and be thorough when researching the problem you hope to solve because careful and methodical research will pay huge dividends. Once you feel you've done enough research to not only clearly define your problem, but also serve as the knowledge base for potential answers to that problem, you're ready to begin working toward a solution!

Chapter 5

Brainstorm Solutions

In Chapter 4, you learned how to research a problem in order to gain a better understanding of the scope of the issue, its history, and the major contributory and complicating factors. Now that you have a clearer picture of the situation, it's time to begin thinking about the method you'll employ to bring about the positive change you'd like to see. In other words, what will you *do* to try to solve the problem?

This is a critical question because the strategy you intend to implement will play a large part in determining the success or failure of your efforts. This isn't meant to intimidate you; it's just a warning encouraging you to stop and think before rushing to take action. There are many, many ways to tackle an issue, and you should carefully consider each one before proceeding. For example, if you've decided your goal is to increase the rate of seat belt usage in your community, you could take a number of different approaches to achieve this end: launch an ad campaign, partner with local driving schools to increase the emphasis on seat belt usage in the driver's ed curriculum, or work to pass legislation making penalties for driving without a seat belt more severe, just to name a few possibilities.

This chapter will help you generate a long list of ideas for addressing the problem you've trying to solve. Once you've identified as many options as possible, you'll be ready to begin the process of slowly whittling down these choices until you've zeroed in on the best approach to take, given your unique situation and resources.

What Distinguishes an Idea from a Solution?

The general rule of brainstorming is that "there is no such thing as a bad idea." That's true. But you can also prime yourself to recognize a *great* idea when you hear it. Consider skipping ahead and reading Chapters 6 though 9. These chapters address Step 1 of the Do Good Well method for social innovation—Do What Works. While you should strive to think up as many ideas as possible (no matter how unlikely they might seem) in the brainstorming phase, you'll ultimately seek to implement the idea with the best odds of succeeding—a solution that actually works. You might be thinking, "Don't I need to test the idea out first to know whether or not it is a solution?" Yes, but you can apply what you learned in Chapter 4 to determine if the idea will make the type of lasting change you're trying to create, if it will put a "band-aid" on the problem or actually *solve* the problem. Chapters 6 through 9 outline the basic principles behind solutions that work, principles to later use to narrow down your list of options. By reading ahead now, though, you can gain key insights that will improve the breadth and depth of your brainstorming session.

Chapters 6 through 9 demonstrate the best solutions are those that:

1. Take into account the larger context of the problem and interact synergistically with existing efforts in order to attack the problem from as many angles as possible (Chapter 6)
2. Incorporate and improve upon existing evidence-based solutions (Chapter 7)
3. Evolve to take into account new information and improve efficacy and efficiency (Chapter 8)
4. Innovate in response to specific challenges or roadblocks, or when existing solutions prove inadequate (Chapter 9)

Of course, as you go about your work, you'll continuously be brainstorming so feel free to flip around and come back to this chapter as needed.

Begin to Brainstorm

Brainstorming is a problem-solving strategy that encourages creativity and unfettered thinking. The goal is to generate a lot of potential solutions, to think as broadly and as inclusively as possible to ensure no possibility is missed. And don't be afraid to get creative!

While you'll ultimately decide that some of these solutions are great (practical, appropriate, and effective), and others are awful (impractical, inappropriate, and ineffective), try not to evaluate your ideas with regard to these metrics right at the outset. Again, save assessments of your ideas for later—the point of brainstorming is to come up with as many options as possible in a nonjudgmental environment. An idea you might dismiss as impractical might actually be wonderful if modified by a suggestion from a peer. Or it might inspire a far better idea. Idea generation is the birthplace of innovation.

Note The term *brainstorming* became popular through the work of Alex Osborn, an advertising executive who wrote the book *Applied Imagination* in 1953 about how groups can come up with creative and quality ideas. He espoused four rules for group brainstorming: (1) Focus on quantity, (2) Withhold criticism, (3) Welcome unusual ideas, and (4) Combine and improve ideas.[1]

While brainstorming can be a solo activity—something you focus on in a quiet location, just you and your journal or letting your mind wander right before going to bed—it's usually most productive when undertaken as a group activity. The more people you can assemble, the more perspectives, experiences, and creativities you can draw from. Oftentimes, good ideas will feed off one another, and a group dynamic is critical for this type of positive interplay.

Below you'll find descriptions of three different types of brainstorming sessions. You don't need to try them out in any particular order, though you should consider trying each type at least once, as you may find each type generates a unique set of ideas. Keep careful records of the suggestions made at each session. After you've run out of ideas at your next session, you may want to pull out the list of ideas from previous sessions to compare answers, as well as bring up any unique suggestions for the group's consideration. By pointing out a solution the group missed, you may spawn additional ideas along similar lines of thinking.

Back-of-the-Napkin Brainstorming

Think of the conversations that arise over dinner or drinks; you start coming up with interesting ideas and find the closest thing to jot these ideas down on—a napkin, scrap sheet of paper, or your smartphone. That's back-of-the-napkin brainstorming—a super informal type of brainstorming that can happen anytime, anywhere, with any number of people (though it's particularly well-suited to a small group of two to six people). This type of brainstorming is great if you're out and about and just happen to see something that inspires you or gets you thinking in a new and unexpected way. With the problem and your ultimate end goal in mind, jot down ideas, observations, or associations as they come up so you can review them later.

Whiteboard Brainstorming

From start-ups to science labs, whiteboards line the walls where great ideas are born. This form of brainstorming works well for most sizes of groups in a classroom or conference room environment. The whiteboard is a beacon, bringing together interested parties who want to see results; it conveys action—you're going to generate ideas, work together to refine the ideas, and come up with some end product or decision. There are numerous approaches to whiteboard brainstorming; two are explained in Exercise 5.1.

Exercise 5.1 Whiteboard Brainstorming

1. Start by gathering around a large whiteboard (or a large sheet of butcher's paper taped to the wall). Use a marker to draw two vertical lines, dividing the whiteboard into thirds. In the left-most third, write "Problems," in the middle third, write "Resources," and in the right-most third, write "Solutions." Then, give everyone in your group a pad of Post-it notes and a pen. If your group is small enough, try to give everyone a different color of notes.
2. Begin with the "Problems" column and instruct everyone to reflect on the primary problem you've identified and want to tackle. Ask the following questions:
   - What factors, past or present, have contributed to the problem?
   - What issues make it difficult to tackle?
   - What obstacles are you likely to encounter?

   Ask your team members to write just one idea per Post-it, pinning these up under the corresponding column.
3. Repeat this exercise with the middle column, asking team members to identify all the resources at your group's disposal. These might include finances, skill sets, expertise, partnerships, community assets, etc. Be sure to include groups with similar goals as yours, even if you don't currently work with them directly.
4. Finally, move on to the right-most column, asking team members to reflect on the information in the previous two columns in order to suggest potential solutions.

Note: If your group is larger than 15–20 people, consider breaking up into smaller groups then reconvening to share the best ideas of each group.

(continued)

Here's another great variation of this brainstorming exercise your group may want to try:

1. Start the exercise in the same way, instructing everyone to brainstorm factors that contribute to the problem. Once everyone has added their Post-its to the left-most column, remove any repeat Post-its, thus leaving only the unique set of ideas.
2. Next, tell your group members to vote for the factors they feel contribute most to the problem. Each member will have three votes and can cast their votes by placing a mark next to each selected Post-it. At the end of the exercise, tally up the votes to determine the factor your group believes is the single greatest contributor to the problem.
3. Ask your team to focus only on this contributing factor and move on to brainstorming resources. At the end of this session, ask everyone to cast another three votes each to determine what your top three resources are.
4. Finally, brainstorm solutions that make use of these three assets and then vote for your favorites.

Town Hall Brainstorming

The town hall brainstorming tactic is a bit more formal but can accommodate large groups of people and many varied perspectives. In this scenario, you arrange for a large public gathering of anyone and everyone who might be interested in participating in the problem-solving process. This should include your team, as well as members of the community in which the problem exists. In addition to general community members, invite local political and religious leaders, local business owners, school board officials, etc. Anyone who might be affected by the problem or the solution should be invited to take part in the problem-solving process. This accomplishes two things: (1) it brings in a wide range of perspectives, as well as community-specific knowledge, to the table and (2) it engages the community in a way that promotes a sense of ownership of the solution, which in turn bodes well for the long-term sustainability of that solution. (For more on community ownership, see Chapters 11 and 34.)

Once you've assembled this town hall–style meeting of minds, open the floor up to discussion of the problem. Encourage community members to propose solutions and make a note of each one on a chalkboard, whiteboard, overhead projector, or pad of paper that everyone can see. Once all the solutions are written down, if your group has brainstormed ideas that haven't yet been mentioned, propose these ideas to the community. Ask for their opinions and make careful note of any critiques or advice offered. If the community dismisses an idea, it's unlikely to be successful no matter how much you like it. On the other hand, if the community embraces an idea, it is more likely to meet with success.

Narrow Down the Options

After you've brainstormed a massive list of potential solutions to the problem you've identified, you're ready to begin paring down the possibilities to more accurately reflect the realities of your particular situation and what is likely to prove most effective, efficient, and sustainable.

Figure 5.1. Brainstorm Solutions, Then See What Sticks

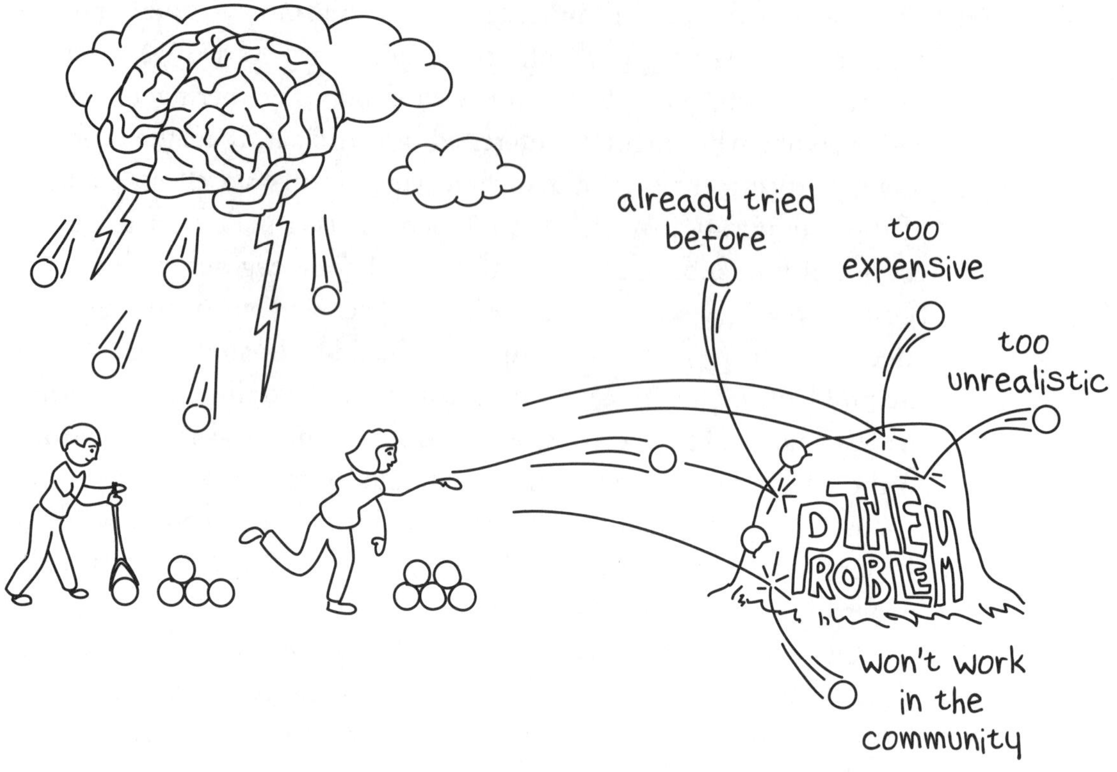

> **Tip** Keep a list of all your ideas, including the ones you decide not to pursue. Periodically refer back to this list; you may find that an idea you previously rejected now seems to have great potential in a new situation or community.

Consider your brainstorming sessions. Did certain solutions pop up again and again in different sessions? This could be a sign they have merit. Were other solutions shot down immediately by community members? These ideas might be particularly difficult to implement. There are likely a host of other possibilities that you and your team will be able to quickly strike from your list, leaving behind perhaps a handful of ideas with true merit and potential.

Once you've narrowed the field to this select few, the next round is tougher. Whittling away the remaining choices will require reflection and much group discussion, all in consultation with the community. Keep these options in mind as you read through the Do Good Well method for social innovation in Part 2. As you learn more about the key elements of successful and sustainable community problem-solving, one idea will likely gain traction, if not emerge as the clear winner.

And remember, when you finally choose a plan of action, there's no need to throw out the list of other solutions you seriously considered. If your plan doesn't pan out, you can always revisit this list for future inspiration. While it's certainly worthwhile to reflect and try to choose the right course of action the first time around, there's no shame in failure. The important thing is that you regroup, understand why the initial idea didn't work, and then try again.

Case Study: Drylands Natural Resource Center

As students at the University of Virginia, Chas Taylor and Daniel Pike learned about a pressing problem: people whose livelihood depends on depleting natural resources are caught in a vicious cycle that harms their environment and decreases their ability to support themselves and their families. Trying to solve this problem, Chas and Daniel cofounded the Drylands Natural Resources Center in Mbumbuni, Kenya, to turn the agro-forestry industry into a sustainable business that simultaneously protects the environment and provides a stable, reliable income to farmers. Chas works for The Earth Partners LP, a land restoration and bioenergy development company, has consulted for the Bill & Melinda Gates Foundation within their agriculture group, and previously worked for McKinsey & Co. Daniel is an MBA candidate at Harvard Business School and previously worked for Astrum Solar, a solar power design and installation company, as well as Analysis Group, an economics consulting firm. In this case study, Chas and Daniel bring together the topics of Chapters 3, 4, and 5—sharing the story of how they went from identifying the problem to brainstorming potential solutions to ultimately taking action that produced lasting results.

Identify a Problem

Chas: Makueni is a district in Kenya that lacks basic infrastructure, such as electricity and running water. Most of the people living there survive by subsistence farming (eating only what they produce). In an attempt to meet their need for fuel and income, people in Makueni have deforested much of their natural woodlands for firewood and charcoal, for which demand in urban areas is booming. These natural woodlands acted as soil and riverbank stabilizers. With their loss, the soils have eroded, rivers have dried up, and less water and fewer nutrients are retained in the ecosystem. Compounded by climate change, which manifests itself in Makueni as less overall rainfall and more rainfall variability, agricultural productivity has declined significantly. As crop yields fall, farmers are forced to further exploit the remaining forest, and the spiral continues. Like many drylands areas in East Africa, Makueni is caught in a vicious cycle of environmental degradation and declining agricultural productivity that leaves food shortages, malnutrition, and sometimes famine in its wake.

Understand the Problem

Daniel: How did we begin thinking about how to address such daunting issues? Once we knew we were interested in dryland areas, we began by trying to understand the basic science around deforestation and agriculture in arid and semi-arid climates. We gathered facts about what was happening on the ground, in terms of farming, technology, and commerce, as best we could through contacts, academic research, the media, and the Internet. Finally, we surveyed how other organizations were trying to combat the problem and tried to assess what was working and what wasn't.

We learned that several groups are trying to solve this problem: environmental programs focused on conservation and sustainable natural resources management; economic aid programs focused on optimizing crop selection, increasing yields, and accessing markets; and social programs focused on women's rights or HIV/AIDS. But few programs tackled these issues in unison. We had the idea that we had identified a missing component: you cannot sustainably increase farmer yields and incomes without simultaneously addressing the long-term environmental issues responsible for the current situation. We wanted something that worked in drylands, something that generated enough revenue for our group and for the farmers that would sustain and grow a program over the long-term.

Brainstorm Solutions

Back-of-the-Napkin Brainstorming

Chas: Through a family friend, I met a Kenyan national named Nicholas Syano, who was getting his master's degree in natural resources management at the University of Wisconsin. Nicholas stayed with my family in Virginia over a Christmas break. Nicholas and I talked for days and days about agriculture, economics, society—and the challenges facing his community. We resolved to do something about it and joined forces with Daniel to form the Drylands Natural Resource Center.

Whiteboard Brainstorming

Daniel: We spent the next six months in the "getting ready to launch" stage, doing research and refining our ideas. We brought friends and classmates together, explained the issues, and together came up with ideas for how to raise money, set up operations, and launch a sustainable program. We spent the summer on the ground with Nicholas and with farmers, which brought about more group discussions and brainstorming of what was needed and what was realistic. Working together, we settled on three main goals for DNRC: first, help farmers restore their land through improving the soil and hydrology; second, generate additional income for farmers through increased agricultural yields and the sale of tree products; and third, develop and disseminate forestry and agriculture best practices for drylands more broadly.

Town Hall Brainstorming

Chas: When we got on the ground in Kenya, our real education began. For example, we realized the scientific program had to be adapted to account for local gender dynamics (e.g., men plowed the land; women did almost everything else), land tenure systems (e.g., farms were difficult to buy and sell and became smaller and smaller as they were divided among sons), and a legal system developed during British colonial times. We went to farmers' homes and surveyed their land, building trust and getting to know them and their unique situations. We gathered the community around, with Nicholas holding large meetings to solicit ideas and input from the community and test interest in our ideas. Town hall discussions—especially those with farmers who had taken part in failed aid projects—helped us refine our ideas and identify what was needed for a lasting solution. For example, we changed the structure to create leadership roles for community members, with a special push for creating women leaders.

Do What Works, Work Together, Make It Last

Daniel: We worked closely with farmers over the first couple years, testing and refining a comprehensive program involving agro-forestry, improved agricultural practices, sustainable wood harvesting, and small business development. Over time, these improved practices have increased the health and productivity of farmers' land, while providing farmers potential income from the sustainable harvesting of firewood, charcoal, and other tree products like forage for livestock. Education is at the heart of this approach, and our program includes biweekly classes, community meetings, and on-site farmer consultation. Today, we are working with over 300 DNRC member families (around 1,800 people). Nicholas oversees the day-to-day management in Kenya, and we have full-time employees who are trained in agro-forestry techniques, community outreach, and operations management. Most importantly, we have earned the community's trust and ongoing commitment to the project's success.

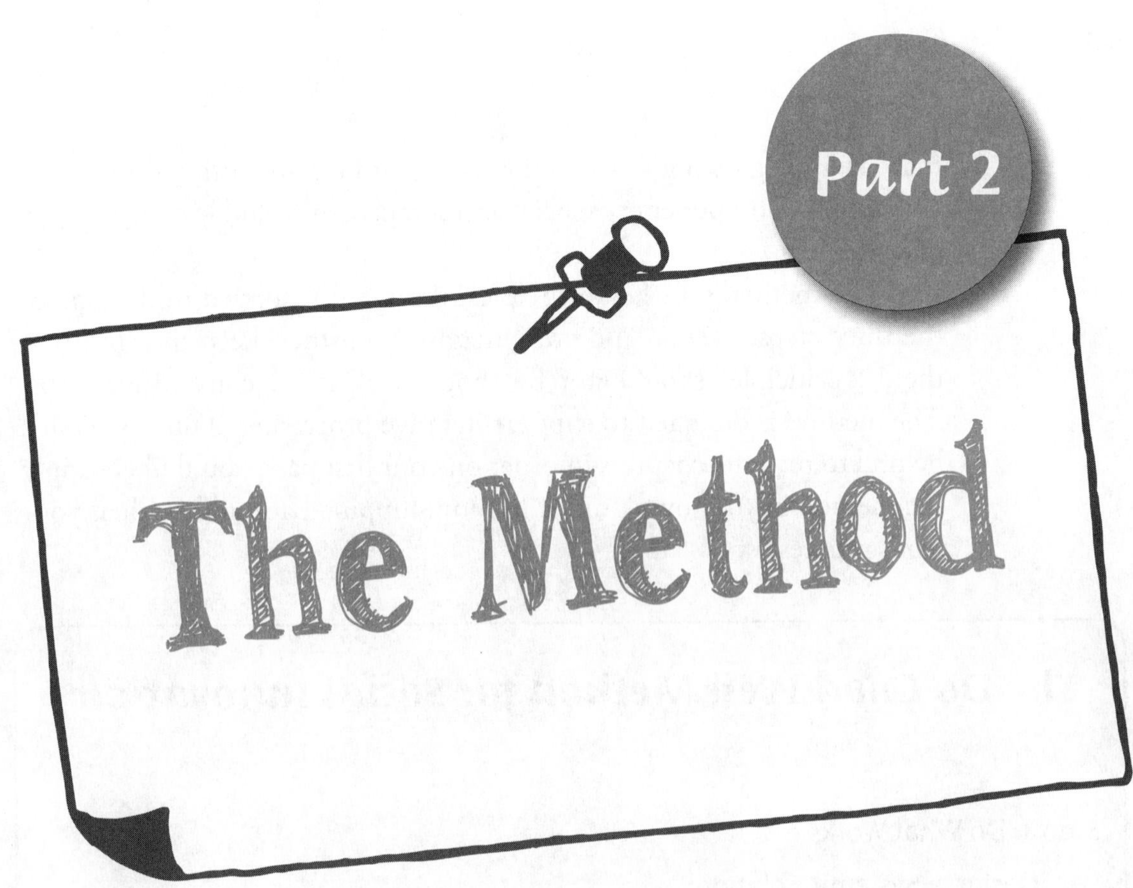

Part 2 presents the Do Good Well method, a simple and flexible framework to use when developing and executing an action plan that can be applied to any idea and any community. Whatever your goal may be, from strengthening a neighborhood through community action to launching a socially conscious product or service, the Do Good Well method's three core steps will help you establish a solid foundation for your unique brand of social innovation.

Step 1: Do What Works guides you to think and plan effectively, implementing evidence-based practices and drawing inspiration from your own and others' mistakes to not only optimize your action plan but also continually reevaluate and refine your solutions. In *Step 2: Work Together,* you'll discover new ways to strengthen and enrich your efforts through collaboration, community ownership, teamwork, and partnerships. *Step 3: Make It Last* helps you ensure the long-term health and sustainability of your efforts by implementing mechanisms that facilitate growing at the right rate, guarding institutional memory, applying the components of social entrepreneurship, and leaving a legacy of leadership.

The method's 12 key principles, though categorized under one of the three steps, overlap and are synergistic. Further, keep in mind that the 12 principles should not be thought of as 12 consecutive steps. The method is designed to support iterative processing. Thus, while it's helpful to read the chapters in order on your first pass, you'll likely apply the method in your own unique fashion, flipping back and forth as your work progresses.

The Do Good Well Method for Social Innovation

Step 1: Do What Works

- Design a Systemic Solution
- Build On What Works
- Measure, Evaluate, Improve, Repeat
- Challenge What Works, Innovate, Keep What Works

Step 2: Work Together

- Balance Starting and Strengthening
- Cultivate Community Ownership
- Foster Team Unity
- Forge Partnerships

Step 3: Make It Last

- Start Small, then Scale What Works
- Engineer Self-sustainable Solutions
- Integrate Social Entrepreneurship
- Share What Works

Do What Works

Admittedly, "do what works" sounds a bit simplistic. And it is, in a way. That's part of its beauty. But when you stop to reflect, the idea is much more nuanced.

You're probably thinking, "Well *of course* I'm going to do what works. Why would I waste time doing something that *doesn't* work?" This mind-set is part of the problem. We take for granted the fact that what we're doing, or what we plan to do, is effective, and never stop to think about whether or not it actually is. This issue is especially rampant in the social sector, where the warm and fuzzy feeling of doing good—as well as the lack of market-based competition—often gives a false sense of efficacy and hampers performing what is the norm in other sectors: continuous data-driven analyses.

In Step 1 of the Do Good Well method for social innovation, we make no assumptions—in itself a key component of "doing what works." These chapters will help you fine-tune the potential solutions you generated in Chapter 5 in order to maximize their chances of efficacy and success.

- *Chapter 6: Design a Systemic Solution*—Explore the broader context of the problem, its root causes, and its relationship to the community. Learn how to integrate your potential solution in a synergistic fashion that embraces other groups trying to solve the same problem as well as multiple modes of problem-solving.

- *Chapter 7: Build on What Works*—Appreciate the value of evidence-based solutions and their potential to be the launch point for your adaptation and improvement.
- *Chapter 8: Measure, Evaluate, Improve, Repeat*—Understand how continuous measurement, assessment, and evolution of the solution you adopt is the basis for improving efficacy, efficiency, and adaptability.
- *Chapter 9: Challenge What Works, Innovate, Keep What Works*—Apply your creativity to meet the critical need for innovative solutions in response to roadblocks and deeply entrenched problems. Test out your brave new ideas and introduce a game changer.

Chapter 6

Design a Systemic Solution

The significant problems we face cannot be solved at the same level of thinking we were at when we created them.

—ALBERT EINSTEIN

Designing a systemic solution is all about expanding your thinking. It means ensuring that the solution you develop takes into account the larger picture—the entire system in which it exists. There is a rich and multilayered context to each problem that includes its multiple, often intertwined causes, its societal and cultural backdrop, and its diverse downstream effects. A thorough understanding of these issues, as well as a familiarity with the various ongoing efforts to address the problem, allows you to adapt your solution to the specific needs of the situation and potentially even magnify the effects of your intervention by recognizing synergistic opportunities. Systemic solutions are likely to prove more effective than those designed around a very narrow understanding of the problem and its context.

The Problem Exists for Multiple Reasons

In all likelihood, the problem you've identified has been around for a while. It took years to create, slowly embedding itself in your community or society as a whole. Numerous factors are responsible for perpetuating it—cultural, economic, social, and political, to name just a few. Take homelessness, for example. There isn't one simple reason why people are homeless. Instead, homelessness is the result of numerous interrelated forces that interact synergistically to create a problem of great magnitude: unemployment, limited affordable housing options, lack of access to health care, domestic abuse, substance abuse, untreated mental illness, physical and learning disabilities, social exclusion, the list goes on.

. . . Therefore Multiple Efforts Are Needed to Solve the Problem

So let's say you've decided to tackle the problem of homelessness. And let's pretend it's an ideal world in which you're armed with a practically limitless amount of power and resources. You snap your fingers and suddenly, unemployment is gone—there's a job for everyone. Would you cure homelessness? No, because many homeless individuals have untreated psychiatric conditions that prevent them from holding down a job. Why can't they seek treatment? Because they may have limited access to mental health resources or lack the social support necessary to access the health system and adhere to a treatment regimen. But what if you snapped your fingers and made health care and social support available to anyone who needed it? Would you end homelessness then? No, because a portion of the homeless population is composed of battered spouses or partners and their children—individuals who have left abusive situations and who may be temporarily homeless as they establish new lives for themselves. The point here is that solutions to deeply entrenched problems require a multipronged plan of attack that addresses all the causes of the problems to be successful.

Of course, this doesn't mean it's entirely up to you and your merry band of social change makers to address all sides of a given problem. That's just not possible. However, as you think about how your group will address a particular issue, keep in mind its multiple etiologies. If you can effectively address more than one of its causes at the same time, great. If not, that's okay too. Regardless of whether your own efforts are single- or multipronged, the important thing is to understand where your group fits in the larger picture, the local- or societal-level multipronged plan of action. In the homelessness example, a multipronged plan of attack might include decreasing unemployment, improving access to and quality of psychiatric care, increasing resources for survivors of domestic abuse, etc.

Coordinate your group's actions with other "prongs" in this multi-pronged approach to ensure you're attacking the problem from all sides with as much force as possible. If one of these prongs is particularly weak (e.g., if domestic abuse awareness and prevention services in your community are almost nonexistent), consider changing your group's approach to the problem in order to meet this need. Or find a way for your group to work with and help another community group already dedicated to this type of work.

Understand the Entire System

Imagine a dam breaks in your community. What would you do to help? You could try to address the immediate problems created by the rising waters. For example, if the flooding forced people from their homes, you could help the displaced citizens relocate to higher ground. You could also look further down the road to address some of the future problems that will result from the flood. For example, how will you clean up the toxic mold that may grow in areas with severe water damage? You could also look backward in time to determine what sorts of preventive measures might have been taken to prevent the dam break in the first place so the situation can be fixed moving forward.

In addition to understanding the time course, it's important to get a sense of the multiple causes and effects by looking "upstream" and "downstream." In the flood example you could (quite literally) look downstream—the riverbed is a mess and filled with debris; perhaps you could get a volunteer crew together to clean it up. You could look upstream—perhaps you could reroute the floodwaters. Finally examine the "origin" itself—find a way to plug the dam.

Like the dam break, the social issue you're trying to address has multiple diverse manifestations, as well as "upstream" and "downstream" causes and effects that lead you to see the problem as it is today in your community. In order to understand the scope of the problem, you need to look back historically. Why was the dam created? In that location? In that style? Using those materials? And with those safety measures? Dig deep to understand each component of the complex system at every step along the "stream." How do the parts interact? If the dam itself is in one town but the most severe water damage is in another, how do those towns work together? If the flood waters are rerouted, how does it impact the area environment and wildlife? So too must you consider the history, contributing factors, societal context, and local impact of the problem and any solution you might envision.

You start to brainstorm potential solutions and decide that the first thing to do is to fix the break. Start by doing your research into the many methods, tools, and materials you could use. Study other dam breaks and what people did to fix them. Let's say you learn many communities used cement to fix the dam. What cement was the fastest acting? Which lasted the longest? What is the cement made out of and do you have access to the same materials? How much did it cost? Whose expertise was needed? Is the cement still working and if not, what was done to replug the hole? Oh, interesting... here's a community that was successful using rubber. The process repeats. Get the picture? For every potential intervention, there are a number of options to research and understand. When you understand the system, you can design a solution that not only works by addressing a specific component but also contributes directly or indirectly to addressing the other points along the stream. In Exercise 6.1, begin to brainstorm potential solutions and draft a game plan for how you will address the problem you're trying to solve.

Exercise 6.1 Draft a Game Plan

Make a list of three factors in each category (upstream, origin, downstream) that are related to the problem you're trying to solve. Then choose one and brainstorm five ways you could address that factor, noting how other factors could be affected. For more guidance on brainstorming, see Chapter 5: Brainstorm Solutions.

Upstream:

Origin:

Downstream:

Chosen factor:

1.

2.

3.

4.

5.

Identify the Root Causes

No matter what solution you implement, make sure it addresses at least one of the root causes of the problem. Too often programs try for a quick fix, targeting what they believe will have the biggest effect in the shortest amount of time. They target symptoms of the problem, rather than causes of the problem. You don't want band-aids—you want solutions! The Whac-a-Mole school of problem solving may rack up instant wins, but that type of victory is fleeting. In order to *solve* a problem, you need to find and address its root cause. For example, scores of programs try to address homelessness by giving out food at shelters and soup kitchens. This is an important and worthwhile service—keep donating to food drives! However, hunger is not the *cause* of homelessness. Handing out food neither empowers those in need nor provides a sustainable solution.

By researching the problem and studying the evidence, here's what you'd find: according to the National Coalition for the Homeless, 20–25% of homeless Americans suffer from mental illness. "Serious mental illnesses disrupt people's ability to carry out essential aspects of daily life, such as self-care and household management … [and] forming and maintaining stable relationships."[1] Further, "a study of people with serious mental illness seen by California's public mental health system found that 15% were homeless at least once in a one-year period."[2] So while soup kitchens and shelters are commendable short-term solutions, the 20–25% of homeless Americans suffering from mental illness might be better served in the long-term by focusing on efforts to improve access to, and compliance with, mental health services. At least part of any solution you devise should address one or more root causes of the problem.

Case Study: Health Leads

When Rebecca Onie was a college student, she volunteered at a large hospital in Boston. While there, she noticed a problem: for many poor families, access to health care alone did not significantly improve health. While a child could be seen by a great pediatrician who properly diagnosed him, often the bigger problem was that the child's family didn't have enough money to feed him, couldn't afford the cost of his medication, or couldn't take the time off work to take him to follow-up visits. Rebecca realized that at times, the root cause of the child's poor health was not an infection, but a lack of resources.

Rebecca's innovative solution was to create an organization staffed by volunteer college students that would allow pediatricians to write prescriptions for resources like food, housing, child care, and transportation assistance, just as they would medications. After seeing the doctor, a family could bring their "resource prescriptions" to student volunteers, who would connect them to the resources they needed. Rebecca's group, Health Leads (formerly Project Health), aims to change the health care system so that the distribution of nonmedical resources becomes a standard service offered by hospitals and clinics. Rather than treating the symptoms, Health Leads aims to treat the cause.

Address Prevention and Treatment

The fields of medicine and public health describe three types of prevention:

- *Primary*: preventing the problem from occurring in the first place (such as vaccines)
- *Secondary*: early detection of a problem and early intervention (such as cancer screenings and cholesterol lowering medications)
- *Tertiary*: minimizing the burden of the problem through treatment and rehabilitation (such as antibiotics and surgery)

When approaching solutions to your social problem, use these levels of prevention to guide your thinking. All three types need to be addressed. In the homelessness example, all points along the stream, from addressing mental illness to increasing affordable housing options to the soup kitchens, play an important role. Or to use a different example, survivors of child abuse face numerous challenges even after the abuse has stopped, including long-term mental health issues and the risk of becoming abusers themselves. So it's equally important to help those who have already faced a problem as it is to prevent the problem from occurring in the first place.

Combine Strategies to Create the Most Effective Solutions

Cancer patients are often treated with multiple different therapies like surgery, radiation, and chemotherapy. Each of these therapeutics provides a unique benefit to the patient so when used in combination, their effects are magnified. This comprehensive "combination therapy" approach is similarly effective on social problems; by combining multiple strategies that target various points along the life cycle of the problem, you'll have the greatest impact.

When researching current interventions, take a step back to identify where the holes are—what aspects of the problem are not being addressed well or at all? What's missing from current solutions? This could be a great place for you to start. All parts of the system need to be addressed—causes, symptoms, preventive measures, and treatments—your role is to determine where in the system your efforts would be best directed in order to ensure the system as a whole is as strong as possible. In other words, if the problem you've identified is only being treated with surgery and radiation, dedicate your efforts to providing the chemotherapy in that combination therapy. By providing a missing component, you augment the collective strength of the system as a whole.

As you learn more about the problem, you'll likely identify many aspects that need additional attention. Don't try to take them all on at once—that would be a big disservice to your cause! Take on only as many components as you can without compromising the quality of your work. In other words, it's better to do two things well than 20 things only so-so. If you find that your solution comfortably addresses two components of the problem and you believe you're up to the challenge of three components, then you should consider expanding the scope of your efforts.

Bring New Players to the Table

The complex nature of these social problems provides an exciting opportunity. Because these issues are so multifaceted, it means that there is a spectrum of avenues through which to make change. Almost anyone can impact a given issue. For example, solving health problems requires a lot more than just what traditional health care professionals like doctors and nurses can do; it needs the involvement of educators, journalists, artists, business leaders, entertainers, lawyers, politicians, engineers, social workers, students, the list goes on. In fact, oftentimes the most innovative solutions come from those who have primary expertise in a different field. Drivers of innovation are everywhere.

Chapter 7

Build on What Works

If I have seen further it is by standing on the shoulders of giants.

—SIR ISAAC NEWTON

When you bake a cake, you don't mix together random ingredients. You use a recipe—the end product of a lot of experimenting and trial-and-error on the part of those who came before you. You do this because you know the recipe will work, and it'd be silly to try to reinvent the wheel, or cake, as it were. Of course, once you have the basics down, you can tweak the recipe to personalize or improve it, but you always start off by familiarizing yourself with the basics—the things that have been shown to work.

Similarly, when working to address a problem in your community, you don't need to start from scratch. Instead, pick up where others have left off. The social problems you're trying to address aren't new. Many other people have tried to solve them; some things they've done have worked and others haven't. Even if you eventually decide to scrap everything and reinvent the very notion of a cake, it's still useful to have a basic understanding of the historical context—what has been tried before, why it did or didn't work, and why a completely novel approach might be necessary.

The idea behind building on what works is simple. First, gather information about what solutions have been tried before. Second,

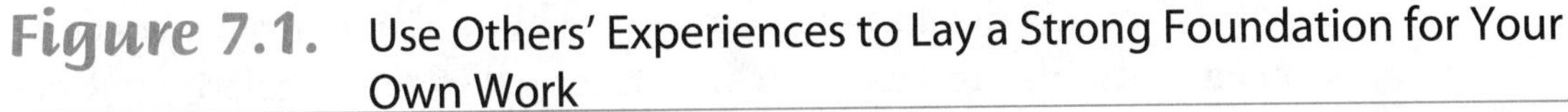

Figure 7.1. Use Others' Experiences to Lay a Strong Foundation for Your Own Work

determine whether these solutions were effective or ineffective. This judgment should be based on objective evidence and reasoned analysis. Third, use this knowledge as a launch pad for your own work. Discard ideas with no proven impact. Keep the ideas that work and build on them or adapt them for your specific circumstances. This is the recipe for progress.

Define What Works

A solution that works is one that is effective—it produces the desired result. Of course, when evaluating whether or not a solution works, you will have to define what the desired result is, as well as the costs you're willing to accept to achieve it. As a result, something that works in one situation may not work in another, due to different desired results or fewer resources. When assessing whether or not solutions implemented by others are effective, try to find out what the initial objectives were and whether or not these objectives were achieved. If so, by what margin? If not, how big was the shortfall? Look for data or studies that provide evidence of the effectiveness of the solution.

Effectiveness is absolutely critical. Think about breast cancer—women and girls are taught to do breast self-exams regularly and get mammograms to try to detect the cancer early. It seems like a great idea. If the norm is for women to do nothing, then of course educating them to do self-exams and launching a public awareness campaign promoting mammograms should be effective, right? Well it turns out that's not the case. When researchers objectively studied the data, they found that mammograms are only effective for older women; in younger women they often result in costly unnecessary surgical procedures and have no impact on survival.[1] So a program to give free mammograms to high school girls might sound like it would make an impact—and it's certainly a "solution," but it isn't an *effective* solution, as the evidence shows that it doesn't work.

Effective solutions are found by asking a question (e.g., Does this work?), collecting data, and then analyzing that data to reach a conclusion (it *didn't* work, or it *did* work). This experimental process of collecting and evaluating data to answer questions is a tried-and-true way of figuring out evidence-based solutions, or solutions backed up by proof.

To maximize the chances that your efforts make an impact, seek out and incorporate evidence-based solutions whenever possible. You'll also need to adopt this type of reasoned evaluation when assessing the efficacy of whatever solution you ultimately employ, both to chart your progress and to identify areas of improvement. You'll learn more about this in Chapter 8: Measure, Evaluate, Improve, Repeat.

Learn What Works

To learn what strategies might prove effective against the problem you've identified, you'll need to do some research to find out what types of solutions have already been tried and with what success. Read about the issue in newspapers, journals, official reports, and on the websites of groups already attempting to address the problem. Whenever possible, seek out analyses based on data collected from studies that attempted to answer whether a solution worked or not. Find both praise and criticism of previous programs and initiatives. Most important, always talk to the people who are directly affected by the problem or who have worked to alleviate it in the past.

When researching, it's important to recognize that you can apply many types of findings to your work. Let's say your goal is *to increase employment rates for ex-prisoners in Dallas through a 501(c)(3) nonprofit.* You'll likely start by reaching out to other nonprofits working to advance the same cause to find out what strategies they've found effective, so in this case you'd look into other Dallas-area 501(c)(3) organizations working to get jobs for ex-prisoners, then break the problem down into its most basic components to guide your research.

- *Increase employment rates:* Your next step might be to find out more about initiatives designed to increase employment rates for other demographics like single moms, and determine if you can apply some of these lessons to your case. What are other sectors, like local government and businesses, doing to increase jobs?
- *...for ex-prisoners:* An Internet search might reveal a newspaper article about a group trying to help ex-prisoners adjust back into life with their families, or a research study showing how a group was able to successfully decrease recidivism rates. What works for this unique demographic?
- *... in Dallas:* Get a sense of what works in Dallas and how geography affects possible solutions. Perhaps the Dallas Meals on Wheels program has found an effective way of delivering goods and services to a population dispersed throughout the city. How can you apply what worked for them to your efforts?
- *... through a nonprofit:* What strategies have been successfully implemented that are unique to the abilities of a nonprofit? How do ex-prisoners respond to outreach programs from nonprofits, and what changes when nonprofits partner with churches, businesses, governments, and the prisons themselves?

The point is that you can consult many different sources, applying relevant components of their results or experiences to your work. And while you should weight published studies with data and figures to back up their results more heavily than a single anecdotal testimonial, there are many types of evidence available for your consideration. For example, you could contact your local parole board to arrange a meeting with currently employed and unemployed ex-prisoners to learn about their experiences looking for employment. As you begin your research, consider the following questions:

- How have others tried to solve this problem?

- What methods did they use?
- How effective were these methods, and what evidence is available to demonstrate their efficacy?
- What worked, what didn't, and why?
- What is missing from their approach?
- How can you build on their success?
- How can you work with them?
- What can you do differently to solve the problem?
- What makes you think your new approach will work?

Once you've collected this information, take time to process it. With all the evidence in front of you, you may find that ex-prisoners have a hard time finding employment not because companies aren't willing to hire them, but because the ex-prisoners aren't properly prepared for their job interviews. This information may drastically change how you approach the problem, preventing you from spending lots of time and money on solutions that don't work to meet your end goal.

Improve on What Works

Once you've identified solutions that work, you can take this information to the next level. Often the best solutions aren't completely new game changers but are existing solutions that have been changed slightly with dramatic effects. For example, how might you implement a given solution in a way that's easier, faster, or cheaper? How can you take what worked in one area and apply it to another cause, demographic, or region? Incremental improvement is smart and sustainable. Deepen your impact by building on others' successes.

Case Study: Land Mine Detection

Sean Genis is a lieutenant in the US Navy who hails from Sharon, Pennsylvania. He graduated with distinction from the US Naval Academy, where he conducted research in nonlinear acoustic land mine detection, which he describes in this case study. As a Rhodes Scholar, Sean graduated with first-class honors after reading philosophy, politics, and economics at Oxford University. He is currently serving as an officer aboard the nuclear-powered submarine USS *Jimmy Carter*. In this case study, Sean demonstrates why it's important to keep in mind that effective social change need not always start from scratch; making a good idea better can prove just as rewarding.

Understand the Problem

Sean: Land mines are present in more than 80 nations. The number of indiscriminate casualties caused by land mines is estimated at more than 17 per day. Land mines also create tremendous economic problems: the threat of a single mine often renders fertile farmland useless and restricts the movement of goods and resources. Although the 140 signatories of the 1997 Ottawa Mine Ban Treaty are undertaking mine clearance efforts, complete demining will take 450 to 500 years at the current rate of progress.[2]

Finding land mines is actually more difficult than carefully unearthing them. Most minefields were poorly documented, if at all, and using metal detectors became much less effective following the advent of plastic mines after World War II. Currently, no single detection method is universally suited to the diverse environmental conditions in which land mines are found.[3]

Learn What Works

Sean: In the course of researching the state of current efforts to address the worldwide problem of land mines, I happened upon the promising work of Murray S. Korman, a physics professor at the US Naval Academy and a leader in the field of acoustic land mine detection. Korman had published the results of several successful land mine detection experiments in partnership with James Sabatier, a senior research scientist at the University of Mississippi's National Center for Physical Acoustics.[4] Unfortunately, much of Korman and Sabatier's work was limited to one-dimensional analyses using devices that must be placed in physical contact with the soil surface.

Improve on What Works

Sean: Drawn to the prospect of addressing a problem faced by not only my fellow members of the military but also civilians in former war zones, I joined Korman's lab in my sophomore year at the US Naval Academy. Because physical contact with mine-laden areas is problematic, I aimed to design and construct a noncontact device capable of measuring soil vibrations in two dimensions. A forward-looking laser enabled me to measure soil surface vibrations without physical contact and could be programmed to automatically survey a two-dimensional grid, enabling me to search for buried land mines with greater reliability and precision than before.

Admittedly, my efforts have not single-handedly revolutionized land mine detection. The actual time required to scan an area effectively using my apparatus is prohibitively slow. Additionally, significant research and development would be required to adapt my experimental device into a practical, readily usable form. Nonetheless, my work is a small step in the right direction, improving on a proven concept in order to bring the dream of reliable land mine detection a bit closer to reality. Many such small steps forward may eventually save lives while giving new economic opportunities to entire communities currently held captive by the unmarked dangers in their fields and forests.

Chapter 8

Measure, Evaluate, Improve, Repeat

Here's the truth that some organizations don't want you to know: a lot of the time and money pledged to worthy causes is wasted because it's spent on programs that, while well-meaning, are ineffective. For example, in the popular Drug Abuse Resistance Education (D.A.R.E.) program, police officers teach K–12 students how to say "no" to drugs. However, in 2001, after almost 20 years and millions of dollars, D.A.R.E. was evaluated by the surgeon general, who determined it did *not* decrease drug use.[1] Yet for years afterward, D.A.R.E. continued to be implemented in its original form in the majority of US school districts, as well as dozens of countries around the world. In 2004, D.A.R.E. finally instituted changes to its curriculum.[2] Unfortunately, no studies demonstrating the efficacy of these changes have emerged.

In 2009, the D.A.R.E. program took a major step in the right direction when it adopted the "keepin' it REAL" curriculum for middle school students, an evidence-based prevention program developed by Pennsylvania State University.[3] Unlike the traditional D.A.R.E. curriculum, which routinely failed to demonstrate its effectiveness,[4] the "keepin' it REAL" curriculum, when evaluated by the US Substance Abuse and Mental Health Services Administration, was ranked among the top three most cost-effective drug prevention programs, delivering 28 dollars in benefits for every dollar spent.[5]

The original D.A.R.E. program is a great example of good intentions that just never produced concrete results. While it's wonderful D.A.R.E. has finally begun moving toward evidence-based practices, a staggering amount of time and money was devoted to ineffective solutions.

In this chapter, you will learn how to measure and evaluate the performance of the solutions you implement so that you can be sure your group is making active progress toward your goal in a way that effectively utilizes your resources. You'll also learn how to regroup and improve your group's action plan when you identify areas of weakness. More important, you'll come to appreciate the continuous need to measure, evaluate, and improve your work.

Figure 8.1. Measure, Evaluate, Improve, and Repeat

Measure What Matters

There are a lot of things you can measure: the number of members you have, dollars you've raised, kids you've tutored, and so on. But what you should really focus on measuring are those things that will best demonstrate your impact. For example, what's more important: the number of kids you've tutored or the average change in test scores of the kids you've tutored? Number of hours volunteered or number of trees planted in those hours? Amount of money raised or what you did with the money? It's not just about finding something to measure; it's about measuring the right thing.

Take some time to think about what you're trying to accomplish and what you can measure to gauge your progress toward that goal. For example, in Chapter 7: Build on What Works, we discussed the example of working to decrease the unemployment rate of ex-prisoners in Dallas. In this case, let's say you decide to help these ex-prisoners by offering a series of job hunting and interview skills workshops designed to make them more competitive applicants. There are many measurements you could use to determine the effectiveness of your program:

- Number of ex-prisoners who attend the first of three job hunting and interview skills workshops
- Percentage of ex-prisoners who complete all three workshops
- Number of interviews extended to ex-prisoners per 10 job applications
- Average number of interviews before receiving a job offer
- Average salary of an ex-prisoner employed full-time
- Percentage of prisoners employed within six months of release
- Number of businesses willing to hire ex-prisoners
- Self-reported confidence level of the average prisoner before and after attending your workshops

And the list goes on. The key is to clearly define the goals of your intervention and then take measurements that are likely to be informative. Keep in mind that in some cases, you will want to take a series of baseline measurements before starting your intervention in order to clearly demonstrate the effects of your program.

WARNING In *The Lean Startup*, Eric Ries warns against what he called "vanity metrics": "measurements like registered users, downloads, and website hits ... that give the rosiest picture possible and do not necessarily correlate with numbers that actually matter."[6] Make sure your metrics matter.

Of course, not everything you measure will speak to the effectiveness of your program. In some cases, the statistics you collect may be intended only to help you better understand the needs of the population you serve or lend insight into patterns of usage or adoption. For example, counting the number of ex-prisoners who attend your information sessions won't necessarily gauge the impact of your services, but comparing these numbers over time will give you some idea of whether or not word is spreading about your program. You may need to adjust the way you advertise your workshops to potential participants.

Tip When collecting data, pay attention to how you are gathering the information. In-person interviews allow you to get a sense of how a person responds and feels, but people may also feel more pressure to give particular answers that are more supportive of your work because they don't want to hurt your feelings.

Once you've determined what you'd like to measure, you'll need to decide the best way to measure it. For example, if you want to measure whether a tutoring program improves a child's performance in school, how do you intend to measure school performance? Letter grades at the end of the quarter? Teacher comments on report cards? Average score on weekly exams? Yearly standardized tests? Does the measurement actually quantify what you think it does? If you don't know where to begin, look to see if there are standard metrics already used in your field. Using accepted metrics has an added advantage of having consistency, allowing you to evaluate your work compared to that of others.

Next, how will you collect data and where will you keep track of it? At the outset, decide how you will record and track your measurements easily and accurately. Will you devote a notebook to the cause with different sections for different measurements or maintain a spreadsheet on your computer with tabs for each type of measurement? How often will you record this data?

Tip

Need a quick answer? Do an online survey. In one day, you can gauge public opinion and get some data to inform a debate you and your team have been having. Note that with surveys there is huge bias based on who you send it to and how you ask the questions, but for certain types of decisions, it's a good starting point.

Another important consideration is how you will avoid (or at least minimize) bias in your measurements in order to ensure your analysis is as accurate as possible. Objective measures like test scores are usually less biased than subjective measures like interviewing students and asking them what they think about the tutoring program. However, because subjective data is often quite valuable, run any subjective questions by a few individuals unaffiliated with your project to make sure you're not asking any leading questions. As much as possible, seek to standardize the way subjective questions are asked, as well as the environments in which they are asked.

Evaluate the Evidence

Once you've gathered the data, the next step is evaluation. But before examining any of the data, before even collecting the data, you should work together with your group to devise an evaluation plan. This document should address how you will use the results, who will run the analysis, how the results will be shared and with whom, what changes might be expected based on the results, and in what time frame these changes will be made. You may not end up following it exactly, but it's wise to have a plan nonetheless.

Next, examine the data. For qualitative data like interviews, you can look for trends and pull out quotes that give valuable insight. For quantitative data, crunch the numbers, do simple statistical analyses, and make a few tables and graphs in Excel. Depending on the type of statistic or complexity of the question, you may want to consult a statistician if you have access to one.

Whether the results seem to support your intervention or not, assemble your entire team to go over the results again together. Solicit as many perspectives as possible to ensure you aren't misinterpreting the data or drawing false conclusions. Strive to be as detailed as possible when determining what specific aspects of your approach worked and what aspects fell short. Work together to understand the reasons behind your results. It isn't enough to say, "This worked." You need to have a sense of *why* it worked.

Keep good records of your findings. If you can show that what you're doing is working, your stats will come in handy when approaching investors, grantors, and donors interested in the social return on their investment. If you can, include a cost-benefit analysis in your evaluation.

Case Study: Change.org

The popular petition site Change.org was originally much more diverse in its offerings than it currently is. As a result of careful measurement and analysis, the leaders of Change.org realized that their users felt the site's group petitions were the most used and helpful of the various tools offered. The group then focused its efforts on this one key aspect, and resolved to provide a better quality group petition than other sites.

Today, Change.org continues to evaluate its performance, tracking how many people have signed a given petition and, more notably, any progress resulting from the petition. For example, petitions on the site protesting Bank of America's proposed five-dollar-a-month fee for customers gathered 300,000 signatures. These petitions, in conjunction with a strong national outcry, convinced the bank to drop its plans for the fee.

Improve Your Approach

Based on your collective evaluation of the data, you will likely have results that leave you at a crossroads: if you find that your approach was successful, making satisfactory progress toward your goal, you may decide to continue along the same path, or make just a few minor adjustments here and there. If you find that your plan didn't work at all or failed to produce the results you'd hoped for, you'd be wise to reflect a bit. If you determine your goals and expectations weren't unrealistic, you may want to take the opportunity to change course, or "pivot." Pivot is business speak for making a thoughtful change in direction that is aimed at testing out a new hypothesis you have about how to improve your product or service. Perhaps your data point to a specific flaw in your reasoning that might be corrected with only a slight adjustment, or perhaps they suggest that an entirely different plan of attack is necessary.

In consultation with your team, decide on your next course of action. If you decide to make changes to your approach, open up discussion on the topic. What types of changes are suggested by the evidence before you? Who within the group will take charge of this effort and oversee its implementation?

Though some negative results or disappointing numbers might seem disheartening, keep in mind that measuring and evaluating are what provide you with the tools to grow and improve. Take advantage of these opportunities to evolve so that you can increase your impact on the world around you.

Repeat, Repeat, Repeat

Once you've measured, evaluated, and improved your approach, repeat the process all over again! The most effective programs are those that constantly assess and reflect on their own work in order to adjust to changing demands or new conditions.

Case Study: Population Media Center

Tova Reichel is a doctoral candidate at the George Washington University School of Public Health and Health Services. She has expertise in community-based program monitoring and evaluation, with an emphasis on behavior change communication. In this case study, Tova shares how she used evaluation to improve the impact of the Population Media Center.

The Approach

Tova: Population Media Center (PMC) is an international nongovernmental organization that uses the media to promote gender equality and women's empowerment around the world. Ascribing to an entertainment-education model, PMC uses the media to educate and encourage social change while entertaining its audiences.[7] PMC's programs make heavy use of positive role models, who are interspersed throughout its radio and television stories for audience members to look up to and emulate. PMC's long-term goal is to reduce population growth rates and raise the status of women in developing countries by encouraging positive behavior change among its listeners.

Measure What Matters

Tova: I worked with PMC to measure and evaluate the impact of its program in Ethiopia. We used a case study approach and collected in-depth information about the impact of one of PMC's radio dramas on a sample of women listeners in Addis Ababa, Ethiopia. The methods were primarily qualitative, including in-depth interviews with clients and care providers, all of them adult women, at six health care clinics in and around Addis Ababa. The interviews were done to gain an understanding of women's access to reproductive health care in Ethiopia and what women's empowerment means in the context of Ethiopian women's lives.

Focus group discussions were used as a method of data collection based on the premise that listeners of PMC's radio programs can provide valuable information regarding the impact of these programs on their own lives. Finally, a content analysis was done of a sample of radio program scripts. Indicators of women's empowerment were compiled and a checklist created using these concepts to assist with the analysis of the scripts. Key terms, phrases, and concepts in the scripts that matched these indicators of empowerment were identified and tallied.

Evaluate the Evidence

Tova: A significant finding emerged during the analysis phase of the research: married women in one focus group explained that their husbands were not listening to PMC's radio program because the drama's male characters were being portrayed in a negative light. This research indicated that something needed to change in order to capture the male audience.

Improve Your Approach

Tova: I reported this finding, which was then used to develop a similar pilot program in Nigeria. PMC's revised approach now stresses the importance of creating positive male role models in radio scripts so that the program can effectively target both women and men.

Chapter 9

Challenge What Works, Innovate, Keep What Works

> *There is no doubt that creativity is the most important human resource of all. Without creativity, there would be no progress, and we would be forever repeating the same patterns.*
>
> —EDWARD DE BONO

In Chapter 7: Build on What Works, you learned to modify and improve strategies and techniques with a proven track record. In this chapter, you'll learn about challenging the conventional and trying something entirely different—being an innovator.

Innovation can seem intimidating, but it shouldn't be. Admittedly, when most people hear the word *innovation*, they conjure up images of scientists frantically scribbling on chalkboards or engineers in white jumpsuits creating a prototype of the next "it" gadget. Sure, some innovations are born in these environments, but most are not. As long as you keep your eyes and ears open, remain receptive to new ideas (no matter how crazy they might seem at first), and demonstrate a willingness to test out these often unlikely solutions, you, too, can innovate!

Of course, after throwing the rules out the window and letting your creative juices flow, you'll need to subject your new ideas to careful scrutiny. A new solution isn't an *innovation* unless it actually works. Experienced innovators know that innovation is as much about

Figure 9.1. Challenge the Way Things Are Done and Seek to Innovate, Keeping What Works

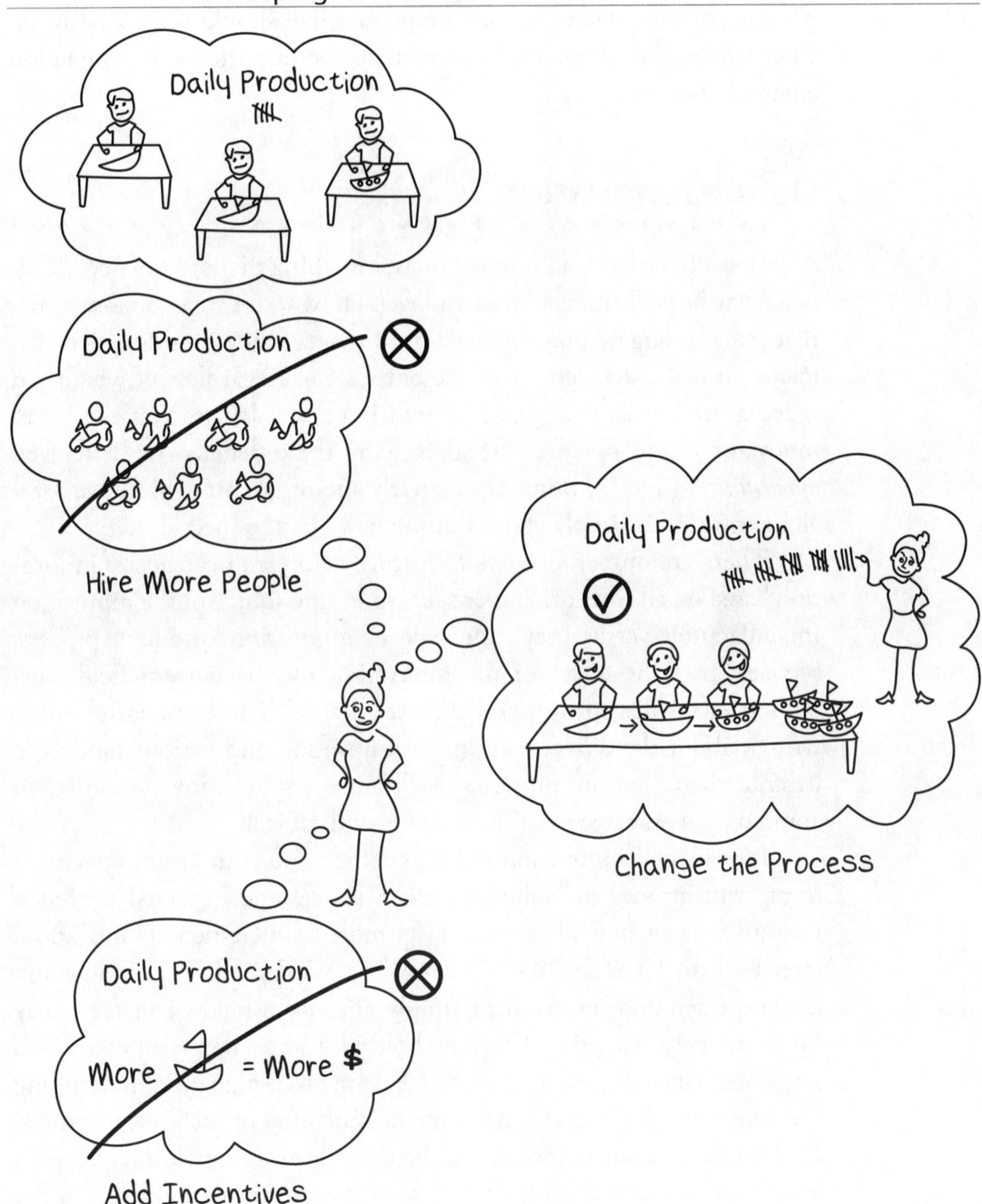

measuring, evaluating, improving, and repeating (see Chapter 8) as it is about applying new perspectives to shake up the status quo. Careful assessment of your new ideas will provide you with the information you need to determine when they work, how to improve them, ... and when to discard them. Because your objective should always be to do what works, this chapter will emphasize the importance of evaluation alongside innovation.

Define Innovation

At its most basic level, an innovation is something that meets a need. This need may be well characterized and well known, or it may be something that remains largely unrecognized until a new solution is designed that makes clear the deficiencies of the old system. Regardless of whether it is recognized or unrecognized, a need implies a deficit. You can be an innovator if you practice: (1) identifying these deficits (or better yet, *opportunities)* and (2) thinking creatively about potential solutions. After all, innovation is simply about finding new ways to meet needs.

There are numerous ways to further define and categorize innovation based on all sorts of different measures: the source of the innovation (manufacturer versus user), the type of innovation (product, process, service, etc.), the effect of the innovation on the current field (sustaining versus disruptive), and the list goes on. There are entire books written about the different forms of innovation and various models to describe them. For our purposes, we'll broadly split innovation into two commonly used categories: incremental and radical.

Incremental innovation typically either results in an improvement to an existing idea, or solution or is a logical and expected next step forward for a given field or market (for more on incremental innovation, refer back to Chapter 7: Build on What Works). Radical innovation is unexpected and, rather than simply advance a field or market, may fundamentally change it. These are bold ideas that have the potential to be game-changers. That said, these ideas are often high-risk, underlining the importance of carefully assessing the outcomes of such interventions. In this chapter, our emphasis will be on radical innovation. Here we'll encourage you to challenge existing solutions, to think big and "stir the pot." On the other hand, incremental innovation also has great potential for change, and you may find many of the ideas presented in this chapter useful when thinking about incremental change.

Challenge What Works

It's time to get critical. Identifying deficits is a key part of innovation. When an obvious problem exists, this means better defining all the individual components of the problem. For example, if the rate of gang initiations has increased in your neighborhood, why are so many teenagers turning to this violent lifestyle? Is it a lack of safe after-school options, an unstable home life, the glamorization of gang culture, a lack of jobs and educational opportunities for high school graduates in your community, etc.?

Most problems are complex and multifactorial, and it can sometimes be difficult to tease out either the primary contributing factors or the nature of the interactions among these factors (see Chapter 4: Understand the Problem to learn more about better defining an issue and Chapter 6: Design a Systemic Solution for a multipronged approach to solving the problem). The better you can break down the problem and define its many interconnected pieces, the more likely it is you'll either recognize a piece of the puzzle that hasn't yet been properly addressed or see a connection others have missed entirely. Your innovation may be a completely new way of attacking the problem that is based on these insights and your unique perspective.

In other cases, a problem may not be as readily apparent, and it may take some research and careful scrutiny to uncover an unmet need. For example, if a new after-school program has markedly decreased gang membership in your area, why are some students still joining gangs? What could be improved about the after-school program to attract more students, and what other solutions need to be explored to further reduce the rate of gang initiations? You'll often find that this type of problem identification boils down to an evaluation of whether current solutions can be implemented in ways that are faster, cheaper, more efficient, or of higher quality. In this case, your innovation may be a novel and unexpected technology that improves outcomes generated by current methodologies or an entirely new methodology whose results surpass those of currently employed solutions.

Innovate

While there's no set formula for innovation, there are actions you can take and behaviors you can promote to maximize the likelihood of both coming up with creative ideas and recognizing their potential. Remember that your goal is to challenge what works. Keep as open a mind as possible, considering not only new methods or strategies but also novel methods, tools, technologies, new groups of people to involve or partner with, and unusual skills or perspectives you might integrate.

In *The Innovator's DNA*, Jeff Dyer, Hal Gregersen, and Clayton Christensen identify five skills of innovators, summarized below.[1] Internalize these skills and you will be well on your way to thinking outside the box in a productive way:

1. *Associate*: Make connections between seemingly unrelated ideas, problems, questions, or fields.
2. *Question*: Challenge convention by asking why things are done the way that they are, and how they can be done differently.
3. *Observe*: Analyze the behavior of people and systems to identify new ways of doing things.
4. *Network*: Seek out people with diverse backgrounds to discuss the problem and potential solutions.
5. *Experiment*: Create opportunities to test ideas, and then take action based on these results.

For practice applying these skills, work through Exercise 9.1

Exercise 9.1 Get Started Innovating

Start cultivating the five key skills outlined in *The Innovator's DNA* by applying them to a problem you'd like to solve.

1. *Associate*: Think of solutions that have been devised to solve problems in fields or causes outside your own. How might they be applied to your problem?

2. *Question*: If there are already efforts in place to try to address the problem you've identified, what evidence are they based on? What might make them good solutions, compared to various alternatives? If you could change one aspect of the solution or solutions currently in place, what would you change and why? What do you think the impact of that change would be?

3. *Observe*: What does your target population (the group affected by the problem) need that it isn't currently receiving? Does this group possess any special skills or engage in particular behaviors that could be used to help address this unmet need?

4. *Network*: Talk to as many people as possible about the problem and any new ideas you formulate. Keep a written or online journal to organize the ideas and feedback you get.
5. *Experiment*: Once you've zeroed in on an idea, give yourself no more than one to two months to pilot your initial plan. Note that while you will continue to test and refine over many months, it's valuable to get the ball rolling and build momentum by experimenting in a relatively short time frame.

It's worth noting that the ability to associate and question are especially critical skills to cultivate, as many fantastic innovations aren't entirely new ideas but rather old ideas repackaged or applied in new circumstances. For example, wiki technology had already been created and proven to work as a collaborative tool for six years before Jimmy Wales used it to challenge the long-established reference book industry. His innovation democratized the act of information collection by creating a free, open-source online encyclopedia written collaboratively by thousands of volunteers. Wikipedia not only challenged what for years had worked, but also revolutionized the way we collect and access information (not to mention study for exams and impress our friends!).

Take It for a Test Drive

Once inspiration strikes and you've identified a great idea, you'll need to figure out if it works or not. While thinking through your solution and the potential obstacles you might encounter is helpful, there's just no replacement for testing out your idea in the real world, albeit on a small scale. If your new idea works well, you can roll it out on a larger scale. If it doesn't, you save yourself the time and energy you would have invested in a failed large-scale implementation. You'll also gain valuable information that you can use to adjust your future approach to the problem.

So by all means, build your idea! Whether it's a prototype, pilot, trial, or beta test, get some version of it up and running for a test drive. The business term for this is a *minimum viable product*; it will allow you to determine if your novel idea works and will give you the opportunity to measure, evaluate, improve, and repeat. Eric Ries, author of *The Lean Startup*, says, "Contrary to traditional product development, which usually involves a long, thoughtful incubation period and strives for product perfection, the goal of the MVP [minimal viable product] is to begin the process of learning, not end it."[2] Then keep what works, and repeat.

Failed innovations often result from an imbalance in one or more of the following three areas:

1. *Time*: If your efforts are too slow or isolated, you won't gain meaningful traction. If they're too hurried, you may overlook important details while rushing to obtain results.
2. *Confidence*: If you have too little confidence, you won't ever get started testing out your idea. If you have too much, you may deny or ignore aspects of your solution that aren't working.
3. *Focus*: If you have too little focus, you'll be easily distracted and lose sight of your goals. If you have too much, you lose the flexibility necessary to explore potential pivot points and other options as they arise.

Keep What Works

Every new beginning comes from some other beginning's end.

SENECA

If you take your new idea out for a test drive and it looks like a winner, that's great! Keep what worked and continue improving. But if it ends up in a flaming heap by the side of the road, don't panic. Not every new idea you have will work, and there's no shame in failure. Most of us learn more from what *didn't* work than from what *did.* These lessons stay with us and give us insight into how to do things better the next time around.

For example, Facebook is constantly testing out new ideas. Some of these ideas, like the "wall" feature, are instant successes. Others take a bit longer to sink in before they're embraced. And still others are abject failures. Take Beacon, for example. Beacon was a service that shared your web activity with friends and facilitated targeted advertising from businesses. It was an innovative idea, but it didn't go over well with users, and Facebook wisely eliminated it.

Of course, Facebook can easily track, measure, and evaluate if something is working. This is much harder outside the world of information technology, but it's no less important. You'll need to make every effort to ensure that the solutions you test out produce results you can measure and evaluate. Armed with this data, you'll

Man's mind stretched to a new idea never goes back to its original dimensions.

OLIVER WENDELL HOLMES

be able to determine with certainty whether or not something worked, and if not, why that might have been. Use what you've learned to either improve your next trial run, or cross off one possibility on your list of potential solutions. At the very least, you will have entertained a new idea, and that is in and of itself a valuable exercise by any measure.

Work Together

It isn't just action but *united* action that drives social progress. For that reason, Step 2 is focused on collaboration—working together. The competitive mentality of "us versus them" is a barrier to progress; it wastes time and resources, which slows down advancement and innovation. The team spirit you feel when working with your closest friends and allies needs to be extended to everyone, starting with the community you're working to improve all the way up to the other organizations trying to solve the same problem, even—rather especially—if they're tackling it in a similar way. Why? Because broadly speaking, we're all on the same team; the enemy is the social problem, not other well-intentioned individuals or organizations. Building bridges should be a part of your group's culture. This will facilitate change that leverages the strengths of individual people and groups to the maximal benefit of the greater cause.

- *Chapter 10: Balance Strengthening and Starting*—Finding the right balance between strengthening existing efforts versus starting something new will be necessary not only from the get-go, but also as your work progresses. On Day 1, many budding leaders are too eager to start their own groups; all too often, novel ideas that spawn new groups would be better served by more mature organizational frameworks. Beyond the initial launch of your group, as new projects arise there will always be opportunities to make a greater impact by joining forces.

- *Chapter 11: Cultivate Community Ownership*—From development to implementation of any potential solution, the success and sustainability of your efforts begins and ends with the participation of the target community and shared responsibility.
- *Chapter 12: Foster Team Unity*—Cultivate another type of community, in this case by developing cohesive, collegial bonds within your group. Reach your leadership potential by prioritizing quality communication and bringing out the best in others.
- *Chapter 13: Forge Partnerships*—With the roots of your solution embedded deeply in the community and a strong team leading the way, it's time to strategically partner with other groups for the purpose of advancing one another's objectives. Turn competition into collaboration.

Chapter 10

Balance Strengthening and Starting

Once you've developed ideas for solutions to the problem you've identified, it's time to consider what framework would be best suited to implementing them: Should you join a well-established group, working from within to implement your ideas, or start a new group? This chapter will guide you through this decision, presenting the pros and cons of each approach. It will also highlight the most important points to consider when making your decision.

It's also worth noting that this question of strengthening versus starting will routinely resurface, whether you choose to start a new organization or join an existing one to implement your initial idea. In any organization (whether well-established or relatively new), as fresh ideas come up and new projects are proposed, you'll need to once again assess whether the goals of the project would be best served by starting from scratch in-house, despite perhaps not having the optimal resources or setup for the task, or by partnering with another organization that has similar goals, along with the knowledge or resources to help make your project a success. This decision process is similar, as ultimately, you always want to choose the structure that will best allow you to execute your plans and realize your vision. You'll find that you can maximize your chances of success by striking the right balance between strengthening and starting… and that's where this chapter comes in handy.

Strengthening

Advantages of Strengthening

Whatever problem you've chosen to tackle, chances are lots of other people and groups are already working to solve it. And if you choose to join an existing effort, you'll enjoy some major advantages. Established organizations have already gone through the trouble of recruiting people with similar interests, developing an organizational structure that works, and securing funding. In most cases, these groups have forged strong community ties, fostered partnerships with similar or allied organizations, and developed a strong sense of organizational identity. When joining an existing group, you use the machinery that's already in place to effect change rather than dedicating your efforts to reinventing the same machinery. Rather than worry about the day-to-day concerns of running an organization, you'll be able to focus your energies on making your idea a reality. Change is about collective action, and collective action is about pooling energies, not splintering efforts.

There are additional practical benefits to joining an established group. For one, groups with longevity are more likely to have already obtained legal status as an official business or nonprofit, which can be a fairly cumbersome, lengthy process (but it *can* be done; see Chapters 38 and 39 for details), so it's a plus if you can avoid the added hassle and expense. Second, some large organizations like the Red Cross and Kiwanis have chapters throughout the country or even the world, providing a network through which your idea, if successful, could naturally spread. Third, joining an established group, and particularly a large and well-respected group, affords a name recognition and instant credibility that might be particularly helpful when trying to build community support for your idea.

Another key practical benefit of joining a preexisting group is that a large or international organization's network can help ensure the continuity of your efforts. In particular, if you're a student, school organizations are especially vulnerable to fizzling and dying out because of graduating members and the natural ebb and flow of membership. Academic commitments and holidays can leave important projects suspended for long periods of time. A national affiliation can alleviate these problems by continuing to move your projects forward, even when you temporarily cannot. Moreover, large organizations tend to be more stable than small, informal groups, so there is a greater chance your project will continue into the future uninterrupted.

Finally, there's something to be said for experience and the associated concept of institutional memory. A battle-tested group that knows the cause thoroughly and also has experience working for change in your area is a valuable asset. By joining such a group, you'd have access to its major benefits (people, resources, and experience, to name just a few), which you could use to nurture your idea. You'd be able to hit the ground running.

Disadvantages of Strengthening

That said, joining forces isn't all rainbows and sunshine. In exchange for the resources, experience, and connections of an established group, you'll have little to no control over the structure of the group or the group's overall direction. As a staff or volunteer member, you'll have some input, but your voice won't carry more weight than those of the other members. And while you can suggest new projects, partnerships, and community alliances, you'll need to seek approval from the group or the group's leadership. Sometimes the organization's priorities won't align with yours, and you may not be able to garner the support you need for your ideas.

A determined leader can make good things happen in an organization, regardless of whether he or she is at the top of the ladder or on the bottom rung. However, it requires time and effort to become a trusted voice in an existing organization. By contrast, when starting your own organization from scratch, it's natural to have much more control over the group's direction and actions.

Starting

Advantages of Starting

You're the master of your destiny, but you're also starting from square one. You'll recruit members, fundraise, build bridges to the community, and track down mentors all on your own. It can be a bit intimidating, but it also means you'll have a great deal of influence over how your group develops and also the way the group goes about implementing your great idea. You'll be able to tailor the group and its activities to the specific problem or types of problems you hope to address. You'll also learn a great deal from the process of starting a group, especially about yourself.

While there may be a steep learning curve at the beginning, you can always reach out to more established organizations for help and advice. You might consider partnering directly with another group to implement your action plan. In fact, it's almost always a good idea to form partnerships in your community, especially when you're getting started. Just remember that if you're planning on partnering with an established organization right out of the gate, you should be able to clearly identify why it is you need to start a separate group and enter into a partnership, rather than join the existing group directly. For more on partnerships, see Chapters 13 and 31.

Disadvantages of Starting

If you start your own group, you give up the built-in staff, resources, and experience that a well-established group can offer. You'll have to recruit members, identify and secure your own sources of funding, and determine an organizational and team structure that works. If you don't know much about leadership or team dynamics, you'll need to learn along the way. You'll also be taking on a lot of responsibility because you'll be shepherding not only your problem-solving efforts but also the group as a whole. A sad but true reality is that a lot of new groups don't last very long, and even those that find their footing may require a lot of time to mature to the point where they're ready to begin taking on major projects and initiatives.

Choose a Vehicle

Now that you understand the pros and cons of strengthening and starting, you need to ask yourself: Do I want to be in the driver's seat or do I want to carpool? The driver gets to choose the music, but carpoolers get to use the fast lane. What is the right fit for your trip? Whether you decide to join an existing group or create your own, whether you embark on a project by yourself or with multiple partners, you should do so because you feel that structure will best allow you to develop and execute your ideas. Remember to keep your focus on solving the problem, not on starting an organization or initiative for its own sake.

Many leaders are too quick to start their own organizations. There is value (and maturity) in strengthening existing efforts over starting

Figure 10.1. The Advantages of Strengthening versus Starting Will Be Weighted Differently in Each Case

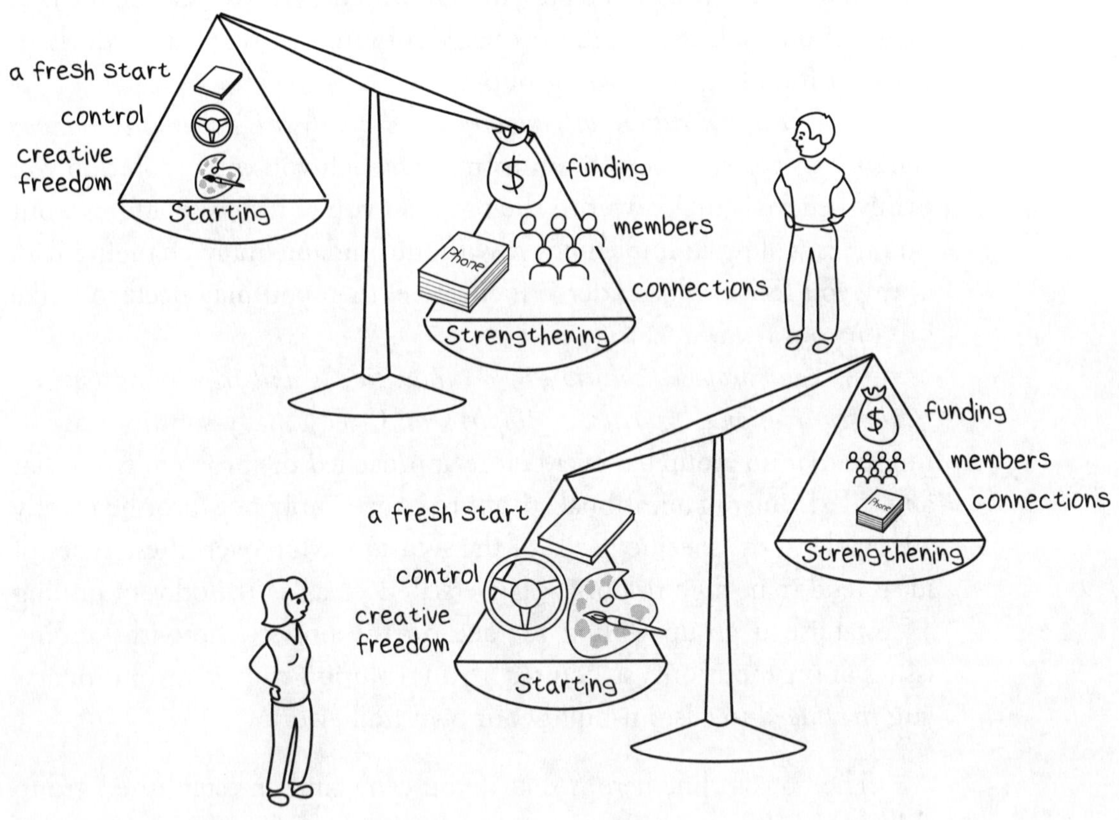

something new, which can often divide community resources and accountability. In general, we recommend that your default should be to strengthen an existing group, but if you find yourself at a roadblock and you can justify the need to start your own group, then go for it.

There are several specific situations when it might be necessary to start a new group. If you find yourself in any of the following situations, striking out on your own may be the best way to see your idea through:

- *The organizations you approach aren't willing to support your proposed plan of action.* This could happen for any number of reasons: the change proposed might not fit the group's mission statement, the method proposed might depart from the group's usual area of expertise, or the organization might be overcommitted already or lack the funds to take on additional initiatives. Sometimes you can work out a compromise. For example, you might consider expanding the scope of your solution to include additional demographics more in line with the group's mission statement. Or perhaps the group might not have the resources to commit to your project at present but would agree to take it on in a couple months. If there's no reasonable compromise that can be devised, consider founding your own group.

- *The organization will adopt your idea only if it's changed in a way you strongly oppose.* If your brainstorming has left you with a solution you firmly believe is the answer to the problem you're trying to address, but no one is willing to implement it without fundamentally changing it in a way you feel would render it ineffective, then you may need to strike out on your own.
- *Your proposed solution is so innovative it will require an entirely new organizational structure to implement.* Occasionally solutions are so unique that no group has ever before approached the problem from that angle. Existing organizational structures may simply not fit or be readily adaptable to the specific needs of the solution. Moreover, these types of ideas tend to be high risk or controversial, decreasing the odds of finding an established group willing to take on the project, notwithstanding issues of organizational structure. If your solution truly is revolutionary, you may need to custom-build your own framework.

The bottom line here is that if you can't find an established group willing to help you implement your idea (within a reasonable degree of what you envision), consider why that might be. Reevaluate both your needs and approach to attempt to find a compromise. If this fails and you determine your solution has great potential but just hasn't found a good organizational match or is unique and requires its own unique group structure, give yourself the green light to create your own group.

WARNING

Founder, president, or *CEO* before your name certainly has a nice ring to it, but if being the boss is first, second, or third on the list of reasons for starting your own organization, reevaluate your priorities. More often than not, you'll make more of an impact by joining forces than by going off on your own.

Strike a Balance

There is no right answer to the question "Should I strengthen or start?" You actually have to do both, finding a balance between creating new things and improving existing efforts. For example, perhaps you've started a new organization that brings together senior citizens to help the community (starting). Your group of volunteers typically focuses on community garden projects and environmental clean-up efforts. However, for your summer project, you decide to contribute your volunteers and funding to a well-established civic group that puts on an annual festival in the town (strengthening). Here you've balanced strengthening and starting.

The Polaris Project, a nonprofit organization that fights sex trafficking, is a great example of an organization that has struck a balance between strengthening and starting. It has a mix of projects: the Polaris Fellowship program for students (started internally for the group), the US Campaign Against Commercial Sexual Exploitation of Children, which oversees a 24-hour toll-free hotline in four languages (started with other organizations), and writing state legislation to change laws and regulations for sex trafficking (strengthening existing efforts and building on the past successes of other groups).

However, when you're first starting out, you don't want to spread yourself too thin by developing multiple projects; instead, start by considering the needs of the very first project or action plan you'd like to implement. Would it be best served by a new organization, or an existing one? Remember that there will always be opportunities to balance strengthening and starting down the line. Right now, just focus on what the best decision is at this particular time, for this particular project, then go from there.

Chapter 11

Cultivate Community Ownership

"[We don't] tell the communities we serve what they need—they tell us."

—*EXCERPT FROM THE PIH MODEL OF PARTNERS IN HEALTH, A LEADING INTERNATIONAL HEALTH AND SOCIAL JUSTICE ORGANIZATION*[1]

Many well-intentioned social efforts are spearheaded by individuals who are not members of the communities they intend to benefit. For example, Americans concerned by the plight of those in developing nations may focus their efforts on improving the lives of people halfway around the globe. Even when our attentions remain domestically focused, we may find inspiration in communities outside our own. For example, a teacher from a high-scoring school district may organize a group of students to help tutor children in a neighborhood with low-scoring schools. Although such actions are well meaning, history has shown that when done independently, they don't work or work only temporarily.

Why? Because in many of these externally directed efforts, the critical element of community ownership is overlooked. In fact, even if the efforts are started internally by a member of the community, if the ownership is with an individual and not multiple members of the broader community, progress is similarly unsustainable. Community ownership is an inclusive, collaborative form of problem solving that draws upon the insights, motivations, and commitment of the community itself to

Figure 11.1. Cultivate Community Ownership

not only maximize the chances of a successful intervention but also ensure its continuation long after the founding members have left.

Community ownership is a critical component of lasting social change, whether that change is initiated by community members themselves or kindly "outsiders." In this chapter, we'll give you a broad overview of what community ownership is and why it's so essential to any type of work you might hope to do. You'll find a more extensive discussion of community ownership, as well as practical advice on how to interact with and engage communities, in Chapter 34.

Learn about the Community

A community can be defined by almost any criterion: geography, culture, race, ethnicity, gender, faith, age, profession, interests, or any combination thereof. Before engaging the community you'd like to help, even if that community is your own, take some time to step back and learn a bit about it. Focus on its history, politics, socioeconomics, demographics, and any other attributes you think might be relevant. Additionally, find out as much as you can about the context of the problem you've identified—how it arose, what has been done about it before, and why past interventions did or didn't work.

Case Study: Generation Citizen

Scott Warren and Alison Cohen are the executive director and director of evaluation, respectively, of Generation Citizen, a 501(c)(3) organization that partners college student volunteers with classroom teachers to provide an action civics curriculum that empowers youth with the knowledge, skills, and motivation to solve the problems they face in their own communities.

Scott: Recognizing the larger societal context through personal experience and research is an important first step in developing solutions. Growing up in five different countries in Latin America and Africa, I witnessed the power of democracy and the importance of promoting democracy among traditionally underrepresented populations. When I was 17, I became involved in advocacy to end the Darfur genocide and joined STAND, a national student anti-genocide organization. At 20, I became STAND's national student director. However, we had a diversity problem: our movement was composed primarily of students at top-ranked universities and wealthy high schools. This civic engagement gap is a more general phenomenon; Harvard professor Meira Levinson has documented that poor and minority students are less educated about the political process than their wealthier, white counterparts.[2] These students are also less likely to vote and more likely to believe that government is not responsive to their needs.[3] Research confirms that elected officials rarely work in the interest of the poorest 20%.[4]

Generation Citizen teaches civics by *doing* civics and targets historically underrepresented populations—low-income youth and youth of color in urban centers. Cofounder Scott realized that for his target community: (1) public schools were an important place to work and (2) getting the students involved by taking action—writing letters to the editor, lobbying politicians, meeting local and state representatives—would simultaneously teach them content and engage them in their neighborhood. At the end of the semester, the teenagers choose a local problem they want to address in their community and work together to try to solve it.

Scott: Local community insight and buy-in is key to successful implementation. From meeting with school staff—key gatekeepers to our target community—I learned that it would be important to align our curriculum with state educational standards. Generation Citizen is now unique in teaching "action civics" in a simultaneously engaging and standards-aligned approach.

Alison: Community-responsive action civics programming has an impact. Our quasi-experimental evaluation has found that participation in Generation Citizen increases student civic engagement by more than one standard deviation. Additionally, college student volunteers report increased civic action skills and teaching skills, which 96% of them intend to apply to careers in the public sector.

Generation Citizen's successful outcomes are due to its commitment to learning about and addressing the assets, needs, and ideas of both the members of its target community—the students with which it works—and the key gatekeepers to its community—school staff and other leaders.

Get the Community Perspective

Just as in the business world's market research and consumer focus groups that drive product development, in the world of social innovation, the community's perspective on a problem is absolutely essential. No solution, no matter how great it seems, should ever be put into motion without first understanding the community's perspective on the problem itself. For example, if you plan to drill water wells for a remote farming community that has been struck by a devastating drought, you might reconsider your plan if you learn that the community members believe the drought is a punishment from God that they must accept. You could certainly drill wells, but no one would use them.

The community's perspective is thus necessary when evaluating the appropriateness of a solution in a given context. Solutions that are not deemed appropriate by the community in which they're implemented will be unlikely to meet with success. Think of it this way: you've likely heard the Chinese proverb "Give a man a fish and you feed him for a day. Teach a man to fish and you feed him for a lifetime." Teaching a man to fish so he can provide for himself seems like a good thing... but what if the man is a vegetarian? Take the time to understand the perspectives of those you wish to help and you're less likely to encounter problems when you implement your solution later down the road.

Another reason to actively seek out the community perspective is to benefit from firsthand knowledge of the problem. Community members may be able to shed some light on the causes of the problem or complicating factors you had never considered. They may suggest solutions or see opportunities that you missed or point you toward helpful resources.

The importance of getting the community perspective and how it results in community ownership is well illustrated by the site DonorsChoose.org. Charles Best saw that public school teachers were frustrated by not having adequate financial support and having to pay out of their own pockets to get necessary supplies such as crayons, glue, and rulers for their classrooms. The teachers had no organized way to ask for money, no way to let potential donors know what their needs were. And from the donors' perspective, Best saw that many philanthropists were committed to improving education; however, while they could donate to universities easily, there was no good system for them to donate to public schools and no way to know what individual schools or classrooms needed. Using his understanding of the perspectives of both teachers and donors, Best created DonorsChoose.org, a community-driven venue where teachers explain exactly what items they need to help their students. The teachers post their requests online, then donors choose which teacher to donate to and how much to give. DonorsChoose.org has full transparency; the teachers record how the money was used and measure the progress students make thanks to the donation. They send this information back to the donor, giving the donor a clear sense of his impact. By understanding the needs of the two communities, Best was able to build a bridge between the teachers and donors in a way that not only gives the community members a sense of ownership, but also maximizes the impact of donations.

Promote Shared Responsibility

Community ownership is built on a shared sense of responsibility between your group and the community; both are invested and committed to working together to produce better outcomes. Sharing responsibility translates into sharing accountability, which results in more buy-in and long-term participation from the various stakeholders.

The key to promoting shared responsibility is involving the community in all aspects from start to finish. Your interactions should not feel like "us" and "them" but rather a large, collective "we". Work together to determine what an ideal solution would look like for the community.

What would be the end goal, who would take an active role in implementing the solution, how will the stakeholders share responsibility and accountability for the short-term and long-term results?

The more community involvement you can encourage, the more invested the community will be in implementing and maintaining the solution. This is critical to enacting lasting change because a self-directed community infrastructure will be necessary to keep the wheels of your solution turning years and even decades after you have moved on.

There is no power for change greater than a community discovering what it cares about.

MARGARET WHEATLEY

One of the best ways to encourage a sense of community investment in a problem is to involve community members in the design and implementation of its solution. Brainstorm solutions with community members, come to a community consensus about the solution, and then take action as a team. As a result of being involved at every step in the process, community members feel a sense of responsibility, accountability, and ownership over the solution. Remember: your role is not to bring change to the community; your role is to *empower* the community to make the change itself. This is the secret to lasting progress.

Chapter 12

Foster Team Unity

> *The way a team plays as a whole determines its success. You may have the greatest bunch of individual stars in the world, but if they don't play together, the club won't be worth a dime.*
>
> —BABE RUTH

Much of the discussion about working together has thus far focused on your team as a whole working with another organization or community. But internal collaboration is just as critical to your success. Creating a harmonious and cohesive team facilitates creativity, accountability, and ultimately, efficacy.

Nurture a Sense of Community

On a very basic level, everyone likes to feel that they belong, that there is a group of people who want and need them and a place where they can meaningfully contribute and thrive. Success is sweeter when shared, and tough times are easier to ride out together.

Appeal to this natural human inclination by fostering a strong sense of community within your group. If you can provide your members with a more emotionally fulfilling group experience, you increase the likelihood that your members will find their work personally rewarding while simultaneously engendering a greater sense of loyalty to the group.

Figure 12.1. Becoming Closer as a Team Increases Your Efficacy as a Team

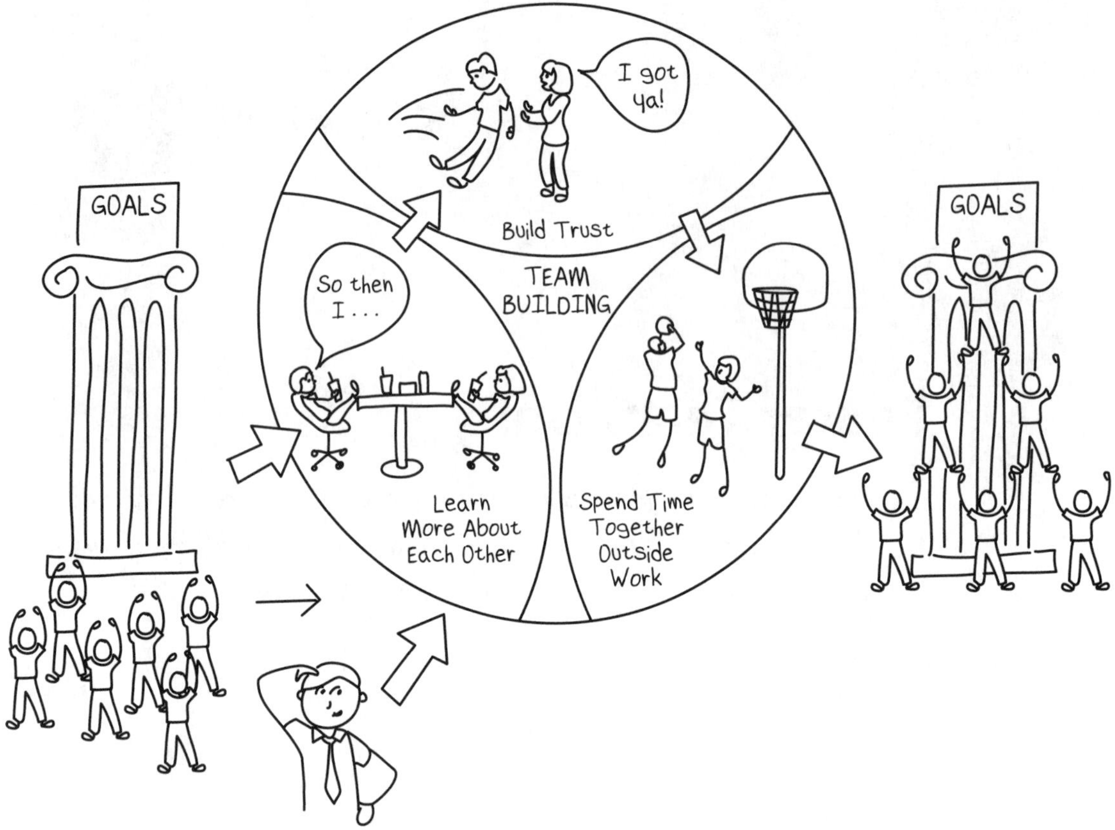

Psychologists David McMillian and David Chavis identify four key components of a sense of community:

1. *Integration and fulfillment of needs*—"shared values [and] rewards that are effective reinforcers"
2. *Shared emotional connection*—"the commitment and belief that members have shared and will share history, common places, time together, and similar experiences."
3. *Membership*—"the feeling of belonging"
4. *Influence*—"a sense of mattering, of making a difference to a group"[1]

In groups that seek to bring about positive social change, a shared value for the cause is generally the first thing to bring people together. This aspect of your work is a natural adhesive, according to McMillian and Chavis. Reinforce this bond by encouraging team members to share their personal motivations and what inspired them to join the team.

Further cement this shared emotional connection by providing group members with ample opportunities to spend time together outside of work. Forming friendships translates into better teamwork and also contributes to a greater sense of membership and belonging. Moreover, when we're in a nurturing and supportive community, we're more likely to feel free to open up, express creative thoughts, and identify and voice potential problems. When your teammates do open up and express new ideas, make sure to recognize them for contributing useful points and perspectives. This will reassure them of their influence within the group and encourage future active participation.

Encourage Ownership of the Solution

As a leader, you'll frequently need to delegate, assigning various group members with the responsibility for a host of tasks. Though it might occasionally be tempting, refrain from micromanaging at all costs. If you trust in the capability and resourcefulness of your group members, you'll give them the leeway to get creative and truly take ownership of the solution, or at least one component of it.

Group members who feel a sense of ownership of the solution, who feel engaged in the cause and valued for their contributions, believe that they matter—and they do! Encouraging this sense of influence is a critical component of community building, as noted by McMillian and Chavis. And as we've discussed, a sense of community is key to member retention and promotion of team spirit.

Facilitate Quality Communication

Communication is very much at the foundation of a unified and well-functioning team. When computational scientist Alex Pentland, director of the MIT Media Lab Entrepreneurship Program, wanted to identify the most important predictor of a team's success, he considered a number of factors: intelligence, personality, and talent, to name a few. But in the end, it was communication that emerged the clear winner. Pentland also learned that *what* was said by a team member wasn't nearly as important as *how* it was said. That is, patterns of communication could predict outcomes so well that, without even meeting potential team members, Pentland and his team could predict which groups would outperform their peers just by analyzing their communication patterns. He determined that the most beneficial modes of communication could be distinguished by their high levels of:

1. *Energy*—the frequency and quality of exchanges among team members
2. *Engagement*—the degree to which all members are involved in dialogue
3. *Exploration*—the amount of communication between members and individuals outside the team[2]

An important note about energy is that the exchanges measured were face-to-face communications. Pentland and his team are quick to stress that the best teams benefit from in-person sharing of ideas, not a barrage of e-mails and text messages. So spend a little less time writing e-mails and get out and talk to your team more.

Another interesting finding was that it wasn't the communication of one or even a handful of leaders that mattered, but the degree to which all members were involved in the dialogue. This means you should strive to encourage open lines of communication among all team members, independent of group hierarchy.

Finally, Pentland and his colleagues found that a strong sense of exploration and willingness to solicit ideas and opinions from nongroup members boded well for team communication and effectiveness, so encourage your team members to get out and share ideas. As Pentland's research showed, exploration breeds success.

Note For more specifics on how to communicate effectively with your team, turn to Chapter 30.

Bring Out the Best in Others

As a leader, one of your top priorities should be to help everyone around you reach their full potential. In this vein, encourage frequent, constructive, and actionable feedback as a building block for continuous improvement and personal growth. Take time to recognize people's skills and give them the freedom and space to excel. A nurturing environment in which your members are encouraged to develop their skills as leaders is a powerful draw that deepens the sense of commitment your members have both to your group and to each other.

Promote Happiness

In *The Happiness Advantage*, psychologist Shawn Achor shows that when people are happy, they work better, are more productive, and are more creative.[3] According to Achor, "A decade of research proves that happiness raises nearly every business and educational outcome, raising sales by 37%, productivity by 31%, and accuracy on tasks by 19%, as well as a myriad of health and quality of life improvements."[4]

Fostering a nurturing environment that is positive and optimistic can go a long way. How can you increase happiness among your team members? Achor gives five simple suggestions that have been shown to correlate with increased well-being and satisfaction:

- Write down three things you're grateful for.
- Write a positive message to someone in your social network.
- Meditate for two minutes.
- Exercise for 10 minutes.
- Spend two minutes writing down the most meaningful experience of the past day.[5]

Pass this information on to your members, and consider incorporating some of the advice into your meetings. For example, you might start each meeting by instructing members to write down or think of three things they're grateful for. As Achor notes, "Happiness fuels success, not the other way around."

Chapter 13

Forge Partnerships

If everyone is moving forward together, then success takes care of itself.

—HENRY FORD

An essential part of learning to work together is learning to forge partnerships. Partnerships are absolutely indispensable; they accelerate your journey toward meaningful, lasting change while expanding your personal network of similarly motivated and committed individuals. By teaming up to work toward a common goal, you instantly expand your access to a wealth of resources, from specialized knowledge and experience, to raw manpower and distribution networks.

Rewind back to elementary school, when you memorized the different types of symbiotic relationships between organisms:

- *Parasitic*: one benefits at the expense of the other (survival of the fittest, or win-lose)
- *Commensal*: one benefits while the other is unchanged (win-annoyed)
- *Mutualistic*: both benefit (win-win).

In the best partnerships, the relationship is mutualistic, with each party contributing something unique or valuable to the mix, thus benefitting both groups. Why focus on forging partnerships? Because the ideal partnership leads to the magic buzzword—synergy. That is, the products of the partnership are far greater than the sum of what both groups could achieve working alone.

This chapter serves as a brief introduction to partnerships. Specifically, it addresses key points to keep in mind when considering potential partnerships. A much more extensive primer on identifying, building, and maintaining productive partnerships can be found in Chapter 31.

Turn Competition into Collaboration

Competition between similar groups is a major (and unnecessary) barrier to meaningful collaboration. That said, it's easy to see how competition arises. New groups are created each day, and the vast majority of these new groups share a cause or objective either with each other or with other established organizations. Because similar groups struggle for the same limited resources (e.g., funding, members, political goodwill), it's understandable they might regard each other as competitors.

However, while a little competition can occasionally be healthy, this type of competition is often counterproductive, ultimately working against your cause. For example, let's say you buy five boxes of Girl Scout cookies from Juliette, your 12-year-old next-door neighbor. When Ana, another girl in Juliette's troop, knocks on your door the following afternoon, you're likely to turn her down. Although both girls are working toward the same goal of raising money for their troop, Ana feels like she has lost out to Juliette and starts thinking about how she can outsell Juliette next year.

When you look at resources from the perspective of the cause (in this case, the Girl Scouts), it's a waste of time for Ana to canvass an area Juliette has already covered. If she had collaborated even loosely with Juliette, Ana could have focused her efforts on a different neighborhood. Perhaps, realizing her tech savvy was wasted knocking on doors, Ana could have built a website for online cookie sales, an approach none of the local troops had tried. If Juliette and Ana had partnered up, they could have covered more ground, and the Girl Scouts would have benefitted from more funding.

You may be thinking that this sounds a bit naïve. We're not going to wake up tomorrow and find competitors holding hands and giving out free hugs. Plus, you think, doesn't competition drive innovation (not to mention the free market)? Absolutely. So what's the difference between good and bad types of competition? *Constructive* competition challenges us to do better, try harder, and create more effective solutions. In contrast, *constrictive* competition limits your potential impact and turns the world into a zero-sum game. In constrictive competition, you lose sight of the larger goal, focusing on doing better than your neighbor, rather than just doing better for the world.

This competitive "us versus them" mentality is a barrier to social progress. It results in wasted time and resources and slows advancement and innovation. The key is recognizing constrictive competition when you see it. If you feel like your group and another group are doubling up your efforts (or reinventing the wheel) a lot, this is an excellent sign you should join forces.

You should also consider a partnership if an opportunity arises that would benefit from your combined skill sets. For this reason, it's good to be aware of the strengths and weaknesses of both your group and similar groups, so you can recognize when a partnership might be especially beneficial. Above all, challenge yourself to begin looking at similar groups not as competitors, but as potential partners. Exercise 13.1 will help you start to make this critical shift in thinking.

Exercise 13.1 Seeing Competitors as Partners

List five groups you might currently view as competitors. What do you have in common? How are you duplicating each other's efforts? What unique skills or resources do they have that you admire? In what ways could you potentially collaborate so that both groups benefit?

Group	Commonalities	Duplicated Efforts	Unique Skills/ Resources	Collaboration Opportunities

Case Study: ReSight

Sheel Tyle is the executive director of ReSight and a venture capitalist at New Enterprise Associates. A graduate of Stanford University, he is a founding partner of S2 Capital, a social investment fund that invests in the promising companies built by young people that advance gender equity, improve health care delivery, and amplify economic growth in low-resource countries. In this case study, he discusses how he forged valuable partnerships that increased the impact of his efforts.

The Problem

Sheel: There are over 161 million people in the world who are visually impaired. 87% of them live in the developing world, and for 80% of these individuals, their impairment is treatable.[1] The problem is pretty simple: if you can't see, it's tough to work. Moreover, visually impaired women in the developing world, approximately 80% of whom are self-employed or unemployed, are marginalized and abused. They are considered burdens on their family and suffer from low self-esteem.[2]

The Solution

Sheel: In response to this problem, I started ReSight, a 501(c)(3) nonprofit devoted to eradicating treatable blindness. ReSight trains and employs individuals who underwent procedures to restore their sight. These people, the majority of whom are women, educate their communities and screen for vision problems as well as other health conditions (like diabetes and hypertension) that can produce visual impairments if left untreated. ReSight thus helps prevent and treat visual impairments in the developing world while empowering formerly blind individuals, transforming them into symbols of hope for their communities.

The Partnership

Sheel: As we were preparing to launch our first programs, we realized there was only so much we could do on our own. We needed advice, so we turned to other vision care NGOs and international bodies like SEVA, Sight Savers, and the International Council for Education of People with Visual Impairment, to learn about their experiences working with patients with low vision. They offered us resources and advice; in return, we offered to institute our programs in their locations.

Consider a Range of Partnership Opportunities

Partnering with another group isn't an all-or-nothing proposition. You don't need to collaborate on every project, and you certainly don't need to stay partners forever. Partnership opportunities come in a wide range of sizes and shapes.

These seemingly endless options can be boiled down to five essential organizational relationships, as described by the Working Together Continuum for organizations. Working Together: A Continuum (Figure 13.1) was adapted by consultant Chris Kloth from Ohio State University School of Social Work from Professor Richard Boettcher's model for the five types of organizational relationships.

Understanding this continuum is integral to building a variety of mutually beneficial partnerships. When working with a partner, you may choose to integrate your operations, joining forces completely; collaborate to build something together, sharing best practices freely; cooperate to take advantage of each group's individual strengths, sharing only limited information; or simply coordinate your efforts, remaining largely independent. You can also return to a state of complete organizational independence in between specific projects or partnership opportunities—partnering doesn't mean you have to do everything

Figure 13.1. Working Together: A Continuum[3]

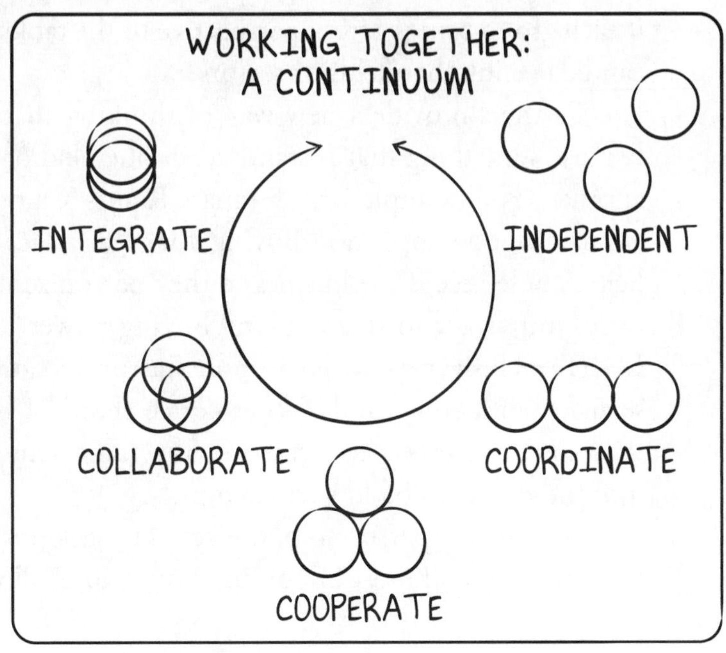

together all the time. Moreover, the nature of your partnership may change over time—you may completely integrate your groups for a short period, then move toward collaboration later. Partnerships are often dynamic, changing according to the needs of specific projects or the emergence of new opportunities.

Thus, you can be competitors and collaborators at the same time. Take Microsoft and Apple, for example. Thinking about the continuum of working together, they wouldn't (and shouldn't) integrate and merge into one supercompany. But they could, and did, collaborate (they created Microsoft Office for the Mac) and cooperate (with third partner Intel to create a processor that runs both Apple and Microsoft operating systems on one Apple machine). Intel's creation of the new processor resulted in progress for all three companies. Not only did they drive technological innovation forward; they produced a better product for users. They still have projects where they are in direct competition, as well as projects where they are independent, but they have found ways to work together and build partnerships that benefit both and solve problems better.

Seek Out Unique Partners

Always keep an eye out for potential partnerships. Keep in mind that partners don't need to be similar or even have similar goals—there may be unusual and mutually beneficial areas of overlap. The trick is to keep an open mind and remain receptive to unique possibilities, particularly if each group brings a fresh perspective to the table. In this vein, consider candidates in other fields or sectors.

Partners provide a new way of thinking that can be revolutionary because something that is standard in one field or region can transform another. For example, the Human Rights Campaign (HRC) created a smart phone app, the "Buying for Workplace Equality Guide," to help people "see if the businesses they patronize understand and honor issues important to them, giving buying power to issues ranging from LGBT inclusiveness to environmental protection."[4] "Equality for all sexual orientations" and "What coffee should I buy?" are two phrases that you'd never expect to see in the same sentence. HRC found an innovative way to build partnerships.

As with any partnership, the key is to seek out situations where you, your partner, and most important, your cause, all win.

Make It Last

One of the most overlooked aspects of many promising ideas is sustainability—perhaps it works, but does it last? The third and final step of the Do Good Well method is about ensuring your efforts do not lead to temporary gains but rather long-term, lasting change. A good solution should continue to work even after you the individual or you the larger group has moved on. To achieve this longevity, specific mechanisms needs to be in place, incorporated into the structure and evaluation of your work.

- *Chapter 14: Start Small, Then Scale What Works*—It's exciting to brainstorm save the world–type efforts and imagine your group quickly blossoming into a multinational organization. Think big, but start small. By testing out your ideas and expanding only those aspects that definitely work, you'll maximize resources and the likelihood of sustainability.
- *Chapter 15: Engineer Self-Sustainable Solutions*—Optimize your group's long-term impact by building systems to support planning for the future, institutional memory, financial independence, and adaptability.
- *Chapter 16: Integrate Social Entrepreneurship*—The biggest game-changer in the nonprofit world has been restructuring the way social problems are solved. We've moved away from the old charity model

to the sustainable social enterprise model, which applies the best of the business sector to produce social change with limited resources, market principles, and, yes, even profit.

- *Chapter 17: Share What Works*—This final component of the Do Good Well method actually brings together all three steps (do what works, work together, and make it last) by sharing what works. Share ideas, outcomes, resources, and mentorship with others. Leave a legacy by paying it forward.

Chapter 14

Start Small, Then Scale What Works

Companies that grow for the sake of growth or that expand into areas outside their core business strategy often stumble. On the other hand, companies that build scale for the benefit of their customers and shareholders more often succeed over time.

—JAMIE DIMON

You care deeply about the problem you're trying to solve. It affects many people, and you have a brilliant idea that has the potential to improve the lives of thousands, maybe even millions! You're sitting on a gold mine of social impact. If you could just get the word out, everyone would want in. The funding and media attention would pour in and soon you could have a branch of your organization in every country …

Time out.

It's certainly tempting to plan a large debut of your organization, but such an ambitious strategy most likely won't work and absolutely won't last. To make a lasting impact, your group needs to grow at the right rate. Grow too slowly and you're out of touch, irrelevant, and unable to keep up with the needs of the community. Grow too quickly and you spread resources too thin, lose the ability to deliver quality products and services, and implode. Only in mythology do fully formed adults appear overnight; in the real world, all good ideas and organizations need an incubation period, a time for testing out what works (Chapters 7, 8, and 9 guide you through the incubation period).

Think about it: organizations that last start small. Today Teach For America has nearly 5,000 teachers spread over 40 geographic regions, but it grew to that size from an inaugural class of 500 teachers in a half dozen cities. Facebook's predecessors, MySpace and Friendster, tried to start big, using the top-down approach. They targeted the general population, trying to reach as many people as possible. Anyone anywhere could join the social networking sites. Facebook was the opposite. It had a bottom-up approach; it started small, initially built for a single, limited community—a few thousand students at one university. As it began to expand, it "scaled," from school to school, creating deep roots in just a few college communities. The level of buy-in that resulted gave it the strength to branch out without losing its core vitality. Scaling has many different meanings in the business world, but here when we discuss scaling your idea or organization, we're talking about this ability to grow at a rate that maintains the quality of your original idea or group. Scaling is vital to sustainability. Just look at Facebook—big, lasting ideas start small.

This chapter explains the framework for growing in a manner that strengthens your impact and promotes sustainability.

Think Big, Start Small

There are two primary reasons not to start big. First, as discussed in Step 1, you need to know your proposed solution actually works. (For more on how to figure out if your idea works, see Chapter 8.) By starting small, you make the best use of your early resources and have the opportunity to improve and innovate on a manageable level. You add more value by doing something well rather than by doing it big.

Second, there is generally no one-size-fits-all model that works in every location and for every demographic. You'll need to tailor your plans to each new community as you expand. Even megafranchises like McDonald's and Starbucks vary both their menus and decors in different communities, taking into account regional tastes and how customers at each location like to consume their food and coffee.

But while it's more effective to start small, you should still think big! Teach For America and Facebook are huge ideas, but even while starting

Figure 14.1. Start Small, Then Scale What Works

small, their creators saw the potential for revolutionary change. It's okay to have a bold and ambitious vision for your team. By all means, invest your efforts in an idea with immense potential ... but test it out before you decide to expand, and when you do, take into account the specific needs of each new community you enter.

Scale What Works

Types of Scaling

You have done some great work, have done the analysis to show that your idea does actually work, and now would like to increase your impact. But just *how* would you like to increase your impact? Gregory Dees and colleagues from Duke University's Center for the Advancement of Social Entrepreneurship identify two types of growth:

1. *Scale deep:* Deepen your impact in your existing community (new solution, existing community)
2. *Scale out:* Widen your impact to new communities (existing solution, new community).[1]

There are many ways to increase your impact: by scaling deep you provide greater services and exert influence on more areas such as research, policy, and public opinion; by scaling out, you broaden your target audience and serve more communities. But don't expand just to get bigger. When scaling, keep the same principles in mind that this method endorses: have evidence of what is needed by the community and that what you're proposing can meet those needs.

Case Study: Gay-Straight Alliance Network

Scale deep or scale out? The answer is both. Needs, resources, and environment will contribute heavily to your choice of how to grow. Carolyn Laub founded the Gay-Straight Alliance Network (GSA) with 40 school-based clubs in the San Francisco Bay Area in 2000. The GSA has done a great job of scaling out: it now has 850 clubs in California and has created a scalable model of organizing youth-led efforts against homophobia and transphobia used by schools in New Mexico and Texas.

When the political environment called for scaling deep, GSA took action by promoting the California Student Safety and Violence Prevention Act, groundbreaking legislation that was among the first to prohibit discrimination based on sexual orientation and gender identity. This traction paved the way for GSA to "work together" and "make it last" by launching the National Association of GSA Networks, uniting organizations in 29 states that support GSAs.[2]

Types of Spread

When scaling out, there are multiple ways you can spread out your efforts. Dees et al. place types of spread on a continuum "requiring an increasing degree of central coordination and typically greater resources":

- *Dissemination*: "Actively providing information and sometimes technical assistance to others looking to bring an innovation to their community"
- *Affiliation*: "A formal relationship defined by an ongoing agreement ... to be a part of an identifiable network [ranging] from a loose coalition of organizations committed to the same goals, to tighter systems operating similar to business franchises"
- *Branching*: "Creation of local sites through one large organization, much like company-owned stores in the business world"[3]

The type of spread you choose will depend on the nature of your solution, the amount of control you want to have, and the skills of the people who will be leading the new expanded efforts.

> **Tip** Keep a written record of what didn't work. When scaling, you may find that certain aspects of an idea that failed initially may work in a different context. The reverse is just as true: as you measure and improve and find that what works varies by community, try to discover why.

When you are expanding your organization, keep in mind the balance of strengthening and creating discussed in Chapter 10. Will you make more of an impact by creating a new branch in another community or by partnering with similarly minded groups already in that community? At this time, is it better for your group to take on an entirely new aspect of the problem, or strengthen an existing effort?

Remember that as you scale, you need to continue measuring, evaluating, and improving. What works in the original implementation may be completely different from what works in scaled efforts. Use the assessment to rev up or slow down your expansion efforts. With this deliberate and results-driven approach to scaling what works, you will generate the force necessary to make it last.

Assess Supply and Demand

You've figured out a solution that works (at least once). Now analyze the supply and demand of your group's solution. Note that the questions that follow are written for efforts that scale out (existing solution, new community) but also apply to those that scale deep (new solution, existing community).

Supply: Do We Have What They Need?

- *Preparation*: Does the evidence prove that your idea works? Is it ready to scale? Which elements must stay? Which will be changed and how?
- *Resources*: Do you have the people, time, and money to implement expansion properly? Will the growth result in enough of an increase in donations or profit to sustain the expansion? What additional resources are required, and what resources may be gained?
- *Stakeholder consensus*: Do your team, advisors, partners, and funders agree that expansion is in the best interest of the group and supports the mission?
- *Quality control*: Will the ongoing work continue at the same level or better? Can you facilitate communication between your team now and a new team for sharing of ideas, resources, and knowledge?

Demand: Do They Want What We Have?

- *Need*: Is there evidence suggesting that the community needs your proposed solution? Are you solving the problem for it better than anyone else?
- *Want*: Does the community want your solution? Dees et al. warn, "If an innovation is complex, represents a radical departure from accepted practice, threatens influential local parties, or clashes with dominant values or ideologies in different comminutes, it will likely be met with resistance."[4] Will the community take ownership and accountability?
- *Certainty*: Can the success you've had be replicated in a different community? Does that community have the resources and environment to nurture the project? Is it likely that implementation will be done correctly?
- *Impact*: Will it show a measured impact? Dees et al. warn, "Impact should not just be about serving more people—it should be about serving them well"[5]

Do the supply and demand balance out? In biology, when cells are replicating, there are certain checkpoints to regulate that everything is growing in proportion to itself and its broader needs. The cells need both external growth signals telling them to multiply, as well as the nutrients, resources, and internal machinery to accommodate that growth. If there is a disconnect, the replication can't proceed. Let this analysis be the checkpoint. Don't expand if you don't have both supply and demand.

Tip If you can't have both, choose quality (a top-notch organization doing good work in a limited area) over quantity (multiple branches).

Not ready to scale? No problem! Scaling is by no means a prerequisite for impact. A high-quality group with a measured impact on 100 people or on one small component of the problem is much better than an ineffective group trying to help 1,000 people or take on a problem out of balance with its resources. Better to solve a small problem than make no progress on a large problem. If you still want to expand, pursue strategic partnerships. You may not necessarily develop your brand, but you will strengthen it and your impact.

Chapter 15

Engineer Self-Sustainable Solutions

In 2010, Haiti was hit by a catastrophic earthquake. In the aftermath of this devastating event, the world gave generously. Countries pledged millions of dollars in humanitarian aid, religious and philanthropic groups organized efforts to help with everything from providing clean water to building housing for the newly orphaned children, and scores of professionals and volunteers of all ages and skill sets left their homes and flocked to the island, committed to lending a hand however it was needed.

Numerous programs and initiatives were launched. All were replete with money, resources, and well-intentioned individuals who put an enormous amount of time and effort into helping Haiti and her people. A few years later, some programs, like Partners in Health, are strong pillars of Haiti's recovering communities. Others no longer exist. Why?

The answer is that in the world's speedy response to the devastating natural disaster, little thought was given to the sustainability of the efforts. In a way, this is understandable given the immediacy of the situation. But the sad consequence is that for many of the groups, the problems they set out to solve remain rampant, and much of the progress those groups made in the early months is now lost, the potential for long-term change never realized. This problem is in no way unique to the Haiti disaster; indeed most organizations struggle with sustainability.

Engineering self-sustainable solutions is a crucial component of social change that lasts. Think of it this way: let's say your doctor advises you to lose 10 pounds. Your first idea to solve this problem is to do a juice cleanse; it requires a bit of money and a lot of willpower but by the end of two weeks you've lost the weight. However, you then return to your usual eating habits and a month later you've gained the 10 pounds back—your money, time, and energy all wasted. In contrast, a sustainable solution would be replacing your afternoon snack of soda and chips with water and fruit, adding in a regular 30-minute jog after work. After two weeks you don't notice much but a few months later, you've lost the 10 pounds. More importantly, because the changes were small and sustainable over the long-term, the impact is lasting—you keep the weight off, even continue to lose a little bit more by the end of the year, and overall feel healthier. In the same way, when trying to solve social problems, you need to design solutions that are self-sustaining, as this not only maximizes your precious resources of time, money, and energy, but also leads to long-term social progress.

In this chapter, we present the key features of sustainable solutions that you should incorporate in your organization's design and culture. It is important to note that "sustainable solutions" encompasses two aspects: (1) sustainability of the organization as an entity and (2) sustainability of the organization's impact. The distinction to make here is that a good solution can mean your organization is no longer involved but that the effects of your work persist, and ideally continue to make an impact in your absence. Thus the goal is to engineer both your organization and your ideas as systems that are self-sustainable; in so doing, you optimize the longevity of your impact.

Plan for Tomorrow

The first principle of self-sustainability is strategically planning for the future. Start by engaging in a little daydreaming: Where do you see your organization in six months? One year? Five years? What do you think the state of the problem and community will be like at those future times? With these ideas in mind, think about what short- and long-term success would look like for your team.

Figure 15.1. Design Solutions That Will Last Long After Your Involvement Ends

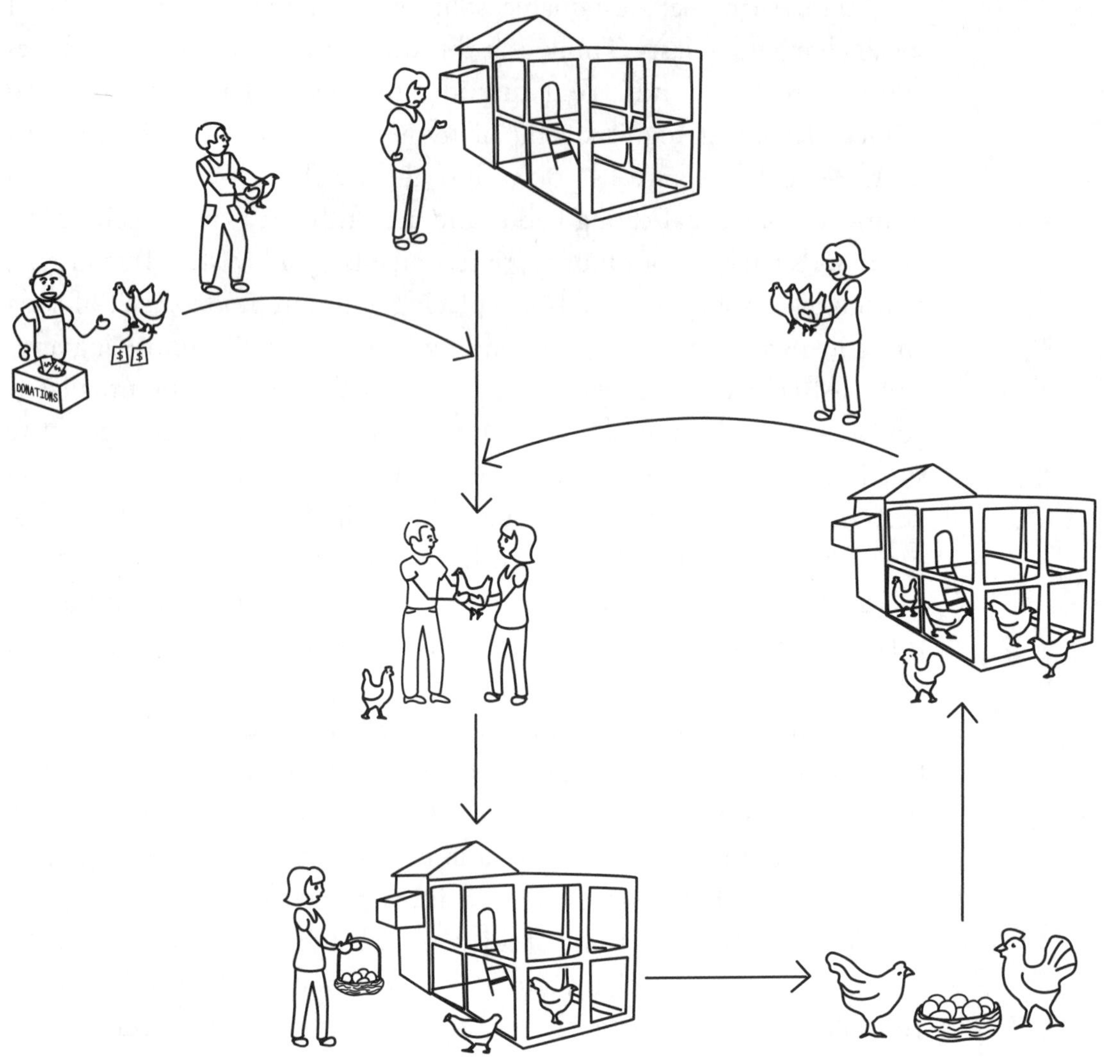

As you did in Chapter 5: Brainstorm Solutions, bring together a diverse group of people interested in solving the problem to brainstorm and discuss anticipated issues. Then actively engage with your team and target community to determine how to best construct your solution to take these issues into account. What timetable is realistic to accomplish each step? How may current assumptions change in the foreseeable future and what can be done today to ensure you have enough flexibility to accommodate these changes?

> **Note** For more on specifics of planning and setting realistic goals, refer to Chapter 21: What Works in Goals and Planning.

Of course, even the best planning will be faced with unexpected situations, but the more you can prepare for what may happen in the future, the more likely you are to create a solution that is sustainable in the community.

Build Institutional Knowledge

Many organizations are heavily dependent on their founder or a key leader. One powerful voice can change the group, revitalize it, and serve as the driving force for change and growth. What commonly occurs is that this one person or small group is a silo of knowledge, the only one who understands the specifics of how things work for the team. So when that leader departs, groups flounder, essentially have to start from scratch, and may find it difficult to build back momentum. Thus for sustainability, proper mechanisms need to be in place to transfer knowledge, making sure the understanding is embedded within the broader group and not isolated to an individual. This is called institutional knowledge, which refers to a system that ensures all parties are well informed on ideas, tools, and resources relevant to the organization, project, or both.

Lack of institutional knowledge is a problem that is just as prevalent in organizations as it is in the target communities. As discussed in the Haiti scenario at the beginning of this chapter, often well-intentioned groups enter a community and come up with a good way to solve a local problem; however, the institutional knowledge and understanding remains with the outside group, not the community. That is, no one in the community is familiar with how the solution was designed and what is necessary to maintain it should problems arise in the future. In the case study at the end of this chapter, you'll read about an effort by the University of Pennsylvania's Engineers Without Borders to design a system to bring clean water and irrigation to a village of farmers in Honduras and the steps they took to ensure the knowledge was deeply embedded in the community so that the group's work would be self-sustainable and lead to long-term impact.

In Chapter 37: Transition Leadership, you will learn how to ensure smooth transitions and build institutional knowledge, including how to facilitate open and frequent communication, transparent record-keeping, a seamless transfer of resources, and a leadership succession plan. But for now, keep this in mind: efforts—both the community's and organization's—should be able to not only sustain themselves but also to thrive in the absence of any one person or group. Remember that the true test of leadership is not just creating something great yourself but also ensuring that the great work can continue after you are gone because you have put the right systems in place for sustainability.

Secure Financial Stability

For organizations aiming to solve social problems, one of the biggest unknown variables is funding. In the past, a predominantly charity-based financial model resulted in the nonstop need for fundraising and little certainty of the amount of money that would be collected. As a result, it was hard to plan new projects, ensure sustainability of ongoing projects, and even guarantee staff members a salary. As the social entrepreneurship model takes hold, ventures can be less reliant on outside sources for funding and can aim for long-term financial independence; however, they can still have difficulty predicting revenue and ensuring market share. Thus while challenging, securing financial stability is a worthwhile goal in the quest for self-sustainability.

While full financial independence of the organization or its individual projects is ideal, it is rare. Realistically, it's almost impossible to guarantee an organization's financial health. But what you can do is strive for as much financial stability as possible.

This begins with evaluating the value of current and proposed expenses and how much they contribute to solving the problem. As described in Chapter 8: Measure, Evaluate, Improve, Repeat, an important component of determining which aspects of your ideas are working is cost. Scrutinize your expenses and look for ways to make the same impact with less money.

Next, address the incoming funds, which may include donations, grants, funding from investors, and generated income. A good place to start is by working to minimize large variations in income as much as possible, as it gives you greater certainty as you make future plans. Consider seeking long-term commitments from donors or applying for multiyear grants. Perhaps the best strategy is incorporating entrepreneurship into your solution by producing a product or service that can generate profit. Thriving organizations often combine all of the above approaches and more to achieve financial stability. To learn more about these specific approaches, see Chapter 22: What Works in Fundraising.

Frequently take a step back and look at the big picture. What financial sources are you missing out on? What inefficiencies are you continuing to struggle with? Research the financials of other groups to get ideas for improving your own. Determine the right timing for incorporating as an official business or nonprofit. Read through Chapter 38: Incorporate as a Business and Chapter 39: Incorporate as a Nonprofit with your team and discuss which is the best fit to achieve your mission. Finally, be on the lookout as new funding opportunities are always emerging.

Adapt and Evolve

The rules of organizational longevity are no different from biological: survival of the fittest. Just as in nature, the ability of both your organization and your ideas to adapt and evolve is critical. The social landscape is dynamic; the needs of a community, the cultural and political milieu, and the available technologies are always changing. Thus while we emphasize being prepared in the earlier part of this chapter, it is equally important that you be able to respond readily to the unexpected.

It is easy for even the most successful and thriving of groups to lose relevance and feel dated when innovation is not a priority. Adding new life to an organization or project is a critical component of sustainability. Learn strategies for this in Chapter 36: Revitalize Your Efforts.

Welcome the opportunity to leave your comfort zone and to work together with people who think differently. Be flexible and in touch with emerging trends. As you'll see illustrated in the case study that follows, the flexibility and willingness to embrace the unexpected can lead to innovations with an impact far beyond what was originally intended.

Case Study: University of Pennsylvania's Engineers Without Borders

Alexander Mittal and his friends were students at the University of Pennsylvania when they founded UPenn's chapter of Engineers Without Borders. Their goal: to improve water and sanitation issues through engineering. The nonprofit group successfully built a water system in the village of Terreritos, Honduras. But Alex didn't stop there; he continued thinking about ways to improve the sustainability of clean water projects like his, and went on to develop an innovative technology for water pipes that he turned into a thriving social business. In the case study below, Alex discusses his experiences and how he incorporated principles of self-sustainability into his solutions.

Plan For Tomorrow

Alex: In order to solve the problem and bring clean water to the village of Terreritos, we had to successfully achieve multiple steps: excavate and protect a natural spring water source, ensure that the water was safe to drink, transport it across five kilometers of mountainous terrain via piping, and bring the water to the center of the community to a tank we had built for distribution to individual homes. When brainstorming ideas and refining our solution, we made sustainability a top priority. We as PennEWB would go to Terreritos and our work would be done over the course of several months; however, we wanted to create a water system that would last in the village for several years, something that would continue to address the problem long after we had left. With this in mind, we settled on what is called a gravity flow system, which would transport water from the spring to the center of the community. In contrast to commonly used water pump-based systems that have moving parts, require electricity or fuel, and as such are more subject to failure, gravity flow systems have no moving parts, have an expected lifetime of 30 years, and do not require complicated maintenance procedures. This system would be better for the future of the community; it was a truly self-sustainable solution.

Build Institutional Knowledge

Alex: Since our involvement in Terreritos began, we have attempted to transfer knowledge to the community as much as possible. We shared and discussed interpretations of data, demonstrated surveying and implementation techniques, shared maps and diagrams, and provided a laptop for future use by community members. In a display of local engineering ingenuity, the community members who helped to dig the pipeline were able to save over half a kilometer of pipe by laying the pipe in a way that partially deviated from the plans we had created. We ourselves did not include the route they chose in the specifications because it would supposedly have required implementation accuracy attainable only with modern surveying equipment. However, by combining their knowledge of the lay of the land with water engineering concepts, the community members were able to engineer the better solution.

Secure Financial Stability

Alex: We participated in a meeting in which the villagers voted in near unanimous support of the project, and each family agreed to pay one dollar per month for its upkeep, a sizeable portion of their income. Taking advantage of a regional politician's nearby campaign stop, we also received a verbal pledge from the government official that she would try to secure partial funding for the project. Prior to our departure to Honduras, we also initiated a press and media campaign in Philadelphia, which we would continue throughout the project's existence. Once a plan of action was established, significant fundraising work began. We approached local businesses, university groups, and individuals for sponsorship who shared our vision of applying technology in a sustainable way to solve water and sanitation issues.

Adapt and Evolve

Alex: After two months of using the improved water supply, families noticed fewer skin problems in the children and fewer incidences of diarrhea. They also demonstrated an understanding of the role of proper hygiene on health. I was proud of the work we did with PennEWB and the impact the system had on the community. But one of the nagging questions for me while building sustainable water systems was why we were separating out water delivery from water filtration. Water flowing through pipe makes contact with the pipe sidewalls over kilometers of distance. I reasoned that if the sidewalls could be made to have some sort of active effect on the water to purify it, water could be transported and purified simultaneously. I decided to change course and pursue this promising idea. Over a one-year period, I set out with a team of researchers at Penn to build our new type of pipe. We incorporated as a business, and our social enterprise continued experimenting with where else we could apply the technology we invented. We were surprised to learn that while it did not work in our originally intended purpose, it actually had a number of other applications to water, energy, electronics, and other industries.

Chapter 16

Integrate Social Entrepreneurship

Whenever society is stuck or has an opportunity to seize a new opportunity, it needs an entrepreneur to see the opportunity and then to turn that vision into a realistic idea and then a reality and then, indeed, the new pattern all across society. We need such entrepreneurial leadership at least as much in education and human rights as we do in communications and hotels. This is the work of social entrepreneurs.

—*BILL DRAYTON*

Consider two groups, each delivering products and services that improve lives. The Red Cross, a traditional nonprofit, collects and distributes blood that volunteers have donated. The other group is a pharmaceutical company that makes money by manufacturing and selling a drug that speeds the growth of blood cells at $20 per pill. Both contribute to saving lives with a product that increases the amount of blood in people's bodies.

According to a very old school way of thinking, the nonprofit is helping people, improving health, and addressing a social problem, while the business is exploiting a social problem to make money. At the same time, since the business has to support itself with profits, it makes profits the bottom line and prioritizes efficiency and evidence-based outcomes so that money isn't wasted on things that don't work. In contrast, the nonprofit is dependent on the money, time, and resources donated by those who in turn feel good about their philanthropic contributions. For the nonprofit, as long as donors feel good about what they're doing, the donations will keep coming, so there is little incentive in their model to prioritize efficacy or efficiency.

Both groups are in essence delivering the same benefit, but they are doing so using different models. Now let's look at the pros and cons of each model. The pro of the nonprofit is that it measures progress by the number of people helped; the end goal is social good. However, the con is that it is not self-sustainable and is dependent instead on constant donations. For the business, the pro is the efficiency; because profit is the driving force, doing what works is paramount. However, at the end of the day, profit is the bottom line, so profit is prioritized over solving the social problem and helping more people (a definite con).

In the past decade, we've seen a revolution that has combined the best of nonprofits and businesses into a new framework: the social enterprise. Social enterprises merge the profit and evidence-driven sustainability model from businesses with the social good mission of nonprofits. They use the power of profit to solve social problems—and measure success by social impact. The social enterprise views profit not as the end game but as a tool to achieve social change; profit is good in that it promotes more efficiency and sustainability.

Social entrepreneurship is a related but not identical idea. A social enterprise is the entity, whereas social entrepreneurship is the mindset. It's very important to note that we title this chapter "Integrate Social Entrepreneurship" and not "Start a Social Enterprise." Starting a company isn't right for everyone, nor should it be. However, the *spirit* of social entrepreneurship is something that can still permeate a nonprofit, activism campaign, or even school club.

Social entrepreneurship has four key principles:

1. Add social value.
2. Innovate to turn a problem into an opportunity.
3. Solve problems using business principles.
4. Remain accountable to the community, cultivating community ownership.

This chapter provides an overview of these principles and the mindset to adopt when approaching a social problem. Chapter 35: Apply

Social Entrepreneurship guides you through the business model in more depth.

Add Social Value

Tip Organizations that offer great support to social entrepreneurs include Ashoka, the Skoll Foundation, and Echoing Green.

The core motivation of social entrepreneurship is to solve a social problem and contribute to the social good. There are myriad ways to do this, of course, one of which is through a social enterprise, as described earlier. But launching a business is by no means the only—or necessarily best—way to embrace the spirit of social entrepreneurship. What's more important is creating a system that fundamentally changes the status quo and develops a new way to problem-solve that empowers people to help themselves.

In his landmark book *How to Change the World: Social Entrepreneurs and the Power of New Ideas,* journalist David Bornstein explains, "Social entrepreneurs have existed throughout history. St. Francis of Assisi, the founder of the Franciscan Order, would qualify as a social entrepreneur—having built multiple organizations that advanced pattern changes in his 'field.' Similarly, Florence Nightingale created the first professional school for nurses and established standards for hygiene and hospital care that have shaped norms worldwide. What is different today is that social entrepreneurship is developing into a mainstream vocation."[1]

Thus there are numerous ways to add social value, through all fields: standard business, politics, nonprofits, and also science, engineering, arts, academia, law, media, and more.

Note Social entrepreneurship was popularized by the revolutionary Bill Drayton, founder and CEO of Ashoka: Innovators for the Public.

Innovate to Turn a Problem into an Opportunity

Social entrepreneurship encourages finding radically new approaches to problem solving, even at times creating entire new systems. For example, Muhammad Yunus, an economist and recipient of the Nobel Peace

"What does an entrepreneur do? The first thing is they've given themselves permission to see a problem. Most people don't want to see problems … Once you see a problem and you keep looking at it you'll find an answer."[2]

BILL DRAYTON

Prize, saw a problem in Bangladesh in the way banks distributed loans. Banks required customers to have a good employment and credit history in order to get a loan, so only the wealthy were able to get money, relegating the poor—and especially women—who lacked this history, to rely on often unethical loan sharks who would charge interest rates so high no one could ever get out of debt. As a result, even a motivated, bright individual had no means to get herself out of poverty.

Yunus's game-changing innovation was microcredit: giving small loans to people who did not necessarily have a strong or any credit history. This small amount of money empowered the poor to start businesses and get themselves and their families out of poverty. Yunus showed that this entire sector of society that had been considered incapable or too uneducated to be trusted with repaying loans was actually filled with talented entrepreneurs who, with a bit of empowerment, could transform adversity into opportunity.

Solve Problems with Business Principles

"It's the combination: big idea with a good entrepreneur: there's nothing more powerful. That's just as true [for] education and human rights as it is for hotel or steels."[3]

BILL DRAYTON

As explained in the beginning of the chapter, social entrepreneurship tries to use business principles to address social problems. For example, think back to Muhammad Yunus's idea of microcredit. The poor need money to pay for their basic needs like food and clothing. How could you fix this problem? You could give out free food at a food bank. Or, you could give a few dollars directly to a homeless man to help him buy dinner or a warm coat for himself. But neither of these solves the problem; they are just temporary fixes.

Yunus lent money to individuals to support the development of their own small businesses. In this way, the actual root of the problem—an insufficient regular income—was addressed. The poor were empowered to start businesses that would help them earn this regular income. Then, they had a sustainable way to buy the things they needed, like food and clothing, by themselves. By using business principles to solve the problem, Yunus turned what could have been a handout into empowerment. If Yunus just gave out the money as charity, the funds would eventually run out. But since the loans are paid back, there is more money to loan out, thus perpetuating the cycle of poverty alleviation through empowerment.

Cultivate Community Ownership

"Social entrepreneurs identify resources where people only see problems. They view the villagers as the solution, not the passive beneficiary. They begin with the assumption of competence and unleash resources in the communities they're serving."[4]

DAVID BORNSTEIN

Finally, social entrepreneurship celebrates the community and makes leaders of those affected by the social problem. The community is not thought of as those who need help but rather those who will rise to the occasion when empowered. Work with the community as partners and value their insights and commitment. Remember that the community is where the solution will be housed and run, so the community is needed to make it last. Community ownership, as it relates to the Do Good Well method, is discussed in more detail in Chapter 11, and practical tips are shared in Chapter 34.

Figure 16.1. You Can Make a Profit and a Difference

Case Study: Home Water Filtration System

Kelydra Welcker is a scientist and social entrepreneur from West Virginia whose innovative work has been recognized by numerous groups including *Oprah Magazine*, DoSomething.org, Intel, and the Prudential Spirit of Community Awards. She was one of three young scientists who were featured in the documentary film *Whiz Kids*. She is an MD student at West Virginia University School of Medicine. In this case study, she explains how she used the key principles of social entrepreneurship to solve the problem of water contamination in her community along the Ohio River.

Identify a Problem

Kelydra: Perfluorooctanoic acid (also referred to as C8) is a chemical used to make Teflon. For the past 50 years, a major chemical company has used it in everything from the liners of pizza boxes to fire extinguisher foam. As a part of the manufacturing process, the company released C8 into the Ohio River as waste. As a result, C8 was in the water my neighbors and I drank and swam in. The pervasiveness of this chemical was a problem: the US Environmental Protection Agency (EPA) labeled it a "potential carcinogen" and fined the company over $10 million.

Innovate to Turn a Problem into an Opportunity

Kelydra: When news of this pollution and its potential health hazards broke, I listened to the media debate and activist voices discussing who was responsible and how it got there. I realized that though they were working to prevent future reoccurrences, they weren't solving the immediate problem—C8 was still in my community's drinking water. I wanted to take action and fix things so my neighbors and family could identify whether there was C8 in their water and, if so, remove it to keep their water clean and safe.

While professional chemical detection and purification systems use fancy, expensive equipment and large-scale processing, I wanted to design something that was simple, cheap, and effective. Using just what I knew from high school chemistry class and working in an old trailer in my backyard, I was able to develop a test to detect C8 in drinking water that anyone could perform at home with the tools they already had in their kitchens. All they had to do was collect a half liter of the sample of water and boil it down. Then by measuring the foam that resulted, my tester could measure the concentrations of C8 with 92% accuracy when compared with confirmed C8 reports from professional labs.

Solve Problems with Business Principles

Kelydra: Cost and practicality are important components of sustainability. If residents of my community were to have a professional lab test their water for C8, it would cost $4,500 and take months to get the results. In comparison, my test costs only 60 cents for the bottle to run the sample in and takes only 30 minutes to run. The technique I developed provides individuals with a method to test their own water for C8, which is perfect for neighbors who draw their water from wells and cisterns and don't have the benefit of filtered drinking water.

Cultivate Community Ownership

Kelydra: It would be easy to paint the company as the "big bad polluting company," but it is one of the largest employers in my community. In fact, my father and sister had worked there for years. The company is an integral part of the town. I felt accountable to my community and, as a member of the community, wanted to ensure that any potential solution I designed had the backing and understanding of my neighbors. Given the delicate political situation, it was important that I keep the lines of communication open between the industry and the community, and make clear that I was not trying to fight the company but work with them to ensure the chemical would not cause harm to the health of others, so that we could have both jobs and a healthy environment.

Add Social Value

Kelydra: After developing this method of testing for this chemical in drinking water and in the environment, the next step was to find a way of removing C8 from people's drinking water. I came up with a now patented design to remove and recover C8. I continued developing, refining, and improving my idea and increased my removal rate of C8 from 6 percent to 100 percent, leading to my second and third patents. Armed with the science, I started a group that tests low-income and elderly people's water for C8.

Chapter 17

Share What Works

Once you've developed a thriving organization that has made a meaningful impact, take the time to share what you've learned with the rest of the world. Just as scholars publish and disseminate their research findings within the academic community and to the general public, you need to make your progress known. Sharing what works is a vital component of sustainability because it ensures that others can use and improve on your work.

Just as you began by building on what works, you are now contributing to collective knowledge so fellow leaders and social innovators can build on what you found to work. This is the ultimate way to make something last: others can improve their own work because of what you've learned. You've come full circle. By sharing what works, you're leaving a legacy. This chapter focuses on sharing what works with an audience outside your organization, but creating institutional knowledge is also a vital component of sustainability for your group. Learn more about it in Chapter 37.

Share Outcomes

What worked for you? What didn't? The technical term for this information is *best practices*—processes, techniques, or methods that experience and evidence show are effective at delivering a desired outcome. In the field of social innovation, sharing outcomes is common within an organization but needs to extend to include the broader community.

The American Productivity and Quality Center reports that the primary barriers to the use of best practices are: (1) not knowing what the current best practices are and (2) lacking the knowledge, skills, or motivation to implement them. It's your job to make this information easily accessible and implementable.

Thus, once you've finished evaluating your own work (particularly with respect to efficacy and efficiency), you should broadcast your findings to others so they can learn from what you've done. Share your insights so others can understand not only what worked for you but also why it worked and in what context. It's important to note that sharing what didn't work is just as important as sharing your successes, so don't be shy about admitting to a few stumbling blocks.

To share your findings, look for opportunities to interact with fellow leaders. This can be at conferences or meetings, with local groups, in publications like research journals and official reports, through membership in cause-related professional organizations, and, most commonly, by disseminating your knowledge online. It's your responsibility to make your outcomes known to your field. To get started, explore the following opportunities.

Conferences

Conferences and meetings are a good place to get started sharing your results because they give you an interested audience to interact with and the chance to get "real-time" feedback. These formal gatherings range from annual large national meetings of organizations, such as Unite for Sight's Global Health and Innovation Conference, to school summits, such as Harvard Business School's Social Enterprise Conference. If you want to share your work formally, you can apply to be a speaker, workshop or panel discussion participant, or oral or poster presenter. If you are just starting off, you can test out the water by registering as an attendee and listening, sharing your ideas more one-on-one with the presenters. Generally, in order to present you have to write up a brief abstract of your findings and submit it a few months in advance, then wait to see if you're accepted. If you aren't accepted or missed the deadline, some conferences also have exhibition areas for groups to reach out to conference participants. Conference participation generally comes with a relatively hefty registration fee (anywhere from a few hundred up to $1,000, plus travel and lodging expenses). If you are a student or nonprofit, you may be able to get a discount; and even if reduced prices aren't advertised it's a good idea to ask the organizers if you can get a discount or apply for a scholarship to help cover the costs. You may even decide to organize a conference of your own and create the space for others to share what works; for more on how to organize a conference, see Chapter 32. Finally, be on the lookout for informal gatherings such as local Meetup.com groups.

Publications

Writing up your results for a journal or newsletter allows you to share your work with the publication's readership. Many of the same groups that put on conferences also have affiliated journals, similarly ranging from national groups to school clubs; one of the most respected publications is the *Stanford Social Innovation Review*. Beyond professional publications, popular publications (magazines, newspapers, etc.) let you reach out to a more general audience. These stories are often human interest stories and typically tell a narrative of your group or the people you're trying to help. Chapter 23 has helpful tips for reaching out to the media.

Online

The fastest and cheapest way to share your outcomes is online. You can start simply by uploading results on your group's website or posting in discussion forums about your cause. E-mail a brief blurb about your work to organizations or individuals you think may be interested and inquire about ways to share your results with or through their group. A number of websites are working to promote online sharing of best practices and create communities of leaders and social entrepreneurs, including GOOD.is, DoSomething.org, and TakingITGlobal.org.

Sharing outcomes is not a one-time effort. Populations and their problems are always changing, and with change come new opportunities for innovation—new ways to make or do something better, cheaper, and faster. Similarly, your group and the way you take action will always be changing as you refine your methods or expand your efforts. Regular and frequent reflection and sharing of best practices is how you achieve continuous improvement.

Figure 17.1. Share What You've Learned with Others

Share Resources

Just as valuable as sharing outcomes is sharing resources—the tools and materials you've created to improve your work and further your cause. Examples of resources include: a checklist of action steps to take before approaching potential investors, a compilation of "getting to know you" games for team bonding, or an entire educational curriculum aimed at increasing civic responsibility among high school students. If you made it and it has worked, share it. Think about the fellow classmate who always took the best lecture notes and then sent them out to the class over e-mail, or the coworker whose PowerPoint templates helped the entire department be presentation stars. When you've done something really well, you help out everyone else by passing it on.

The archetype of sharing resources online is open content. Developed by David Wiley, a professor at Brigham Young University, open content centers around the 4Rs Framework:

- *Reuse*: the right to reuse the content in its unaltered/verbatim form (e.g., make a copy of the content)

- *Revise*: the right to adapt, adjust, modify, or alter the content itself (e.g., translate the content into another language)
- *Remix*: the right to combine the original or revised content with other content to create something new (e.g., incorporate the content into a mashup)
- *Redistribute*: the right to share copies of the original content, your revisions, or your remixes with others (e.g., give a copy of the content to a friend)[1]

Tip It's helpful to include a way to track who is using your materials. This is a perfect opportunity to identify a potential future partnership. In addition, you'll add a lot of value to your work by keeping in touch with others who adapt your materials. These individuals can provide valuable feedback on how your original ideas translated into other communities.

When you've created and refined useful materials, consider posting them online, so others can follow the open source framework to use or perhaps even adapt your materials for another community or social problem. There are many websites trying to provide a platform to encourage sharing for social causes, including Jumo, TakingITGlobal, and IdeaEncore. A great education-specific tool is Curriki (Curriculum Wiki), which lets anyone upload and use curricula and collaborate with each other to share advice and progress. At a minimum, you could create a Google document and put it on your website, encouraging others to use it. Technology brings new collaboration tools seemingly daily. Always be on the lookout for tools and venues that can help you better receive and share what works.

WARNING Be sure to discuss any legal or copyright issues with a lawyer before making your materials publicly accessible, as there may be certain restrictions you wish to place on them.

Pay It Forward

Sharing what works is not just about sharing the results of your work or the resources you've developed to advance it. It's also about sharing yourself: your ideas, your insights, your mentorship. Your own leadership is inevitably the result of many people lifting you up, introducing you to potential partners, developing skills in you that led to your success.

Pay them back by paying it forward. So whether it's a younger social innovator seeking guidance or a company looking for your expertise, be generous with your time.

You will likely find many creative ways to pay it forward. Consider Amos Winter. As a graduate student in engineering at MIT, Amos designed the leveraged freedom chair, a manually powered wheelchair for people in the developing world that can function on all types of terrain. The beauty of Amos's design is that the leverage freedom chair is constructed from materials produced by local companies in the developing countries. Thus, it can be created and used by people anywhere in the world, and because each local company is community owned, its manufacturing activities stimulate the local economy.

But Amos didn't stop there. He developed a class for MIT students to discuss disabilities in the developing world and allow them to discover their inner social innovator and launch projects aimed at improving mobility. He continued paying it forward by founding the MIT Mobility Lab (M-Lab) to provide resources and expertise to any student looking to improve the lives of disabled people. What started with one technological innovation turned into a movement, catalyzing the development of a specific lab devoted to furthering social innovation in the field. By sharing what works, Amos created opportunities for new leadership, collaboration, and progress.

Sharing outcomes, resources, and mentorship creates a lasting legacy, giving others a foundation on which to build and strengthen their work, which not only circles back to help you improve your own efforts but also ensures your work disseminates beyond your community and breeds synergy. Sharing what works actually brings together all three steps of the method—you contribute to promoting what works, working together, and making a lasting impact. By ending the Do Good Well method with sharing what works, we turn what may look like a linear path into a cycle, empowering you to turn change into progress.

Chapter 18

The Method in Action

***We searched for a young leader** who could help "bring it all together" by demonstrating step-by-step the Do Good Well method in action. When we interviewed Alia Whitney-Johnson, we found an insightful innovator whose work embodies creativity, entrepreneurship, and social responsibility. As a 19-year-old college student, Alia transformed a simple hobby of hers—creating beaded jewelry—into a tool for empowering teenage survivors of sexual abuse with the skills to achieve financial independence and break the cycle of violence. Today, Alia's organization, Emerge Global, is an award-winning social enterprise working to provide greater opportunity and freedom for young survivors of abuse and their children. This unique chapter guides you through all 12 parts of the method by presenting an extended case study of Emerge. What follows is Alia's first-person account of her journey from start to self-sustainable solution.*

The Problem

Her 11-year-old body didn't seem to be capable of bearing a child. Yet there she was, nursing her baby boy, a child conceived with her own father. Renuka (her name is changed here to protect her identity) had a story similar to that of many of the girls I met while volunteering for a summer in Sri Lanka. When her mother had left their village to find work abroad, Renuka's father and uncle began to sexually abuse her.

Pregnant as a result of rape, she was removed from society and placed in a shelter for her own protection, allowing her abusers to remain free for years as their trial continued. Because abortion is illegal in Sri Lanka, Renuka had her baby but was unable to give him up for adoption because she was a minor.

I remember standing in awe of Renuka's courage to go to court and testify against her abusers, fighting for a better life for her younger sisters despite societal stigma. But she also faced challenges. Like other girls who have survived abuse in Sri Lanka, she faced psychological trauma, alienation from family and community, and a loss of educational and career opportunities. At the age of 18, she would be expected to make her way in the world without education, a family, a job, or a network of support. My stomach churned as I imagined her future. Worldwide, girls who have survived childhood sexual abuse are significantly more likely than other young women to experience future abuse.[1] Moreover, girls who have been abused in the home are more likely to allow the cycle of abuse to continue with their own children.[2]

The Opportunity

By standing up to her abusers, Renuka had demonstrated great courage and strength. I wanted to get to know her, to be a mirror that could reflect her resilience. But that goal did not seem easy … We were from two different worlds, speaking two different languages. How could we connect? I thought about the universality and healing powers of art and remembered my childhood activity for creativity and expression—beading. At age seven, I began a jewelry business, designing jewelry to sell at craft fairs and on a commissioned basis. In addition to the joy beading brought me, it taught me very valuable skills—the fundamentals of business strategy, organizational development, and working with customers.

As I stood watching Renuka in admiration, I realized that beading could be a fun activity that would allow us to become friends. This simple idea soon evolved into a plan with great potential: teaching Renuka to create a business of her own. Little did I know that my plan to support Renuka would soon transform the lives of many.

The Do Good Well Method in Action

As a college freshman, Alia knew herself—she was a civil and environmental engineering student from MIT, a passionate problem-solver, and, in her spare time, a jewelry designer. And she knew her world—her commitment to improving the lives of people who struggled to get from day to day is what drew her to engineering and also what led her to Sri Lanka for the summer as a tsunami relief volunteer. On an unrelated but serendipitous volunteer assignment, Alia unexpectedly discovered the heart-breaking reality faced by girls her age and younger who were survivors of sexual abuse. While she had no formal training in poverty alleviation or experience working with survivors of sexual violence, she could not walk away. Committed to understanding the problem, she befriended Renuka and other girls in Renuka's shelter. Inspired by their strength, Alia developed a vision: to equip these girls with the tools they needed for self-sufficiency and to help them bring about their own visions of change for their country. Join Alia as she uses the Do Good Well method to share her path from vision to progress.

Step 1: Do What Works

Design a Systemic Solution

At the age of 19, I had discovered a reality that I knew I wanted to change. To design a systemic solution, I needed to understand the many factors that led to abuse and what interventions could contribute to long-term social change.

Why does this problem exist? The World Health Organization and the Centers for Disease Control and Prevention use an ecological model to describe the complex interplay of factors that contribute to sexual violence. Like many social problems, sexual abuse is the result of multiple overlapping spheres of influence: individual, relationships, community, and society.[3] I wanted to design a systemic solution that began with a girl but would ultimately affect all of these dimensions:

Individual

Problem: Experiencing sexual violence as a child makes these girls vulnerable to experiencing or perpetrating violence in the future.[4]

Intervention: Help them heal from past abuse by increasing their confidence, decision-making capabilities, skills, and resources for self-sufficiency.

Relationships

Problem: A person's closest relationships (especially family or partners) can affect their norms and behaviors.[5] Unhealthy relationships can lead to tolerance of abuse or inability to leave abusive situations.

Intervention: Educate women about physical and reproductive health, their rights, and their own values around relationships. Help them become financially self-sufficient so that they can support themselves and avoid being trapped in unhealthy relationships.

Community

Problem: In Sri Lanka, survivors of abuse find themselves isolated, without resources, opportunities, or a network for emotional support outside the shelter.

Intervention: Connect the girls to one another, empowering them to unite and advocate for themselves. Build allies with local female mentors, service providers, and job opportunities that will support the girls in their adult lives.

Society

Problem: Current policies and cultural norms allow abuse to go unnoticed, perpetuating destructive norms.

Intervention: Increase societal awareness about sexual violence and advocate for government policy change.

Ultimately, starting with the individual, it was possible to transform all of the spheres that perpetuate a cycle of violence. We believe that these are the girls who will create long-term societal change. Indeed, as they testify in court and defend younger sisters, they have already begun to do so.

Build on What Works

Based on my research, I wanted our intervention to build a community of support for these young women and also increase their confidence, self-sufficiency, decision-making capabilities, and knowledge of their rights and bodies. I recognized that many groups had developed models for economic empowerment to achieve these goals and more. So, I began to explore the methodologies and outcomes of other projects with the hope that I could build on them.

Organizations like Grameen Bank have helped women by connecting them to microfinance. Because many women in developing countries lack the ability to access formal loans and are vulnerable to being scammed by loan sharks with high interest rates, this model of economic empowerment provides women with small loans (called "microcredit") to start their own businesses. Another approach is embodied by groups like Mercado Global, who support artisan cooperatives (such as a group of textile weavers in Guatemala) by connecting them to the global market where they can earn more for their trade.

When designing our programs, I built off these models of economic empowerment, improving on and adapting them for our target community. There were challenges: the girls I had met were not already artisans, and they didn't have the network or knowledge to access microcredit. I wanted to find a way to combine the concept of empowering girls to generate money (like Mercado Global does with women's cooperatives) while also helping them use this money to start their own businesses (in the way microcredit can). By combining these concepts, we could empower girls to generate, rather than borrow, money for their own businesses and futures.

This concept, which we later coined "collaborative capital," was the foundation of the organization I founded, Emerge Global. Through our concept of "collaborative capital," we would collaborate with the girls to help them generate their own capital—money that they could invest in their futures—through the creation and sale of unique jewelry in a safe, low-risk environment. This empowers the girls to know the value of the money they generate without the potential risks associated with repayment of a loan (in many areas, accessing capital through credit has been associated with corrupt loan sharks who demand exorbitant interest rates and/or force women into prostitution to pay off the loans). Furthermore, to maximize our impact, we would teach the girls how to leverage this money to pay for their children's education, start a business, or buy a house where they can always have refuge.

Today, Emerge has used this concept as the foundation of its four programs:

1. *Beads-to-Business*—enables girls to generate savings and develop business knowledge through beading
2. *Life Skills*—teaches reproductive health, job readiness, goal setting, and other critical topics
3. *Mentorship*—connects girls to local women
4. *Reintegration*—provides individualized support as girls transition from shelter into the community

In our model, jewelry is collected each week by the program coordinator and is then sold in Sri Lanka, the US, and online by Emerge. 50% of the jewelry's selling price goes directly to the girls. In addition, $0.25 from each sale is invested in a community fund that finances ideas the girls have for community projects, enabling them to effect change collectively. (More on the Emerge business model can be found in the section "Integrate Social Entrepreneurship.") By building on the proven successes of Grameen Bank and Mercado Global and adapting their models for our target group, we were able to design a model that is effective and safe.

Measure, Evaluate, Improve, Repeat

As an engineer, I value the process of continuous improvement, adjusting our work based on data and results. While our metrics have evolved over time, our initial evaluation systems were relatively informal: we collected individual and group feedback, observed self-reported emotional changes as well as those demonstrated through behavior (for example, willingness to talk or be open with their ideas and feelings), and tracked the amount of savings generated.

Through initial observations, we realized that our initial approach—teaching all participants business concepts together—was not an effective way to meet individual girls' needs. Girls came and left the shelter at different times (depending on their court cases) and had varied educational backgrounds (some had never been to school, others had done high school math). We realized that we needed to build a program that could be tailored to the needs and pace of every participant. So, we transformed our business training into a self-paced workbook (for an overview of this workbook, see Teaching Business at the Right Pace).

Teaching Business at the Right Pace: The Emerge Beads-to-Business Workbook

The Beads-to-Business workbook is divided into four self-paced stages:

- *Stage 1:* Girls learn jewelry techniques and are introduced to the workshop's simulated economy, which includes a store and bank. While selecting jewelry supplies to use each week, they learn how to set a budget within a spending limit and to fill out order forms.

- *Stage 2:* Participants lead the simulation, playing both shopkeeper and banker, and mentoring another girl in the program.
- *Stage 3:* Girls are guided through the process of designing their own jewelry products and planning a jewelry business.
- *Stage 4:* Participants plan a business unrelated to jewelry. This connects skills learned in the program to their own goals for life outside the shelter.

Each week, in order to turn in jewelry, girls must have completed a page in their workbooks. By linking jewelry creation (which the girls love) to their progress in the business curriculum, we are able to ensure that girls are learning to make the most of the money earned. The workbook has gone through several iterations, based on participant feedback (for example, correcting unclear wording and diagrams) as well as areas that staff identified as challenging concepts to master.

During the initial phases of program development, girls who left the shelter expressed a need for skills beyond business management and jewelry design. This feedback prompted us to develop our supplemental Life Skills curriculum, with units on job readiness, goal setting, reproductive health, money management, crisis management, and community development. We also launched a Mentorship Program to help girls develop supportive relationships with women role models.

As we gained confidence in our programs, we started to standardize our monitoring and evaluation methods. We now have several goals and indicators for each program (an example can be found in Example of a Beads-to-Business Programmatic Goal and Indicators), which are measured through a variety of surveys taken before, during, and after the program; regular observational data by trained staff; and workbook progress. We also host annual reunions and follow-up with alumni to track program outcomes (how they've spent their money, how financially secure they are post-shelter, if they've experienced repeat episodes of violence, etc.). Data evaluation and program improvement are continual iterative processes.

Example of a Beads-to-Business Programmatic Goal and Indicators

Goal: Empower each girl to manage her finances responsibly

Indicators:

- Knowledge:
  - Knows how to make a budget within a spending limit
  - Knows how to read a bank book
- Experience:
  - Has planned a budget for life outside of the shelter
  - Has made a plan for how she will leverage money saved in the program
  - Has successfully served as the banker and shopkeeper three times each
- Confidence in personal skills:
  - Has expressed increased confidence with banking knowledge
  - Has expressed increased confidence in budgeting

Note We struggled at first with balancing quantitative data (i.e., amount of jewelry sold and dollars earned) with qualitative data (i.e., feeling a sense of growing community among the girls). We realized that to ensure an evidence-based approach, we needed to find ways to quantify the qualitative. We now use images of faces as a scale (from frowning to beaming) to measure questions like: "How happy do you feel when you think about your future?" or "How comfortable do you feel sharing your ideas with others?" The pictures are easily understandable and correlate nicely with numbers for analysis.

Challenge What Works, Innovate, Keep What Works

When I arrived in Sri Lanka, I was shocked to find such courageous girls locked behind the walls of shelters, excluded from society and lacking the resources they needed to achieve their goals. Unfortunately, sexual violence was being addressed by removing from society the very girls who could fight to change it. While the girls had been brought to shelters for their own "protection," it felt as though society was being protected from them. Society's answer to the problem, its version of what worked, didn't really seem to be working.

I began doing research to understand the landscape of nonprofits working on our issue in Sri Lanka. While some focused on violence against adult women, none specialized in addressing the multifaceted needs of minors who had survived abuse. There were no groups thinking about the complexity of an 11-year-old child giving birth to another child out of rape at an age when she was both too young to work and too young to give up her child for adoption; no organizations thinking about the impact of removing girls from school for their protection; and no groups considering the emotional effects of denying girls the agency to choose how and where to protect themselves because of their status as minors. While there were organizations that ran shelters for girls who had survived rape, they lacked targeted programming and failed to consider the girls' lives beyond the shelter, such as their need for reintegration support. Furthermore, no organizations were working with the government to consider the policies and duration of court cases that kept girls out of school and in shelters. In short, we found a void that deserved its own organization and infrastructure to push for change.

The traditional model of "protection" through shelters wasn't going to create the change that was needed. We needed to challenge this notion and transform shelters into spaces of healing and learning, spaces of opportunity rather than exclusion. Through this innovation, we could equip every girl in the system with the skills needed to become self-sufficient and end violence in their spheres of influence. And, by partnering with the government to reach these girls and presenting the positive results of our work, we could encourage the government to think proactively about policies that affect these young women. By challenging the status quo of the current shelter system, we would be able to develop a solution that not only improved the lives of the girls in the system but would also transform the system itself.

Step 2: Work Together

Balance Strengthening and Starting

Emerge did not begin with a perfect blueprint or a goal to reach girls around the world. I began my journey as a volunteer for another nongovernmental organization (NGO), doing office work and venturing to its home for teenage mothers whenever I could. Emerge's first program began with 18 girls in that home. I could have started a new organization; instead, I chose to pilot my program in collaboration with the organization running the home—they understood the girls' needs much better than I did. I felt this partnership would be more effective and sustainable than creating a new entity, especially since I was still a student in the US. So I worked with the NGO running the home to execute our operations, and I connected with another like-minded nonprofit in the US to help raise funds.

As our programmatic success began to receive international press, I started receiving requests from other shelters in Sri Lanka and around the world. I realized it was unreasonable to expect that our NGO partner in Sri Lanka could scale our programs to reach other organizations' homes, as they were already stretched with their own programming. We needed two entities of our own: one in Sri Lanka that could partner with shelters run by many different organizations and one in the US to focus on achieving a global vision. Three years after launching our programs, we therefore incorporated as the Emerge Lanka Foundation in Sri Lanka and Emerge Global in the US. We still look to partner with as many groups as possible, knowing that our impact together will be much greater than what we achieve alone.

Cultivate Community Ownership

As I developed Emerge, I realized that long-term change in Sri Lanka wasn't going to come from me, a foreigner with a foreign way of looking at the world. Rather, change would come from the talented young women we work with every day. Furthermore, long-term support for these girls was not going to come from endless volunteer trips from the US to Sri Lanka. To truly cultivate community ownership, we needed a local team (including staff, board, and volunteers) to run operations and set the group's vision, local outlets to sell the jewelry, funding opportunities in Sri Lanka, and government support to enable us to reach all girls who were in government protection and to eventually push for policy change. Our goal was to develop a structure and incentives for local leadership.

While Emerge Global in the US initially sent volunteers and funds to support Emerge Lanka's development, it has empowered our Sri Lanka operations to run more independently over time. Each year, the Sri Lanka team maps out its vision, including planned steps towards financial and operational independence from Emerge Global. Emerge Global issues quarterly grants to Emerge Lanka based on its successful achievement of these goals. Our work in Sri Lanka will therefore soon be locally sustained and owned, led by a dynamic group of local leaders who will ensure the longevity of our work.

Foster Team Unity

Initially, as we implemented our programs through the existing shelter system, we were met with some resistance. There were questions about our qualifications and programmatic content, skepticism about the girls' potential, and jealousy from shelter staff, individuals who lacked the opportunities that we were providing the girls. The result was that our program was just that: a program, separate from the day-to-day routine of the home itself. We needed to build trust, to excite our partners by proactively sharing the girls' progress, and to create opportunities for development of the homes and their staff beyond our programs for the girls. In order to succeed, we needed to envision our programming as a holistic solution to transform the homes themselves, rather than just a set of independent programs to benefit participants.

While we are still learning the best ways to build multipartner team unity, we now have great relationships with our partner shelters. We go through our curricula in detail with shelter staff so that they understand what we are teaching the girls and can reinforce lessons outside of class. When possible, we try to engage the shelter staff in our programs, soliciting their feedback and allowing them to join relevant trainings with participants, such as CPR and first aid. We also provide regular progress reports to our partner organizations so that they understand our impact and are able to leverage details of this success when speaking with their own donors, supporters, and supervisors. Our successes become their successes as well. Finally, we look for ways to improve the homes themselves, seeking out donations and volunteers from our own networks. These contributions often support the girls as well as quality of life in the home for staff and have therefore made our partners excited to work with us.

Through this process, we learned that advancing team unity was not only about our own team but also ensuring that we took the needs and situations of our partners into consideration. Today, we are committed to maintaining a culture of collaboration and opportunity that both serves the girls and supports the shelter system serving the girls.

Forge Partnerships

When I began Emerge, I dreamed of building our own utopian children's village for survivors of abuse. I remember sitting at a friend's table in Sri Lanka, with him generously pouring endless cups of coffee as we mapped out our dream. As we began to do research, however, we realized that there were many existing homes and that an additional home would compete for limited resources without adding much new value. Instead, we began to envision ourselves as a mobile classroom that would improve the experience in existing centers, adding value rather than competing. Through partnerships, we could provide transformational change for more girls than we could serve in our own children's village. Furthermore, we could focus on becoming excellent at one thing rather than trying to provide everything.

Tip Be sure to document the logistics of any partnership in a signed agreement. This ensures that expectations are clear and will set you up for successful collaboration.

We began to focus on partnerships with shelters that served our target group. Every week, our staff members climb into a dilapidated van with boxes of beads, program supplies, and a commitment to transform isolated shelters into creative and healing spaces where girls develop critical business and life skills. By partnering with established shelters that serve our target group, we save time and money on space rental and participant identification, and increase our network and credibility. In return, our partners receive free programming and a variety of goods and services that benefit their homes. We've also engaged the girls themselves in contributing to their homes through their community fund. They've used this fund to paint the homes, fix toilets, and to promote healthy living for future girls in their home by purchasing sports equipment (they have also used the fund to support community projects outside of the home, such as delivering lunch to the elderly). Through collaboration, Emerge and our partners have had a bigger impact with fewer costs than we would have independently.

Step 3: Make It Last

Start Small, Then Scale What Works

Emerge began with 18 girls. Our initial pace felt fast: in just five months, we launched our first program, built a website, developed the first products and brought them to market, and hired our first staff person. At the time, I imagined we would be in three countries within our first five years. However, nearly eight years later, it's clear that scaling an initiative is a bit more complicated.

After initial programmatic success, organizations across Sri Lanka wanted to partner with us to reach many target communities that were outside of our original scope: children with disabilities, orphans, and widows. Excited by the prospect of scaling, we piloted our program with a group of children with disabilities. However, this pilot did not have the impact that we had previously seen—the children were uninterested in the educational and therapeutic effects of creating jewelry and simply wanted to earn money. We realized that the needs of children with disabilities were very different from those of girls who had survived abuse. Our programs had been designed to address a particular target group and were not effective for other groups. While we were eager to scale, this type of scaling simply did not work. We decided to stay focused, to develop quality over quantity, and to become the best we could at changing one very specific issue. We therefore took a new approach to scaling: first, we would scale deep, developing a suite of curricula to support the complex needs of teenage survivors of abuse. Then, we would scale out to reach new girls, but only at a pace that would ensure quality programming.

As we prepared to scale, we focused on ensuring our program curricula and teacher training were well-documented, our administrative structures (such as systems to manage our finances, programmatic data, and donors and customers) were in place, and that the appropriate sales infrastructure had been developed to accommodate growth.

To date, jewelry sales have been the hardest component to scale. While they have always been a core part of our vision, they were initially a secondary priority to our program development. Now that we have excellent programs, we are turning to sales as the key to both scaling and sustaining our work.

The challenge we face in sales is also our strength: each piece of jewelry is unique (though it fits certain design specifications, such as length and style). While customers love that the jewelry reflects the artist, this also means that it is difficult to sell in bulk to stores. We are in the process of determining whether our current sales methods will be sufficiently scalable, or if we will also need to develop a standardized line made by alumni or adult women to help fund our work for younger girls. Because our sales must grow at the same rate as our programs, the answer to this question will be key to the scalability of our work. Ultimately, we will only scale our programs as large as we can scale the business component of our work.

Engineer Self-Sustainable Solutions

With the goal to make long-term change in Sri Lanka, we have focused on developing our organizational sustainability. In addition to using our business model as a mechanism for financial sustainability (see the next section called "Integrate Social Entrepreneurship"), we have increased our organizational sustainability through our institutional memory and organizational structure. We also have ensured sustainable impact of our programs through long-term engagement with participants.

To ensure we have sustainable impact, I believe that Emerge needs to have a life of its own beyond me as its founder. An organization's ability to remain strong even with new leadership is an essential test of an organization's longevity. This has forced me to think about developing methods for institutional memory—documenting and sharing the types of knowledge that are hard to share: relationships and key lessons learned, for example. Part of this process has required maintaining organized files online, and another part has required equipping other team members with the knowledge needed to lead Emerge. This approach gives me great hope that our transformative work will continue.

At an organizational level, having an entity in the US and in Sri Lanka has enabled us to develop local ownership that will sustain Emerge in Sri Lanka long-term, even if US volunteers and support wane over time.

We also want to ensure that our impact on the young women we serve is sustainable. Emerge is not a one-time intervention; we become the girls' families and are there for their successes and challenges as they go out into the world. In addition to supporting their reintegration process, we invite them back to teach and mentor other girls in our programs, and we keep them connected to one another through reunions. In this way, Emerge is not just a set of programs—it's a community.

Ultimately, we think about creating self-sustainable solutions in almost everything we do. Whether considering programmatic or administrative operations, the key to long-term success is thinking through how our systems and impact can last long-term.

Note Short and regular communications keep people invested in our work. This is also a core part of our strategy for sustainability. We send out quarterly e-newsletters and maintain an active presence online via Facebook, a blog on our website, Twitter, and Flickr. In a time when most communication is done online, we've found personalized correspondence such as handwritten cards or phone calls can go a long way.

Integrate Social Entrepreneurship

At the core of Emerge is a social entrepreneurship business model that increases our impact, sustainability, and scalability. The money Emerge participants have saved is not a gift or a handout; it's money they've *earned* and is therefore a core component of the empowerment process. The girls beam when they realize that they themselves earned this money. Furthermore, we have linked this process to education that empowers girls to make the most of their savings and to become leaders in issues that matter to them. In this way, our business model impacts girls financially and educationally.

Tip We have found that small costs add up quickly and can change over time. We revisit our pricing regularly, keeping data current and looking for ways to cut costs.

So, how does our model work? While Emerge participants only make one or two products per week, the emotional and financial impact of this process is significant. Girls have saved thousands of dollars during our programs and have used this money to start businesses, finance education, support children, and build homes. In our current business model, 50% of Emerge jewelry's selling price goes directly to the girl who made the product, and the remaining 50% supports Emerge's sustainability by covering the cost of making and selling the jewelry as well as the girls' community fund (which is composed of $0.25 for each product).

Tip Branding and packaging are as important as our product. Customers love our Emerge jewelry bags (designed by a former participant and made by alumnae) and they add credibility to our organization and value to our product.

Long-term, our ability to grow our sales channels will enable us to scale our work. We have utilized a number of sales outlets, selling to stores, on consignment, online, through craft fairs, and through an agent model where individuals host "jewelry parties," acting as ambassadors for our cause and selling Emerge jewelry. In Sri Lanka, we are currently focusing on selling through stores. In the US, we are focusing on online and agent sales. We aim to sell an increasing amount of our jewelry in Sri Lanka as a strategy to decrease reliance on foreign support, increase local awareness of our cause, and minimize our carbon footprint and costs.

While our model continues to undergo improvements, social entrepreneurship has been a great way to build a scalable and sustainable solution that enhances the ownership and impact of the Emerge empowerment process.

Key Steps To-Date in Designing Our Business Model

Step 1: Piloting Our Concept—We utilized donations to buy beading supplies to pilot our programs. This pilot enabled us to understand product development possibilities based on the girls' interests, attention spans, and abilities. We then designed a line of jewelry and packaging (both tags and bags) for our initial target market: socially conscious college women.

Step 2: Bringing Products to Market and Collecting Data—We began exporting products to the US to sell at craft fairs. Direct customer feedback along with sales data (what products and colors were selling well) helped us understand our customers' preferences. We also realized we had additional markets: college administrators and staff, as well as mothers.

Step 3: Developing a Business Plan—We created a business plan based on preliminary sales data. We also began to look for places to source supplies in larger quantities for cheaper prices.

Step 4: Round Two of Product Development and Sales Distribution—Based on feedback, we refined our designs and packaging. We also created a signature lotus bead (our logo) to be used in every product. We launched our Emerge Agent program and our online store. We then revised our business plan as we received more data.

Step 5: Selling Locally in Sri Lanka—With the end of a civil war in Sri Lanka and an increasing tourism industry, we realized there was a growing local market for our jewelry. We therefore began selling on consignment to stores in Sri Lanka.

Step 6: Next Steps: Developing a Strategy for Scale—Today, we are in the process of considering a wholesale model and examining ways to increase our financial sustainability through sales. And yes, this means revising our business plan … again. To be sustainable, it is important to continuously adapt.

Share What Works

Just as we benefitted from others sharing what worked (and didn't work), we are committed to sharing our results, insights, experiences, and resources with others. Publicly, we have shared our work through our website, blogs, articles, videos, conferences, and public presentations. Eventually, we aim to make our curriculum open source, available for free to other organizations. But, for me, the most meaningful lessons I've learned are often the hardest to talk about publicly—lessons about handling sexual harassment, about corruption and developing safeguards to mitigate it, about cultivating the confidence of people who are much older than I am, about the discouraging competition in the social sector, and about creating and balancing personal and professional boundaries. These, among others, are the lessons I like to share one-on-one, where we can discuss their relevance to others as they start or grow their own projects.

Emerge would not exist were it not for countless individuals who sat down with me to share their successes and failures, their ideas, lessons learned, and frustrations. Good mentors are invaluable—people who will not judge but simply listen, support, advise, and share. I try to play this role with others, offering a safe space where we can be authentic and vulnerable with one another, able to get to the root of our challenges openly and to develop real solutions together. This work is too important to not face the tough, unpolished, and unglamorous questions of getting our work done effectively and meaningfully head on. And, we need to do it together.

Today, through learning from my peers and mentors and sharing my own lessons learned, I am more confident than ever that our generation has the energy and capacity to effect great change. The girls of Emerge have already shown me this. And, if we share our successes and failures, stay humble and open to learning, remain authentic to ourselves but open to collaboration, I believe we have a very exciting future ahead.

Note Sharing what hasn't worked helps others avoid our mistakes and enables us to utilize our failures as learning opportunities. Engineers Without Borders in Canada does a particularly good job of this—every year, they produce a public "Failure Report." Transparency and authenticity can increase support and belief in your work, and true and honest reflection can lead to improvement.

Alia Whitney-Johnson is an engineer, entrepreneur, and the founder of Emerge Gl[illegible] (www.emergeglobal.org). She is grateful to the Emerge team, its supporters, and he[illegible] for believing in her and making Emerge a reality. Alia loves traveling, salsa [illegible] she still steps on toes), and the inspiring girls of Emerge.

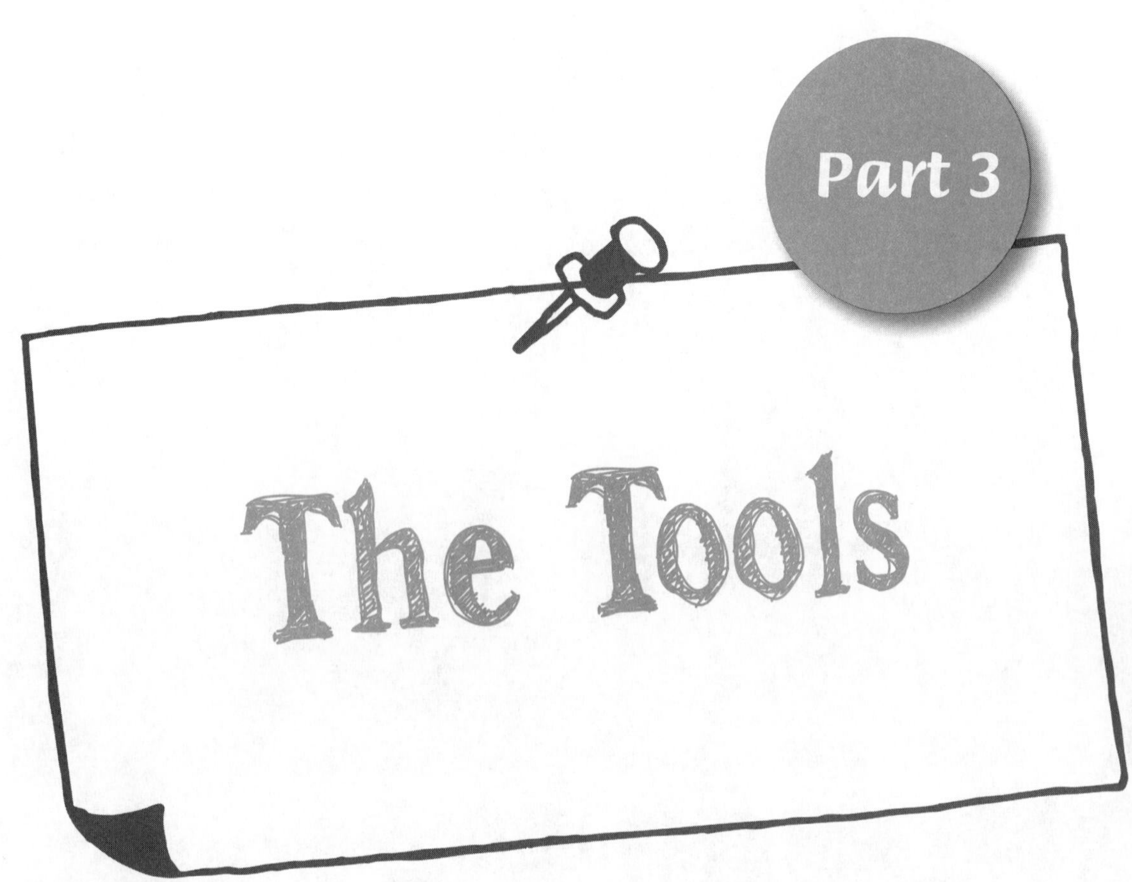

Part 3 is packed with the step-by-step practical advice and nitty-gritty details necessary to not only execute your action plan, but do so in the most effective, efficient way possible. Each chapter is devoted to a very specific task or skill, from those you'll need when just starting off (finding mentors, choosing a group name, building a team), to those you'll need further down the road when growing (securing funding, fostering partnerships, incorporating as a nonprofit or for-profit) and engineering sustainability (transitioning leadership, revitalizing a group, cultivating community ownership). And because each chapter in Part 3 features pearls of wisdom from young leaders who have established themselves as experts in their respective fields, you'll benefit from their experiences and anecdotes as well as tried-and-true tips inspired by their successes (and occasional mistakes!).

Do What Works

Proven Strategies to Increase Your Impact

Chapter 19

What Works in Choosing a Name

Names have power. They can make an impression—good or bad—before you ever set foot inside the door. Of course, we won't "name names" here, but you know a bad name when you hear it. On the opposite end of the spectrum are names that stand out because they're distinctive in an entirely different way. Maybe they sound beautiful, are novel and pleasantly unexpected, or just seem to fit. Names can be unique and memorable or common and forgettable. Think 50 Cent would have had much street cred with a name like Curtis James Jackson III? Would Coca-Cola still be the most recognized company in the world if its founder had chosen a name like Fizzwater?

The name you give your effort is just as important. The word or short set of words that make up your name will be emblazoned on everything from your group's T-shirts to your future job applications. Taking the time to think about your group's name is a worthwhile investment of energy. And with that in mind, let's examine the naming process in a bit more detail.

Break it Down: Tone and Function

Tone

Your name will have a tone—a mood or feeling it inspires when someone sees or hears it. The tone helps shape the image you project to the world. Does your group want to be seen as serious? Playful? Happy? Bashful? Sneezy? The tone can also say a lot about your group's style and institutional culture. Take Google, for example. The name is fun and creative—not necessarily what you'd expect of a multibillion-dollar tech company. That's pretty much how Google rolls—fun and creative—from a whimsical guiding principle ("Don't Be Evil"), to always changing themed logos to celebrate holidays and birthdays. Google's name reflects its values and personality.

Whether you hope to invest your organization with the seriousness of the issue you're tackling, inspire followers to join something epic, or appeal to people who believe socially innovative work doesn't have to be somber to be effective, the sentiment should come through in the name you choose.

There Is No Best Way to Pick a Name

It's important to understand why you choose the name you do and how it connects to both the goals and style of your organization.

Here are some examples:

- *Explanatory:* TED: Technology, Entertainment, Design
- *Serious:* Human Rights Campaign
- *Purposeful:* Teach For America
- *Playful:* Just Naïve Enough
- *Techy:* Change.org

Function

Your name clearly has a meaning, but you can convey that meaning in many different ways, accomplishing many different things. Your name might be:

- Exhortative, issuing a call to action: Save the Whales
- Descriptive, giving information about your group's activities or how it functions: Save the Whales Through Film
- Exclusive, defining the membership of your group: Vegan Single Dads for Saving the Whales

- Referential, including another name or organization to add credibility, suggest an approach, or identify institutional alliances: The PETA-Vegan Single Dads Fund for Saving the Whales

Choose a Name

To start the process of choosing a name, here are some questions to ask yourself and your team.

What's the Structure of Your Organization?

Form follows function. Are you an institute, a community, a campaign, a network, a company? The answer to this question will help define your group. Say you want to prevent gecko abuse. Is your group a short-term project, a coalition of different parties working to prevent abuse, or a fund raising money to prevent abuse?

Examples: Bill & Melinda Gates *Foundation*, Make Our Food Safe *Coalition*, United Negro College *Fund*, Gay & Lesbian Leadership *Institute*

What's Your Cause?

The issue you're trying to address should factor into the name you choose. This might seem like an obvious point, but what's important to note is how many different ways you can do this.

First, how specific do you want to be when defining your cause? Let's say your group works with local farmers to provide food shelters with produce the farmers are unable to sell. The cause you're specifically addressing is hunger. But if your group is planning to, or might one day, tackle additional related issues like unemployment, it might be better to reframe your cause as something more general, for example, poverty.

Second, are you open to getting a bit creative with your group's name? There are ways of alluding to a cause without actually flat-out stating it, so you'll need to decide if you want to be explicit or implicit. In the example, if you decided your group's cause was hunger, an explicit name might be something like Hunger Relief Partnership and an implicit name might be No Empty Plate. The latter name uses the image of an empty plate to communicate the associated idea of hunger, and though hunger is never explicitly mentioned, it's clear to anyone hearing "No Empty Plate" that the group works toward hunger relief. Of course, whenever you use a more creative name, there's a chance some people won't immediately understand, but your name will stand out and be that much more memorable for those who do.

Here are some examples:

Explicit	Implicit
Environmental Defense Fund	Keep America Beautiful: This exhortative name hints at the environmental cause at the heart of the organization.
Center for Reproductive Rights	Planned Parenthood: If parenthood is planned, this implies exercising one's reproductive rights, the organization's primary reason for being.
National Society to Prevent Blindness	Helen Keller International: This group, cofounded by Helen Keller (the famous and inspiring deaf-blind woman who overcame huge odds to go on to accomplish great things), didn't include its cause of blindness prevention in the group name because Helen Keller's name is already so strongly associated that the connection is implicit.

What Do You Do?

What type of activity are you involved in? Think of verbs to describe what your group does on a day-to-day basis. Do you build, teach, organize, create, gather, feed, mediate, heal? The type of activity may become an important part of your name.

Examples: *School* Yourself, *Feed* America, DonorsChoose.org

Who Are Your Primary Members or Customers?

Are you a faith-based organization? Are your members drawn from a specific gender, professional field, or ethnic group?

Examples: *Indi*corps, *Transgender* Law Center, *Girl*Tank

What Makes Your Group Special or Different?

What is it that really matters to you? What's the word or phrase you want people to associate with your organization? Is there some aspect of what you do that makes it unique, or some aspect of what you do that you'd like to emphasize?

Examples: *Revolving Fund* Pharmacy, *Peer 2 Peer* University, *Generation* Citizen

Don't Choose a Bad Name

The motto of brainstorming is that there is no such thing as a bad idea. The same outlook does *not* apply to names. Although there's no single right way to pick a name, there are a lot of ways to pick a bad name. And if you mistakenly choose a bad name, it could damage your credibility, turn off potential funders or customers, and make it more difficult for you to recruit others to your cause. Here are some of the biggest name mistakes.

Overused Words and Phrases

Nothing is more annoying than generic-sounding names, and this is especially true in the world of socially conscious businesses and organizations. Certain words come up more often than others (*international*, for example), and in some cases, they are unavoidable. But the more you steer away from clichéd phrases and words, the more you'll distinguish your group from the pack.

Use with Caution

"_______ Without Borders." Médecins Sans Frontierès (Doctors Without Borders) is not only the founding father of latter-day humanitarian organizations, it's also the epitome of a well-established humanitarian organization with a great name—so great that variations on it have popped up everywhere. Move on.

In the same vein is [Group of People] for/against [Cause]; for example, Students for Choice, Meteorologists Against Global Warming, Cylons for Equality. These names are straightforward and practical, but also rather formulaic. Use with caution.

Following is a list of words that you shouldn't necessarily avoid—they come up so frequently that sometimes it's impossible not to use them—but if you can, think of a way around them. Note that using words like *global* or *international* actually often misrepresents the scope or focus of the organization.

international	global
world	aid
change	empower
relief	assistance
movement	help

Words That Mean Something You Don't Mean Them to Mean

Nathaniel: Sometimes a word used in an organization's name suggests something about the organization's mission that's actually not correct or is misleading in some way. As an example, "The Innovation Network" sounds as if it would be a social entrepreneurship institute—a funder or developer of innovative change agents. In reality, it's an organization that sells impact assessment tools. While impact assessment may be an important part of innovation, it's certainly not what you think of first or would go to the organization seeking.

Another example is "Genocide Intervention Network." Originally called The Genocide Intervention Fund, this group got its start raising money directly for African Union peacekeepers in Darfur. As the organization extended its mission to advocacy, education, and other activities, its leaders adopted the name Genocide Intervention Network to better reflect the group's new goals.

Trying-Too-Hard (or Inadvertent) Acronyms

One of the most common (and annoying) problems of group naming occurs when groups choose names explicitly to have a specific acronym. Flip through any student group directory, and you'll have to fight the urge to laugh at all the bad acronyms: LEAD, HELP, CARE, GIVE, YOUTH. The problem isn't limited to student groups: a few well-established, successful organizations are guilty of this naming gaffe. Consider Action on Smoking and Health, or ASH. It's too much of a coincidence to think ASH just happened to be the acronym that resulted from their first-choice name. Now it should be noted that ASH is a highly accomplished group championing a worthwhile cause, so clearly its choice of name hasn't served as too much of an impediment. But highly contrived acronyms tend to give the impression that your group lacks maturity or creativity (even if it has plenty of both), so avoid the temptation to go with the easy answer. Think your parents named you so you'd have catchy initials for monogrammed towels? Probably not (unless, of course, your name is Ophelia Molly Gordon or Upton Gary Luther-York).

It's also worth noting that while you shouldn't choose a name for the acronym it produces, you *should* at least consider what the resulting acronym will be. Choosing a name without thinking through its acronym can result in a really awkward abbreviation. Think abbreviations that spell out curse words, body parts, or, um, actions.

Name Your Baby

When you feel that you've got the name that might just be "The One," run through these steps before finalizing your decision.

1. *Write it down.* Write your potential name down on paper, and then type it out. Sometimes taking a step back helps you identify major flaws that are hard to see when you're caught up in the naming process. Once you've done this, go do something else and then come back. What's your gut reaction when you see the name again? Is it stuffy or too silly, or just right?
2. *Google it.* Double-check there isn't another "Gecko Abuse Prevention Society" already.
3. *URL it.* Go to whois.net to make sure your potential domain name isn't already taken, keeping in mind that geckoabusepreventionsoci-etyofsouthernflorida.org is not an ideal URL.
4. *Share it.* See how your friends and family members react to your group's name. Say it aloud to see if it has the right ring to it.
5. *Sleep on it.* Give yourself time before you carve your group's name in stone. If it's a good name now, it will still be a good name a week from now.

Figure 19.1. After You've Picked a Name

In *Bury the Chains: The British Struggle to Abolish Slavery*, Adam Hochschild conveys a story of one unfortunate naming.[1] In the early decades of the nineteenth century, a Birmingham woman who wanted to form a women's antislavery society wrote to Thomas Clarkson, the leading English abolitionist of the day, asking him for suggestions for naming her group. He suggested the name: "Female Society for Ameliorating the Condition of Female Slaves in the British Colonies, but with a view ultimately to their final emancipation there."

Even in one of the world's first great international social movements, they were thinking deeply about names. Luckily for you, the fashions have changed a bit, and a simple two to four words should be just fine. But make those few words count.

Nathaniel Whittemore is a founding director of the Northwestern University Center for Global Engagement. He spends altogether too much time thinking about marketing and perception, and his previous and current projects have had names including Just Naïve Enough, OpenShutter Project, The Passenger Magazine, Refugee Connect, and Beyond Bangalore.

Chapter 20

What Works in Writing a Mission Statement

If your name is the heart of your enterprise, your mission is its soul. Your mission statement is one or two sentences that explain what your group seeks to accomplish and why. It's the thesis statement for the novel of your action. Much more than a description of your organization, it's something others can refer to in order to learn about and differentiate your group from others. You'll also reference it when making important organizational decisions like who you do and don't partner with and how you allocate scarce resources and prioritize programs.

This is the mission statement for the Genocide Intervention Network:

> The Genocide Intervention Network envisions a world in which the global community is willing and able to protect civilians from genocide and mass atrocities. Our mission is to empower individuals and communities with the tools to prevent and stop genocide.

Imagine the Genocide Intervention Network is looking to adopt a new initiative. Several suggestions have been made, and the group must decide which one to implement. Among numerous considerations (finances, staffing, and feasibility, for example), whether the proposed program fits with the group's mission statement is a key consideration. Among equally feasible ideas, which one does the most to "empower individuals and communities with the tools to prevent and stop genocide"?

Perhaps the Genocide Intervention Network is considering two proposals for implementation in a country with a history of ethnically motivated violence. One proposal would place greater restrictions on the sale of handguns; the other would seek to teach tolerance and appreciation of ethnic diversity to schoolchildren. You could reason that restricting handguns would help check violent acts of all kinds, particularly in the case of a mass uprising or civil war. However, the group would probably instead implement the educational curriculum, which would attack the root of the problem: instilling positive attitudes and values at odds with a mentality capable of genocide. This program would most clearly fit its mission "to empower individuals and communities with the tools to prevent and stop genocide."

Your mission statement is in many ways the thesis statement for the essay of your action. When you learned how to write a five-paragraph essay, your teacher no doubt seared into your memory that the entire essay should revolve around the thesis statement. Each paragraph both flows from it and supports it. The development of the whole essay is dependent on the thesis statement, just as the development of your organization is dependent on your mission statement. Why? Well, as your group grows and matures, adding paragraphs or chapters, you'll constantly refer back to your mission statement to guide your actions and make the right decisions —those that support the ideas and principles set forth in your mission statement. That's why it's vital to write a concise, clear, and well-considered mission statement.

Tip A mission statement is a bit like the US Constitution in that it's a document you constantly return to for guidance.

To help you with this task, we'll outline characteristics of a great mission statement, review some missions that exemplify these characteristics, and offer some exercises to use when writing your mission.

Characteristics of a Great Mission Statement

Although not every great mission statement will possess all the characteristics we address here, understanding these elements and why they're important is indispensable as you begin crafting your own statement.

Brevity

Keep it short and to the point. Your mission shouldn't use more words than are absolutely necessary to get its point across about who you are, what you're doing, and why you're doing it. A good mission will cut to the chase. This doesn't mean you can't use descriptive language or add a sentence or two to set the scene before delivering the punch, but the punch is what people remember.

Clarity

Missions are frequently muddled in vague language that reflects the difference between good intentions and understanding how to put good intentions into practice. So it's vital to use words that are clear and easy to understand. Avoid jargon and technical terms. Find words that convey your meaning precisely and don't have ambiguous meanings.

Focus

Your mission statement should distill your group's efforts into an easily communicable central statement of purpose. Don't try to fit in more than you need; find that core idea that underlies everything you're attempting to do.

Note At its core, your mission statement defines what you seek to do in the world: the problem you seek to solve and the change you wish to create. Your mission is an articulation of your organization's goals and its beliefs about what can be achieved.

Examples of Mission Statements

Please note that our examples are real ones because they are better than anything we could invent. Each of these organizations represents an incredible group of people doing incredible work; no criticism with the missions discussed here should in any way indicate anything less than our total admiration for each of these organizations.

To get a sense of what a good mission statement looks like, read as many as you can. Here's a sampling of missions from young organizations and a short analysis of each.

This is the mission statement of Americans for Informed Democracy:

> Americans for Informed Democracy (AID) is a non-partisan 501(c)(3) organization that brings the world home through programming on more than 1,000 U.S. university campuses and in more than 10 countries. AID fulfills its mission by coordinating town hall meetings on America's role in the world, hosting leadership retreats, and publishing opinion pieces and reports on issues of global importance. Through these efforts, AID seeks to build a new generation of globally conscious leaders who can shape an American foreign policy appropriate for our increasingly interdependent world.

- *The good*: The final sentence situates both what AID seeks to develop ("a new generation of globally conscious leaders") and why (to "shape an American foreign policy appropriate for our increasingly interdependent world").
- *Room for improvement*: The phrase "brings the world home" is vague. Even with the rest of the statement providing context, it's ambiguous.

Here is the mission statement for Appropriate Infrastructure Development Group:

> Roughly 2 billion people do not have access to basic services such as electricity, clean drinking water and sanitation. Development of this infrastructure is essential to breaking the cycle of poverty in developing countries. The Appropriate Infrastructure Development Group (AIDG) works to provide rural villages in developing countries with affordable and environmentally sound technologies that meet these needs. Through a combination of business incubation, education, training, and outreach, the AIDG helps individuals and communities gain access to technology that will improve their lives. Our model provides a novel approach to sustainable development by empowering people with the physical tools and practical knowledge to solve infrastructure problems in their own communities.

- *The good*: The words used are simple, direct. It's clear the organization's focus is providing "technology that will improve lives."
- *Room for improvement*: The mission statement is much too long, containing more information than needed.

This is a reworked version:

> The Appropriate Infrastructure Development Group (AIDG) works to provide rural villages in developing countries with affordable and environmentally sound technologies that meet basic needs such as electricity, clean drinking water and sanitation. Through a combination of business incubation, education, training, and outreach, the AIDG helps individuals and communities gain access to technology that will improve their lives.

Vision Versus Mission

The difference between a vision statement and a mission statement is simple but often confused: *vision* is your sense of the world as it should be; your *mission* outlines your approach to achieving this vision. When you share your mission with people, they will ask, "Well, how're you going to do that?"

There is a tendency for people writing missions to confuse means and ends, including the means (the how) in the mission statements. Remember that at its core, your mission is about the change you seek to make, not necessarily how you plan on making it.

Note how Genocide Intervention Network's one-sentence mission statement is preceded by a one-sentence vision statement:

> The Genocide Intervention Network envisions a world in which the global community is willing and able to protect civilians from genocide and mass atrocities. Our mission is to empower individuals and communities with the tools to prevent and stop genocide.

- *The good*: This is a model of succinctness, clarity, and focus. It articulates who the organization is focused on empowering and to what ends, and it uses easily understood words and provides a framework for focusing its activities.
- *Room for improvement*: Round of applause, this is a good statement.

Also effective is the vision statement for the Interfaith Youth Core (IFYC):

> Interfaith Youth Core seeks to build a movement that encourages religious young people to strengthen their religious identities, foster inter-religious understanding and cooperate to serve the common good.

- *The good*: Like the Genocide Intervention Network mission, the IFYC mission is a model of succinctness, clarity, and focus. Moreover, the mission is a good example of how a mission can articulate a set of goals and bring them together under the overarching banner of the organization. For IFYC, "strengthening religious identities," "fostering interreligious understanding," and "cooperation to serve the common good" are all central and mutually reinforcing components of their mission, which organize and situate a myriad of activities.
- *Room for improvement*: Nothing to say here either. This, too, is a good statement.

Write Your Mission Statement

The question that matters more than anything else when writing your mission is this: What do you care about most?

Most young organizations articulate missions that are much broader than they should be and suggest an organizational capacity much greater than is actually the case.

We all want to end global poverty and realize world peace, but realistically these are missions beyond the scope of any one organization. So what do you care about *most*? What *specifically* does your organization seek to do? For whom? Articulate this, and you have your mission.

If you're having problems figuring out what your group cares about most, ask the following questions:

1. *What's the problem we've identified? What's the problem we seek to fix, the gap we intend to fill?*

> *Nathaniel*: For the Center for Global Engagement (CGE), it's that young people who want to create global change don't have the educational resources and tools necessary to do so.

2. *What does the world look like with that problem solved? In other words, what's our vision?*

> *Nathaniel*: A great way to home in on your mission is to first describe your vision. What does the world look like with your problem solved? For CGE, it's a world in which students who care about the world have access to the learning resources they need to fully leverage their passions and energies to create change.

3. *Who will we work with to achieve our vision?*

> *Nathaniel*: What group, community, or type of individual will help you achieve your vision? For the CGE, it's young people who care about global problem solving.

4. *How will we achieve our vision?*

> *Nathaniel*: Once you've identified the people you'll work with, what do you intend to do? Capacity building through education? Direct provision of services? For CGE, the fundamental activity is educational: to develop students' capacities to enact change.

Most missions are a combination of the answers to these four questions. Try to answer these questions with your own group in mind, and then combine your answers into a brief, clear, focused mission statement.

Exercise 20.1 will serve as a tutorial on developing your own mission statement.

Figure 20.1. Figure Out What Your Group Cares About Most

What's the Problem?

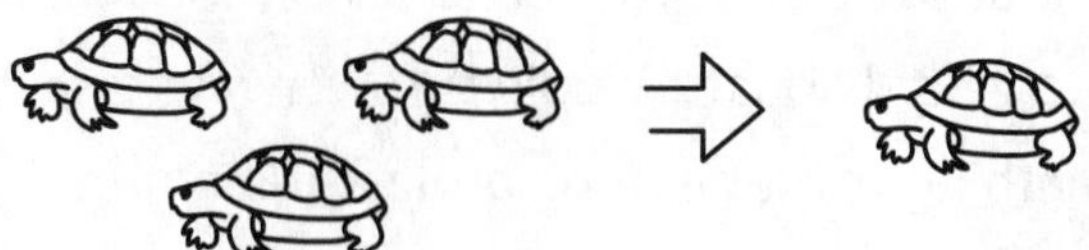

What's Your Vision?

Who Will You Work With?

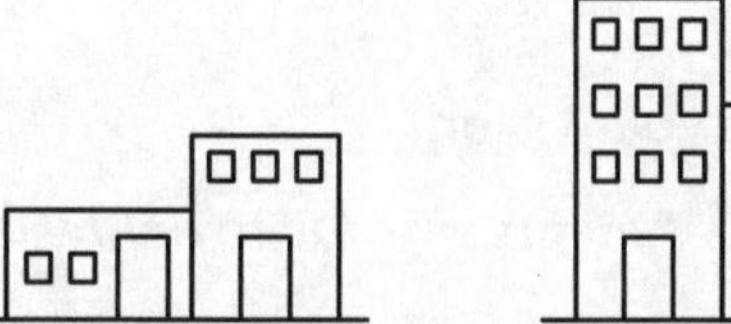

Local Gov't. Condominium Owners Local Volunteers

How Will You Achieve Your Vision?

Exercise 20.1 Mission Development Tutorial

You've noticed that people on your school's campus treat squirrels poorly. Squirrels are subject to verbal abuse. People throw away trash near squirrel homes. You decide that something must be done and recruit a group of students who share your concerns and begin with writing a mission statement.

Run through the following questions:

1. What's the problem?

   Squirrels are unappreciated by the university community, contributing to the degradation of squirrel livelihood.

2. What's your vision?

   We envision a world where squirrels are appreciated for all they offer to our diverse campus environment.

3. Who will you work with to achieve your vision?

   We will focus our activities on the students who fail to appreciate the beauty of the squirrel.

4. How will you achieve your vision?

   We will design educational and marketing programs to improve student understanding and appreciation of squirrels.

And here is your sample mission statement:

The squirrel today is threatened from all sides—loggers, builders, and now, our student body. The University Squirrel Union seeks to design educational and marketing programs to improve student understanding of and appreciation for the majestic squirrel.

(continued)

Now it's your turn:

1. What's the problem?

2. What's your vision?

3. Who will you work with to achieve your vision?

4. How will you achieve your vision?

Your Sample Mission Statement

Words Matter

Your mission speaks volumes about your organization, defining who you are, what you do, and how you intend to leave an impact on the world. A great mission statement will capture the spirit of your enterprise, providing guidance for your future growth and development. Take time to craft the right statement. And you might just find that in the process, you learn something new about who you are and what you truly want to do.

Nathaniel Whittemore is a founding director of the Northwestern University Center for Global Engagement, whose mission states, "The Center for Global Engagement builds the capacity of young people to cross borders of nation, race, faith, and more to develop responsible, sustainable solutions to shared global problems."

Chapter 21

What Works in Goals and Planning

A goal without a plan is just a wish.

—ANTOINE DE SAINT-EXUPÉRY

- ☐ Vision
- ☐ Problem
- ☐ Potential solution
- ☐ Name
- ☐ Mission statement

Check, check, check, check, check, done.

You've committed to fulfilling your social responsibility and want to make an impact. Now it's time to turn those good intentions into an action plan. This chapter will help you answer two fundamental questions:

1. What are you going to do?
2. How are you doing to do it?

The key to successful execution is successful planning. It's time to organize your organization.

Step 1: Design Goals

Goals guide the actions you take. They help you identify what needs to happen and in what order. Moreover, creating concrete goals (both long- and short-term) and the process of writing them down foster personal and team accountability. When everyone knows what's supposed to be done and when, they are literally on the same page.

We've drawn upon the principles presented in Part 2 to design a simple mnemonic to help you identify the characteristics your goals should have. Choose goals that have MERITS:

Mission-driven
Evidence-based
Realistic, based on **R**esources
Impactful and **I**nnovative
Tangible and **T**rackable
Specific

Let's break down the mnemonic.

Mission-Driven

Chapter 20 gave you guidelines for creating a mission statement; this is a great place to start thinking about your organization's goals. Create goals that reflect your mission statement. For example, the American Cancer Society Teens mission states that it will fight cancer through "advocacy, education, fundraising, and service." So when discussing the goals for the year, members tried to develop at least one project to reflect each of the four broad categories. Referring to your mission or vision as the building block for goals not only ensures that you're addressing the problems you set out to solve, but also helps you identify areas you've missed.

Evidence-Based

Make sure the work you're doing is efficient and effective. Build on what others have shown works in the past, and make sure that the goals you choose are proven to target the problem you're discussing. Let's say your mission is to provide crisis relief to countries struck by natural disasters. It might sound like a heroic thing to fly out to devastated countries to help relief efforts, but if you lack training in relief work or the region is resistant to outside help, your airfare might be better spent as a donation to the Red Cross, an organization with a well-developed infrastructure for crisis response. Something may sound like a great idea and have the best intentions, but what is more meaningful is having at least some evidence that it will work. Don't waste your time or energy on something that just feels good.

Realistic, Based on Resources

Design goals that are ambitious but achievable. It's great to dream big, but if you overshoot practicality, you and your team will end up disappointed that you fell short of your lofty goal and may not recognize the positive contribution you did make. When determining how realistic your goal is, take into account resources like time, money, and staffing.

Impactful and Innovative

Prioritize work that adds value to the cause and the field. Projects that have the potential to affect a lot of people or attack a problem from a completely new angle are those that should pique your interest. Of course, if you are going to try something completely new, make sure you have a plan to evaluate its effectiveness so that you can figure out if it's working.

Tangible and Trackable

When setting goals, write a plan for how you'll measure your progress along the way. You need to be able to measure, evaluate, and improve on your work. Tangible goals can be measured, which means they can be evaluated and subsequently improved. For example, "improve opportunity for low-income students" is not measurable, whereas "increase the high school graduation rate in all three county public schools by five percent in two years" is.

In addition, when considering funding requests, investors and donors look for evidence of measurable success. Keep a detailed record of your goals and progress so you can regularly evaluate your work. Designate a person who will be responsible for collecting, analyzing, and sharing the data. Remember that improvement is just as valuable as raw numbers—maybe even more.

> **Note** Don't think of group assessments as final exams. Think of them as pop quizzes: periodic check-ins to see how your group is doing and what progress you've made. These little quizzes will help you figure out if you're on track or if you need to adjust your course.

Specific

Goals should be specific, for example: "Collect $10,000 for program to help survivors of domestic violence secure legal representation for court cases against abusers." It's a good idea to have goals that are both internal ("Raise membership in the group to 50 members by September") and external ("Apply for two grants to fund refugee education program").

Step 2: Prioritize Goals

Now that you've set some goals, you need to prioritize them. When you have multiple things you want to accomplish, which is the most important? When prioritizing, consider timing. Does one goal need to get done before another goal can be attempted?

Differentiate between long-term and short-term goals. A long-term goal is one that may take from several months to over a year to accomplish ("Develop a working relationship with a state representative in the next three years"). Once you have your long-term goals in place, set the short-term goals that will help you reach each long-term goal. Short-term goals can be done relatively quickly ("Research state representatives to determine whose interests most align with ours by the end of this week. Call their offices to find out about volunteer opportunities by the end of next week").

Step 3: Brainstorm Execution

Once you have your goals decided and prioritized, it's time to figure out how you're going to accomplish them. Get your team together and brainstorm. You'll all have different ideas about the necessary actions to accomplish the goals, and that's fine. There are always multiple ways to address a problem. Make a list of these different ways, and figure out what steps you'll need to take to achieve each goal. Which path is the most effective and efficient for you and your group based on your resources?

Step 4: Develop an Action Plan

Armed with your ideas, it's time to develop your strategy for accomplishing goals: your action plan.

First focus on the basics of what, how, who, and when.

- What?
  Determine the specific steps and tasks necessary to complete each goal and how you'll measure each outcome. How will you define success?
- How?
  What resources do you need? In your plan, outline how you'll attain and manage each resource.
- Who?
  Who will be responsible and accountable for each task? While on the topic of who, also think about with whom. With whom can you collaborate?
- When?
  In many ways, the core of a plan is determining when, so we'll spend some time detailing this aspect of creating an action plan.

Note Use data to guide your actions. In order to create a solution, you need to know whether the data support your planned intervention. If not, why might this be? If there are no data, plan a pilot study for your proposed intervention.

Deadlines and Calendars

Once you've written down your tasks, assign a deadline for each. This will help you pace both long-term and short-term goals and allow you to plan ahead and balance your leadership role with other commitments. If you need to rely on outside groups in order to achieve your goal, allow extra time.

Tip No matter how much you plan, surprises will arise, you'll make mistakes, and you'll have to try again. Budget extra time for the unpredictable, particularly when scheduling to meet set deadlines, and account for potential barriers that may come your way.

Use the talents of your team members and the resources of your community as best you can. When you're constructing the time frame, make sure it doesn't conflict with school and community events. Read "Potential Scheduling Conflicts" for some tips on days and times to consider when arranging meetings or programs. Plan accordingly to avoid scheduling conflicts.

Make a year-long calendar with your goals and deadlines, as well as meeting dates and times. Distribute copies to all members and sponsors.

Depending on their own schedules and interests, they may want to be particularly active in one specific program or at a certain time of the year. Planning is crucial to leadership: the more you plan and the more people you involve in your planning, the better your result will be.

Potential Scheduling Conflicts

Days of the Week

Keep these days and times in mind when scheduling:

- Common days of religious observance include: Wednesday evenings, Friday evenings, Saturday mornings, and Sundays.
- Most people set aside Friday and Saturday nights for social and family commitments. Don't try to compete with date night or game night.
- Students often take standardized tests like the SATs and LSATs on Saturday mornings.

Times of the Year

In addition to regularly scheduled holidays, pay attention to these:

- Community leaders and most organizations are busy with vacations and holiday commitments from Thanksgiving to New Year's. Avoid trying to start something new from mid-November through mid-January.
- When working with a diverse group or people in other countries, be observant of their cultural and religious holidays.
- Many people, especially those with school-aged children, take vacations in August. As a result, businesses and nonprofits are notoriously slow moving at this time since so many staff are out.
- If you're working with students in several states, remember that spring break dates vary, as do summer holidays. Schools in the South may start in early August, and schools in the North may continue until the middle to end of June. On the topic of students, keep in mind that in the fall semester, students are busy with applications for colleges, graduate schools, and jobs.

Scheduling

Tip: Make a point of identifying the special skills and relevant contacts of your team members, and be sure to utilize them to benefit your cause. If one of your members is a management consultant who majored in statistics, she can be in charge of analyzing the survey and creating graphs. If your roommate's dad is a middle school teacher, he can help get you on the agenda at the board of education meeting. Keep all of these in mind when creating your group's action plan.

When fundraising, account for the schedules of major fundraisers in the community. If the Red Cross or United Way holds fundraisers in your town during a certain week, schedule your fundraiser a few weeks earlier or later. This will help you minimize the number of potential donors who choose not to donate to your cause because they have recently donated to another. While you may not be able to avoid all other events, be sure to schedule around the large-scale fundraisers in your community or on your campus.

Plan around the grant application cycle. If you're thinking about applying for grants, make sure that you'll have some concrete data on your progress and success before applying. A proven track record speaks volumes to grant committees.

Interested in politics? Plan around the election cycle, particularly every two and four years when more prominent races have elections. The media tend to be more in tune with political issues around election time, and politicians may be more responsive. If you're looking for media attention (of course you are!), understand the news cycle and what gets covered when. For example, you may not get much coverage if you hold an event the day of an election. But launching a campaign to help single moms find jobs around Mother's Day would be timely.

WARNING: Know when to say no. Don't overdo your goals and set more than you can handle. To quote former British Prime Minister Tony Blair, "The art of leadership is saying no, not yes. It is very easy to say yes."

Step 5: Evaluate

> *When it is obvious that the goals cannot be reached, don't adjust the goals, adjust the action steps.*
>
> CONFUCIUS

After each project, debrief with your group. Compare your outcome with your initial goals and draft a follow-up report. If you didn't meet your goals, think about why that might be. Were they too ambitious? Did you run into problems that you didn't expect? Brainstorm new ways to meet the same goals. Keep these reports, along with your goals and checklists, in a binder. You can refer to them when you make your new lists, assess your progress, search for funding, and train a new group of young leaders.

Figure 21.1. If You Fall Short of Your Goal, Adjust Your Action Plan Not Your Goal

Sample Action Plan

Mission Statement: The Chicago Students for Community Health is dedicated to working with schools, businesses, and the government in Illinois to improve the access, quality, and cost of nutritious foods for Chicago residents.

Long-term goal 1: Get more nutritious foods (all under 200 calories per package) in high school vending machines by April 1.

Long-term goal 2: Organize a community healthy eating fair to take place in June in the public park, with booths from at least 10 local farmers and vendors.

Long-term goal 3: Increase food subsidies to farmers of organic fruits and vegetables by the next election.

Long-Term Goal 1

Short-term goal 1: Set date to speak to board of education. (Deadline: October 1)

Short-term goal 2: Research how other school systems have reformed vending machine selections, look up data on health effects of popular children's snacks, and compare the cost of healthy and unhealthy snacks. (Deadline: January 1)

Short-term goal 3: Survey 500 students in area schools on what healthy snacks they would buy (ask health and physical education teachers to help distribute surveys). Create graphs of the results.
(Deadline: February 1)

Short-term goal 4: Start a petition. Ask 10 members to each collect 100 names each on the petition, and ask a public health professor to join you in talking to the board of education. (Deadline: March 1)

Short-term goal 5: Decide who will give the speech. Write a rough draft of the five-minute speech. Practice presenting it three times to friends, and have them ask questions and give feedback. (Deadline: March 15)

Short-term goal 6 (follow-up): Send thank-you notes to board members. Discuss with team how we felt about the process, evaluate our progress, and determine next steps. (Deadline: May 1)

Now that you have seen an example, it is time to focus on your own leadership. Use Exercise 21.1 to set long- and short-term team goals as well as some personal goals.

Exercise 21.1 Set Goals

Long-Term Goals

List five long-term goals for your organization:

1.

2.

3.

4.

5.

Short-Term Goals

Choose one of your long-term goals and expand on the steps it will take to reach that goal. Remember to set deadlines. Brainstorm five short-term goals necessary to reach your long-term goal:

1.

2.

3.

4.

5.

(continued)

Personal Goals

In addition to drafting goals for your organization, create some personal goals. Make a list of five things you want to accomplish as a leader. While you are at it, make a list of things you want to get done outside your organization, perhaps in school or at home.

1.

2.

3.

4.

5.

Now it's time to stop planning, and start doing!

Chapter 22

What Works in Fundraising

When we recognize that a better word for fundraising is "friend raising," we open limitless doors to creativity in support of our causes.

—SUE VINEYARD

Asking for money or material donations for your cause can seem pretty intimidating—but it shouldn't be! Fundraising is a two-way street. Yes, you're asking for something, but you're also providing something in return. Try to think about it this way: let's say you want to bake a pie but you've run out of sugar and the store is closed. You can let the ingredients you've already prepared go to waste, or you can ask your neighbor if he has sugar to share. When you ask your neighbor, he's more than happy to help. He even gives you a baking tip to help you get the perfect pie crust. Later, when the pie is ready, you return with a slice for your new friend.

Fundraising is like this in many ways. Although it might feel awkward to ask a stranger for help, the person you've approached might truly be happy to help. He may even give useful advice or offer to help in some other way. In exchange, he gets a return on his investment: an emotional return—the warm feeling that comes with sharing and investing in a good cause—and perhaps even a material return (in this case, a literal piece of the pie). It's win-win.

Of course, you won't always get what you've asked for. But even in the worst case scenario, you'll just get a simple "no." Whether you fundraise by soliciting donations, selling goods and services, or attracting investors, the same principle holds true: there's no harm in asking, and you'll often be pleasantly surprised.

This chapter introduces a number of tried-and-true fundraising strategies and is divided into three main parts. The first section will prepare you to fundraise. This involves a lot of planning, gathering documents, and teamwork to ensure that everything's in place. The second section will discuss how to solicit donations from individuals (friends, family, strangers, etc.) and businesses, both directly (letters, personal appeals, etc.) and indirectly (classic fundraising events). The third section is an in-depth guide to securing grants and monetary awards. This chapter contains all the basic tools and insights necessary to raise the money and material donations your group needs.

Prepare to Fundraise

Know Your Financial Needs

Even if your organization is staffed by volunteers, you'll need to pay for things along the way, including products and services that aren't typically donated (for example, materials, space, and utilities). Tally up your costs and make a budget for the year (see the "Budget" section later in this chapter). If your group exists to raise money for another organization, what's your goal for the year? You don't need to have a definite number in mind, but you should have a good estimate.

Identify Potential Sources of Funding

There are many types of funding available, so familiarize yourself with all the options at the outset. You'll likely end up with some combination of the funding sources outlined here:

Donations

Donations are essentially gifts (financial or otherwise) that are given to your organization with minimal (if any) stipulations. While you may solicit donations from corporate or other institutional donors, individual donors remain the largest, most consistent source of funding for social causes.

Fellowships

While other sources of funding are directly for your organization, fellowships are often more focused on you as the leader of the business or nonprofit. In addition to funding, fellowships provide many forms of support including mentors, media attention, leadership training, and a strong network of alumni.

Here's just a sampling of groups that award fellowships: Acumen Fund, Ashoka, Echoing Green, Skoll Foundation, TED, Unreasonable Institute, Draper Richards Foundation, and the Kauffman Foundation.

Grants

Grants are a form of competitive funding awarded by process of application. The funding body (government organizations, foundations, corporations, etc.) considers the merits of your group's proposal as well as whether or not your objectives are in line with its own goals. If you are awarded a grant, your funding will be contingent upon your abiding by a set of criteria established by the funding body.

- *Public grants*: Grants.gov is the best place to start for all things pertaining to government grants.
- *Private Grants:* Philanthropically-minded foundations abound at the local, state, national, and international levels. Foundationcenter.org is a good starting point.

Crowd funding

Crowd funding harnesses the power of small donations, or micropatronage. Your group submits an idea or project proposal to an online community where individual users can browse through projects, donating as much or as little as they'd like to those ideas they find most compelling. To dive right in, check out donorschoose.org, Pepsi Refresh Project, Chase Community Giving, or Global Giving.

Investors

If your idea could potentially turn a profit and you're considering the route of the socially conscious start-up, consider approaching investors to raise the funds you need. Angel investors, incubators, accelerators, and venture capital firms provide early financial backing to promising businesses in exchange for a small amount of equity (partial ownership) in the company. To learn more about pitching to venture capitalists, turn to "A Primer on Venture Capital" later in this chapter.

Student- or University-based

Your school's career services or public service office should have listings of funding opportunities for both current students and alumni. Look into business plan competitions (especially prevalent at universities with business schools), as well as a new trend—university centers for innovation.

> **Note** A far more extensive list of funding sources can be found online in an up-to-date database maintained by DoSomething.org, a fantastic organization that works to inspire and support youth innovation.

Perfect Your Pitch

A fundraising pitch is your well-reasoned argument for why a certain person or group should fund your organization. Whether you're making your case in writing or in person, online or at an event, follow these guidelines to sell your audience on what you're doing and why they need to support you:

- *Explain the pressing problem you're trying to solve and why you're the best one to solve it.* Why is your cause so crucial and compelling that it must be addressed now? Did something happen recently in the news or in your organization? Are you seeing a trend that will only get worse over time if it's not dealt with now? Why should your organization be the one to address it?
- *Highlight your organization's capacity, effectiveness, and professionalism.* You want to impress your potential donors. Convince them that you know what you're talking about and will be effective carrying out your work.
- *Point out what makes you unique.* How is your organization special? Perhaps you're working in an area that has been neglected, taking a new approach to an age-old problem, or playing a novel role in a collaborative effort. Is your organization a leader, the only one of its kind, or the go-to organization for a specific issue?

- *Present the proposed solution.* Which specific services, programs, and processes will you use to tackle the problem? Give specific details and include why you chose that path.
- *Describe why your organization is a good investment.* The funder is looking for a solid social return in exchange for giving you money or resources. Explain how you'll make the most of the donation.

Review these points with your team and encourage discussion. Make an effort to see things from your potential donor's perspective and at the very least, be sure you're able to answer the following likely questions:

- How does your organization's work affect my life?
- How exactly will my money be used? How much will be for the cause? For administrative overhead?
- How much say do I have in how the funds are used?
- What has the impact been of past investments?
- Who else is already funding your work?
- When can I expect to see results from the project I'm funding?
- How will my donation be recognized?

Once you have a good sense of your donor's perspective and the main points you'd like to highlight, type up a draft of your pitch and then turn to Exercise 22.1 to help you refine it. If you're having trouble figuring out what to prioritize, read "Perfect Your Pitch" at the beginning of Chapter 24.

Tip It's helpful to have pitches of various lengths, so that you can tailor your pitch to the situation. Create the following versions of your pitch: one sentence, one minute, and five minutes.

Exercise 22.1 Improve Your Pitch

Give your pitch to a friend or advisor whose feedback you trust will be honest and constructive. Ask him or her to evaluate your pitch as a prospective funder. Provide your evaluator with a feedback sheet like the one below. After reviewing the comments, take another crack at revising your pitch and then repeat the process, first with the same evaluator, and then with another.

What worked well?

What could use improvement?

How do you feel after reading the piece?

Other suggestions for improvement:

Illustrate with Examples

The most successful fundraisers and pitches feature true stories that illustrate the impact their organization makes and how their work has improved people's lives. Show your donors how additional money will be put to good use. Don't be afraid to incorporate pictures, videos, testimonials, and guest speakers as well.

Gather Your Paperwork

Keep all critical documents in one place and keep them up-to-date. This includes your tax forms, income and expense records, budgets, receipts, list of board members, signed agreements, and so on. If you have an Internal Revenue Service designation (e.g., if you are a tax-exempt 501(c)(3)), these papers should also be kept close at hand. You may need to produce these records for potential donors and you'll definitely need to reference them when applying for grants.

Plan, Plan, Plan

Planning a fundraising event or campaign should start weeks to months in advance. Solid preparation will also help you cope with any difficulties that arise. For hints on scheduling fundraising efforts, see Chapter 21: What Works in Goals and Planning.

Ask!

If you want something, you have to ask for it. Make your needs known. Clearly identify the purpose of your work, demonstrate the need, and then make your specific request. If the individual says no, thank him or her for considering your proposal and move on.

Express Gratitude

When you receive any type of funding, always send a short thank-you note, make a follow-up phone call, or mention the contribution on your website or in your next newsletter. If you can, share a success story that the funding helped make happen. Demonstrating gratitude empowers both the donor and the recipient. By thanking your donor, you acknowledge their critically important role in your work. You also build additional goodwill, increasing the likelihood the donor or funder will say "yes" when you next ask them for support.

Solicit Donations

Donations, contributions, or gifts all mean the same thing: resources. In the traditional sense, these resources tend to take the form of money, products, services, or facilities. However, other resources that may be donated include time, expertise, contacts, and advice. Donors may be individuals, community groups, corporations, or any number of other types of organizations. Most donations come with no strings attached, but some may be earmarked for specific purposes.

Individual Donors

Individual donations can be solicited from anyone and everyone—your family, friends, friends of friends, and even people you have no connection to whatsoever. However, before approaching individuals you don't know, try to determine if you have any shared interests that might help you tailor your pitch. This isn't possible in many settings, but in some cases, you might be able to do a quick Google search prior to meeting with a potential new donor. If you can learn a bit more about the things they care about, you can better demonstrate how your group's goals match the potential donor's values.

Business Donors

When approaching businesses, while you might at first be tempted to approach large, wealthy corporations, your first stop should be small local businesses. If your group shares a home base with the business, and especially if your project is tackling a local problem, a local business will generally be more inclined to get on board. If you do hear a "no" when requesting a monetary donation, try another tack. Businesses are often willing to give in-kind donations, that is, goods and services such as food or meeting space. Sometimes you can establish a partnership with a business that will donate a percentage of its earnings to your project (this is often called "cause marketing"). For example, a local restaurant might donate 10% of the proceeds from dinners served on Thursday nights, or even a single Thursday night, to your organization.

To partner with a business, emphasize how the goals of the business and your group intersect. Often businesses are willing to sponsor entire projects, programs, or events if you can show that the relationship will be mutually beneficial. Explain how you will publicly acknowledge their patronage to help them gain a bit of additional advertising and a lot of positive press. The sponsorship benefits you offer should scale up with increasing amounts of support for your group. For example, you could put the company logo on your group's promotional material in exchange for sponsorship of a single project. If a business sponsors two projects, offer to put the company's contact information on your group website or include their name in a speech you're giving. Be creative!

So what do donors get from this interaction? Remember that fundraising is a two-way street, benefitting both your group and the donor. In addition to the warm, fuzzy feeling of helping a good cause, donors may qualify for a tax write-off if your group is a tax-exempt organization (see Chapter 39 for more information on applying for tax-exempt status). In addition, businesses that donate to your cause may experience a financial benefit from the positive press your group can offer. Publicly supporting a good cause (particularly a local one) may engender goodwill in the community, which in turn may translate into increased sales. For example, some local sports leagues are sponsored by local businesses. Such teams are often named after a particularly supportive business or feature the business's logo on their T-shirts. Parents and passersby who see the logo on the shirts of the children may take note of the business's benefaction and make a point to frequent that business in the future.

Sejal: While serving on the Mayoral Youth Commission, I organized a Leadership Conference, an event involving several hundred students from local school districts. To cut costs, I contacted a few restaurants to ask if they could subsidize or provide free food for the participants. I also asked local stores if they could donate raffle prizes. Before calling these local businesses, I drafted a quick description of the conference and the benefits of a corporate sponsorship, which I used in my phone conversations. Several of the store managers (this is crucial—I always requested to speak to the manager) were eager to support a community event geared toward students. Within a matter of weeks, I'd secured enough meals for all conference participants and had gift certificates, coupons, and other goodies for raffles. Not every business was willing to help and a few franchise stores redirected me to the national office, which often manages sponsorship requests. However, even at the national level, I was able to secure extra donations by following up with voicemails, e-mails, and snail mail.

Write an Effective Fundraising Letter

Convincing potential donors to open their hearts (and pocketbooks) can be as simple as sending a well-crafted, polite request by mail or e-mail.

However, because individuals and companies receive funding requests all the time, it's critical that any letter you write be as persuasive and appealing as possible in as few words as possible. Strive to personalize the request to your potential donor whenever you are able to do so. Use the guidelines below and the example provided to help you craft an effective fundraising letter of your own:

- *Clearly identify your group, yourself, and your role.* Sound official.
- *In one or two sentences, explain the purpose of your project or initiative.* Briefly explain how it's relevant to the individual, company, or community.
- *Be specific.* How will you use the contribution to make an impact in your community?
- *Point out the tangible and intangible benefits to your reader.* If an individual or business makes a donation, what can they expect? This might be a membership, public recognition, regular newsletter, or simply the satisfaction of making a difference.
- *Cite a compelling statistic or two.* Is there a credible statistic you've heard recently about your work or the larger field that is particularly thought-provoking or persuasive? If it's easy to understand (without too much background) and makes a point about your work, use it.
- *Humanize the problem with personal anecdotes.* To help your readers experience your cause on an emotional level, introduce them to the people behind your statistics. Illustrate how the problem has affected a particular person or group of people with a powerful picture or story.
- *List current donors.* Mention the individuals, foundations, or corporations that already support you in the manner you're asking of your reader. Testimonials from previous or current donors can go a long way to reassure the reader that their donation will be effective.
- *Personalize your request.* Your letter should have a personal, conversational tone. Try to include at least one line at the beginning or end of the letter to make it clear you're not sending a form letter—for example, "On a personal note, I read about your company's recent partnership with our town's local farmers and was inspired to purchase more local food," or, "Our mutual friend Adam McArthur advised me to reach out to you because of your prior philanthropic commitment to local orchestras."

Sejal: When sending out fundraising letters for my organization, Girls Helping Girls, I include an explanation of exactly how a potential donation could be used. I've found that it encourages more donations when giving a range of dollar amounts so that donors see how even $25 can make an impact. For my project raising funds to build a library for girls, I added this description at the end of the fundraising letter:

$8,500 will fund the building of a library and required infrastructure

$500 can help provide a nutritious lunch program for the girls

$450 can provide 1,000 books to the girls

$150 can sponsor one girl's education for one year in India

$50 can sponsor one girl's education for one year in Africa

$25 can help purchase classroom supplies

Host a Memorable Fundraiser

Fundraising events are a great way to bring together your team and your supporters to earn a relatively large amount of money in a short amount of time. In addition, fundraisers increase your group's visibility in the community and raise awareness of your cause. They give you the freedom to engage your target donors and present your case in whatever setting you might like. Here are 10 ideas for fundraising events, just to get you started.

Note Many fundraising events require money to produce, so look for ways to minimize the cost of throwing the event and maximize potential donations.

1. Hold a bake sale in an area with heavy foot traffic.
2. Organize a benefit concert featuring local artists and bands willing to donate their time.
3. Throw a bash for your organization's birthday, and ask guests to bring donations for your project.
4. Host a movie night, and feature a film that's related to your project.
5. Organize an online auction that features continuously rotating items. Ask board members and friends to provide initial auction items.

6. If you have a product to sell, register for vendor tables at popular conferences and events, or try neighborhood gathering spots. Encourage your supporters to stop by.
7. Hold a "phantom event": a scheduled nonevent that asks attendees to donate the money they would have spent if the event were real.
8. Hold a 50–50 raffle in which proceeds are split evenly between the winner and your organization.
9. Organize a walk-a-thon or dance-a-thon.
10. Hold a letter-writing campaign within your organization to solicit either in-kind or monetary donations from individuals, community groups, or companies. Reward the person whose letters raised the most money with a prize. Use their letters as templates for future letter-writing campaigns.

A Primer on Venture Capital

Ernestine Fu is a social entrepreneur, author, and venture capitalist. She became Silicon Valley's youngest venture capitalist at the age of 19 when she sourced and funded her first deal within two months of joining Alsop Louie Partners. An engineering student at Stanford, she is currently coauthoring *What You Can Do for Your Country* with the former dean of Stanford Law School, Thomas Ehrlich. We interviewed Ernestine to get a better sense of what funders are looking for when evaluating your proposal.

Why would a social entrepreneur seek venture capital funding?

Ernestine: If you're an entrepreneur in need of significant funds to build your socially conscious business (generally at least $1 to $5 million) but are deemed too risky to be financed by commercial banks like Bank of America or insurance companies like Prudential, then consider venture capital (VC) funding. Unlike donations, grants, or fellowships, VC funding is not a gift: it's an investment. VCs use funds from wealthy third-party investors, known as limited partners (LPs), to finance entrepreneurs. In working with LPs, VCs need to maximize the return on their investments. Thus, VCs invest in relatively high-risk businesses in exchange for an equity stake in the company. This means that when the businesses succeed, the VCs and LPs do, as well.

Why would you want to give up part of the ownership of your business?

Ernestine: Entrepreneurs give up ownership in order to develop their businesses rapidly and become leaders in their respective industries. VC funding is not a gift in the usual sense; it's a *smart* gift. VCs help businesses scale by transforming small start-ups with fewer than a dozen employees, to large organizations with thousands of employees around the world. Some entrepreneurs worry that "giving up ownership" to VCs also means giving up control. However, VCs don't want to run your company; they simply want your company to run well. As long as you run the company well, you can stay in control.

What are some of the nonfinancial benefits of VC funding?

Ernestine: Beyond financial backing, VCs can provide mentorship and critical industry contacts. Although there's no set formula for building a successful company, most successful start-ups in each industry demonstrate similar basic principles and general patterns: start with the right team, develop the right product, and build momentum despite changing markets. The right team has complementary skills and an ability to attract great talent. The right product does the job effectively and efficiently, while delighting users through an elegant customer experience. The markets change due to new technology, natural disasters, government policies, and, more frequently, changing customer needs.

As you build your organization, you will inevitably encounter problems. These problems might include employees fighting with one another, customers complaining about your product, and competitors surpassing you. That's where the experience and insight of your VC mentors are invaluable. I like to tell entrepreneurs, "Good entrepreneurs respond intelligently to changes in the environment. Great entrepreneurs anticipate changes in the environment and adapt proactively before they need to." As a mentor, I try to be an entrepreneur's best friend during challenging times, helping to understand and work through problems. But when things are going well, I like to challenge entrepreneurs to outperform expectations.

In addition to mentorship, contacts are important because the potential and success of an enterprise often depend on its ability to recruit top-notch employees. As a growing company adds new services and the need for talent becomes more complex, VCs can tap into their networks to help entrepreneurs recruit talent.

Are there any special considerations socially conscious companies should keep in mind when applying for VC funding?

Ernestine: From alternative energy sources to socially responsible consumer products, socially conscious companies are funded by VCs. However, socially-minded companies require different objectives for assessment. Social enterprises are a hybrid between for-profit corporations and traditional nonprofits. There are many ways you can make money and do good. The Corporations Code created two new types of business entities in California, effective as of January 2012: the flexible purpose corporation and the benefit corporation.?? Both of these subtypes of traditional business organizations allow entrepreneurs to strive not only for economic profit but also social welfare objectives.

These two factors can be measured through financial return on investment and social return on investment. Examples of the latter might include a reduction of carbon emissions, an increase in the number of people who have access to clean water, or a decline in the number of malnourished children in third-world countries. When raising funds, socially conscious start-ups need to consider how to provide both an attractive return to investors and solutions to social issues.

What are the three most important things venture capitalists look for when evaluating a team to invest in?

Ernestine: All venture capitalists look at talent. Does this person have a track record of success? Does this person have the foundational knowledge to build this business?

The first deal I sourced for Alsop Louie Partners was a search and analytics platform, Jetlore, with a social media search engine product called Qwhisper. The seven-person team led by two Stanford PhD students had applied for patents, written award-winning papers, and presented at numerous renowned conferences.

Beyond talent, the founders of Qwhisper were also passionate, flexible, and optimistic, the three key traits I look for when evaluating a team to invest in. Passion drives teams to make vision a reality, even when things get rough. Flexibility allows teams to be prepared to change plans quickly and adapt to changing markets. Optimism allows teams to think big, have the strength to endure the hardships associated with starting a business, and inspire employees, customers, and investors during tough times.

What makes a start-up pitch stand out?

Ernestine: Humility. Humility magnifies all other positive attributes. While venture capitalists love to invest in big ideas with big markets, exaggeration and overconfidence can hurt rather than help entrepreneurs. People who display authentic humility tend to wield more respect and influence than those who don't.

What are the three most common mistakes young social entrepreneurs make when pitching to investors?

Ernestine: The biggest mistakes aren't generational. Regardless of age, common mistakes I see when entrepreneurs pitch to investors are poor communication, exaggeration, and poor self-assessment. First, even the greatest idea may become the worst pitch if you can't communicate it clearly. Hone your communication skills so that you master the "60-second elevator pitch" and produce well-written, concise documents. Second, don't exaggerate your opportunity because this suggests ignorance and arrogance. Rather than claim a giant market, clearly identify your target customers and partners. And third, no team is perfect, so be honest in your self-assessment. Be ready to identify weaknesses in your team and product, and ask for help from investors to strengthen your company.

Apply for Grants

A grant is a monetary award given by a foundation, corporation, or government agency to support a specific project or organization. Typically, grants support new initiatives or novel programs that run for a defined time period; they are less likely to support ongoing operating costs or administrative overhead.

To receive a grant, you must describe your project or organization, as well as your plans for the requested grant money, in a written proposal. While writing a grant can be a lot of work, try to approach the task as an opportunity to reflect on the current state and envisioned future of your organization. What follows is a practical guide to the grant-writing process.

Step 1: Identify Appropriate Grants

The individuals and institutions who provide the funding for a grant usually have a very clear idea of the types of organizations or social problems they want to fund (e.g., funding projects led only by students or organizations working to tackle elder abuse). Identifying the right grants for your group is thus a matter of ensuring your group's mission and proposed project align with the specific criteria set out by the grant maker. For example, a grant may only fund projects spearheaded by youth under the age of 25 or may only support organizations that target rural areas.

This means that you'll need to do some research to find the right grants for you. The following websites are great places to get started:

- Grants.gov—Search an up-to-date database of federal grants and submit your applications through the same site.
- Catalog of Federal Domestic Assistance (CFDA) (www.cfda.gov)—The CFDA, issued annually and updated continuously on the Web, describes some 1600 federal grants and nonfinancial assistance programs.
- USASpending.gov—Search this site to find out what grants have already been awarded to groups in your area. Knowing who in your area has been funded can help identify other groups that you might contact for a potential partnership or to ask for their advice when applying for your own grants.
- The Foundation Center (www.foundationcenter.org)—You'll find a comprehensive database of private grants as well as free tutorials and classes on grant writing and the application process.
- The Grantsmanship Center (www.tgci.com/funding)—Click on the state map to find links to information about your state's local funding sources.

Types of Grants

Grant money comes in two basic flavors: public or private.

Public grants are awarded by government agencies and departments at the federal, state, and local levels. They are the primary source of support for domestic nonprofit social, health, educational, and cultural programs.

Federal grants: There are more than 1,000 grant programs that give away some $400 billion every year. However, the aims and objectives of these grants are determined by legislation and, therefore, can vary based on who is in office and how the economy is faring. Government agencies provide detailed information on grants they offer, qualifying guidelines, and application procedures on their websites.

State and local grants: Like federal grants, the distribution of grant funds at the state and local government levels varies with the political and economic climate. However, these smaller grants may be less competitive than those at the federal level.

Private grants are awarded by foundations, community groups, direct-giving programs of for-profit corporations, businesses, and, of course, individual donors.

Step 2: Learn about the Grant Makers

Once you've identified appropriate grants, spend time learning about the grant-making institutions that are sponsoring them. With this knowledge, you'll be better able to explain why your proposed project is compatible with their missions and goals. To learn about the grant makers:

- Read their publications
- Comb through their websites
- Go over their grant guidelines closely
- Find out what projects they've supported previously
- Call or e-mail to clarify any questions you might have

Dalya: In my role as Founder of Writing for Community Success, I've learned that knowing your audience is vital. The people who first read your grant proposal are likely professionals in the field of grant making.

- They probably know significant background information about your issue but may be unfamiliar with your organization's particular slant or niche.
- They're time-pressed and prefer succinct answers to their questions.
- They want to be inspired by your vision.
- They're experienced and frequently talk to each other (so be honest and upfront).

Step 3: Understand the Application Process

Before beginning, learn about the grant application process generally. Although there are many different types of grants, there are some standard procedures that you'll need to know. Explore grant-writing tutorials and explanations online. And pay attention to deadlines!

Step 4: Make Sure You Meet the Eligibility Criteria

Double-check the specific grant's eligibility requirements to be sure your group qualifies. For example, your group might be required to involve or benefit people in a certain city or already have nonprofit status. If you don't qualify, move on.

Step 5: Complete the Application

When you're writing a grant application, identify the problem you want to address, outline a detailed project plan, describe the expected impact, explain how that impact will be measured, and discuss your plans for long-term project sustainability.

Step 6: Review, Review, Review!

Review the application thoroughly. Have you answered all of the questions? Have you provided all the required forms and supplemental materials? Have you adhered to word and page limits and checked your spelling and grammar? Have a few additional sets of eyes read your application after reviewing the grant guidelines.

Step 7: Stay Optimistic!

> *Ravneet*: Don't be discouraged by rejections. When I've been rejected for a grant, I find out who received the grant and try to learn from their application. Don't hesitate to ask for feedback. In my experience, some grant makers are willing to go over your proposal with you and explain why you weren't funded. Knowing why they decided not to fund us has given us valuable insight for writing subsequent, winning proposals.

Grants Checklist

Review

- General application instructions
- Formatting guidelines (required content, length, spacing)
- Submission deadlines

Special considerations

- Key points to emphasize
- Terms you need to research or double-check before including them in the proposal
- Supplemental documents for submission (tax forms, compliance statements)

Deadlines for yourself

- Completing background research and organizing any resources you'll need for the proposal
- Writing the first draft
- Making revisions
- Tracking down supplemental documents

Finishing touches

- Checking that all references are correct
- Double-checking the grant requirements to be sure you've included all necessary information and forms
- Having a team member double-check the proposal

Anatomy of a Grant Application

Grant applications typically include the following sections, though they often have their own variations.

Letter of Inquiry

Some grant applications begin with a prescreening process in the form of a brief letter of inquiry (or letter of intent). The letter is an opportunity to summarize clearly and succinctly your group's mission, the purpose of the project for which you are requesting funding, and the project's relevance to the specific grant maker. Grant makers read these letters in order to screen out projects that don't meet the grant criteria. This practice saves your organization the time and effort required to assemble a full grant proposal in the event your objectives don't quite match those of the grant maker. If a letter of inquiry is required, the grant maker will note that on its website and application materials. (See the LOI Components and Sample Letter of Inquiry.)

LOI Components

First Paragraph

- State who you are: organization name, project title, mission of project
- Ask for the gift: specifically mention requested amount
- Essential what-where-when: what you want to do, geographic location, time period of project, length of requested support

Paragraph 2

- Provide an overview of your organization: mission statement, goals, history, and accomplishments

Paragraphs 3–4

- State the problem and need.
- What will you do with the money? Explain exactly how you intend to use the funds requested.
- If you already have outside support for your project, detail those contributions and explain how this grant would complement existing funding.

Last Paragraph

- Why should the funder consider you? Show that you know about the funding organization, its mission, the intent of the specific grant, etc.
- Always express your appreciation for the opportunity.

Sample Letter of Inquiry

Save the Sea Bass
1234 Nearthewater Road
Smalltown, WA, USA

Ms. Generous Grantor
Environmental Foundation
ABC Inland Street
Major City, NY, USA

Dear Ms. Generous Grantor,

I am writing to inquire about submitting a proposal for Save the Sea Bass for $10,000 to help produce a documentary about the plight of the endangered Sea Bass (aka Patagonia tooth fish).

Save the Sea Bass is a 501(c)(3) nonprofit organization founded in 2010, the same year the Sea Bass was added to Greenpeace International's "red list" of endangered species. Since its inception, Save the Sea Bass has conducted over 300 educational seminars about overfishing and its devastation to the Sea Bass populations of the Pacific Northwest. Of the over 30,000 that have attended Save the Sea Bass seminars, nearly one-third or 8,613 have been motivated enough to write letters to local and international governments requesting legislative action to, well, *save* the Sea Bass. Save the Sea Bass Board members have spoken before governmental bodies and Congress half a dozen times and established themselves as the premier organization for Sea Bass conservation by speaking before the United Nations General Assembly in favor of stricter worldwide quotas for Sea Bass fishing.

Now, Save the Sea Bass wants to speak to a wide audience as the recognized authority it is by producing a documentary film. Save the Sea Bass has already secured time with PBS and the National Geographic Channel to air the final product at least 3 times in the regular television season. The anticipated audience is intended to be some 400,000 people during each airing, an exponential increase in the size of audience Save the Sea Bass has reached through its existing efforts.

Save the Sea Bass believes our goals with this project are very much aligned with your organization's "mission to help create quality educational documentary features." Our organization has already secured financial support for this project from the Environmental Media Fund and Film for Action as well as the Ocean Foundation and we hope you'll consider joining these funders in support of the production of our documentary feature.

Thank you for taking the time to read this letter. Please feel free to contact me directly at sally@savetheseabass.org should you have any questions about Save the Sea Bass or our documentary project. I look forward to hearing from you and submitting a full proposal at your request.

Sincerely,
Sally Sherlock
CEO, Save the Sea Bass

Title Page

Make a good impression with your title and the title page of your grant proposal. The title should reference the central idea or project you would like funded. Include basic contact information for your organization, including an e-mail address and phone number.

Abstract or Executive Summary

An abstract or executive summary is a brief summary of the major components of your grant proposal and includes: the purpose, needs, procedures, and evaluation sections. A grant reviewer uses the abstract to determine if the rest of the proposal is worth reading.

An abstract explains the basics of your proposal:

- *Problem:* What's the problem you're addressing or the need you'll fulfill? Why does the situation exist (root causes)? Use any facts and figures you can find that document the specific issue in your region.
- *Value:* Why should the grant maker care about this problem? What's at stake? To be blunt, "So what?"
- *Results:* What are you aiming to do to solve the problem? What would success look like?
- *Solution:* What's your specific plan of action? Include the necessary steps or components, time frame, and means of evaluation.

- *Qualifications:* How is your organization uniquely suited to the task?
- *Finances:* Why does your group need funding? How much does it need? What other sources of funding do you already have or plan to seek?

Organizational Description

Introduce your group. Include the organization's full name, location, purpose, history, target population (including demographics), services provided, major successes, and number of people served and how they've benefited.

Eventually you'll need to update this section to reflect growth or new projects you've undertaken. If you're collaborating with another organization, each of the groups requesting funding should be described separately before detailing your joint efforts.

Statement of Purpose

The statement of purpose is a description of the problems that your group seeks to resolve, both generally (for example, poverty) and specifically (for example, neighborhood childhood hunger).

Need Statement

The need statement is where you convince the grantor of the importance of the problem, and the potential impact your proposed plan can make. Give the readers the impetus to take action immediately by providing facts and figures that support your arguments. The more evidence you provide, the better.

Think of yourself as a prosecutor, pleading your case to the jury (in this case, the grant maker). Make a compelling argument backed by factual evidence that ensures the jury's verdict will be in your favor. Let's say you need money to expand an after-school program for children in high-risk neighborhoods. Assume your argument is that you need to expand the program to give more children a productive after-school environment, which, you believe, will help them stay out of trouble. Do you have any statistics that show the benefits of such after-school programs? Are participants less likely to join gangs, do drugs, or drop out of school? Even better, do you have any statistics that show the benefits of your own program, for example, a 5% increase in students attending two- or four-year colleges? How likely are your students to stay in school when compared with the average student? Quantifiable results make a strong case.

Statistics describing a population's need anchor a need statement. They are among the most memorable aspects of a grant proposal to a reviewer. However, as powerful as numbers are, the unquantifiable personal stories, perspectives, and quotations of real people helped by your work are oftentimes the most powerful evidence. What changes did they see happen, and why are those changes so important to them? If written with the right emphasis, personal stories are just as motivating to the reviewer as statistics.

Try to show why the problem you're addressing is more urgent or important now than ever before. Moreover, explain why you are approaching this grantor—why the outcomes your organization will achieve are particularly important to the grantor and why your organization is well qualified to attempt to resolve this issue.

Program Description

A program description typically includes four subsections:

- Goals and objectives
- Methodology or plan of action
- Staffing
- Evaluation

Goals and Objectives

In the goals and objectives section, discuss the anticipated results of carrying out your project. Goals are typically broad statements about how you hope to improve the situation by addressing the problem; for example, "We aim to improve the reading skills of elementary school students in the community."

Objectives focus on single actions or steps that are taken along the way to achieving goals; for example, "Objective 1 is to provide academic support for up to 50 students failing English by instituting an after-school peer tutoring program in the fall semester." Objectives should be more specific in terms of focus and time than goals, and they should have MERITS: mission driven, evidence based, realistic based on resources, impactful and innovative, tangible and trackable, and specific (see Chapter 21 for more details). A well-written objective should include the estimated number of people you will serve and the specific short-term change that you expect will result as a measurable output.

Your goals and objectives should tie into your need statement. If they don't, this suggests that you or your organization may not know the community, the problem, or the funder as well as you think you do. When writing the objectives, think about indicators and features of the problem and its circumstances that you can measure, so you will know if you've succeeded.

Be realistic. Objectives need to be achievable within the grant period (usually one year). You should show that you've considered relevant factors, such as location, community-specific features, any bureaucracy you may have to deal with, and your own organizational capacities.

Methodology or Plan of Action

Here you explicitly identify the methods you'll use to carry out your proposed activities and achieve the goals outlined in your statement of purpose. The methodology or plan of action addresses three fundamental questions:

How: Provide a detailed description of all activities that links specific steps in your method to the objectives you've already specified.

When: Present tasks as a chronological time line, with clear deadlines attached to critical project milestones or checkpoints that confirm progress toward your goal.

Why: Explain why you chose the methods you did by citing recent research or experience.

Finally, identify and describe any potential problems you may encounter. This attention shows you've thought about these potential challenges and are prepared to address them. Describe contingency plans should these problems arise.

Staffing

Identify the individuals responsible for implementing and managing your project, both paid and volunteer staff. Include two or three sentences about each person that explain how the people you've selected suit their roles.

Evaluation

An evaluation plan should include your areas of evaluation, how you'll assess them, and what you expect to learn. It will determine if your project met its goals and objectives as well as identify areas for improvement.

Once you're awarded a grant, some grantors evaluate your progress themselves or employ external auditors to receive an unbiased assessment of your group's work. However, you'll be expected to do your own assessment as well, using the standards set in your evaluation plan.

Two major types of evaluation are quantitative (counting numbers) and qualitative (reviewing experiences). Data gathered through quantitative methods (surveys, questionnaires, administrative records) can be analyzed with statistics and then represented using charts, tables, and graphs. Let's say you're starting a mentoring program for at-risk students. You might argue that the positive influence of a mentor would result in mentees' earning better grades. To measure this, you could collect copies of the mentees' report cards at the start of the program and then again at the end of semester and end of the year. Any improvements could be quantified with a number (for example, "We found a 15% increase in average grades of students in the program, compared to students not in the program who had a 5% increase").

Qualitative data are expressed in terms of themes, ideas, events, personalities, and histories. You can gather these data through observation, interviews, and document analysis. For example, you might expect to see an increase in the confidence levels of mentees who've been in the program for a few months or more. You could assess this by interviewing the students' teachers to see if they've noticed any changes in the mentees' behavior since entering the program.

Depending on what you measure, you'll also need to indicate when you'll be doing the measuring and how often. You may also need to evaluate progress according to the funder's reporting requirements. For more about measuring and evaluating your work, see Chapter 8.

You don't actually have to be 100% successful in producing your projected results 100% of the time. While we want success, sometimes what we learn from mistakes can be even more valuable! Sometimes unexpected results actually teach much more than the results we initially sought. Funders know that and are interested in organizations that are constantly learning. They rely on us to report our findings regardless of whether we accurately predicted what they would be. They especially like to fund organizations that are actively addressing their weaknesses, finding new and better pathways to success. Finally, always make a point to share those pathways with your colleagues. See Chapter 17 for more on how to share what works.

Budget

The budget is your account of how your organization plans to spend its money. A well-thought-out budget is comprehensive, accounting for all expenses you expect to incur. It should show your grant and nongrant income sources (both committed and pending), including a separate column for donations that are not money (referred to as "in-kind donations"). This gives the funder a sense of how its grant will be part of your overall financial plan.

The budget needs to be realistic and should tie closely with the rest of your proposal. This financial snapshot is often one of the first parts of a proposal that a funder will read, and it may be the most carefully scrutinized.

The budget can actually be one of the easier parts of the grant proposal. The plan of action or methodology section should ideally explain the who, when, and where of your project. Your budget is essentially a reiteration of this same information but with dollar amounts specified.

Your budget should differentiate between personnel expenses (salaries and benefits) and nonpersonnel expenses (rent or mortgage, utilities, maintenance, taxes, fundraising expenses, travel, postage, equipment costs, supplies, and insurance). For specific project budgets, you'll need to separate out direct costs (people and materials that are devoted to the project) and indirect costs (administrative or overhead costs that the overall organization incurs so it can operate the specific project). Indirect costs are often listed as a percentage of the total grant request and should never total more than 15%. Some funders don't fund indirect costs, so be sure to check the grant guidelines for that information.

A budget narrative (that is, your justification) needs to accompany a budget and contains detailed descriptions for every item in the budget. The narrative can accompany your budget as one or two lines of notes following each line item in the budget table itself, or a detailed list with each item on the budget summary table referenced and explained in one or two paragraphs.

Conclusion

Your grant proposal should end with a brief conclusion that summarizes the proposal's main points and makes one last appeal for your project. Remember that a grant proposal is a piece of persuasive writing, not just a descriptive document about the work you want to do. It has to convincingly make two arguments in order to get the funder to give you money (1) that there's much needed work to be done that is uniquely relevant to the funder's mission and (2) that your organization is the best one to do the work. Your conclusion should explicitly state these arguments.

> **Tip** Before submitting your application, remember to proofread for errors, check the math in your budget summary, and make a copy of your submission to keep for your records.

Unless the application instructions indicate otherwise, your conclusion should also discuss your project's sustainability, or what will happen when the money you're requesting runs out. Share your plan for after the grant period, including cost projections for continuing operations or starting the next phase.

Overall, the idea is for your reviewer to finish your proposal with a sense of faith in your project and your organization's future.

After You Click Submit

Once you've submitted your proposal, reflect on your work and express gratitude for the experience. Regardless of whether the proposal is funded or not, preparing it is a valuable learning experience and you should thank those who helped you, including the funder. If your proposal is funded, fantastic! If not, you'll have the chance to ask for feedback in order to better prepare for your next grant application.

However, keep in mind that grants are just one type of vehicle for funding. Successful fundraising efforts are almost always multipronged, incorporating a number of different resource-raising strategies like direct-mail campaigns, fundraisers, income-earning partnerships with for-profits, and in some cases, venture capital. Moreover, successful fundraising is about much more than just resources. It's about raising a constituency in support of your mission. Donations and grants flow from the relationships you create and it is those relationships that ultimately give legitimacy and sustainability to your work.

Ravneet Kaur graduated from Stanford University. She founded the South Asian Community Health Project, which provides free cancer and cardiovascular screenings for underserved, uninsured immigrants in New York City through a partnership with New York University Medical School.

Sejal Hathi is a senior at Yale University. The founder of Girls Helping Girls and cofounder of global social enterprise girltank, she has also worked as advisor or ambassador for Ashoka's Youth Venture, UNICEF, the World Bank, State Farm Insurance, Youth Service America, and others, on gender-sensitive development and youth entrepreneurship.

Dalya Massachi, founder of Writing for Community Success, specializes in helping community-minded professionals advance their work through outstanding written materials. She serves as a writing trainer and coach, grantwriter, and editor. Her award-winning book is entitled *Writing to Make a Difference: Twenty-Five Powerful Techniques to Boost Your Community Impact.*

Chapter 23

What Works in Media and Marketing

You can have the greatest idea in the world, but if you can't promote and communicate it effectively, it might as well not exist.

Media is changing. We find ourselves in a time where both new and old media are morphing to fit our communication needs, and so we should approach media as mechanisms of mass communication: whether it's TV, radio, newspapers, Facebook, or Twitter, media answers this question: *How do I get my message out there?* Media is the way your voice or idea reaches other people. Your media strategy is all about creating, packaging, and delivering your message to be heard by as many people as possible.

This chapter shows you how to plan and execute your efforts in media and marketing.

Plan Your Media Strategy

Draft Your Campaign: Identify Your Audience and Goals

Maximize Resources

You have two critical resources: time and money. Having an abundance of one will offset a shortage of the other. Figure out what venues will offer you the highest return for your investment of each resource. For all forms of media, there are a few key universal metrics:

- *Reach*: the number of people receiving your message
- *Frequency*: the number of times an individual receives your message
- *Message*: what your audience hears
- *Noise*: all of the other marketing messages that an individual is receiving[1]

Develop Media Goals

What's your vision of the ideal media campaign? Getting 100 additional members? 5,000 "likes" on Facebook? $10,000 in donations? When you define your goals, think big. Look at what other similar organizations have done. Examine their Facebook pages, Twitter accounts, and news coverage. Aim to do even better than they did, perhaps setting a goal of 20% more raised than a similar organization or even your own group compared with last year.

Know Your Audience

Your goals must parallel your intended audience. Say you're looking to reach Internet-savvy teens. An online campaign would make more sense than a traditional print newspaper campaign which has an older user demographic. Tailor your media campaign and goals to the media consumption pattern of your intended audience. Keep your budget in mind. If you don't have enough money to spend on advertising, you can get your story out for free online.

Select Your Media Mix

Media mix is the combination of media (online, radio, television, etc.) you'll use. Will you be primarily an online viral video sensation? Do you want to launch simultaneously in the local newspapers and online? Remember that media consumption patterns are different for each audience; if you're targeting multiple demographics at the same time, using a media mix is particularly important.

Identify Your Audience

What characteristics describe your target group of interest? Young, urban, college educated? What kinds of media do they consume?

Research by looking at official statistics and speaking to members of your target audience and finding out what forms of media they consume and how.

With defined goals you will be better equipped to measure success.

Measure Success

After identifying your audience and media goals, set benchmarks for success. Aside from meeting your goals, there are some nuances of measuring media success that are essential but not necessarily intuitive.

Membership

The better measure of membership success than head count is the number of members who are engaged with your organization and are recruiting others. Measure membership in terms of enthusiastic active members.

Donations and Sales

The highest form of marketing success is in consumers' brand loyalty, where they have had such a positive experience interacting with your brand that they would happily return. This can be encouraged through special discounts or promotions for a user's next purchase. For example, you may be selling T-shirts and offer a deal that those who buy one get a discount for a future purchase. Loyal supporters or customers are the lifeblood of many businesses and nonprofits.

Develop Awareness

If you are working toward awareness, success can be gauged in a variety of ways. For social media, measuring success is quantitative: Facebook likes, Twitter followers, and YouTube views, for instance. For all other forms of media, a good gauge of your success for an awareness campaign is in brand recognition, which can be done through surveying your target demographic to see if they recognize your organization's name and cause.

Create a Memorable Message

Messages in the media need to be clear, crisp, and short. Like President Obama's 2008 campaign slogan of "Change We Can Believe In" and Pepsi's "For Those Who Think Young" catchphrase, consumer marketing is short, catchy, and aspirational. Catchphrases stick with consumers because they're crafted to strike the nerve of "Yeah, I want that!" and then the person associates that positive feeling with the brand, person, or idea every time he or she encounters it.

The catchphrase or buzzword should convey the mission of your organization, why what you're doing is important, and why others are joining in. A good example is the American Lung Association catchphrase "Fighting for Air,"[2]which demonstrates the mission (activism), the importance of it (air), and why others are joining in (everyone needs air).

Find out what messages organizations similar to yours are using. Then figure out a way to do it better and make it your own. Coupling it with an icon or image is very important: many people are visual learners and associate graphics with brands. Start brainstorming some buzzwords and catchphrases. If you have ideas about powerful images, go ahead and sketch them out.

Traditional and Social Media

Media can be divided into two camps: traditional and new. Traditional media are newspapers, radio, television, and magazines. They are generally about informing the audience. New media, mostly online, are about informing and *are* the audience. Examples are social media like Facebook and Twitter, websites, blogs, and online versions of traditional media like TV and newspapers (especially because user commenting is now possible in most every online interface). Understanding and leveraging the nuances of both types of media offer the greatest return on your media campaign investment.

The key to getting your message out in each of these formats is to understand how consumers use them. With so many competing media outlets vying for the same consumer attention, your message needs to stand out. Part of that is in crafting your message—simple, catchy messages work best—and the other part is using both traditional and new media together to build momentum surrounding your message. Ideally your campaign will be so exciting that it will self-perpetuate (go viral), with people posting links to your articles, YouTube videos, and website on their own.

Budget for Your Campaign

Most social and online media can be used for free, though if you do decide to pursue traditional forms of media, you will need to understand how advertising pricing works.

Traditional Media

The essential thing to understand about advertising is its monetization. The general metric for advertising is the *cost per mille* (CPM) or cost per thousand impressions. This is different for all media and is different within media outlets too. The more popular the TV show, newspaper, radio program, or magazine is, the higher the CPM it commands. Therefore, media campaigns, especially in working with traditional media, are expensive. Average CPMs vary across media. Mary Meeker, an analyst at Morgan Stanley, recently published approximate average CPMs across media as of 2010: broadcast TV, $28; magazine, $17; newspaper, $17; cable TV, $12; radio, $10; out-of-home (outdoor advertising), $5; and Internet, $2.[3]

If you do have funding and want to proceed with an advertising campaign that encompasses both new and old media, it helps to work on a traditional advertising campaign with an agent, agency, or someone who has experience in creating high-quality content. Because advertising in traditional media is usually used by well-established brands and companies, this chapter focuses on figuring out how to advertise for little to no cost through interviews and social media engagement.

The Internet

Internet advertising is often the most financially feasible way to advertise, for both businesses and nonprofits. What's unique to the Internet and social media is that you can promote your brand for free simply by being popular and engaged with your users. In addition, you can pay a little money to advertise on different websites through either display or banner advertisements by working directly with the websites of interest or with an advertising intermediary like Google's AdSense. Social media are an excellent way to engage users and promote your idea.

Become a Media Personality

Alert the Media and Submit Press Releases

In order to get into the media and generate buzz, one of the best ways is to start locally. The more local you are, the more likely it is that you can simply send an e-mail and the less need there is to create a press release. Let's say you're a college student and want the campus newspaper to run a story about your cause. One way to do it is to write a letter to the editor to be published in the opinion editorials (op-ed) section that mentions your cause (see a sample letter to the editor in Chapter 24). Or get your story in the newspaper as news. If you know reporters, you can e-mail them directly or ask for an introduction (in person or in an e-mail). When approaching a reporter, keep these guidelines in mind:

- *Reporters need news in order to write articles.* When composing your e-mail, stress the news factor of your cause. Is it the first campus organization of its kind? Did it just win an award? Emphasize why this is news and why people would want to know.
- *Sometimes a particular reporter won't take your story.* It's okay. Press on. Approach other reporters and see if someone else will. This works best with a personal connection from the inside out, but if you don't have one, try going from the outside in for press coverage. Approach multiple media outlets: newspapers, radio, magazines, and so on.
- *All press is good press.* Your story is a story with any media outlet that publishes it. Pursue every avenue for publicity.

If you can't approach local media outlets like campus newspapers and instead have to (or want to) directly approach larger newspapers and other media outlets in your area, create a press release. The purpose of a press release is to send various media outlets a summary of your news story along with contact information for a quote or follow-up information. Essentially it is a prewritten news article for media outlets to publish as soon as they see fit, if they see fit. Here are the key components:[4]

- Your contact information and the timing notation: for example, "FOR IMMEDIATE RELEASE."
- An action-oriented title and detailed subtitle.
- The body of the press release, limited to a few paragraphs, that tells your story in action words. This is the place to emphasize how exciting and newsworthy this story is.

Once the press release is written, e-mail it to the editors or reporters of all the media outlets you think would be appropriate: newspaper, magazine, TV, radio, online, etc. If no one contacts you, it may be that there is insufficient space for or interest in your story. It doesn't hurt to send a follow-up e-mail or call to remind them about you story, though be careful not to spam anyone. As with any relationship, be polite, professional, and respectful when dealing with the media.

If a media outlet runs your story, you are most likely going to be interviewed. In the following sections, we'll discuss how to talk to different media outlets to get your message heard.

Television Interviews

Being interviewed on television, especially live television, can be an exciting but nerve-wracking situation.

> *Mackenzie*: In college, I was interviewed on live national television for the *Today Show* and thought I was going to faint as I was walking on set! It was the biggest television interview I had ever done, and it was one of the best experiences of my life. It taught me the value of creating a short, simple message that is said slowly and with a smile.

- *Before speaking to a reporter, have your message ready.* Ask yourself, What is my message? What do I want people to hear the most?
- *Boil down that message, the most important thing to you, to a 10-second sound bite.* Frequently television interviews get cut short, and you get asked something like, "We only have a few seconds left. What is the most interesting part of your campaign?" Be prepared. Get your message out there in a clear, concise way that can be quoted or played on a 20-second clip.
- *Slow. Down. When. Speaking.* This is true for all forms of media, especially for television. Slow down, say your words deliberately, use expression in your face, and enunciate clearly.

> *Mackenzie*: For me, on the *Today Show*, it was most important to me that people heard about how significant continuing to work for a tobacco-free tomorrow is, not just because I am personally driven by my father's death from tobacco-related lung cancer but because it is a critical public health issue.

- *Smile.* Television is the mix of information with appearance, and being a happy, friendly person makes everything you do and say much more palatable.
- *Listen to the question before you start answering.* This helps the conversation flow and helps you organize your thoughts as you are speaking. If a reporter says to you, "What is the most rewarding part of what you do?" answer by saying, "The most rewarding part of what I do is work with disadvantaged children and youth and help ensure that they have a better future." That way, if your response is edited to a sound bite, the editor can pick the key part of your answer, and it sounds natural instead of your stumbling over your answer with something like, "Working with disadvantaged children. It's really cool." That gives the reporter and the news editors nothing to work with.

Fashion for Television

When being interviewed on television, dress as if you are going to a job interview, because that's essentially what this is: your job of being the spokesperson of your organization. This generally means business casual (for women, a suit or a dress; for men, a suit). Here are some style pointers:

Women

- *Suits*: They are timeless, classy, and stylish. Buy a suit that makes you walk with a little bit more confidence. The choice of pants versus skirt is yours, just make sure it fits you well.
- *Dresses*: Flattering, tasteful dresses look wonderful. Choose colors or prints that are smart and simple. Aim for a look that will pop on screen and make you feel great.
- *Shoes*: A proper business casual shoe is closed-toe, not too high, and not too flashy. Avoid flip-flops or sneakers.

- *Jewelry and accessories*: Jewelry for television can add some flair without being distracting. The famous designer Coco Chanel is credited as saying, "Before you leave the house, take one thing off,"[5]asaway to convey that understated elegance is the better way to go. As a rule, you have earrings, a necklace, and a pin: pick two.
- *Hair and makeup*: This is the most important part of your appearance because people will be looking at your face as they listen to you. Your hair and makeup should be neat, one step above your normal routine, and make you feel confident. For hair, a little bit of styling goes a long way. With makeup, aim for perfect skin and softly enhanced features. Wear at least a lip balm because when our lips are dry, we often subconsciously lick them and don't smile as much. Avoid shimmer or glitter anywhere. When you are finished, you should look like you but *just a little bit* better than usual.

Men

Guys should suit up. If you have facial hair, make sure it's tidy. Keep your hair simply styled. Generally, dressing in neutral colors like black or shades of blue is recommended, along with a corresponding tie.

- *Suit, shirt, and tie*: Easy shirt-tie color combinations are either contrasting colors (black and white) or colors in the same family (light blue and navy blue). Make sure you can tie your tie well; if not, ask for help.
- *Fit*: Your shirt should fit you well, and your pants should touch the top of your shoes but not the ground.
- *Socks*: Your socks will show when you sit down, and they should be a color that matches or is close to your pants.
- *Belt and shoes*: It's best to stay in the same color theme throughout your outfit, as in: black pants, black belt, and black shoes.

Print Interviews

When you are being interviewed for print, much of the same holds true as when being interviewed on television, except that you're able to take the time and choose your words carefully. If a photo will be taken for the article, the same dress rules apply to print as they do television. When being interviewed in print:

- *Have a sound bite ready of the exact message you want to convey.* Figure out the wording beforehand. Find a way to work that phrase into the interview, particularly early on. One of the worst things to say in an interview is "I'm not sure," or "I don't know" when you are asked about an important statistic or figure related to your work. Have examples and data on hand. If you don't know, you can say something like "I'm not familiar with that particular figure, but I do know that four out of five people . . . [insert new statistic here]." The point of the print interview is to give clear, concise, well-informed quotes that can easily be peppered into a story.
- *Choose your words carefully.* Generally during an interview, anything you say to a reporter may end up in a newspaper article, so take your time in replying. You are not on live TV. Figure out how you want to phrase your answer to the question, and be precise in your language. You may very well be quoted exactly, with every "um" or "uh" included (especially if the reporter is not crazy about you). Be deliberate and exact during a newspaper interview. Every word counts.
- *Never say "off the record."* Some reporters honor it, and some don't. The general rule is that if you are saying something to a reporter that is off the record, you probably shouldn't be saying it at all.

Some reporters will allow you to see the article before publication and approve all of the quotes and information in it, but others don't. Assume that you won't have the final word on the story, which is why it's incredibly important to be prepared, poised, and deliberate in your interview.

Radio Interviews

Radio interviews are often conducted in person or over the phone where you call in and talk to the radio host. Here are some tips for radio interviews:

- *Provide clear and concise messaging.* This is particularly salient on live radio because you get only a few seconds to speak in between radio host banter. Have your message boiled down to a one-sentence statement like "I founded the State University Cancer Organization to increase awareness regarding early detection of cancer so that fewer people would have to suffer from a disease that, if caught early, is very treatable." Bam. That's it. Try to tie every answer back to your main message.
- *Smile as you speak.* People hear it in your voice, and it makes a big difference on the impression you leave on listeners.
- *Say less, and say it slowly.* The key to a good radio interview is enunciation and simple messaging. No long stories or inside jokes here; you just want to get the message out.
- *Repeat your message in different ways throughout the interview.* It does more than help the message sink in for listeners; it also catches people up who tune in during your interview. Tie your message back to every answer you give, and you'll be golden.

Crisis Management

Here's some advice for dealing with controversial interviewers, mitigating bad press, and correcting marketing mistakes.

Deal with Difficult Interviewers

Although it's common sense not to accept interviews with people you know are going to be rude or will argue with you, sometimes it happens. Maybe you accepted an interview with someone, and moments into the interview you realize that this person is not on your side. Occasionally you will find yourself in this situation with a reporter who is grumpy or confrontational, asks you belittling questions, tries to get a reaction out of you, or tries to put you down. *The most important thing is not to lose your cool.* Often people who are trying to get a rise out of you are looking for a bad reaction because the negative reaction or controversy will pull in more readers and listeners.

Suppose you are advocating for animal rights and you're in a radio interview where the host says, "So you're advocating for animal rights, huh? Well I just love meat. I would kill it myself. Would you like a steak sandwich? I'll have my assistant get you one right away." Something inflammatory like that is intended to make you react defensively and lead to a debate. Resist. *Don't get into an argument.* The best response is to politely say something that brings the conversation back to your message—something like this: "I'm so glad we're jumping right into this topic. I know that vegetarianism isn't for everyone, but I'm hoping that even meat eaters will agree that things can be done to avoid the unnecessary excessive suffering of animals who give their lives for the meat on our dinner table. That's why I founded this group." It's important to stay positive and professional even in the ugliest of conversations. If you react negatively, the sound bite can be edited to make *you* look petty, confrontational, and extreme. Don't give your critics any ammunition.

Mitigate Bad Press

You no doubt will some time have an event, a show, or some sort of publicity that garners a bad review or a critical article. It's just part of marketing and media, so don't take it personally. Instead use it as a learning experience. If you are in charge of an organization that is criticized in the media, look at your critics' objections and figure out how to refine your message to take the focus off their message.

For example, if you start an organization dealing with hunger in America and a critical newspaper article attacks your cause using American obesity statistics, make sure that the next time you focus on food insecurity for low-income children in your next media push. Don't ignore your critics; use them as a barometer to see how clearly your message is coming through and if it's addressing the most pressing part of your cause.

You'll always have to deal with people who disagree with you and your approach to solving the problem. Just make sure that they are dissenting because you two genuinely disagree, not because your message is not properly being conveyed.

Correct Marketing Mistakes

Maybe you have given an interview and the next day you realize you've been misquoted, said the wrong thing, recited a statistic incorrectly, or something else that makes your stomach drop as you read it. *Don't panic.* Here are some ways to correct media mistakes:

- If the article is online or in print, call or e-mail immediately to have it corrected. Most media outlets will fix anything that is incorrectly published because it also reflects on them. For both your sake and that of the publisher's integrity, don't hesitate to offer a correction.

- If it was a television, radio, or other live interview, you can't go back in time to change it, but you can use other forms of media to correct the mistake and smooth it over for future interviews. Suppose you incorrectly cite a statistic in a television interview. You could use social media to acknowledge and correct your mistake or make sure that you recite the correct statistic in your next interview.

Nobody's perfect, but it's imperative to correct your mistakes when you have the opportunity.

Create an Online Brand Through Social Media

Online and social media are means to both inform and engage your audience. Social media focuses on a continuous influx of new content that is interactive and frequently updated. It gives users the opportunity to get involved in ways previously unavailable to supporters or customers.

Create a Website

One of the most critical parts of developing your brand through online media is creating a website. If you're a novice to website creation and don't know how to code, the best approach might be to find a friend or classmate who has experience in this area and will create the website for free or less money than if you approached a professional. If your contact won't do it for free, you can expect to pay at least $100 for the creation of a website.

For the design, the general layout should be organized and professional, especially for the home page. Figure 23.1 shows an example and contains several key components that every website should have:

> **Tip** Creating a logo is one of the most significant things you will do for your brand. If you have friends with experience or expertise in creating logos, reach out to them. Otherwise, you can design your logo with readily available logo design software. Avoid using clichés or clip art, and keep the design as clean as possible.

Logo. The logo is most often in the upper-left corner.

Ways to donate. For all nonprofits, fundraising is essential, so instructions about donating are visible and easy. Start-ups generally include a list of funders and major investors.

Figure 23.1. Create a Website

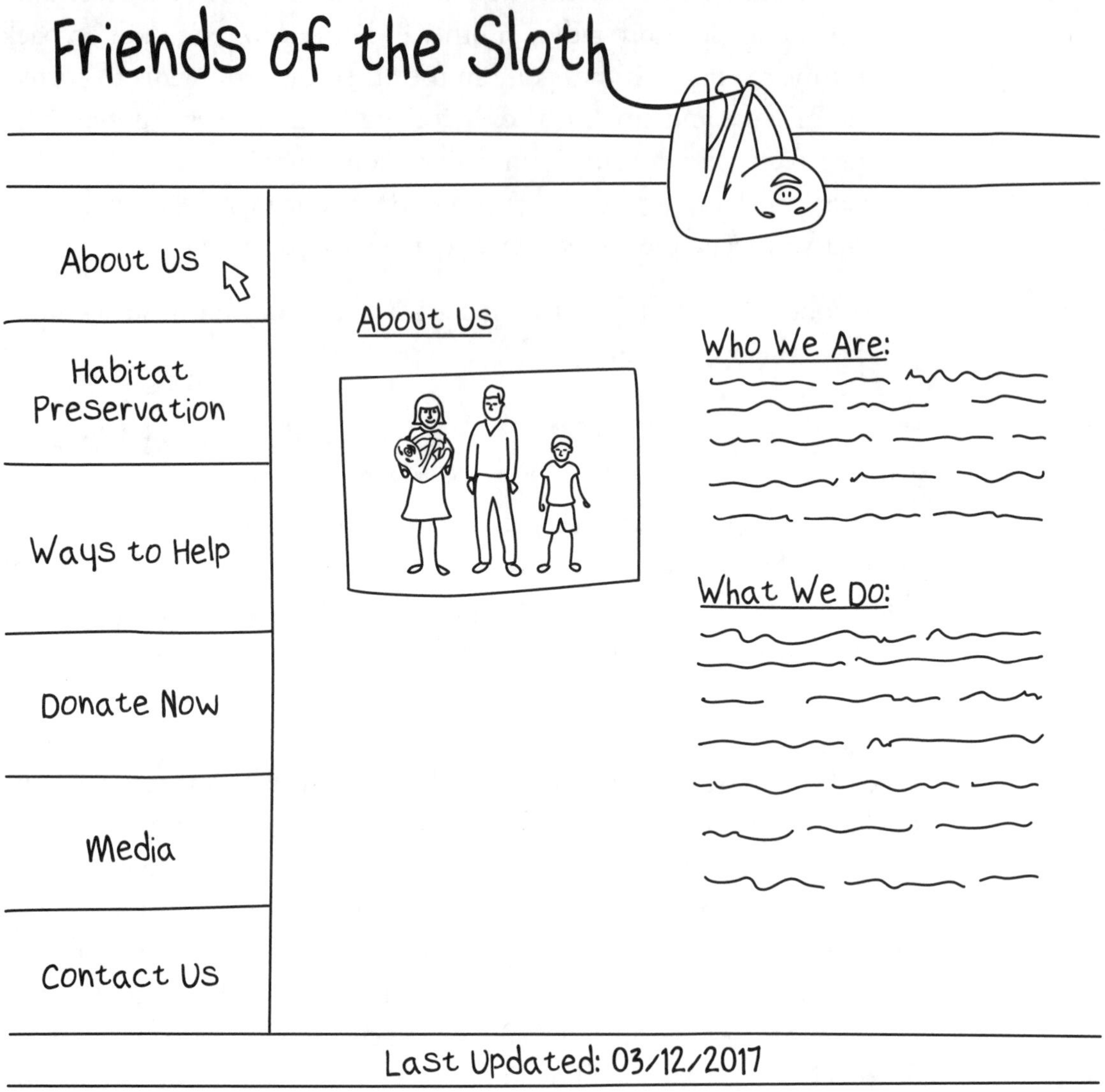

Communicative photo. Include a photo that conveys what your group does.

About us. This part of the website describes your mission and story.

Pictures and media. This is a place to showcase photos, events, and videos of your organization.

Contact us. This lists the best ways to contact you, as well as your social media links.

Those are the basic components, but you're free to add other tabs like "Get Involved," "Shop," or "Tell a Friend," depending on the media goals you outlined. Your website should be clean, neat, organized, and exactly as long and detailed as it needs to be.

First, choose and register a domain name. When thinking of your domain name, check out whois.net to see if someone else already owns the domain name you had in mind. If so, sometimes you can contact them and see if they are willing to sell it. Other times it is just better to select another domain name idea. There are two keys to registering a domain name: (1) finding a server that is in your price range (.com and .org domains generally cost $10 a year) and (2) creating a domain name that suits your organization's brand. Once you have selected a name, say, humanrightsaction.com, it's worth it to also register the .org and .net domains in order to make sure that your organization is the only one that people may stumble across with "humanrightsaction" in the address.

After choosing and registering your domain name, find a hosting platform on which to build your website. Website hosting platforms are where you can build and modify your website. Sometimes it's included in the domain name registration, other times you need to find the Web platform separately.

Next, design and build your website. Either build the website yourself or work with a Web developer to create it. Your website's design must be user friendly, as people will quickly get frustrated and leave your site if it is difficult to navigate, takes too long to use (use flash media sparingly), or is too text heavy.

Your website should be classic and timeless so it won't have to be updated constantly like a social media site (though when you do update your website, perhaps once every month or so, announce your update through your social media forms). In your design, use lots of pictures if possible. People find photos, especially photos of people, more engaging than clip art graphics.

If your organization is seeking donations, you can easily set up the donation section of your website. It's best if you allow people to donate directly through PayPal or some other online or credit card intermediary. Finally, be sure to link your social media back to your website and vice versa. Your social media mix is a web where everything is connected.

Facebook

Facebook may be equally or more important than your website, depending on your campaign (and it's free). A Facebook page both informs and engages users, keeping them up-to-date with news, information, photos, and more. Make sure everyone in your organization "likes" your Facebook page and posts it as *their* Facebook status. The more people who are talking about it, the better, as it will "trend" on your Facebook newsfeed. Note that if most of the people in your social circles are not on Facebook and instead are on another form of social media, these same principles hold true. In any social media platform, you want people to be talking about and interacting with your organization in that online space.

With that, you can use Facebook to aggregate other media forms that you have ventured into: Twitter and YouTube, for instance. Creating and linking your Twitter account to your Facebook page is a great way to multitask in social media, as well as posting your YouTube videos and photos from events in your Facebook albums. The main goal of social media in general is to create a supportive, socially engaged audience interested in your cause and invested in the success of your organization.

Here are some Facebook tips:

- *Profile or main photo.* Pick something with high resolution that communicates your cause in action, as this is a publicly displayed picture of your organization. Choose an image that speaks volumes about your cause. Another option is to choose something simple, like your logo.
- *Photos.* At your events, conferences, etc., take plenty of pictures, both posed and candid. Make sure it's announced that if you interact with the organization's Facebook page, you'll be able to see and "tag" yourself in the pictures. Almost instantly, you have an increased number of people interacting with your page, and people will get to see the pictures from your event.
- *Videos.* This is a place to showcase a YouTube video, TV appearances, etc. You can also post videos from events and encourage people to "tag" themselves and their friends.
- *Likes, fans, subscribers, and/or members.* This is the number of people who have chosen to interact with your page and follow your updates. This number should be continuously increasing because it shows the number of users who are actively engaging with your cause and seeing your updates.

• *Status updates.* Are you posting status updates only when you want something from your audience: donations or votes, for instance? It's better if you are posting things that are germane to the topic at hand for the benefit of your interested readership.

• *Facebook management.* When you post something, you will often get comments from your readers. Reply to comments made on your photos and videos, and moderate any negative comments or spam. While it's important to encourage dialogue and allow dissenting opinions to be heard, if a user is becoming inflammatory or using profanity, make sure someone is monitoring your Facebook page to quickly delete any such comment and ban that user from making additional comments.

Twitter

Twitter is a microblogging site that stands for "Text Whatever I'm Thinking To Everyone Reading." Twitter users get 140 characters to publish, or "tweet," short messages to all of their readers or "followers." On Twitter, unlike on Facebook, it is more common to Tweet several times a day. Here are some pointers for successfully using Twitter:

- "*Follow*" and be "followed." Subscribing to other people's tweets increases the likelihood they will follow yours. Once you register for a Twitter account, search and follow similar people and organizations.
- *Tweet frequently.* The purpose of Twitter is giving up-to-date news. For example, "Just raised our first $1,000! Every cent will help the homeless! Such a good day!" Or, "We are entering our first nonprofit competition. Vote here [website URL] to support us!"
- *Retweet relevant news even more.* This not only helps your social network on Twitter but also increases the chance that *you* will be retweeted. Being retweeted is meaningful because it gives you far more reach than if you just Tweeted to your own audience. It also helps you appear more engaged with your network.
- *Send direct tweets, reply, and interact with others on Twitter.* The more engaged you are, the higher yield your Twitter account will be.
- *Link Twitter with other social media.* Your Twitter updates can be linked to Facebook and LinkedIn, which allows you to create content in multiple social media outlets with the same effort.

YouTube

YouTube is a place for online video sharing. You can create an account and post videos you have made to be publicly viewable. YouTube also gives you feedback through users being able to "like" or "dislike" your video, as well as comment. Because YouTube commenters are often anonymous, many of the comments are negative and shouldn't be regarded as an accurate reading of the quality of your video. If you prefer not to moderate comments closely, you can disable comments for your video.

When creating a YouTube video, keep it short (ideally one to two minutes), make sure the picture and sound quality are excellent (people will lose interest almost instantly if they cannot clearly see or hear you), and keep it exciting. For its thumbnail view, use the most colorful or attention-getting slide of your video.

You may decide to create your own YouTube channel if you plan on uploading many videos. That way, a user can "subscribe" to your channel and see all of the videos you have ever posted, conveniently organized in chronological order.

Blogs

Blogs are used for a variety of reasons: some people use them to document their lives as an online journal; others use them as a way to write freely about things they find interesting. If you have a great deal of commentary that would be too long to write on Facebook or other social media, a blog may be a good choice for your organization. Creating a blog page is a lot like creating a web page except everything is shorter and divided into chronological sections.

Similar to Twitter, you can follow or subscribe to other people's blogs (both your potential collaborators and competitors) and they in turn may subscribe to yours. Many bloggers post once a day. If you decide to direct that much content onto your blog account, make sure all your other social media sources point readers to your blog. Note that your blog is also a place to post interesting news articles, links to other organizations similar to yours, and solicit donations or volunteers.

Manage Your Media, Gain Supporters, and Go Viral

Managing your media is important because the only thing worse than no media campaign is a bad media campaign. Make sure you carefully and thoughtfully tend to your media mix. If you have a Facebook account, conduct the daily maintenance: update your status, reply to comments, and delete spam or abusive comments. For Twitter, send two or three Tweets per day, retweet one thing, and reply to anyone who Tweets you directly. For YouTube, monitor comments and reply to any inquiries in the comments section. This goes for the other forms of media as well. Update your website as often as you can with the most relevant information. With social media, you truly get what you give.

Create a brand that informs, engages, and captivates your audience. Embody a message and make sure that everything you do in marketing and media reflects that message. Your cause is about your vision of a better tomorrow. With every Tweet, every status update, every video upload, use marketing to get you closer to that idea of a better tomorrow.

Mackenzie Lowry graduated from Harvard College, receiving her degree in history and science with highest honors and a minor in global health and health policy. She is an experienced anti-tobacco advocate and was named one of *Glamour* Magazine's Top 10 College Women 2010 for her efforts. She would like to acknowledge Arhana Chattopadhyay, Hal Hofman, and Ellyn Angelotti for their support and contributions.

Chapter 24

What Works in Activism

I have come to the conclusion that politics are too serious a matter to be left to the politicians.

—CHARLES DE GAULLE

There are many ways to tackle a problem. If you want to help the homeless in your area, you can organize a canned food drive for a food bank, volunteer at a soup kitchen, or donate money to a shelter. All are wonderful, caring options. But if you want to get to the root of the problem, you'll need to follow it all the way back to the bigger society-level factors at play: the high unemployment rate, limited mental health resources, and inadequate permanent housing facilities for low-income individuals. If you want to make such far-reaching societal level change, you'll need to add in a new element to your game plan—influencing public policy. How do you exert such an influence? Through activism.

Activism—speaking out, ideally together, and changing our environment in ways that address the root causes of problems—is about influencing the laws by which we all live. You might respond, "I don't have the time [or energy or money or experience—or all of these] to do this stuff." All the better. Often the less entrenched you are in politics, the more influence you have. That's because you represent "the real America" in an elected official's eyes. You have no ulterior motives (compared to paid lobbyists, for example), so your opinions are seen as more genuine and probably shared by many of your neighbors (i.e., constituents).

But is it worth it? Absolutely. Political activism is exciting because it is a high-stakes game. The impact you can make has the potential to affect thousands, even millions, of lives. We're not saying you should stop volunteering at soup kitchens. But if you're looking to make life easier for a lot of people all at once, to make a difference that will persist long after you've moved on, you'll want to change the rules of society's game.

This chapter teaches you about activism. It will guide you to effectively talk about your cause, influence government officials, and amplify your voice.

Perfect Your Pitch

Boil It Down

Passionate leaders often overestimate the amount of information people can absorb. Several studies have found that a person's working, or short-term, memory can hold five to nine items of information at a time. As the item becomes more complex, from letter to syllables to words to sentences, a person can remember fewer.[1] When the item is a substantive argument or message, then, short-term memory may have difficulty holding onto more than one. Long-term memory may retain even less information.

What's the application of this research? Memory is important because people must remember information in order to act on it. Therefore, you should keep your message simple. Highlight the basics. Especially when people are first introduced to you or your cause, they'll absorb only your most salient points.

Katherine: I learned how to crystallize my thinking at a training run by Golin Harris, a leading PR firm, with a three-pronged approach to messaging:

1. *Identify a problem*: What's wrong? Why should anyone care?
2. *Point to its source*: Why does the problem exist? Who is responsible?
3. *Come to a common solution*: How do you propose this problem be fixed? Your solution should address the root of the problem and include the roles of your organization and audience.

Whittle your ideas down to one sentence for each of the three prompts. These statements are your key messages. Here's an example from Katherine's work fighting the tobacco industry through Ignite, a nonprofit she founded in high school:

1. *Identify the problem*: "Tobacco companies make a deadly, addictive product and market it to youth across the world, creating a public health crisis that costs 440,000 lives each year in the US alone."
2. *Point to its source:* "Public officials have let tobacco companies off the hook."
3. *Come to a common solution:* "That's why we formed Ignite. We're demanding that politicians pass laws that protect people, not profits."

Once you have these fundamentals down, repeat, repeat, repeat! Memorize these three points, and you have a perfect 30-second pitch to give to anyone.

Tell a Story

For most people, a story is much more engaging than a deluge of statistics, however shocking they may be. Adding a human face to your message helps others identify with those who are affected, while statistics engage the more analytical parts of the brain. Whether you're talking to one person or a thousand, always have handy a quick story that is 30 to 90 seconds in length, depending on the context. Pick a personal example that illustrates the problem, the source of the problem, or the solution in real life.

Katherine: Often when nicotine addiction comes up in discussion, I talk about Doug, a guy who stopped to check out one of Ignite's street demonstrations. A decade-long smoker, Doug had developed lung cancer so severe that doctors had to remove part of his lungs. Still, even after invasive surgery and a strong desire to quit smoking, he couldn't. I told him that tobacco companies have increased nicotine by 10 percent over the past seven years, which may have made it more difficult to break free of nicotine's control. "These corporations shouldn't be able to make this any harder for you. That's just not fair," I offered. "You're right," he answered, drawing another puff to get his fix. "It's not."

This story shows the human effects of a big problem: tobacco companies are consciously making deadly, addictive products. Listeners aren't imagining Excel charts or statistical regressions. Instead, they see Doug, ill with cancer, still puffing on a cigarette as he talks on a street corner. They realize that what public officials allow tobacco companies to do has real, very personal consequences.

Avoid a Common Mistake

Katherine: Katya Andresen's book, *Robin Hood Marketing: Stealing Corporate Savvy to Sell Just Causes*, helped me realize one of my pitfalls: forgetting my audience's values. So often, we try to convince people that they want to do what we're asking. "Come out to our next meeting! Global warming has to be stopped," our e-mails might read. Whether we're asking people to learn a new fact, vote, donate money, or join our demonstration, we frequently move from us to them. We figure out what we want and then try to prove to our audience why they should care, why our message is worthy. Andresen points out that we've just missed a big step: adapting our request to include the values and desires of our target.[2]

In other words, imagine wearing your audience's shoes. What are they thinking? What do they want? What would motivate them to join in? With this information, adjust the wording, and sometimes the content, of your request. That way, you meet them where they're at, instead of asking them to come to you.

Focus on the Positive

We take cues from people we see as similar to us. So highlighting any support you have from people with whom your audience identifies can help you snag more support. In contrast, stressing that you're desperate for help may make your audience wonder why their counterparts have stayed away. In a recent study run by behavioral scientists Alan Gerber and Todd Rogers, phone calls to potential voters that stressed how few people were expected to vote decreased the likelihood that a potential voter cast a ballot. Phone conversations that predicted a high turnout increased the odds that a potential voter headed to the polls.[3] Use this insight to your advantage by emphasizing the support you already have, and others will soon follow suit.

Include a Call to Action

Effective activism includes a specific call to action that tells your audience exactly what they can do to help your cause. This could be signing a petition, writing a letter to the editor, voting, or something else entirely. Calls to action are valuable because we tend to block out messages about bad outcomes unless we're also presented with an easy way to avoid these outcomes. For example, social psychologist Howard Leventhal and other researchers found in the 1960s that strong language about tetanus's dire effects increased the likelihood a person received a tetanus shot only when the health information came with clear steps outlining how to get vaccinated.[4] No one wants to hear about a problem they can't do anything about. Give them a potential solution.

Good calls to action begin with verbs like *write, tell*, and *come*. Poor choices are usually too broad; "support the troops" is a poor call to action because the message doesn't explain how to support those in the military. If you can't take a picture of someone executing your call to action, it's not specific enough. A better call to action would be "Send a note to our troops at ThanksArmy.com."

Whatever you ask people, build in an opportunity for them to publicly commit to taking that action. The commitment could be made as simply as by writing their name down on a sign-up sheet, signing a pledge online, or affirming verbally to an organization's leader that they will attend an event. A study run by social psychologist Anthony Greenwald and his colleagues shows that this step matters: the percentage of potential voters in their study asked whether they would go to the polls was 25 points higher than the percentage of those not asked. The mere question alone prompted a behavior change. Participants in another study were given the opportunity to volunteer. In one group, people signed up by completing a form, and in the other group, they indicated their interest by

Tip Good calls to action are also usually local, as are effective activism campaigns. Often the fewer people a legislator represents, the easier it can be to convince her to support you. And that, in turn, can make it easier to sustain interest among your recruits because people want to see a payoff for their efforts. For both reasons, focusing on issues at your city council or state legislature will maximize your impact.

leaving a nonvolunteering form blank. Although both groups had a similar rate of agreeing to volunteer, those who joined actively by writing were significantly more likely to actually show up to volunteer than were those who joined by leaving a form blank.[5] Action breeds action.

Influence People with Power

Testify

Testifying sounds like something you see in a courtroom TV drama. But in the real world, it's actually not in a courtroom and it's not difficult. You simply speak before a few legislators for about three minutes about an issue they're considering and then answer any questions they might have. Here's how to testify:

1. *Find legislation that affects your issue, and learn when elected officials will discuss it.*
   - Do a search using a keyword of the topic and [city name] city council or [state name] legislature.
   - Search an online newspaper for coverage of relevant legislation.
   - Call the relevant government body. Ask the receptionist if a public hearing has been scheduled for the bill that interests you.
   - Contact a local advocacy coalition that works on your issue. These groups often coordinate speakers to testify before elected officials.
2. *Cite nonpartisan, research-focused organizations or government agencies.* These sources usually appear less biased than an advocacy group with a specific agenda. For example, if you're using a fact sheet from the Campaign to End AIDS Now (which might sound a bit biased to a legislator), follow the footnotes and find the information sources; they'll likely be unbiased organizations like the National Institutes of Health or the World Health Organization.
3. *Include a few key facts as you write your remarks.* Practice your comments ahead of time, and consider outlining your key points on an index card to carry with you.
4. *Make your remarks convincing, personal, respectful, sincere, and brief.* Include:
   - Who you are
   - Your three key messages: the problem, the source of the problem, and what you think elected officials should do to solve the problem

- The specific bill or ordinance if possible and the specific impact this change will have on constituents
- The source of any facts you use
- A short story from real life that illustrates your point

5. *Anticipate your audience's criticisms.* Think of the most compelling arguments they could make against your case, and beat them to the punch by explaining why those concerns are unfounded. This is perhaps the most critical component of powerful testimony.

Sample Testimony

Courtney Otto testified before the City Council in Louisville, Kentucky, on a bill to ban smoking in public indoor workplaces and thereby ensure a safe environment for workers and customers alike.

Thank you for granting me this opportunity and your time. Allow me to introduce you to the reason I am here.

This is my mom, Bonnie Jean Otto. In this picture, she is 56. I am 17. From the picture, you can tell that she is pretty and has a great smile. The woman you see here is charming, intelligent, sweet and considerate. She's my biggest fan.

However, if you will look at the audience in front of you, you will notice that she couldn't be with us tonight. This is the first time she's missed one of my speaking engagements before. In the last three months, though, she's been absent from a lot of big events. My 18th birthday. My high school graduation. And what would've been her 57th birthday, just two weeks ago.

My mother died—or, as I have come to think of it, was killed—on May 10 of this year from non–small cell carcinoma, a smoker's disease. But my mother was never a smoker. She abhorred the smell of cigarette smoke, having grown up in a household with a father who smoked and having worked most of her life in smoky newsrooms and offices. Every doctor she saw cited second-hand smoke as the cause for her disease. She fought for seven months. She was strong. But the cancer that she didn't bring upon herself was stronger.

It is your responsibility to keep those in this community safe. That is what you were elected to do. You have failed in this responsibility. Statistically speaking, during the time that this proposal has been debated, during the time that you have failed to act on your words, 304 Louisvillians have died of diseases caused by second-hand smoke. I am here with you tonight to beg you to act. Not by passing a ventilation clause that has been proven in other cities to be completely ineffective. Not by passing a weak "sign tax." But by passing a comprehensive ordinance. I am here as a citizen who believes that everyone should have the right to eat at a restaurant or work in a bar without compromising their health in a deadly way. I am here because I believe, and hope, that this is still a community in which the death of an innocent, like my mom and countless others, is something we are angry about. I am here as a daughter who is heartbroken because her mother will not be at her wedding, although she took every possible precaution to ensure her own health. So for those of you who make excuses not to act, and for those of you who would dare to tell me that second-hand smoke is not dangerous, I hold up the studies and warnings of the surgeon general, the Environmental Protection Agency, and the National Cancer Institute. And I hold up this picture of my mother, who loved me more than life but never dreamed her life with me would be cut short.

The night before my mother died, I was tucking her into bed after a hectic day when she said something that I will never forget—something I hope you never forget. "Tomorrow will be much more peaceful," she said. I didn't understand her remark until the next morning, when I discovered she truly was at peace for the first time in months. Her tomorrow was more peaceful, but tomorrow for those who loved her was a nightmare. You have an amazing opportunity to help bring peace to Louisville. The quality of our tomorrow, as a community, is in your hands tonight.

Katherine: Courtney's testimony was powerful not just because of its content but also because of its style and structure. Notice its length and organization; she wrote her points concisely and used a personal story to show the human side of the choice the city council had to make. She conveyed genuine emotion but stayed professional. Courtney also brought a large picture of her mom, which she held up as she began the second paragraph. (The council passed a smoking ban for many public indoor work sites hours later.)

You don't need to have had a life-changing experience like Courtney's in order to testify. Many public officials are interested in how the issue affects average voters. Presenting the worst tragedies to policymakers is critical, but so is communicating how the issue affects people in a less pronounced way, since this experience is shared by more people. So speak up! You've got something to say, and public officials need to hear it.

Petition

Petitioning someone with power allows you to show how many people want that power used for a specific purpose. That purpose could be to qualify a candidate or initiative on a ballot. (A ballot initiative is a question posed to citizens, not legislators, whose answer takes the effect of law.) Alternatively, a petition could seek to convince a:

- Public official to introduce legislation or vote a certain way on a bill
- Person of influence to attend your event
- University to change a policy
- Store to stop selling a product

You can gather signatures online or in person. Change.org is a fantastic online tool to gather signatures for a petition—either one you create or one someone else created. If you gather signatures in person, consider these steps:

1. At the top, write at most two clear, simple sentences that specify what each person is saying when he or she signs your petition. This statement should reference the name of the person to whom you'll send these petitions and if applicable, the bill number.
2. Make a column for signatures, a second for printed names, and a third for zip codes. You usually don't need each signer's full address; most elected officials just want to know whether that person is a constituent.
3. Get enough people to sign. Fifty signatures will hardly be noticed by a congressional office. Worse, it may tell a politician that fewer people than she expected support your cause. In addition, research the difference in votes between the elected official and her opponent in the last election. This is often a good number of signatures to try to gather; you can argue that the people you've rallied (if they're 18 or older) could potentially decide the next election.
4. Copy the petitions for your records before mailing the originals to legislators who are actually in the position to take the action requested by the petition.
5. Consider leveraging the petition to draw public attention to your issue before mailing or delivering the signatures. For example, you could tape the petition pages together to form a scroll, take pictures unrolling it on the steps of city hall, and then tweet them out.

Sample Petition

Councilwoman Jones, HIV prevention programs help reduce the rates of HIV among many important groups in your constituency. Please oppose any cuts to HIV prevention programs in this year's budget.

Resident's Signature Printed Name Date

1. ______________________________

2. ______________________________

3. ______________________________

etc.

Take It to the Streets

Most efforts for social change engage the public to either shift norms or pressure people with power to do something. This "street activism" is perhaps the most fun because it allows for a lot of creativity. And it doesn't have to be complicated or difficult to plan. Street activism can be as simple as writing a captivating statistic and your group's website address on a poster and then holding it in a subway car for an hour.

Here's one example: a "numbers campaign."

> *Katherine*: A few friends and I wanted to raise the profile of the Iraq War throughout the University of Virginia community shortly before the 2004 election. Through flyers, chalking, and even painting a bridge in the middle of the night, we plastered all over campus the following: "1100: zero." The enigmatic message intrigued students, professors, and staff the next morning. After the buzz built for several days, we returned in the middle of the night to replace all signs of "1100: zero" with "1100 U.S. soldiers killed: zero WMD found." The attention the community paid to the issue was much stronger than if the full message had been pushed without this priming. We literally walked into a classroom a few minutes before the lecture began and heard students talk about these revealed statistics without any prompting.

Katherine's campaign can be easily replicated. You can feature almost any number or word with flyers, chalk, T-shirts, public service announcements, social media posting, and posters held alongside busy intersections. All you need is some imagination.

Whatever form your street activism takes, there are 12 basics that apply to most scenarios:

1. *Train fellow activists to impart key messages and respond to questions.* Have a quick meeting before your event begins, and discuss each of your three key messages, and questions that opponents might pose. This will help ensure a unified narrative.
2. *Designate a point person.* This person will make decisions about the execution of the event as it progresses (for example, sending someone to print additional flyers) and deal with anyone who might cause trouble at your event or with any police should they question your right to be there.

3. *Pick a location that will be busy if you are outdoors or small for your group's size if you're indoors.* If the event is indoors, imagine 20 people inside a small classroom. The room feels overflowing, and there's a lot of interest. But if those same 20 people stood inside a banquet hall, the event would feel empty. There's so much open space that it's easy to envision all the people who aren't there.
4. *Ensure you have any necessary legal permission to use the space.* Some street events require permits; some don't. To check, call your local police department.
5. *Avoid clichéd images.* Surprise people with fresh symbols, graphics, and metaphors in your activism.

Katherine: Ignite steered clear of using body bags, since those have long been associated with the health effects of tobacco, which everyone knows. Rather, we often lit candles to memorialize those who lost their lives that day to tobacco addictions.

6. *Use only one statistic or fact.* Remember that every day we are bombarded with images and messages. Keep yours simple so that people will be more likely to remember your main point.
7. *Give something tangible to passersby.* These are your handouts. Small flyers often work well if they are creative, with little text and maybe a graphic; these are called "palm cards," since they fit in a palm. Simply extend your handout in the direction of the person passing by and say, "This explains what we're doing."

Katherine: Palm cards don't have to be a piece of paper. The handout for one Ignite event was a small pack of M&Ms, affixed to a label with a message like: "The FDA keeps arsenic out of these M&Ms but not out of cigarettes. Tell Rep. Smith to stand up for smokers."

8. *Include just one call to action.* It can be difficult to get someone to respond to even one call to action, so don't overwhelm them with several. Your handouts should include this call to action and directions for completing it (for example, the mailing address to send used cell phones for veterans).
9. *Listen, but keep moving.* You'll usually meet at least one person whose story justifies your work. Ask if you can take a picture with

this person and share it; with their permission, you can tweet it, send it with a thank-you note to your group's donors, and the like. You'll also run into folks who disagree with you. Those who are arguing with you will often try to draw you into a long debate. Hear them out, respectfully state your points, and conclude the conversation. You have a lot of people to reach.

10. *Plan less, act more.* It's easy to get caught up planning an event to perfection. But the return on deliberating sharply declines after the basics are covered. Instead consider spending those additional hours on a street corner.

> *Katherine*: When some Ignite leaders were hanging out together for a couple of days, one morning we decided to hold an activism event later that day. We tossed around ideas, picked one, shopped for supplies, prepared the banner and palm cards, and traveled to our event location, all within six hours. It was one of our most successful events.

11. *Repeat, repeat, repeat!* Save your materials, and roll them out again the following weekend or month. This continuity will help you build recognition in the community, strengthen awareness of your message, and save you a lot of energy preparing for your next event.

12. *Share.* Post your materials online so activists in other parts of the country can adapt your materials for their cause. Describe what worked and what didn't, so others can build on your success and avoid your mistakes.

> More than many other fields, politics involves countless factors influencing a singular outcome, whether that be the vote of a legislator, the passage of a bill, or a candidate's election. Figuring out whether you're individually making a difference can be difficult. Make sure to measure what you can control (and observe). How many people signed a petition? How many actually called their elected official after receiving your palm card?

Vote

In US presidential elections over the past four decades, about half of all citizens 18 to 24 years old voted on average.[6] That's one in every two—not bad. But consistently, the percentage of the broader adult population voting has exceeded that for the youngest voters by about 30 percent. We can do better.

If you'll be 18 by the time of the next election but are not yet registered to vote, get in the game by registering at rockthevote.com.

Educate yourself. Research who is running to represent your area at the local, state, and federal levels by entering your zip code on the home page of vote-smart.org. Then follow the links to get a list of those on the ballot.

Now look at ballot initiatives registered on the website for your state's board of elections, and figure out where candidates stand on your issue. To do the latter, you can:

1. Call, e-mail, or write them a letter. If an election is around the corner, they may be especially likely to give you an answer though less likely to be specific, especially if not asked to be precise. In your original question, ask what dollar amount or range of funding they would support for a particular program, or ask whether they would vote for or against a particular bill.
2. Read through news articles, or call your newspaper's Metro or Politics department and ask to speak with the reporter who covers the upcoming local, state, or federal election.
3. Best of all, ask the candidates in public. Go to a public debate or town hall forum, and respectfully ask the candidates what they would do about your issue, ideally in front of the crowd during the event. This approach not only gets your question answered but also raises awareness of your issue among those who attend the debate or forum.

Finally, don't forget to ask your family, neighbors, and Facebook friends to vote for or against certain candidates or ballot initiatives. You can make a whole campaign of this task!

Why Influence Politicians When You Can Be One?

Don't count yourself out of the game. Young people have run for and won elected office more times than you might think. If you are interested, ask yourself:

- Has the person currently in office announced she will not run for reelection? Or is the politician struggling to maintain support?
- Can you come up with the money? Realistically, you'll need to raise at least a few thousand dollars for a local race, tens of thousands for a state race, and hundreds of thousands for a federal race.
- Does a substantial percentage of voters (or at least adult residents) in your district share your views on what needs to change and how?
- Are you unfazed by most criticism?

If you find yourself answering yes, follow these next steps:

- Get involved with your political party, which usually organizes leaders at the county or town level. Contact the state party headquarters, and ask when local party activists are next meeting. Spend at least a year actively involved at the local level.
- Research the rules for running for office in your area. Go to your state's board of elections website to learn more.
- Research the campaigns of young people who have won election. For example, John Tyler Hammons became mayor of Muskogee, Oklahoma (population of about 38,000), in 2008 when he was 19 and a freshman at the University of Oklahoma. Alex Morse became mayor of Holyoke, Massachusetts (population almost 40,000), at age 22 in 2011, having run his campaign while finishing college. Luke Ravenstahl became city council president in Pittsburgh, Pennsylvania (population over 330,000), at age 25 in 2006 and soon after won election as the city's mayor.

Vote with Your Wallet

In addition to or in place of political activism, economic activism, that is, putting pressure on corporations, can effectively produce change. Consider organizing a widespread "buycott," a collective decision to refrain from giving your business to a particular corporation, to protest unjust practices or products that present a social injustice. If enough customers leave to shop elsewhere, the business will need to change to remain profitable.

You can also force changes at times through a collective decision to take your business to a particular corporation to support practices or products that contribute to social justice. The more profitable you can help that organization be, the more likely it is to continue and expand the efforts you appreciate and the more likely it is that competitors will follow suit.

The linchpin of both these strategies is twofold: get enough people to participate so the business's bottom line is noticeably affected, and ensure the business understands that it gained or lost customers because of the specific issue at hand.

Amplify Your Voice

Make the News

One of the most powerful ways you can flex political power is by snagging the attention of traditional media: TV, radio, and print. The typical news story isn't about young people taking on the government, so it's novel. If you're on the younger side, you have a better shot at media coverage than most older adults.

Getting reporters to cover your event or campaign requires invitations that:

- Are concise.
- Connect with a timely issue that's locally relevant.
- Clearly identify the what, where, when, why, and how.
- Offer an exciting visual (for example, a field of empty shoes representing people who have lost their lives).
- Provide a clear point of contact with e-mail and phone information.
- Come more than once. Consider notifying TV, radio, print, and online journalists a few days before and the day of your "news."

For more on amplifying your voice through the media, including discussion of how to write a press release and navigate interviews, see Chapter 23.

Letters to the Editor

Another way to garner media attention is to write a letter to the editor of a newspaper or magazine. It is a short piece, usually limited to 250 words, that addresses a recent news item. Start by referencing the event or actual article so you make clear that your writing is relevant to the moment. Then use your three key messages to drive home a narrow, targeted point. (See the Sample Letter to the Editor.)

Nearly all publications accept submissions online, either through their websites or by e-mail. Check the publication's website for submission instructions.

Sample Letter to the Editor

For a higher tobacco tax …

Three cheers for Gov. Ernie Fletcher! As a college student, I've witnessed first-hand the tobacco industry's aggressive marketing to young people. We're still being hooked to killing ourselves. That's why I'm thrilled the Governor is open to raising Kentucky's still-low tobacco excise tax.

Making tobacco more expensive absolutely makes it harder for the smokers I knew in high school and now in college to afford a deadly tobacco addiction. Data back this up. For every 10 percent increase in the price of tobacco, youth tobacco use rates drop a whopping 7 percent.

Last session, Kentucky made a long-overdue move to raise the state's tobacco excise tax to 30 cents. Economists estimate that this increase will result in the avoidance of 10,000 premature tobacco-related deaths in Kentucky. It's a great idea, but still woefully inadequate.

Our tobacco excise tax is now the 45th lowest in the country, while our tobacco use rates are some of the highest. We can do better.

I urge Fletcher and state legislators to consider raising the tobacco excise tax to the national average: 91 cents. If public officials really want what's good for the public, and not tobacco companies, they'll do it.

Katherine Klem

Louisville Courier Journal[7]

Social Media

It's fitting to close this chapter with social media. Like political activism broadly, the tools on your iPhone or laptop are just waiting to be tapped. The challenge is using them frequently and in time. Social media allow you to spread and build on the momentum of the moment, so take advantage of that energy before it dissipates. If you're inspired to get the word out about something, do so without delay.

Many applications of social media to social innovation are not closely guarded secrets to decode. Invite your Facebook friends to like your group's page, or challenge activists in your group to get 1,000 people in one day to repost a sentence that educates the public about the problem you're seeking to solve. Tweet out real-time updates from your events. Take video with your phone and post it on YouTube that night. Use LinkedIn to find similarly minded partners who can help you take your work to the next level, even simply by chatting over coffee. Post to your online chat status, and share a link to your group's website when you update its content. Refer to Chapter 23 for more details on using social media for your cause.

These suggestions are perhaps even a bit obvious—an observation that points to a danger of online tools: their novelty wears off as their adoption spreads. Challenge yourself to find ways to cut through the clutter and stand out. The possibilities for social media will evolve over the years and over your experience, but you'll always want to stay creative to ensure a meaningful and lasting impact.

Activism Begins with "Act"

A little rebellion now and then is a good thing.

THOMAS JEFFERSON

The most effective activists are often those who act more than they plan. So get out, and get moving. As Goethe once said, "Whatever you can do, or dream you can, begin it. Boldness has genius, power and magic in it. Begin it now."

Katherine Klem earned a BA with high distinction from the University of Virginia and is now a Dubin Fellow in the Master in Public Policy Program at Harvard's Kennedy School. She also founded Ignite, an organization rallying youth for socially just tobacco policies, and led it through its six-year run.

Chapter 25

What Works in Educational Curricula

A liberal education is at the heart of a civil society, and at the heart of a liberal education is the act of teaching.

—A. BARTLETT GIAMATTI

"Knowledge is power" is an overused phrase, but its message is no less true. And if you're trying to empower others, particularly with regard to deeply seated social problems, knowledge is one of the most potent weapons in your arsenal.

To impart knowledge to others in an efficient, accurate way, use an educational curriculum: a carefully planned, standardized course of study designed to teach someone about a particular topic. There are many more subtle aspects of curricula, but this definition is the essence of a curriculum. While you'll often be able to adjust existing curricula to your needs, you'll sometimes need to develop a curriculum from scratch.

This chapter guides you through the construction of a curriculum, highlighting best practices as well as the continuous refinement process characteristic of the very best curricula.

Determine How Education Can Help Your Cause

There are two ways to think about education: (1) primary—the lack of education *is* the problem you're solving, such as an initiative to educate seniors on how to use computers and (2) secondary—education is a tool to address the problem, for example, violence against women, and one way to do that is by teaching young adults how to deal with anger in appropriate, nonviolent ways. For advice on how you can use education to further your cause, see Exercise 25.1.

Exercise 25.1 How Can I Use Education to Further My Cause?

Brainstorm various aspects of the social problem you're trying to solve and how you could address the problem through an educational program. Think of the different stakeholders—both the people affected by the problem and those who can make a difference—and what types of education they need. Read the example below then fill in the chart using your cause. Note that the example includes both primary and secondary uses of education to address the social problem.

Figure 25.1. Use Education to Further My Cause

Sex Trafficking

Former/Current Sex Workers

Educate them about health protection, human rights, and tools for economic empowerment in addition to public resources for getting out of the trafficking ring.

Legislators

Educate them about trafficking statistics in their jurisdiction and the importance of creating alternate jobs for sex workers.

Introduce the benefits of creating public policy that places harsher consequences for employers in the trafficking ring.

Children of Sex Workers

Provide basic elementary school education to children of sex workers who often do not have access to education given their economic background.

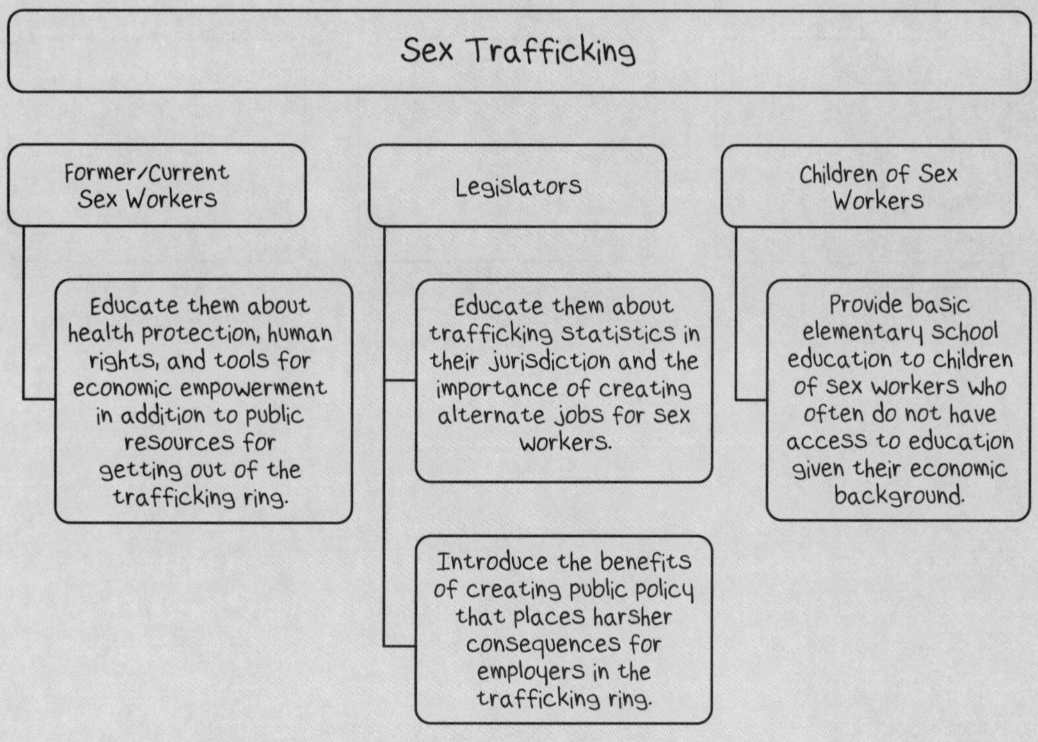

(continued)

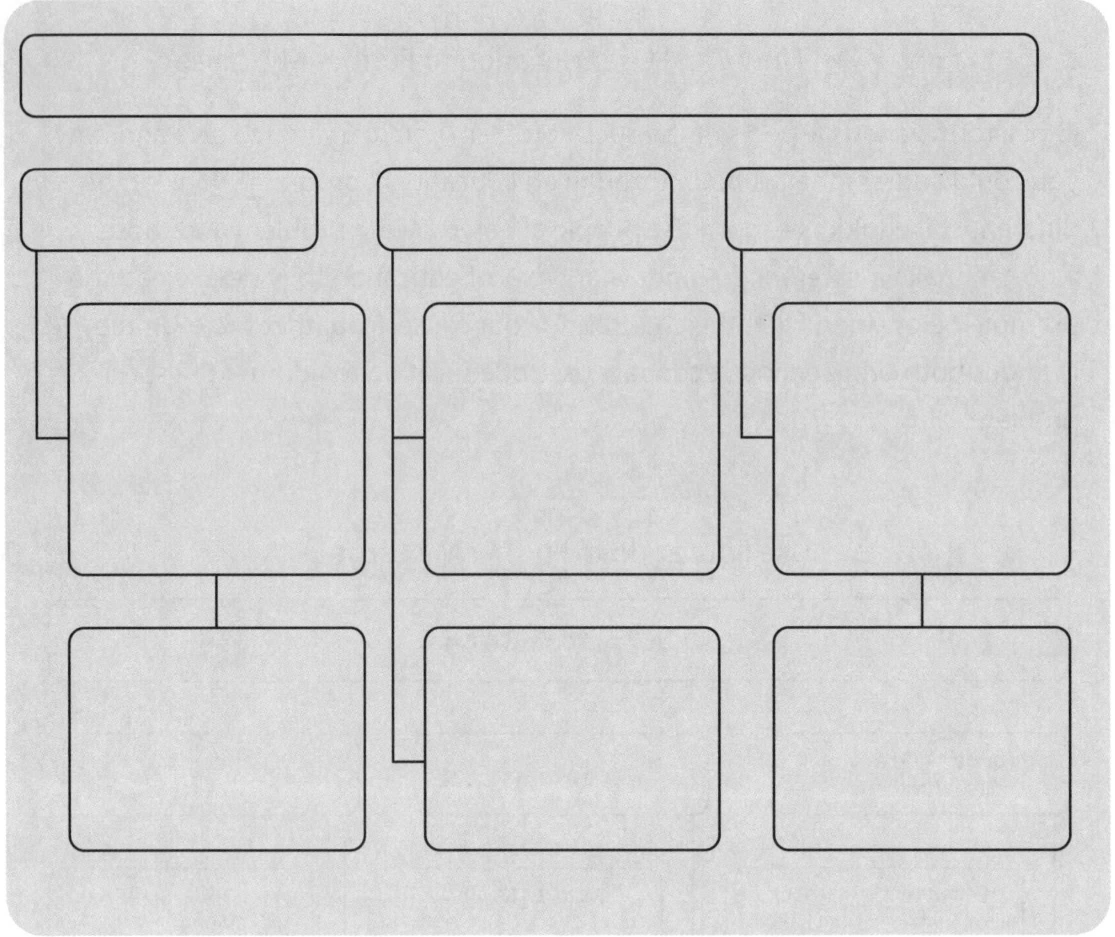

Understand the Purpose of an Educational Curriculum

Underlying most educational systems is the idea that learning must be planned and guided. A curriculum is the road map that organizes teaching and learning processes for teachers and students. It is a standardized way of imparting knowledge that's informed by prior knowledge and refined by experience.

How People Learn

When you're developing a curriculum, it's important to keep in mind how people learn. There are a number of schools of thought with regard to this. One idea is called constructivism, which makes three major assumptions about the learning process:

1. Knowledge must be "constructed" by the learner and incorporated into her current understanding. This means the teacher must be aware of the learner's prior knowledge.
2. Knowledge cannot be transferred intact; higher-order relationships must be recreated. For example, a teacher can point to a ball and tell everyone that the object is called a "ball." Since most kids will have had prior exposure to a ball (the context), they will be able to learn and make higher-order associations (for example, that a ball rolls). Most forms of knowledge are far more complex than this example and do not have a context from which to draw higher-order associations. This means that actively working to build those higher-order associations within the learner's mind is crucial.
3. The learning process is dependent on the learner. Teachers can facilitate learning, but students must take the time and make the effort to learn for themselves, or it is unlikely any significant learning will take place. Thus, the learning process should be made as enjoyable as possible so that the learner wants to participate.

Know Your Audience

In order to create an educational curriculum that can have a positive impact on your audience, it is necessary to understand your audience. This is arguably the most important aspect of the development process and will establish the right foundation for you to subsequently exercise your creative liberties in curriculum design. Educators can effectively structure overarching curriculum goals with a deeper understanding of the needs and sensibilities of their audience. Start by asking these questions:

- *What issues are specific to my audience that need to be addressed?* Example: If you are teaching about sexual health–related topics, is it better to split your audience by gender? Explain your answer.
- *What are some current attitudes relating to my social issue?* Example: If you are teaching about global climate change, is your audience already aware of such environmental trends? If it is new to them, where do you start educating them?
- *What are some common themes and beliefs of my audience members?* Example: If you are teaching teenagers about sexual health, what are some social or cultural values of your audience members? What do they care most about in learning about this topic?

Understanding your audience will allow you to design a curriculum that is congruent and calibrated to the needs of that audience. Use these questions as a starting point and conduct adequate background research to think about how your audience will interact with your initiative.

> **Tip** Communicating widely about the curriculum development process, beginning with audience members themselves, can help create buy-in for your cause and ensure the success of your educational program.

When trying to understand your audience, think about what unique tools can be used to educate that audience. People learn in different ways. Employing online, visual teaching methods, in-person approaches, tactical materials, and other innovative teaching tools can appeal to different learning styles and increase the effectiveness of your curriculum plans. According to the evidence you find, which learning tools are most effective and the best way to deliver your educational plan? A variety of methods, including great visual aids, interactive teaching elements, and thought-provoking reflection, can serve as effective pedagogical tools. The National Education Association also highlights best educational practices, which include cooperative learning, instructional method variation, and project-based learning, which emphasizes student-centered projects rather than teacher-centered instruction.[1]

Keep these characteristics of your target audience in mind:

- *Prior knowledge of material*: Conduct background research to establish a baseline of knowledge and the educational goals for your curriculum based on what your audience already knows and does not know.
- *Cultural background*: Consider the culture and society from which your audience is coming and how this will influence your teaching style and educational curriculum.
- *Delivery of content*: Will your educational curriculum be taught via online tools, interactive elements, written information packets or another medium? Think about the ways your audience is best able to connect to your educational curriculum.
- *Curriculum content*: Thoughtfully outline learning goals and materials that will be included in your curriculum. This is a vital step that will guide curriculum design.
- *Educational plan designers*: Bring the right people on board when creating your curriculum! Who are the experts on your issue? Consider various stakeholders and how their input could be valuable in curriculum design. A diversity of opinion is valuable in content creation and delivery.
- *Teachers*: Who will be educating your audience? Teachers can range from people closely linked to the social cause or outside trainers and organizers. Also think about the venue for instruction (an after-school program, existing group meeting, etc.).
- *Available community resources*: Think about how your audience will be able to move forward *after* and make change with their new educational background given existing community resources.

Multiple Intelligences

Doing what works in education is often your best bet to designing an effective curriculum plan. One of those best practices is to consider *multiple intelligences.* Howard Gardner, professor of cognition and education at Harvard's Graduate School of Education, developed the theory of multiple intelligences explaining that we learn in many different and independent ways.[2] He identified eight categories:

- Visual-spatial
- Linguistic

- Logical-mathematical
- Bodily-kinesthetic
- Musical
- Interpersonal
- Intrapersonal
- Naturalistic

Educational plans that reflect this diversity of intelligence styles can appeal to a broad audience and incorporate fresh and fun activities that can engage others. The multiple intelligences theory is also useful in choosing a variety of approaches for evaluation, which is important for measuring and improving your work. For example, using organizers, playing background music, and journal writing are assessment strategies that employ different intelligences (visual-spatial, musical, and intrapersonal, respectively) and can enable you to evaluate learning. Considering multiple intelligences pushes you to be more creative and inventive with your educational curriculum.

Figure 25.2. Multiple Intelligences

Develop a Curriculum

What follows is a step-by-step guide to curriculum development that is modular, scalable, portable, and interdisciplinary. The flowchart in Figure 25.3 illustrates an eight-step iterative approach to curriculum development. It's important to note that you need to not only develop the curriculum, but also measure its impact to guide future improvements.[3]

Legal Policies and Guidelines for Curricular Programs

Make sure you understand and follow national and local legal policies regarding your program. For example, if you are implementing your curriculum as part of a university-based program and want to provide students with surveys as a mechanism of obtaining feedback on your program, they may be considered "human subjects for nonmedical research." This means that your program will likely fall under the jurisdiction of the Institutional Review Board at your university, and you will have to comply with the board's requirements. It is important to look into this as early as possible because gaining permission can be a tedious process.

Step 1: Requirements Analysis

The first step of the curriculum development process addresses the "why?" question. It's crucial you define a clear motivation behind your curriculum. To do this, sit down with your team and establish the needs that your curriculum is intended to address. What kind of educational gap are you trying to fill? What are you trying to teach? Concisely articulate the requirements for your curriculum since all subsequent steps will be based on meeting these needs.

Step 2: Establishment of Goals

This step of the process is intended to address the "who?" and "what?" questions. Identify your target audience and what you hope they get out of your curriculum. What is the background of your students? What prior knowledge will they have? Keep these questions in your mind as you develop your curriculum so the main goals can be achieved.

Figure 25.3. Curriculum Development

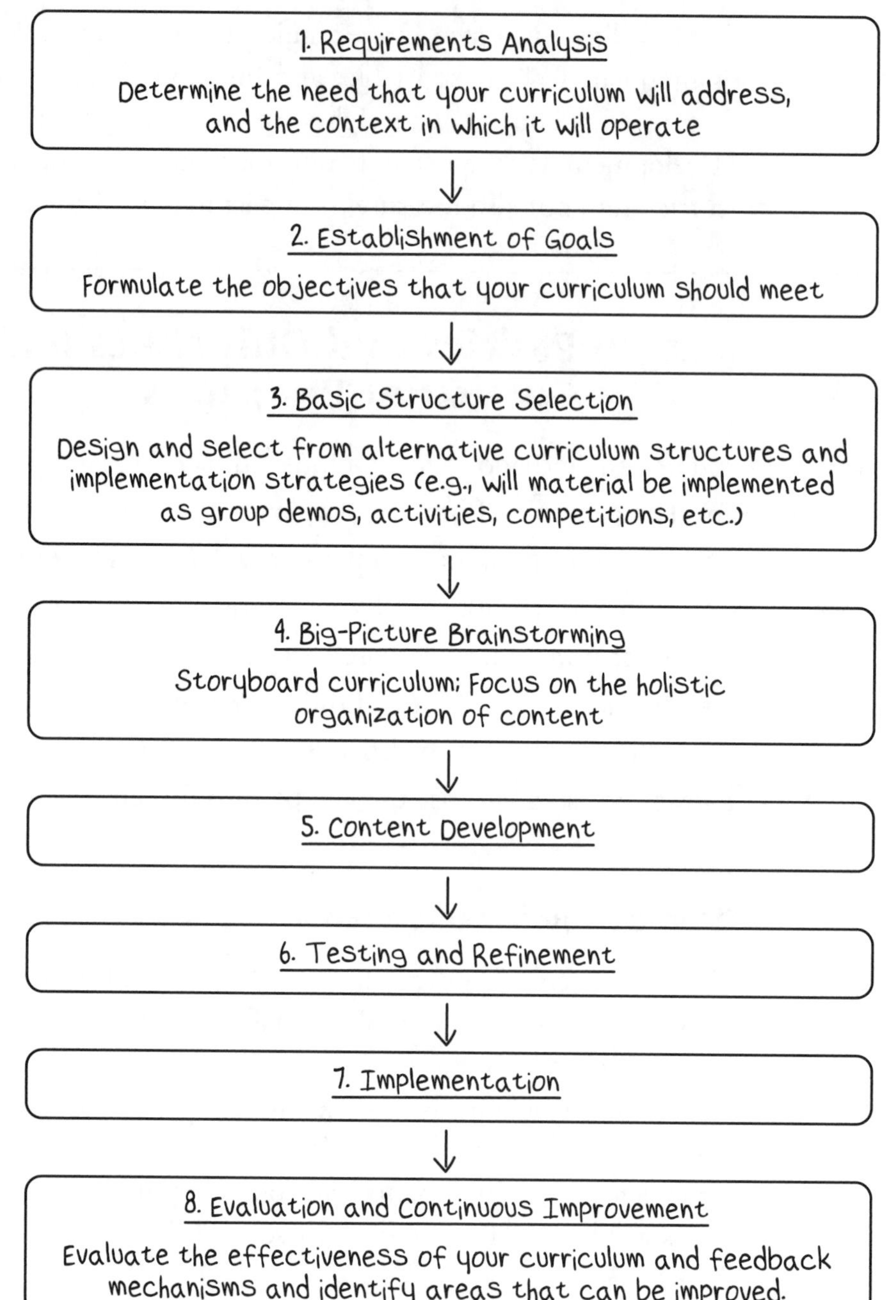

Step 3: Basic Structure Selection

This step starts to answer the critical "how?" question at a basic level. First, list the topics that need to be covered and the breadth and depth of the material with the student reading level and instructor teaching level in mind. Next, list various curriculum structures that may be suitable for teaching the material you've just identified. Finally, ask yourself how the curriculum is to be used in your program. Answering this question will help you determine the optimal structure. However, your decision should also be based on an understanding of your objectives and constraints.

Given the information that you have available, do your best to identify your program's limitations in terms of schedule, resources, and facilities. These constraints are important to factor in at an early stage in curriculum development so that you don't end up with something that can't be realized.

When engineering a structure for your curriculum, strive to answer the following questions:

- Who will be implementing the curriculum (teaching and mentoring)?
- How will the teaching be conducted? Will the students be in small groups, each led by a mentor, or will they be taught by a presenter in a big group?
- What kind of teaching materials will you provide? Will you need to prepare a loose set of online references or a more in-depth workbook for students? Do you need separate versions for your staff and students?
- Who will be responsible for further developing the curriculum?

William: My own experience with designing curricula comes from my work with United InnoWorks Academy, an organization I founded in which college student volunteers teach science and engineering to grade-school students from disadvantaged backgrounds. InnoWorks aims to help remedy the shortage of STEM-educated (science, technology, engineering, and mathematics) individuals and to enable continued science and engineering innovation. For each InnoWorks program, college students are responsible for the instruction. Teaching is conducted in modules, students and teachers receive separate books from which to follow the lessons, and the curriculum is developed through a collaborative effort by college students at InnoWorks chapters around the world. InnoWorks curriculum developers usually generate seven to ten potential modules and eventually narrow these down to the best four or five. Each module follows a set template: a background section introducing the module, followed by a collection of activities and missions. Consider designing a template of your own for various elements of your curriculum; it will provide an easy-to-follow format for your curriculum developers and will also save the editors of the final curriculum a lot of time if all submitted materials are in the desired form.

Step 4: Big-Picture Brainstorming

Once you've identified the group of people who will spearhead curriculum design, set aside some time for unconstrained brainstorming, both individually and as a group. It is essential that the group that is creating the curriculum understand the major goals. Big-picture brainstorming is a good way to break down your objectives into manageable chunks that can be developed in smaller groups and then fit back together to form a cohesive curriculum. If you're designing a thematic curriculum, start by thinking about potential themes and how they can be used to teach concepts that achieve your educational objectives.

Step 5: Content Development

Once you've decided on an overarching structure, you'll need to divide up further content development tasks. See Exercise 25.2 for help in planning your curriculum.

Exercise 25.2 Planning Your Curriculum

To maximize the effectiveness of your curriculum, you need to be able to answer the following questions.

1. What is the motivation for your curriculum? What needs does it address, and what context will it operate in?

2. Who is your target audience? What are their specific needs?

3. What are the major goals of your curriculum?

4. How is your program different from formal education? What advantages do you have that you can draw on to give your students the best possible experience?

5. Is your program founded on an educational philosophy that is not commonly used in the development of already available educational curricula? If so, it may be worthwhile to initiate your own curriculum development effort from scratch.

6. What structure will your curriculum take, and how do you plan on implementing it?

7. How do you plan on ensuring the accuracy of your curriculum?

8. How do you plan on testing and evaluating the efficacy of your curriculum? How will you translate the findings of such analyses into tangible improvements?

William: At InnoWorks, we found it helpful to create a leadership role of curriculum chair—someone to be responsible for the curriculum as a whole and who can serve as the lead editor for the staff handbooks and student workbooks. For the writing and developing team, it is essential to build collaboration and teamwork. A team of people who work well together and believe in the mission and goals is critical for success. For quality control, you should have at least two groups outside your team review the curriculum: the target audience (for example, elementary school students, HIV/AIDS orphans) and professional experts (for example, public health specialists, human rights organizations).

The source of inspiration for lessons, presentations, activities, and missions can come from almost anywhere. Most of the time, your ideas will originate from your own experiences in class, travel, research, watching television, and so on. Even vague ideas can be grounded by doing some library or Web searches. Don't be afraid to be creative and take risks on new methods of teaching. Students will quickly let you know if something is not working in the next phase, testing and refinement.

Experiential learning with a variety of instructional strategies is widely recognized as an effective teaching method. Use field-based elements in a real-world setting, collaborative projects, and active learning experiences in your instructional plan. Teaching with striking visuals is likely to stick with your audience more than just a lecture alone.[4]

Shalini: When I teach my elementary school children, they tend to be more excited about arts-based instruction that involves hands-on crafts. I'm able to motivate, excite, and engage them with this form of curriculum, which also leads to better knowledge retention.

Step 6: Testing and Refinement

A lot of things that look great on paper don't work in real life. Thus, your curriculum committee should be testing its ideas throughout the development process. Try to align your testing strategy with your actual implementation plan. For example, if you plan to implement your curriculum for elementary school children, why not run the prototype material by some of the younger siblings or other relatives of your development team members? More often than not, they'll uncover deficiencies in your curriculum that you would have never even considered.

Observe, observe, and observe! Are the students engaged? Do they get bored or frustrated easily? You might find that an activity is too simple or too difficult for your target audience. Something may not work at all, or it may take too long as written and need to be condensed. The list of possible problems is endless, so the importance of testing your curriculum cannot be overemphasized.

It's also important to note that when developing your projected budget, you'll need to factor in costs associated with curriculum testing. For example, if a particular activity involves students' building energy-efficient toy cars, the relevant committee should be allocated funding to purchase materials and test everything to make sure the activity is safe and works as intended.

> **Tip** Test early: this will give you a sense of what will work and what will not so that the rest of the curriculum can be better developed.

Step 7: Implementation

It's game time! If you've put in the effort to develop a solid curriculum, chances are things will go well. Nevertheless, there is always room for improvement.

Step 8: Evaluation and Continuous Improvement

There are many methods for assessing the efficacy of your curriculum. For example, you may want to survey students and staff to obtain their feedback on the curriculum and how they think it should improve. Curricula that are portable and scalable can be transferred to a wide range of settings. You can also measure outcomes such as changes in student understanding or skills.

Your program can benefit from a long-term strategy for analyzing program impact, such as tracking student performance in school before and after they have participated in your program.

Curriculum evaluation is vital in assessing the efficacy of your educational plan in producing desired results and exploring ways to best improve current curricula. Developing online tools for collaborative curriculum development enables the rapid exchange of ideas, feedback, and evaluations of curricula after programs to guide future implementations. Among various successful evaluation strategies, setting goals and indicators at the outset of your program emphasizes the original objective and creates a clear outline for evaluation.[5] While pretests and posttests for the audience shed light on comprehension and long-term retention, there are also nontesting evaluation methods like behavioral changes and discussion that may prove even more effective than traditional testing and survey-based assessments.[6]

Shalini: In order to evaluate the success of our after-school tutoring program, we used an evaluation plan that examined homework practices (whether a child persisted on a task, sought appropriate help, or worked independently and creatively), engagement in learning (staying focused and alert or contributing to discussions), and relations with peers (working well with others, forming friendships, or showing consideration). Using a scale from 'never' to 'always' we looked at the students over one academic semester and rated their progress in each area.

Sample Evaluation Plan

Using this outline, you can set up a clear method for evaluating and improving on your work for future iterations of your education curriculum.

Evaluation Framework: The Model and Time Frame

1. *What are you going to evaluate?*
   In this section, address your educational model, implementation, and outcome objectives for your curriculum and the context for your evaluation
2. *What questions will you address in the evaluation?*
   In this section, ask yourself whether the implementation and outcome objectives are being attained. If not, why?
3. *What is your timeframe for evaluation?*
   When will you collect data and why? When will you deliver pre- and post-surveys, perhaps?

Implementation Objectives

1. Types of information
   Collect information on types of initiatives implemented in your curriculum
2. Sources of information
   Where are you getting information from?
3. Methods for collecting information
   Questionnaires? Interviews? Observations?
4. Methods for analyzing information
   How will you use this information to improve? This analysis is likely to be descriptive in nature, sorting information with meaningful classifications

Outcome Objectives and Performance Measurements

This section will compare knowledge before and after your educational plan, observing changes in the baseline information. Describe how you will assess audience knowledge and attitudes and determine if a change has occurred.

> *Shalini*: Following the evaluation phase in which we surveyed students and parents with specific questions relating to homework practices, engagement in learning and peer relations over the course of one semester, we created a focus group of volunteers to think about our future strategies. Implementation should be adapted and modified from evaluation outcomes for effectiveness going forward. In my work, we changed curriculum, added more interactive activities to increase peer interactions between children, and incorporated more unstructured social time in response to our evaluation which indicated a need for improvement in peer relations.

Education Lasts a Lifetime

At this point, you might be thinking that creating a curriculum from scratch is too much work for it to be worth the effort. For many types of programs, adapting off-the-shelf materials for a curriculum may be adequate. However, developing your own curriculum allows you to structure it in an optimal fashion and ensure it aligns with your program goals and the needs of your audience.

The whole purpose of education is to turn mirrors into windows.

SYDNEY HARRIS

Engaging your team in this effort can also make them feel more connected to the program and its goals and be prouder of the final result. While it does require extensive research and careful design, curriculum development can be a strong asset in furthering your overarching goal and educating new audiences.

William Hwang founded United InnoWorks Academy and has served as executive director for the past nine years. He is editor of four books on InnoWorks' educational philosophy, methodology, and curricula. He graduated from Duke University with degrees in biomedical engineering, electrical and computer engineering, and physics; received an MSc in chemistry at the University of Oxford as a Rhodes Scholar; and is currently pursuing an MD-PhD at Harvard and MIT.

Shalini Pammal is a Harvard College student who has been involved in education as a founding director for the South Boston After School Program. At the Phillips Brooks House Association, Shalini continues to have a direct impact on youth programming and education, supporting directors in creating sustainable change and closer community connections in the over 80 programs that serve nearly 10,000 low-income youth across Boston and Cambridge, Massachusetts.

Chapter 26

What Works When Running for Office

To be a statesman, you must first get elected.

—*J. WILLIAM FULBRIGHT*

Elections aren't just for politicians or student government leaders. Leadership is needed everywhere and most leadership positions are filled through elections. This means that you'll encounter many situations in which an election stands between you and a position that will provide you with the leverage and resources to make meaningful change.

In this chapter, you'll find helpful tips and strategies to help you come out on top at the polls. Although the chapter primarily focuses on running for a position in student government or a campus organization, the same principles apply to elected positions in any organization (professional societies, community groups, cultural clubs, and so on). Running for political office is a bit beyond the scope of this chapter, but a smaller-scale election campaign like the one outlined here is certainly great training for the big leagues.

> **Note** Elected office is a great vehicle for making change; it allows you to represent your peers and develop your leadership skills while making an impact, both individually and as a team.

Know the Position

Mission Alignment

First, think about whether the mission and programs of the organization are right for you. For example, student government has a specific mission, which most often revolves around improving social and educational opportunities for fellow students and increasing visibility for campus affairs. If your passion is ending human trafficking in Southeast Asia, there are likely more effective groups to be part of than your school's student government. Ask yourself if you can accomplish your goals for social innovation through this position.

Eligibility

What is the organization's leadership structure? What positions are elected, and when do elections take place? Are there certain qualifications that the position officially or unofficially needs? For example, in campus organizations, it's rare for a freshman or new member to hold an executive leadership position because such individuals haven't had the time to develop enough of a track record to be trusted by the members with elected office. However, some groups (and particularly student councils) have a separate first-year leadership team to give new members the opportunity to prove themselves, and have more impact, early on.

Job Description

While the general mission of the organization may be something you're passionate about, it's important to understand just what being a group leader means. For example, if you're on the staff of your school's *Journal on Social Enterprise*, recognize that as an editor, you'll be spending much more time revising submissions and seeking advertisers than writing your own articles. It's also essential to get a sense of the balance between mandatory tasks and freedom for creativity and change. Being an effective elected representative means finding a happy medium between working on larger committee projects and advancing personal passion projects. All organizations have ongoing projects that require engagement from their members. Some of these projects will be more interesting to you than others, but by participating, you help keep the overall mission moving forward.

Shadow

One of the best ways to understand the position is to follow the current office holder and attend a meeting. If you are elected to the office, you will likely be spending the majority of time in meetings you don't currently attend. For example, most member-based organizations have additional smaller meetings consisting of just the leadership or committee members. Check to see if they hold open meetings. If so, sit in on one to gauge how the meetings are run and what the elected leaders are doing. If the position requires not just attending but running a meeting you don't usually attend (such as running for director of the fundraising committee), attend the committee meeting to get a sense of how the current leader runs the meetings, what seems to be working well, and what needs improvement. This will give you ideas about what problems need solving and what potential solutions are reasonable.

To decide if a position is right for you, do the following:

- Research the specific work of the organization and the responsibilities of those in elected office.
- Make sure the position meets your goals of what problems you want to solve and how you want to solve them.
- Attend meetings and observe the current leaders in action. Then share with them your ideas, questions, and concerns.

Know the Voters

Learn about the Priorities and Problems

What are the top items on the organization's to-do list? What issues are most pressing to the current leaders? Are these the same issues of concern to the larger membership?

Attending a meeting will help you identify some of the group's priorities, but you should also talk one-on-one and in small groups to as many current and past office holders, as well as senior members, to get the inside scoop on their priorities and what has mattered to voters in the past. Most important, talk to as many members (voters) as possible to hear their thoughts. In addition to helping you get a sense of what needs to be solved, you'll show them you care about the issue and are motivated to improve the organization.

Brainstorm Ideas

What is it that you most want to see happen at your school or in your organization?

You may know the answer to this question before you ever take office, or you may arrive at an answer only after a few months of involvement. For some, it may be something huge like changing campus party policy or keeping at least one library open 24/7. For others, it may be something with a smaller scope, like creating more awareness of health resources or reallocating funds from one project to another. Your ideas, big and small, expensive and inexpensive, are valuable. After brainstorming, run your ideas by other members and listen to their comments. Use your discussions with voters to refine your ideas and identify potential problems you'll encounter turning the idea into a reality.

Design a Platform

Identify Potential Solutions

Begin by finding out what has already been done. Understanding the history can be tricky because most organizations, especially student organizations, which tend to have frequent turnover, have a short institutional memory. This lack of membership continuity can make it easy for records and practical experience to be lost. See if the organization has an archive system or if any of the older members remember related work. Read old meeting minutes to see what topics have been discussed. Are there ideas that have been brought up year after year but tabled? Often people propose the same ideas but are unaware of why the ideas don't move forward. If this is the case, investigate the reasons. Can you eliminate previous barriers? Is there a new way to approach the problem? Are there other organizations or committees you could team up with to try to push the idea?

If there are no internal archives, another place to look is the campus or local newspaper archives or blog posts. Also check with your school's or city's administration to see if they know of the specific history of your organization. Whenever possible, build on the work of others rather than starting from scratch.

Craft Your Message

Most elections require either a written statement of candidacy or a speech. This message should discuss:

1. Your background and qualifications
2. Your past contributions and successes
3. Problems you've identified and specific ideas for how you propose solving them
4. Your enthusiasm for and commitment to the organization and cause

Campaign!

Every organization handles the election process differently, so it's helpful to find out as much as you can as early as possible. Talk to someone who has run before. E-mail the group's secretary to find out what's typically involved in the campaign process.

Once you know the rules of the election and what others have done in the past, get creative. If there's a particular issue you're passionate about, be sure to incorporate it into your campaign.

> **Note** In a lot of ways, a campus or community election is like a national political campaign: think about what you like and don't like during a presidential election, and the same will usually hold true for your fellow classmates and members.

Share Your Message

Keep an e-mail list of supporters. During the campaign, send them up to four short e-mails:

- *Throw your hat in the ring.* Announce your candidacy, explain briefly why you're running and what you want to change, and list a few key ideas you have. End by asking for their vote.
- *Build a team.* Generally close friends are happy to help you with a few minutes of their time. Accept their generosity. Send a message that includes one or two specific action steps they can take to support you, such as asking three other members to vote for you or helping you put up posters around campus next Monday afternoon.

- *Get out the vote.* Send a reminder the day before or the morning of the election reminding your supporters that now is the time for them to cast their ballot. If voting occurs online, include a link with clear directions of how to log in and vote for you. If voting is in person, include details on where and when the voting will occur. Note that some organizations allow absentee voting, so do everything you can to make sure your votes are counted.
- *Say thank-you.* Shortly after the election, regardless of the outcome, send out a thank-you note acknowledging their support. If you win, include your first item of business (after celebrating!). If you aren't elected, consider adding a note about how you will continue supporting the cause outside of the elected position.

WARNING

While a few short e-mails like these are helpful, do not send many more. People are receiving e-mails like yours from many people and "spamming" can turn off even your biggest supporter.

Advertise

Whatever your issue or campaign style, be sure to have fun with your campaign. Set up a group on Facebook or host a party to meet potential constituents. Even if you aren't elected, this is a great opportunity to hear ideas and concerns and make great friends along the way. And you'll have even more ideas for your next campaign.

Christina: When I ran for a spot on my college's undergraduate council, I wanted to get creative with my campaign posters. I used fun-size candy bars glued to 8.5 by 11 sheets that I hung on everyone's door. The candy bars covered up text, indicated in bold below, so in total the poster read:

Mounds of homework and
things to do? Take a **Fast Break**
from the **Crunch** and vote for
CHRISTINA ADAMS
For the
Undergraduate Council.

She **Promises** to give **Whoppers**
Of effort and enthusiasm serving
Quincy House.
Vote online at uc.fas.harvard.edu

Creating a Campaign Poster

What should you prioritize when making a poster? Richard Lonsdurf presents four key tips to ensure your posters help you earn votes. Richard graduated from Harvard College, where he served as the resident designer for several campus organizations, including the Let's Go series of travel guides.

Richard: In terms of effectiveness, campaign posters (especially on campus) generally rank somewhere between white noise and chain e-mails. Sitting back and hoping your message will be seen is as effective as hoping someone will find Waldo when no one even knows he's missing. But *good* posters can provide your campaign with a sense of legitimacy. And when you make a word-of-mouth contact later, your audience will remember having seen your message before. This can happen only if your posters are widely distributed, easy to see, easy to read, and inspire an emotional response (laughter is a good start) in the people who see them.

To make sure your posters are memorable, keep in mind these guidelines.

Don't Let Visuals Overwhelm Your Message

Richard: Figure out where the text is going first, and design around it. Of course, that isn't to say your text can't be the poster's most attractive feature. Test out various fonts to see what is clean, simple, professional, and, reflects your campaign and personality. Default fonts like Arial or Times New Roman can underwhelm, especially if there is a large amount of text, so try other strong neutral fonts like Franklin Gothic, Palatino, and Gotham. Don't fall into the trap of gimmicky fonts like Curlz, Papyrus, Stencil, Old English Text, and avoid the dreaded yet pervasive Comic Sans.

Keep It Short

Richard: A poster is not a dissertation. Martin Luther may have had 95 theses, but you don't have nearly that much space to get your point across. The bare bones to include are your name, title of the office you're running for, and the name of the organization. Depending on the audience's familiarity with the election, you may also want to include the date and time of election, your picture (be tasteful), and contact information or a campaign website. If necessary, a succinct byline about your purpose or background can provide helpful garnish.

Make It An Easy Read

Richard: A poster is not a subtle statement. Use the 30-foot rule: if you can't read the biggest word from several yards away, it's too small to catch anyone's attention. Big color (or black and white) contrasts will also help you turn heads. Remember that your poster will be surrounded by several other loud contributions.

Use Quality Images

Richard: Some images are saved in formats that look fine on the screen but awful when you blow them up to larger sizes. Don't let sloppy, grainy images ruin your poster. A professional poster implies a professional campaign! If you're in need of additional photographic images, search free or cheap stock photo websites like istockphoto.com before using an image from a search engine.

Consider investing in a quality design program like the Adobe Creative Suite (Photoshop, Illustrator, InDesign), which will revolutionize the way you work. If you're a student, your school may already have copies of the program available on public computers. Adobe's Classroom in a Book series is particularly helpful when learning how to use their programs. If you're looking for some training in graphic design, there are many quality online tutorials and podcasts that will teach you to create beautiful images.

Figure 26.1. Effective Campaign Poster

Christina L. Adams was student body president at Bartlesville High School in Oklahoma. She graduated with a degree in government from Harvard College, where she served as chair of the campus life committee of the undergraduate council and as one of eight class marshals, lifetime class officers.

Chapter 27

Do What's Right

Management is doing things right; leadership is doing the right things.

—PETER DRUCKER

From childhood, we're taught what's right and what's wrong, so by now, acting ethically may seem pretty straightforward. However, sometimes the right thing to do isn't always clear to see or easy to do.

Being successful and being ethical can and should run hand-in-hand, though. You can do both *what works* and *what's right.* It helps to have a framework in place to help guide you along the way. With this in mind, there are three important principles to follow to help ensure that you and your team are acting ethically in making social impact:

1. *Right attitude*: Establish ethical guidelines for your team from the outset.
2. *Right action*: Follow best practices to maintain high ethical standards.
3. *Right reaction*: Address ethical dilemmas in ways that minimize damage and maximize learning potential.

Discuss some recent examples in the news of leaders who have acted unethically. How, why, and when did they go wrong? What should they have done differently?

Right Attitude

Just as you shouldn't set out on a hike without researching the trail, you shouldn't begin work on your enterprise without doing some planning. It's useful to have a direction for ethical as well as logistical reasons. This section outlines some topics to discuss prior to implementing your project to avoid getting lost later.

First, you'll need a map to navigate the moral labyrinth ahead; in organizational management, such maps are called "codes of ethics." A code of ethics is like a group conscience: it guides the team's ethical decision making, even if different individuals have different personal ethical rules.

Creating your code of ethics will give your partners and you a chance to really get to know each other.

Step 1: Learn What Drives Your Team

Have a series of discussions with your group to determine the values that drive your work. Consider leading structured team brainstorming sessions or holding focus groups with community members.

Use the following questions to start your discussion; as people talk, you'll naturally think of more to ask:

- What is your mission? Your vision?
- How would you like to communicate and collaborate with the other stakeholders?
- What are some of the principles that guide the organizations you admire?
- What are some worst-case scenarios for this project? How would you respond to them?

Step 2: Consolidate and Clarify

From these discussions, create a list of principles that drive your work. Include a short explanation of why and how you'll put each principle into practice. Outline contingency plans for ethical dilemmas that may arise.

Continue discussing and refining until you have a polished code of ethics you believe in. It doesn't matter if the final product is in paragraph or list form, as long as it's clear and concise.

Figure 27.1. Formulating a Code of Ethics

Step 3: Get Consensus

Give all group members the chance to read, discuss, and consent to the code of ethics you've collaboratively drafted. Once you're in agreement, share it with other stakeholders (e.g., through online and print publishing) and reference it in partnership agreements.

Right Action

Remember that action should follow intention; it isn't enough just to *know* what's right; you must *do* what's right too. So now that your map is drawn, it's time to start your journey. Watch out for potholes, though. Here are some areas and examples where ethical issues can crop up:

- *Interpersonal*: discrimination, sexual harassment, mistreatment of subordinates, etc.
- *Program design*: misleading promises, excluded stakeholders, inadequate staff training, etc.
- *Financial*: fraud, bribery, stealing, etc.
- *Legal*: breaches of confidentiality, broken safety regulations, lack of necessary certifications, etc.

Follow the steps outlined next to promote ethical practices throughout the course of whatever initiative you undertake, be it founding an NGO or working to get an unjust law repealed.

Step 1: Communicate

Tip

Good communication requires active listening. Pay attention to what your partners are saying—and not saying.

Cultivate a culture where people feel comfortable expressing their feelings. If channels exist for people to express their concerns, potentially thorny ethical issues can be addressed early on. For example, you can create an anonymous comment box and hold regular check-in meetings.

Step 2: Be Transparent

Being open about your intentions and forthright in your actions helps build your reputation as a trustworthy partner. You have nothing to hide and everything to be proud of. Make your financial statements publicly available, and keep electronic and paper records of your work whenever possible.

Not everything should be public, of course, such as sensitive information about clients or private, early-stage negotiations. Use common sense and research confidentiality laws pertaining to your work.

WARNING

Like Hansel and Gretel, you always leave a trail behind you—but this is the 21st century and yours is an electronic trail. Be aware of your online conduct. Once you click Send, your words are permanent. Don't let careless comments come back to haunt you.

Step 3: Be Self-Aware

To be honest with others, you first need to be honest with yourself. Are you following your code of ethics as best you can on an individual and organizational level? If not, how can you do better? Engage in self-reflective activities, such as keeping a journal on your motivations and activities. Remember to accept constructive criticism gracefully too, rather than take it personally.

> *Amy*: Self-reflection can be deeply humbling but also deeply educational. For instance, I've caught myself complaining about poor communication before realizing I was contributing to the problem instead of helping to build the positive atmosphere that I wanted. Striving to be more self-aware helps me stay true to my values, so I can lead by example.

For more on self-reflection, see Chapter 40.

Right Reaction

No matter how prepared you are, things can still go off-road. Maybe you took a wrong turn; maybe a teammate did. Don't panic! Mistakes happen. What's meaningful is how you react and get back on track.

Step 1: Assess

Once you recognize an ethical dilemma, assess the situation as best you can.

First, how did you get into this situation? By determining the factors and decisions that led you astray, you can better address the situation at hand, as well as prevent future occurrences.

Let's say your group has been inadvertently teaching some incorrect facts in the nutrition workshop you run, potentially damaging the health of the workshop participants. You investigate and find out that your group got the facts from an online source that wasn't reliable. So now you know that in the future, you'll double-check your sources.

Second, what is the scale and seriousness of the situation? Investigating the current and potential impacts will help you "triage" what issues to tackle first. Maybe the contact information of your donors was accidentally sent to some mailing lists. You find out what kind of information was sent out, how many people were affected, and who has access to the information now. You will manage the situation differently if you find out the information was only partial cell phone numbers, as opposed to full credit card numbers. Remember that actions have ripple effects, so think broadly about who and what might have been affected when assessing the dilemma.

Third, what are the precedents or protocols for addressing this situation? Imagine one of your staff has been accused by another of using petty cash for personal purchases. Your organization's protocol for this situation is to give both sides a chance to explain themselves before making a decision based on the evidence.

Step 2: Address

After you've assessed the situation, it's time to act. Ignoring a problem only makes it worse.

> **Tip** Create a safe environment in which whistle-blowers are thanked, not punished, for coming forward.

- *Communicate*: Hold frank discussions with your team and work together to find a solution. Don't be afraid to seek outside advice.
- *Be transparent*: Owning up to mistakes will turn a potential disaster into a learning opportunity, prevent the same mistakes from happening again, and increase your reputation for honesty.
- *Follow your conscience*: Step away from a project if you're uncomfortable with the direction it's heading in.

No matter what reasoning you follow, use the same principles from your preparation and practice and refer back to your code of ethics.

Step 3: Learn

After successfully resolving your crisis, learn from your mistakes so history doesn't repeat itself. Write down the key points you learned from your assessment of the situation. Discuss the dilemma and how it was resolved during future team trainings.

Exercise 27.1 Team Ethics

Brainstorm some ethical dilemmas you might find yourself in, using an actual situation that you've experienced or one of the following hypothetical situations:

- Seeing your teammate take credit for something someone else did
- Making up an excuse for your incomplete work when you really just missed the deadline (the classic "the dog ate my homework"/"my computer crashed" line)
- Being told by a superior to fudge facts on a report so your group looks better

Work through this dilemma with each of the stages discussed in this chapter. If you use an actual situation, compare your responses to how you actually reacted.

Right Attitude

1. Write a code of ethics with principles that would be applicable to this situation.
2. Who are the stakeholders with whom you'd need to discuss this code of ethics? How would you discuss it with them?

Right Action

1. How could communication, transparency, and self-awareness have helped prevent this dilemma?
2. Imagine that you are one of the people involved in the dilemma. What are some of the justifications you might have for your actions?

Right Reaction

1. Assess and address the impact of this dilemma. Prioritize what you must do to fix the damage.
2. How can you ensure it will not happen again? Consider different areas of potential change such as individual, organizational, and legal.

Ethics: In Theory, Black and White—in the Real World, Shades of Gray

Have you ever exclaimed, "How could they have done that!?" when hearing about someone who had acted unethically?

Many social psychology experiments have shown that ethical decision-making can be highly affected by situational circumstances. Psychologists Daniel Batson and John Darley found that individuals running late were less likely to stop to help a stranger in need—though they were on their way to a lecture about the Good Samaritan![1]

An infamous study of prison interpersonal dynamics recruited volunteers for a two-week simulation at Stanford University. The subjects were randomly assigned to roles as prisoners who were detained in a makeshift prison or guards who took shifts watching the prisoners. Members of both groups quickly and intensely internalized their roles; the prisoners became traumatized and the guards abusive. The unfolding events disturbed researcher Philip Zimbardo so much that he halted the study after six days.[2]

Consider the effect of authority, peer pressure, or other factors that can make ethical decision making more challenging. Does this affect how you should prevent or address ethical dilemmas?

An Ongoing Dialogue

This chapter isn't meant to be a definitive guide to ethical decision making. Rather, it's here to help get a discussion going. Only you and your team members can understand the challenges you face and work together to address them.

Amy: I've had my fair share of missteps doing community activities—nothing intentional, but plenty of misunderstandings and times when I didn't know how to do the right thing. However, by forcing me to react to new difficulties, these experiences taught me valuable lessons about ethics and service. With the right attitude, your greatest challenges will lead to your greatest personal growth.

Amy Dinh has participated in and designed many university service-learning programs in the United States and abroad; she draws on her experience to advise students, professors, and community organizations about ethical and effective service. She currently works at the Center for Responsible Business at UC Berkeley's Haas School of Business.

Work Together

Start and Strengthen Meaningful Relationships

Chapter 28

Find Mentors

> *[Mentor to Telemachus:] Be strong, that even men hereafter born may speak your praise. … Rely upon yourself, and make my words your guide.*
>
> —*HOMER,* THE ODYSSEY

Homer wrote two epic poems about a wise Greek warrior-king named Odysseus. When Odysseus is called away to fight in the Trojan War, he leaves his newborn son, Telemachus, in the care of an old friend named Mentor. Twenty years later, when Odysseus has neither returned home nor replied to any of Telemachus's texts, Mentor gives Telemachus the wise advice above. He encourages Telemachus to have courage and take the lead in his father's absence, a piece of advice that leads Telemachus on a journey of growth and self-discovery that eventually sees him reunited with his father. It is also revealed (spoiler alert!) that Mentor is actually a disguised Athena, goddess of wisdom, skill, and strategy (among other things). It's no surprise, then, that modern mentors are those who guide others with their wisdom, skill, and strategy.

Mentors are essential to young leaders because they can share advice and best practices with you and your team, saving huge amounts of time and energy. Even if your group is more developed, there are always new decisions to be made and new ideas to consider, and mentors provide valuable insight. Finally, on a personal level, a mentor can help guide you along your dream professional path.

Find an Ideal Mentor

To go about finding a mentor to help you and your organization reach your full potential, start by looking for someone who can:

- *Inspire you.* Your mentor should be a beacon of inspiration to you, and her work and persona should challenge you to be and do better. As Ellen Ensher and Susan Murphy observe in their book *Power Mentoring*, mentees are attracted to mentors because they recognize a kin persona, and that also allows them to regard their mentor as someone they can aspire to be.[3]
- *Impart words of wisdom.* You want someone who can give honest advice on any situation, drawing from past successes and failures to distill little pearls of wisdom. Even if they haven't pursued your career path, they should be able to offer you lessons for your own life.
- *Be your advocate.* Your mentor should act as your key strategist and cheerleader, guiding your goal setting and actively helping you achieve, whether by introducing you to colleagues or singing your praises to others.
- *Guide you through difficult decisions.* You need someone who will ride in the passenger seat as you navigate through steep turns in your life and who will work with you to amass and consider the information you need to make confident choices.

These qualities are applicable to all kinds of mentors, but they're just a starting point. Later in this chapter, you'll further define the specific characteristics you're looking for in your mentor and in your mentoring relationship.

Sujay: A high level of professional success does not necessarily mean someone will be a great mentor. It's imperative to find someone who wants to take the time to invest in you and your mentor-mentee relationship. A great way to assess a mentor's potential is by looking into his past. Has he been a mentor to others in the past? If so, what do they say about their experiences? Are they still in contact or working with this person (generally a good sign), or was there a falling out (not so good)?

Figure 28.1. Characteristics of a Good Mentor

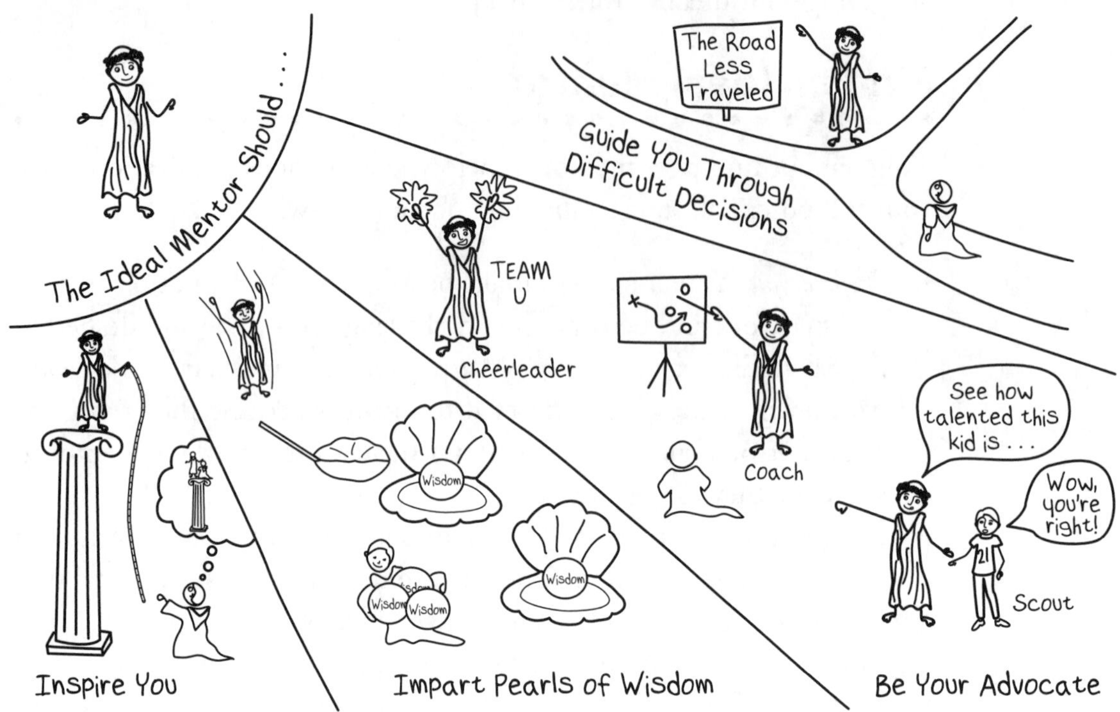

Build a Mentoring Team

The concept of mentorship as a singular, top-down relationship between a single tenured professor and a student, or a high-level executive and a new employee is making its slow march to join the dinosaurs. Just as CEOs rely on their board of directors and the president of the United States draws on his cabinet, you should draw on a diverse team of mentors for your professional and personal development.

Multiple Mentors

One size never has and never will fit all. For example, if you're an aspiring human rights lawyer, you might reach out to a practicing human rights lawyer for guidance on developing your career. But your law school professor, who has probably coached several students like you, might be an excellent source of wisdom as you consider delving into multiple interests within human rights work. Together, these two mentors can do what one alone couldn't have accomplished.

Mentors All Around You

As you begin to build your mentorship team, carefully consider who to approach to be your mentors. While it would be incredible for Suze Orman to be your financial mentor and Steven Spielberg to be your creative advisor, it's not likely—and not even necessary. Constructing a team of mentors requires you to break out of the traditional view of mentorship and consider the people who are around you, not just above you, as mentors too. While Steve Jobs had several mentors in his life, one of his greatest mentors was his father, Paul Jobs, who instilled in him the value of fine craftsmanship that helped him revolutionize technology. The people around you have likely inspired, challenged, and enlightened you in several different aspects of your life, particularly your peers.

Sheba: My peers have been crucial to bolstering my personal and professional development. While studying abroad, I often wished that I could better explain my experiences anthropologically and spend more time considering how social enterprise could revolutionize health in each country. I reached out to a few fellow students who, I felt, exercised these skills well, sparked a conversation about my dilemma, and sought out their advice. This collaborative mentorship radically transformed my thinking during my travels and allowed me to extract greater value from them.

Identify Your Goals and Needs

While it might be tempting to go straight into the mentorship search, first consider why you're approaching a mentor and who in your life is best positioned to advise you. Exercise 28.1 will help you make this decision.

Exercise 28.1 Map Mentors

Building a mentoring team means finding people to address the multiple aspects of your life. In the diagram below, label each circle with an area that is important to you (school, work, religion, family, community, artistic expression, etc.). Then list potential mentors who could help you reach your goals in each area. Highlight the names of people who are in more than one circle.

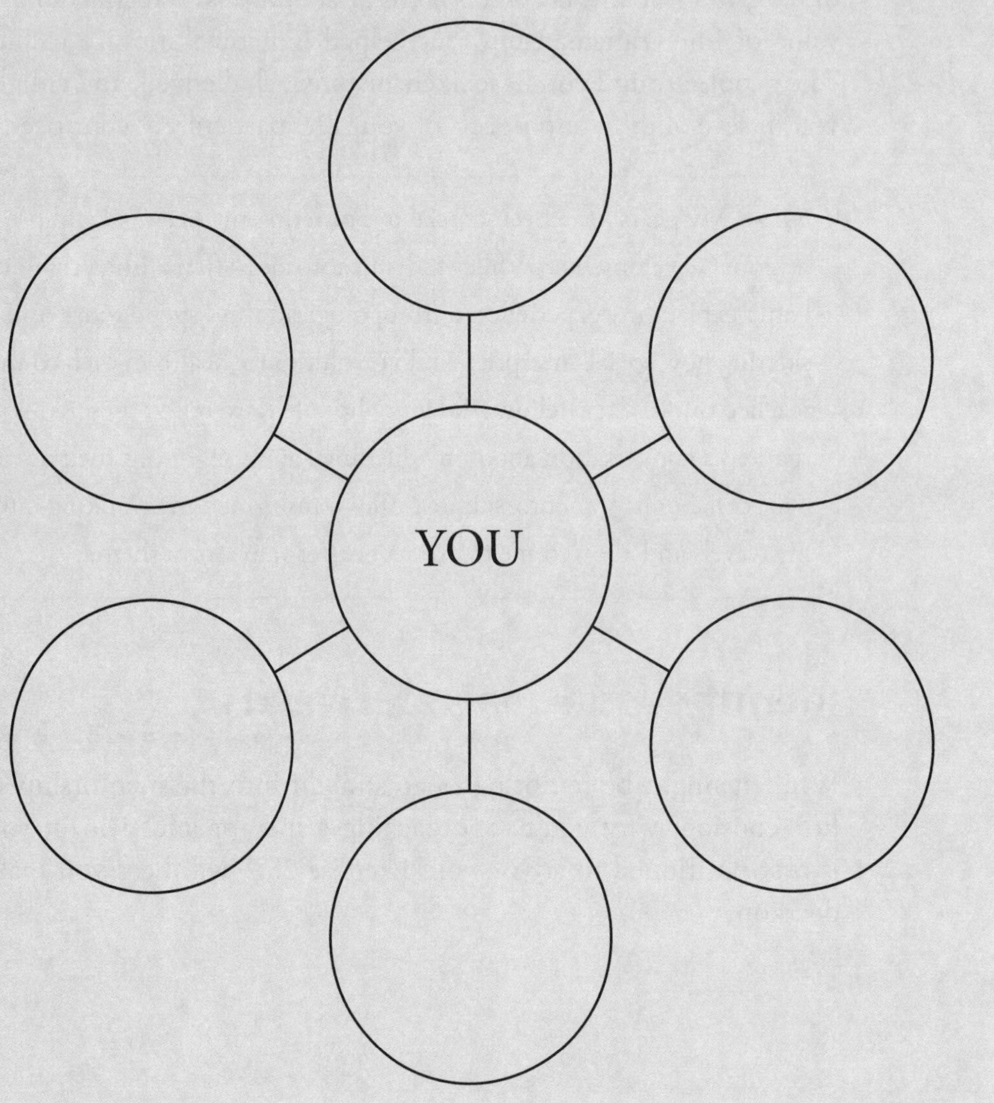

Tie Projects to People

The most effective approach to securing a mentor is to have a goal or project that could directly benefit from their advice and mentorship. As you seek out mentors and prepare to approach them, remember to tightly integrate them with your goals and projects. It could range from something as simple as achieving a greater balance in your life to something as intensive as starting your own enterprise. This sweetens your "Why Mentor Me?" pitch, and it provides the mentor with something tangible to latch onto in order to springboard your relationship. Even once your project is over or your goal is attained, your rapport will most likely be strong enough to maintain a mentoring relationship.

Assess Your Assets

Like any other smart consumer, take stock of the influential people in your life before you dive headfirst into "shopping" for your mentor. Building a strong mentorship relationship takes time and effort. Why duplicate those efforts unnecessarily if you are already connected to someone who can help you attain your goal?

Think about each area of your life and write down who is already a mentor, officially or unofficially. Who has gone out of their way to share their time and energy with you? How can you strengthen your relationships with these people?

Fill in the Gaps

Once you've assessed your assets, focus on the areas where you need mentorship. Within each area, are there any significant goals you're tackling that would greatly benefit from the advice and expertise of someone you look up to? If so, first take a look at the list of mentors you constructed and consider whether one of them could provide you with what you need. If you feel that you need someone new to reinvigorate your life, it's time for your shopping spree to begin.

Create a Core Corps

In your core corps are the mentoring relationships that you are going to prioritize and commit to. Although these individuals may not work together and may not even know each other, treat them like your dream team, your personal board of directors, and work with them to find the best ways to help you and your ideas grow.

Identify New Mentors

Mentors rarely knock on your door hoping to find people to help. This means you'll need to actively search for potential mentors. Exercise 28.2 will help you get started.

Exercise 28.2 Collect Role Models

Make a list of people you've met in the past year, such as a speaker you watched from a distance or a client you worked closely with. Select a few you admire, and think about how they could help you achieve your short- or long-term goals. Use the guidelines below to compile your list.

For more inspiration, make another list of exciting individuals you are planning to or would like to encounter in the coming months Plan how you can approach them and begin building a relationship. Keep this list accessible and add to it periodically. If you have a few minutes to spare, browse LinkedIn or relevant news stories for potential mentors, and add their information.

Name

Title

Why I admire this person

How this person can help me achieve my goals

How I met or can meet this person

How I will maintain a relationship with this person

Use Your Network

Once you've identified a few people you think can advise you in one or more areas of your life, seek out ways to connect to them. Turn to your networks to see if anyone you know can help you get your foot in the door with your role model. If this fails, do a little more research and determine if your potential mentor will be giving a speech or attending a conference near you.

Don't forget the obvious: ask friends and family if they can point you to people who might be able to guide or advise you.

> *Sheba*: When I was designing Synergy, my college's first undergraduate social innovation incubator, I was working with some great mentors but wanted to draw on the expertise of someone who had already created an incubator. By sharing this desire with my friends and existing mentors, I was soon able to collaborate with individuals who had built successful incubators in the past.

Approach New Mentors

It can seem daunting to reach out to a mentor, but you simply have to follow Nike's advice and "Just Do It!" See the Sample Mentor Introductory E-mail for an example of reaching out to a potential mentor.

Your Request

Looking back at your life map, specify the goals that you want to work on with this mentor. This is where having a project can come in handy because it gives your mentor the chance to witness firsthand how you work and a window into who you are as a person. But if you don't have a project for this mentor, all is not lost! Simply articulate a goal that you are working toward or a personal strength you are trying to enhance, and then cite your potential mentor's experience or character traits as reasons for approaching them.

Sheba: While writing an article for my school's *Global Health Review*, I reached out to one of our organization's advisors saying merely that I was "interested in learning more about his experiences." I made the mistake of not connecting my passions—as well as my article—to my mentor's interests, and I didn't explicitly have an "ask." Our conversation was brief and, needless to say, aimless. However, as busy as he was, he was kind enough to meet with me again. When we did, I made sure that I at least had specific areas in my article I wanted to work on and had targeted questions about his work with the Clinton Foundation that could help me expand my interest in strategic philanthropy.

Don't waste your time or the precious time of a potential mentor. Before meeting with someone, have a clear idea of what you're looking to get out of the meeting.

Your Contribution

When you approach a potential mentor, keep in mind that your relationship can have benefits for both of you. If a mentor is senior to you, you might not be able to offer him similar wisdom, but you can at least energize or inspire him in some way. Highlight your relevant past experiences and your personal strengths when you first interact so that your mentor can begin to trust you in their field.

Demonstrate engagement by suggesting new directions for your mentor to push his work. Finally, and most important, show your respect, enthusiasm, and commitment to working with him. That alone can excite a person and make him feel that he is making a positive difference in your life. Remembering your contribution to the relationship will help it flourish in the long run; every time you meet, walk away feeling as if you've gained something and given something in return.

Sample Mentor Introductory E-mail

When e-mailing a potential mentor, establish who you are; how you know him; why you're interested in his research, work, or experience; and what you hope to discuss with him. Then request a meeting. You might also want to attach a copy of your CV. Here's an example:

Dear Ms. Grace,

Your thoughts on delivering mobile health care in South Africa that you shared at the Africa Institute last week allowed me to reimagine the way that health care is being transformed globally. My name is Sheba Mathew, and I'm currently an intern at a small organization that is about to begin a mobile health program in the Northwest Province, which is why your insights had particular resonance with me.

I would love to share more about my project with you and would very much value your advice on how to best implement messaging through a Please Call Me Service. Is there a time that would be good for you to chat in person or on the phone in the next two or three weeks? I am happy to come to a place that is convenient for you.

Looking forward to it!

Sheba Mathew

Forge a Strong Relationship

Know Your Mentor

Make sure to read as much information about your potential mentor before you meet, including publications, any online talks, and blog entries. Ask your contacts what they've heard about your potential mentor or what their impressions are if they've met. Of course, no matter how wonderful you think your mentor is, be careful to not go overboard and cross the line from "researching" your mentor to "sort-of-stalking." For example, wait till you've already met before adding them as a Facebook friend.

Find Common Ground

Treat your mentor like a real person as opposed to someone from whom you want to extract information, advice, or a recommendation. Discover what gets them fired up, and find ways to connect your own interests to theirs.

Sujay: Take note of any shared experiences you might share. Perhaps you went to the same college, grew up in the same town, or are both big baseball fans. Finding some common ground will provide you with conversation starters.

Come Prepared and Ready to Commit

Sure, showing up is half the battle, but the other half is a lot more demanding. When a mentor asks you to prepare something for your meeting, go above and beyond their expectations, especially if it's the first meeting. If he doesn't ask anything of you in advance, you should still go beyond expectations and make sure that you've given significant thought to his previous suggestions for you.

Tip In addition to their wisdom, mentors often have specific recommendations of resources to share with you, such as other people to talk to and books to read. Have a notepad or smart phone handy to jot down any names or ideas your mentor mentions. If you forget, send an e-mail thanking them for their time and make sure you ask to follow-up on their recommendations.

Ask for Feedback

Another way to illustrate your commitment to your relationship is to ask your mentor for feedback on your work or your growth. Talk to your mentors about your leadership skills, and explicitly ask for feedback and recommended changes you can make. Taking the initiative to have this conversation shows that you are interested in learning from your mentor and that you trust what he or she has to say.

Engage in Dialogue

In the book *True North*, Harvard Business School professor Bill George draws attention to the importance of building a two-way relationship with mentors in order to make the relationship last.?? One easy way to do that is to engage in critical dialogue with your mentor. Rather than being a depository for your mentor's suggestions, contextualize and work through them, and challenge your mentor when appropriate. This will help develop your relationship into one of shared respect and learning.

Keep in Touch

Once you've found a mentor, send a thank-you note after your meeting. If you feel you'll need another meeting sooner rather than later, suggest a date. Other than that, set up regular meetings with your mentor when you need his sage help and advice in person. In between meetings, send updates about what you're doing.

Even when you aren't seeking something specific, continue to give back to your mentor and think of ways to include him in your personal life, whether that's sharing an interesting book you read or connecting him with someone of interest.

> *Sheba*: When I was studying abroad in Vietnam, I spent a few minutes writing postcards to some of my mentors sharing highlights from my travels and a few events that reminded me of them. They were all thrilled that I was thinking of them and that I had brought them into a different aspect of my life, and that small act has bolstered our relationships tenfold.

Evaluate

As Lois Zachary and Lori Fischler discuss in *The Mentee's Guide*, it's important to evaluate the extent of a mentoring relationship.?? Once you've connected with your mentor a few times, consider how well the relationship is working for you. Do you trust your mentor, and do you feel that he trusts you? Is the relationship one that you would like to continue to grow, or has your mentor helped you as much as he can? Continuously evaluating your mentoring relationship will help you move it forward or seek new mentors if necessary.

Pay It Forward

One of the best ways to understand how to find and keep a good mentor is to be a mentor yourself.

When you're mentoring, keep in mind the qualities you're looking for in a mentor, and work to embody them for your mentee. Do your best to let the mentee's interest in the relationship guide you, but don't shy away from setting demands or reaching out to the mentee occasionally so it doesn't feel as if she has to be the initiator. This will not only benefit her life but will challenge you to take your own life one step further.

Sheba Mathew, a senior at Harvard College, is the co-founder of Synergy, Harvard's undergraduate social innovation incubator. She has pulled together multiple mentors to develop her interests in anthropology, global health, and social enterprise to solidify a vision of creating technological and business innovations that can promote the health of the underserved.

Sujay Tyle is leading business development at Los Angeles–based start-up Scopely, having left Harvard College with mentor Peter Thiel's 20 Under 20 Fellowship. He was the head of market strategy at Boston-based Kyruus. A recipient of the Presidential Environmental Youth Award from the White House and EPA, he is the cofounder of ReSight, Inc.

Chapter 29

Build a Team

One man can be a crucial ingredient on a team, but one man cannot make a team.

—*KAREEM ABDUL-JABBAR*

You can't be a leader without people to lead. And to make a real and lasting impact, you don't just need people, you need people who work together: a team. While certain components of team building are instinctual ("trusting your gut") and others are serendipitous ("right place, right time"), there are some proven methods you can use to help with this process. This chapter guides you through building and sustaining strong, effective teams that both work hard and work well together.

Identify Your Needs

There are a number of needs to consider when searching for, vetting, and selecting your team members. As always, recognizing talent is a critical skill.

> *Mona*: The best team-building advice I've heard is that you shouldn't be afraid to surround yourself with people who are smarter than you.

Content Expertise

Someone with content expertise knows a specific field inside and out. Depending on the problem you're trying to solve, this might be someone who knows everything about early childhood education or rehabilitating injured manatees. Chances are you've picked a field you're already pretty knowledgeable about, but it never hurts to recruit additional experts.

Process Expertise

People with process expertise have a specific skill set (for example, fundraising, coding, or marketing). They may not know much about your specific problem, but they're stellar at what they do, understand your mission, and know enough about the context to be valuable.

Work Style

Although it may seem intuitive to want to build a team with similar work styles, this can create significant weaknesses that far outweigh the challenge of building rapport across diverse approaches. While different work styles can initially be frustrating, diversity in a team is an asset. In his book *The Tipping Point*, Malcolm Gladwell identifies three archetypal work styles that differ but complement each other and build a team with a well-rounded set of skills:[1]

- The "maven" gathers and feeds key information to achieve the vision
- The "salesperson" builds an exciting shared vision through powerful persuasion
- The "connector" brings all the right players to the table

A well-rounded team needs people with different approaches to the process of working. For example, you don't want a team full of visionaries and no one who thinks about implementation. In addition, a strong team requires diverse work styles as well as people who understand and appreciate others' differences.

Exercise 29.1 How to Evaluate Working Styles

We all have a work style that is natural for us and will influence the dynamics of the teams we're on. As you build your team, strive to create it with diverse work styles and support people to understand and appreciate each other's work personalities. Use the following questions to evaluate a potential team member's work style.

How does the person work in a group? Does he:

- Tend to brainstorm, sort information, or push the group to a final decision?
- Focus on improving the process of the group working together or getting to an outcome?
- Work to maintain the status quo or push the group to grow?

How does the person think about and perform a task? Does she:

- Consider the details of implementation or the big picture context?
- Start brainstorming by listing all the possibilities or all the parameters?
- Prefer to plan everything in advance or to let things unfold organically?

How does the person define success? Does he gain satisfaction from:

- Crossing the T's and dotting the I's?
- Fostering teamwork?
- Defining and accomplishing a task or set of tasks?
- Creating new initiatives or trying new approaches?

How does the person deal with failure? Does she:

- Feel it's a reflection of personal skills or efforts?
- Assign blame to others or take the blame for the entire group?
- Try harder or give up and move on?

Keep in mind that there are no right answers (although your work style will likely create an affinity for others with similar work styles).

Network

You may want to include team members with strong professional connections you can leverage. For example, a health-centered group may want to build connections to health care professionals, and a group trying to improve urban issues may forge relationships with city planners and local officials. Look for team members who can help you establish relationships with these experts.

Start with Who You Already Have

Your enterprise, whether nonprofit or for-profit, will most likely start off with a leadership team and perhaps a loosely knit group of members. Start out with what you have. If you have a few people you can run ideas by, will give you honest feedback, and bring skills that you may not have, ask them to join the leadership team. Even if this group is informal at first, you can still use many of the principles from this chapter to build a strong team. As your organization becomes more established, this inner circle may morph into the more formal board of directors, executive staff, or founding partners. At a minimum, make sure to clearly communicate to your leadership team their roles, responsibilities, and expectations.

Select a Team Structure

Selecting a team structure is an essential step because it affects how you work together and share responsibilities. There are many different structures to use, and the best one for you depends on the goals of your organization and the culture of your team. You may choose a more traditional hierarchy, create a leadership structure of your own, or even find that sharing leadership across the group works best. Most new groups won't need the classic organizational hierarchy of a president, chief executive officer, chief operations officer, and so on. Rather, it may be more practical to begin with a functional structure in which people head up different key areas of work, such as marketing, sales, operations, and program management.

Note When you're starting off, take time to consider the structure, but don't get too caught up in hierarchy and assigning titles, because the structure will likely naturally evolve to fit the needs of your group.

Once your group has gained steam and you're a bit more established, you may want to consider a more formal team structure. Most established organizations have several different teams, including a leadership or executive team, a board of directors or advisors, one or more staff teams, and perhaps volunteers or larger groups of stakeholders. The executive leadership team and board are the backbone of your organization.

As you formalize these roles, take time to vet the inner circle to make sure they're a good fit for the team and the role. Both the executive leadership team and board of directors should be composed of people who share your values and are committed to the mission and vision, though they will have different roles in realizing that vision. The executive leadership team gets the vision off the ground. The members of the board of directors are the trusted advisors the executive leadership turns to when the organization needs to adapt its vision, build community support, and scale. When determining the structure of the board, you may prefer an advisory-oriented board with representatives from each stakeholder group or a working board with task committees.

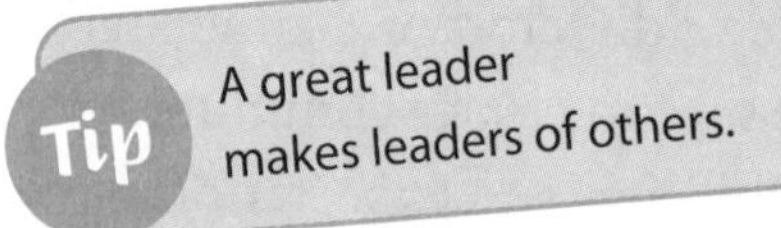

Regardless of how you share responsibility, it's paramount to give the other leaders your trust, respect, and freedom over their committee or project. Help them develop and cultivate their own leadership abilities.

In sum:

- Surround yourself with people smarter than you.
- Know when you need a content or process expert.
- Build a team that spans diverse work styles.
- Design a team structure that suits your specific team goals rather than defaulting to the standard hierarchy.

Recruit

When you are recruiting team members, it's great to have options. Ideally you'd like a large pool of qualified candidates to choose from. So how do you get the word out without spending a lot of money on advertising? Here are some low-cost or free ways to reach people:

- Look for like-minded people through meetup.com groups, community groups, and university associations.

Figure 29.1. Team Structures

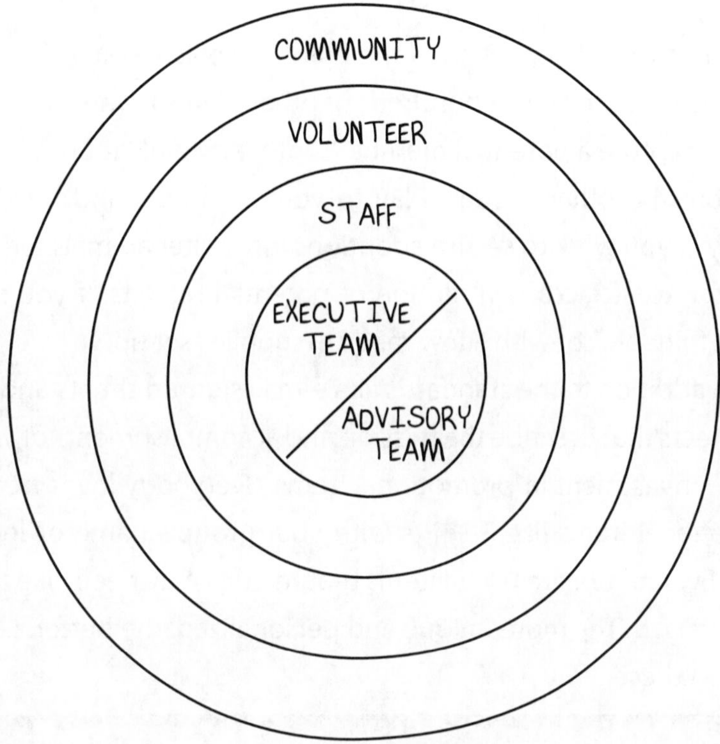

- Leverage low-cost platforms such as Idealist, Craigslist, alumni websites, and professional association job boards.
- Your best free resource is your network. Send a description of the position to helpful contacts with a request to please forward it along to promising candidates.

> *Mona*: Some of my best team members started as a network connection with three or four degrees of separation.

Reaching the right people is only half the battle; you also have to spark their interest. Don't assume everyone knows how awesome your group is, so take the time to articulate why being on your team would be an amazing experience. Whether you're recruiting for a volunteer, board, or paid position, prepare a well-thought-out position description. If you're a nonprofit or start-up that can't offer the most competitive salary (or any salary at all), consider other benefits you can offer candidates—for example, flexible work schedules, growth and professional development opportunities, health care, and retirement benefits.

Winning the Recruitment Fair

If you're trying to recruit a team, a common place to start is a university or career fair. You'll join dozens or hundreds of other teams trying to recruit top talent.

To capture a potential member's interest, think about what makes you stand out from the other groups. Play to your strengths and turn them into a visual display. If you work to secure adoptions for shelter animals, bring a friendly puppy with you to attract the attention of potential recruits. If you started a free clinic, have a foldable cot with a few medical supplies set up.

In addition to the standards like e-mail sign-up sheets and one-page information sheets that describe the mission and accomplishments of your group, consider a small investment in promotional items. Everybody loves free things. Give away promotional items like T-shirts with your group's name or logo emblazoned on them. Even better are useful items that recruits may need, like a clipboard, pens, or a mouse pad. The more unique and personalized, the better. Look online for good deals on these.

Components of a Position Description

A good position description that contains the components listed below will help attract the right candidate. This may be your first impression on interested candidates so take some time to hone your message.

1. A great opening statement that spells out what is particularly interesting about the position and the organization, as well as a description of the values, vision, and mission of your enterprise. Make this compelling and concise.
2. A description of the role, including title, time commitment, and relationship to other team members (that is, who reports to whom).
3. Primary duties that describe day-to-day work. List these in order of importance, and include the occasional duties too.
4. Required skills that are specific, such as, "At least two years of experience managing groups of more than 50 volunteers," rather than, "Experience managing large groups of volunteers."

5. Any educational qualifications that you require or desire, noting when these may substitute for on-the-job experience.
6. Key success factors that spell out how you will evaluate the person in the role.
7. Any other requirements such as having a car or willingness to travel.
8. Who to contact for more information and where to submit the application.

Be sure your job descriptions and interview questions don't break federal, state, or local laws. Never include questions or criteria based on race, gender, age, religion, disability, health status, marital status, or sexual orientation. When in doubt, check the laws in your area.

Interview

Once you've attracted great candidates, how do you choose among them? People usually put their best foot forward in an application and interview, so you'll have to work to get an accurate picture. Use these tips:

- Read candidates' résumés and note specific things in their work history that you want to ask about.
- Ask open-ended questions; then stop talking and listen. Let the candidate paint a picture for you in her own words.
- Ask for specific examples. Don't let the interviewees get by with, "I'm an ethical person." Have them describe a tough ethical dilemma and how they dealt with it.
- Avoid asking leading or obvious questions such as, "Do you work well under pressure?" Instead, present a situation and see how the candidate responds: "Some people are more motivated by a dynamic environment while others are more motivated by a stable environment. Which do you prefer?"

Remember that candidates are also interviewing you. They will want to know a good deal about your leadership and their potential work environment. Here are ten common questions candidates may ask:

1. What are the group's core values, mission, and vision?
2. What are the main daily activities I'll be involved in?
3. What are the core skills you're looking for?
4. Tell me about the clients and partners I'll interact with.

5. Who are the colleagues I'll work with on a daily basis?
6. Who are the key competitors and collaborators?
7. What are the opportunities for growth and professional development?
8. How would you describe the organizational culture?
9. What are your favorite and least favorite parts of working with this particular team?
10. Where do you see the enterprise in one, five, or ten years?

Hire

When you've found Mr. or Ms. Right, be prepared to formalize the relationship with a written agreement. Even if you're an informal group such as a student group, it is still a good idea to document your mutual expectations and agreements. Include the person's role, how he or she is expected to interact with others, and how he or she will be evaluated.

If your organization is established, be prepared to offer the job with a well-thought-out offer letter. Start by researching state laws to ensure that you are fully in compliance with them. If you don't intend to use the offer letter as a contract, make sure you include an "at-will employment" statement (meaning that either party can terminate the relationship without liability) and avoid referencing annual pay rates or implying future job security.

WARNING

Don't burn bridges with the candidates you didn't select. Communicate with them in a timely and respectful manner. It's just plain polite and thoughtful, and you never know when you'll cross paths again with that person in the future.

Components of an Offer Letter

1. Candidate's name
2. Job title
3. Brief overview of job details, including primary task, supervisor, and a reference to the full job description
4. The salary or pay rate
5. The start date
6. Description of any probationary periods and evaluation practices
7. Description of benefits or reference to personnel handbook with this information (include a statement about holidays, sick time, and vacation)
8. The length of time that the offer letter is valid.
9. Any conditions that must be met in order to be eligible for the job (for example, pending proof of eligibility to legally work in the US)
10. An at-will employment statement

Sustain a Team

The way a team plays as a whole determines its success. You may have the greatest bunch of individual stars in the world, but if they don't play together, the club won't be worth a dime.

BABE RUTH

Once you have your team in place, you'll need to make a concerted effort to build up and cement the relationships within it, as well as promote the attitudes and problem-solving skills that will help ensure the long-term success of your group. This takes some effort, but it's well worth the investment. Think of your team as a luxury car: it requires constant maintenance and upkeep, but if you treat it well and look after it, it will outperform even your wildest expectations. The following guidelines will help keep your team in racing form.

Build Team Synergy

To foster good team spirit within your group, first acknowledge that the process of building team rapport is crucial to producing good long-term results. Dedicate some time for people to get to know each other and start building trust and respect. Here are some ideas:

- *Share a meal.* Make one of your meetings a potluck, or arrange to meet at a restaurant.
- *Try an ice-breaker.* Ice-breakers are a great way to uncover interesting facts about team members and promote bonding. A quick Web search will pull up lists of ice-breakers, trust exercises, and team-building activities. Try some of these during a team retreat or at the beginning of every team meeting.
- *Bring in an expert.* If you have the budget, hire a team-building facilitator to lead a workshop or retreat.

What activities have helped *you* bond with teammates? What specifically about the activity made it effective?

Create a Safe Environment

Teamwork requires an open dialogue and an environment where members aren't afraid to speak up. Here are some leadership tips that encourage dialogue and build trust:

- Ask questions rather than always providing answers.
- Acknowledge and show respect for everyone's ideas.
- If an idea isn't the right one for that moment, be diplomatic when turning it down.
- Ask for people's opinions frequently, and then listen.
- Be open to having your mind changed.
- Rather than hiding mistakes or punishing people for them, use mistakes as opportunities to learn.

Provide Opportunities and Reward Achievements

It takes special skills to recognize and use the talent in others. A great leader brings out the best in colleagues and collaborators. In *Team Building: Proven Strategies for Improving Team Performance*, William Dyer, W. G. Dyer, and Jeffrey Dyer note that successful teams have both the appropriate skills and the motivation to achieve their vision, as well as good leaders who foster both of these qualities in their teams. The authors observed that if motivation is the challenge, "empowering skilled team members with greater responsibility for team tasks and performance can be an effective way to increase the team member's commitment to the team and its goals."[2]

However, if the team has plenty of motivation but lacks the appropriate skills, a leader must act as an educator and coach to help them develop the skills. If this is the case, outline a work and learning plan with each team member to develop the necessary skill sets and then offer support. Provide frequent constructive feedback and coaching that helps team members recognize and leverage their strengths.

Finally, reward good performance. This could be a shout-out at a meeting, a small but thoughtful gift, or a party to celebrate a success. The more specific you can be with your praise, the better. Find out what motivates each person on your team. Some people respond well to public recognition, while others are much more moved by private words of praise.

What type of recognition do you respond to? How does a reward change your behavior?

Set Ground Rules and Expect Growing Pains

At the core, teams are relationships between people. Relationships take time and effort to mature. Don't assume everyone understands how to work well together from the start. Sometimes there are growing pains. Take time to discuss what success will look like for your team (in terms of both product and process), what the ground rules are for interacting, how decisions will be made, and how conflicts will be handled. Exercise 29.2 gives you ideas on how to deal with difficult team situations.

It may be hard to imagine that your team would ever need ground rules or a protocol for handling conflict, but if you're tackling something challenging, you'll be pushing people to excel. Before you know it, you could have a stressed-out, tense group on your hands. Don't despair—prepare! Prevent problems by setting some ground rules. These steps are just as relevant for ad hoc teams working together for a short time as they are for well-established teams.

Exercise 29.2 Team Toxins

Take some time, on your own or with your group, to think through situations where team toxins may arise and determine what you can do to prevent and manage these situations.

List a few potentially toxic situations, and make them as realistic and detailed as possible for your group—for example: "We have spent three months planning an event to gain publicity and secure new donors. At the last minute the keynote speaker falls through. During an emergency team meeting one person on the outreach committee accuses the entertainment organizer of not having it together and ruining the whole event."

1. Think about and list three ways to handle the situation in the moment. For example:
   - Call for a break to let people cool off.
   - Ask the entertainment organizer to use "I" statements to explain how the accusation affected him.
   - Ask the outreach committee member to reframe the concern so that it is about the entertainment organizer's actions rather than about him personally.
2. Think about and list three ways that you can prevent the situation beforehand. For example:
   - Educate the team about the concept of team toxins and how they affect people personally and the work of the group.
   - Create a group agreement about how team members will engage with each other during challenges.
   - Role-play difficult situations so that the group members have practice recognizing the toxin they are most likely to use and how to choose alternative behaviors.

Work with Remote Teams

Once your group is up and running, it may reach a tipping point, growing beyond the original core team and expanding into more than one location. As you expand, new responsibilities will arise for you and your group, such as figuring out how to engage in a new level of fundraising, how dispersed locations can work together, or how to ensure quality across multiple sites. Acknowledge the strengths and successes of the team that got you this far while simultaneously planning for new and different circumstances. Creating good rapport and collaboration between dispersed teams requires some extra attention to detail. Use these tips to build a strong organizational culture that can support dispersed teams:

- Make sure team members who work remotely are included in rapport-building activities.
- Try to connect face-to-face as much as possible. Use Skype, Google Hangout, GoToMeeting, and other Web platforms that enable virtual face-to-face connection.
- Avoid siloing. Instead, encourage collaborations across geographical divides by sharing information through a group server or file sharing software such as Dropbox.
- If possible, bring all teams together for quarterly or annual retreats to reinforce relationships.
- Check in frequently with team members or managers to catch and address challenges early.

Give Feedback in a Productive Manner

Occasionally you may need to provide feedback that qualifies as negative feedback. This can be the hardest part of working in a team, and it's a great test of your leadership abilities. In his book *Feedback That Works: How to Build and Deliver Your Message*, Sloan Weitzel points out that many people fail to be helpful because they offer judgmental feedback or interpretations of behaviors, such as, "You need to be more strategic."[3] While this might seem clear to the person providing the feedback, it doesn't describe the behavior that needs to be modified or its impact. Use the information in the following section to give and receive effective feedback.

How do you know when you need to give your team negative feedback? The authors of *The Seven Principles for Making Marriage Work*, John Gottman and Nan Silver, identified the following four "team toxins" to watch for:[4]

- Blaming: Making personal attacks rather than disagreeing with someone's ideas
- Defensiveness: Refusing to own up to mistakes or inappropriate behavior
- Contempt: Behaving in a hostile way that may include sarcasm or demeaning humor
- Stonewalling: Refusing to engage by withdrawing

If you recognize these behaviors, you'll need to step quickly to correct the problem: pause, name the issue, and then take some time to educate the team about the impact of the behavior. Come to an agreement on how to handle such future situations.

Give Feedback

The following tips will help you give effective feedback to your team members:

1. Find a good time and ask for permission to give feedback. No one wants to be caught off guard or given negative feedback in a public setting.
2. Start out by noting what you observed. Giving a specific example helps people remember their actions.
3. Share what you observed about the impact of the person's behaviors. Use "I" statements and stick to observational facts rather than judgments and interpretations.
4. Help the person understand what didn't work and what should be done differently by asking for his reaction and thoughts.
5. Work together to establish a few specific alternative actions or behaviors that would be more appropriate and support this person's change efforts by giving him recognition for improvements.

Receive Feedback

As a leader it is just as critical to be able to receive feedback as it is to give feedback. You are modeling the ability to remain open to learning and improvements. Keep the following tips in mind when you are receiving feedback:

1. As a leader, you may have to take the lead in soliciting feedback. Regularly ask people what they think, and put structures in place to get regular, timely feedback, perhaps using a leadership evaluation or a suggestion box.
2. Notice your automatic reactions, and be aware of your own biases. We all have buttons that can be pushed and make us less able to hear feedback.
3. Ask clarifying questions that help you understand how your behavior was perceived and the impact it had on others.
4. Thank the person for offering feedback to you. Feedback is a gift and a chance to become even better at what you do, but it is difficult to give someone feedback, particularly if that person is your boss. Be kind and acknowledge the effort it took this person to talk to you.
5. No matter what, don't get defensive. Even if you feel the feedback is totally off the mark or it makes you mad, don't react in the moment. Take a breath and give yourself some private time to process what you heard before reacting.

Work with Friends

Vinod Nambudiri is a graduate of Harvard College, Harvard Medical School, and Harvard Business School. He is completing his medical residency training in internal medicine and dermatology. Highlights of past experiences working with friends have included consulting on a start-up hospital chain in India and running the finances for a conference for 1200 attendees.

When it comes to building a team, one of the first places we turn to is our own circle of friends. Working with close friends—teaming up for a class project, codirecting a community event, or founding a business—presents a wonderful opportunity. Whether in academic, extracurricular, or professional contexts, friends can be tremendous assets, supporting your dreams and helping you accomplish your goals. However, working with close friends can also be awkward and difficult. Such working relationships present a unique set of challenges, including to maintain the line between work and fun, personal and professional. But with clear communication and a mature attitude, both friends, as well as the group itself, can benefit from the friendship.

Given leadership positions within a group, three potential situations might exist:

1. You are in a leadership position.
2. Your friend is in a leadership position.
3. You are both in leadership positions.

Here we'll examine each of these circumstances in greater depth, illustrating how to make the most of working with friends.

Navigating Friendships When You're at the Helm

Value Your Role
Vinod: Leading a group that your friends belong to means you'll occupy a position of authority and respect among your peers. Your role as a leader among friends is a privilege not to be taken for granted. Take your responsibility seriously, but enjoy the experience while doing so. Your leadership role will likely be for a finite period, whereas close friendships have the potential to last a lifetime.

Be Fair
Vinod: Treat your friends in the group the same way you'd treat others to maintain an unbiased leadership style. Group members who sense favoritism is at play will lose respect for you as a leader.

Recognize Boundaries
Vinod: Never take advantage of friends who are a part of your team. Though you should feel free to solicit feedback on your leadership, never ask them to give you insider information on other people in the group. This places them in a potentially compromising position due to their friendship with you. Asking your friends to "spy" on other group members will only cultivate ill will and resentment.

Bring Out the Best in Others
Vinod: It is possible to develop a synergy between your roles as a leader and as a friend. Think about what has strengthened your friendship in the past, and try

to apply this to the group setting. I found myself in charge of organizing a large gala for 500 attendees. My friend was also on the organizing committee. While many perceived her as a quiet, reserved professional, I knew she was a skilled negotiator with a deliberate, persistent, respectful style. I assigned her the task of identifying the appropriate vendors for the event, and she secured excellent prices for high-quality services that impressed the entire organizing committee and all the gala attendees.

Following Your Friend, the Leader

Give Honest Feedback

Vinod: As a member of a team under your friend's leadership, you have the chance to provide valuable feedback. If your friend's leadership skills need improvement—perhaps her communication is lacking or she makes hasty decisions—you should bring this to her attention. She cannot improve her leadership if she's unaware that a problem exists. Though providing a friend with constructive criticism can be uncomfortable, doing so is the mark of true friendship. Offer concrete, specific suggestions for how she can best address her shortcomings.

Similarly, if your friend is leading the group wisely, making sound decisions and implementing good policies, offer support by following her direction and recognizing her accomplishments. Positive feedback is as valuable as constructive criticism. By identifying her strengths, you enhance her confidence as a leader and reinforce her positive attributes.

Respect Authority

Vinod: Awkwardness may arise when taking orders or being assigned tasks from someone you consider a peer or friend. Initially this may seem to throw off your friendship dynamic. If you feel your relationship is being strained, to bring this to your friend's attention; open communication is always appreciated. Also, remember that the skewed distribution of responsibility is dictated by the hierarchical organizational structure, not your friend.

Sharing Friendship, Sharing Responsibility

Build on Strengths

Vinod: Leading with others is a skill that, once learned, is a powerful tool. Collaboration underlies virtually all successful accomplishments, capitalizing on the strengths of each individual. An advantage of sharing leadership responsibilities with friends is knowing, even before you ever work together, what the strengths and weaknesses of your collaboration will be. Do you both love to work around firm deadlines? Is one more organized than the other? Early on, discuss areas of leadership differences, and incorporate strategies to resolve or work around them.

Communicate Often and Well

Vinod: Clear, consistent communication is critical to maintaining the strength of your friendship and the effectiveness of your collaboration. Make sure you're both clear on the goals of the organization, tasks at hand, and how the collaboration will affect your friendship.

Even with clear communication, however, it's sometimes the case that one (or both) of you fails to meet certain responsibilities. If your friend is at fault, be sure to address the issue directly though tactfully, and identify what allowed the lapse to occur. Discuss what happened—perhaps a problem with communication—and devise plans to rectify the underlying cause for the future.

Approach the interaction with the level of respect you'd want to be shown in similar circumstances. If you happen to be the one to drop the ball, be honest and forthcoming with your friend. While this may be difficult, you should initiate the dialogue rather than place your friend in the position of having to bring up the matter.

Learn from Others

Vinod: Most important, when you work with friends, view the experience as an opportunity to learn. In such collaborations, you may discover leadership traits in each other that inspire new-found respect. At the end of the leadership collaboration, take time to reflect on the experience together.

Better Together

Vinod: By taking a balanced and open approach to working with your friends—by respecting your past relationship with them and by being willing to learn from the new experience of working together—you can help ensure that working with friends ends up being more comfortable than cumbersome. Whether as a leader, member, or co-leader, working with your friends affords you the unique opportunity to emerge from the experience better friends because of it.

Exercise 29.3 Be a Great Leader and Friend

You're leading an organization that several of your friends are members of. List three challenges you anticipate in this context. Then tell how you would address each one.

1.

2.

3.

While working with friends, unique leadership challenges are sure to present themselves.[5] Thinking through the scenarios below and identifying ways to address these potential obstacles will help prepare you for such future situations and strengthen your leadership skills.

1. You're leading a team of five individuals starting a new company. Three of the members are your friends from a previous company, and the final member of the team is new to you and the others in the group. The new member of the company remarks that he is feeling somewhat isolated at work. What steps do you take to foster a successful group dynamic as you begin your start-up?

(continued)

2. A close friend on your team tells you that your leadership during the last meeting was perceived as dominating and disregarded some of her key ideas. You felt that her visions for the project at the last meeting were not the best ones for the organization and had instead selected those of a coworker. How do you discuss this with her, mindful of your longstanding prior friendship?

If Necessary, Recalibrate Your Team

The boss drives people; the leader coaches them. The boss depends on authority; the leader on good will. The boss inspires fear; the leader inspires enthusiasm. The boss says I; the leader says WE. The boss fixes the blame for the breakdown; the leader fixes the breakdown. The boss says, GO; the leader says Let's GO!

H. GORDON SELFRIDGE

Sometimes even the best preparation, feedback, and conflict mediation won't solve the problem, and the best thing you can do for your team and your organization is to let someone go. If this is the case and the person is an employee, first and foremost educate yourself on the federal and state employment laws that pertain to firing employees. There are a number of steps you must take to protect yourself from a wrongful termination suit. Once you know you are in compliance with the law or if the person is informally part of your organization, use the following tips to get through the ordeal as painlessly as possible:

- Don't initiate the conversation until you have exhausted corrective measures. Let him or her know explicitly what needs to change and what actions will be taken if requested changes are not made.
- Set up a one-on-one meeting with the person, and make sure it is private.
- Start the meeting with a direct explanation of your decision. Be concise, and after you've imparted the information, give the person time to absorb the information and respond.

Figure 29.2. Navigating Friendships When You're at the Helm

- Be prepared to back up your decision with data if necessary. You don't want someone to try to talk you out of your decision.
- Be compassionate but don't sugarcoat the reasons for your decision.

Mona Jones-Romansic has worked with diverse enterprises for over a decade to improve organizational management, operations, and culture. As director of Olive Grove's Learning and People Practice, Mona supports leaders to align organizational culture, systems, and strategy to increase mission impact.

Chapter 30

Optimize Communication

The art of communication is the language of leadership.

—JAMES HUMES

Effective communication within a team is the glue that holds the team together. Good communication goes beyond stating this week's goals or outlining projects; it spans everything from collaborating and setting group goals, to promoting strong team rapport and maximizing knowledge retention. Good communication keeps your team knowledgeable, engaged, and focused on group goals. This chapter will help you establish and maintain effective communication within your team.

Why Good Communication Is Important

Good communication allows you to express your goals for the group clearly, ensuring everyone is on the same page. It:

1. Prevents mistakes and misunderstandings, which saves you time, money, and other valuable resources.
2. Keeps your group organized and focused, increasing productivity.
3. Is key to effective conflict resolution.
4. Is the hallmark of a good leader.

Essentials of Team Communication

Maintain a Unified Front

This is harder than it sounds and more valuable than it seems. It has real potential to boost the productivity of your team. Whether it's communication from the leaders to the members, from one committee to another, or externally between your group and another organization, unity is essential. Disunity will derail the achievement of your goals and the effectiveness of your leadership.

> *Trent*: Mixed messages from a group's leader can cause damage. Once the leader of a group I was in failed to come to a consensus on changing membership requirements. Rather than table it for a later meeting, the president presented the changes to the members, and officers who disagreed openly challenged the proposal. This created considerable confusion among the members and discord among the leaders that took weeks to resolve.

This doesn't mean there should never be disagreement. Disagreement is a valuable tool to discover the pros and cons of various issues, which generally makes your final decision better. However, it should be done professionally and at the right time. At a meeting's conclusion, your group should all be ready to work toward your goals and projects. This ensures consistency and a more professional image both inside and outside the group.

Key Communication Points

During executive board or committee meetings, determine key communication points:

- Agree on what will be communicated to the members: "We will organize a gala fundraiser to benefit cancer research."
- Decide how the information will be communicated: "We will announce it in our group meeting, send out e-mails, and include it in our newsletter."

- Agree on what specific details to include or omit: "The date will be October 12, from 8:00 p.m. until midnight at the KJ Ranch. The cost will be $125 per person."
- Plan how to handle feedback from the group: "Jane will answer questions and serve as the point person for event information; John will discuss member responsibilities and answer questions about any requirements."
- Discuss the necessity of the project, and how it will benefit the group: "The event achieves our goals of promoting cancer awareness and fundraising for cancer research. It is also a great opportunity to recruit new members to the organization."
- Encourage members to be positive about the experience: "This will be a lot of work, but will have an incredible impact on our community. It will be a great night we'll all enjoy!"

Be a Leader Rather Than a Dictator

There is no communication in this world except between equals.

KEN BURNS

Eventually every team experiences a moment of great conflict where no one can come to an agreement on the issue. In situations like this, it's tempting to pull rank to resolve the problem quickly. This, however, will increase confusion, frustration, and resentment. Instead of saying, "Because I'm the president and I said so," if there's a problem, take the time to fully address the situation. In this way, you may realize something you missed or help someone better understand what's going on. This promotes a healthy environment for your team and ensures focus on your team goals rather than hurt feelings. Use these tips:[1]

- Is the conflict about a specific issue? Or is it a result of personality differences?
- Is the conflict due to lack of full understanding or lack of information?
- What are the key issues at the center of the dispute? What does everyone agree on?
- Are emotions too high to effectively address the situation? Should it be tabled and addressed later?

Figure 30.1. Be Leaders, Not Dictators

Encourage Two-Way Communication

While it's important that members of an organization listen to and understand what leaders are communicating, it's equally important for leaders to hear what the members are saying. Encouraging open, two-way communication, both in and outside meetings, not only increases overall understanding of the issues at hand; it also promotes ownership from team members. Don't wait for your members to come to you; actively seek out feedback from your team. Make meaningful efforts to address their concerns and questions.

Be Open-Minded

Remaining open to new ideas and being amenable to change is essential. Studies have suggested that by keeping to this rule of communication, both individual and team goals will be realized and overall attitudes will remain positive.[2] Be open to suggestions for improvement and alternative ideas.

Stay Positive

Negativity increases stress levels, leading to shorter tempers, greater frustration, and decreased productivity. Unnecessarily negative criticism causes people to get defensive or shut down, which is counterproductive to your goal. Set a positive tone to ensure your communication is received effectively.

Give Fair Notice

Relay information to the relevant parties far enough in advance so they have a reasonable amount of time to prepare, especially if it's something they'll need to plan around.

Keep It Simple, But Be Thorough

Be sure to cover all the necessary information without becoming overly repetitive. Simply state the who, what, where, when, why, how, and who to contact for more information. For example, if your group is planning a new project, you might make the following announcement: "The project will entail [description], will require members to do [details], and will benefit the organization and public in the following ways: [examples]. Any questions? Thanks, and remember to meet at [place] at [time]. Check your e-mail for updates."

Don't overstate each point. If your members start tuning you out, they may miss something crucial you address later on. If you don't give enough detail, your members can always ask clarifying questions. Present, discuss, and conclude. This can be challenging, but the better you can do it, the more effective your communication is.

Accuracy Is Key

Even if you are pressed for time, always double-check the details before sending out any communication. Following up with corrections creates confusion and risks critical information not being received.

Effective Team Meetings

Physically coming together as a team is vital for effective communication. In-person working time is critical and limited. Good communication practices will ensure your meetings are effective and efficient.

Agendas

Provide meeting expectations for attendees using an agenda to list goals and items to discuss. Members can take notes on each item, write reminders for later, and have a record of the meeting. The agenda provides structure for your meeting.

E-mail agendas a few days in advance or distribute them to members as they enter the meeting so they have time to read the information and form questions. Your agenda should be designed in a way that is most effective for your group. You may want to bullet-point each item of business and who will present it. Consider giving a time estimate for each section. Be clear about what it is you expect to accomplish during the meeting.

Sample Agenda

Young Professionals Against Cancer Quarterly Board Meeting, April 25

I. Welcome: Yang (2 minutes)

II. Introduction of New Mission and Advocacy Chair—Noor (2 minutes)

III. Membership Changes—Sasha (10 minutes)

   a. Membership standings/requirements
   b. Committee meetings—intent and committee selection
   c. Membership social: *Thursday, June 23* at Noch's Pizza
   d. Kickball tournament: *Saturday, August 6* at Metro Parks on Fifty Street

IV. Special Projects—Trey (5 minutes)

   a. Downtown City Marathon: *Saturday, April 30* Cheer Station on Mile 11
   b. Second Annual Purple Tie Gala: *October 12*
      - Planning Committee
      - Venue and Theme Update

V. Mission support projects—Chelsea and Paul (5 minutes)

   a. Cancer Patient Visits: *Monday, May 23*
      - Volunteers to arrive @ 6:00 p.m. See volunteer sign-up sheet
      - Pizza night—pizza and dessert donated

VI. Announcements and Close—Yang (2 minutes)

   a. Nominations for executive committee due in July
   b. Next quarterly board meeting: Monday, July 25

Use handouts when any major items will be discussed or voted on. For example, if a new bylaw is being presented to the members for discussion, print up copies of the bylaw along with a brief synopsis describing its purpose, why it's important, and the impact it will have on the organization. Handouts should also be distributed before the meeting or as members arrive to allow time for them to review the information.

Records, Records, Records

Comprehensive meeting minutes and other organizational records are essential. Meeting minutes describe what happened during the meeting, including what topics were discussed, what actions will be taken, and any questions that are still outstanding. Meeting minutes should enable absentees members to know precisely what happened at the meeting. A thorough set of meeting minutes eliminates confusion and safeguards against memory lapses.

Sample Meeting Minutes

Young Professionals Against Cancer Executive Committee Meeting
Monday June 28—6:00 pm

Attendees: Yang, Sasha, Juan, Paul, Noor, Lacey, Mark

Next meeting: Monday, July 19, at Main Office

- Networking at 5:30 p.m.
- Meeting at 6:00 p.m.
- Lacey and Mark will not be in attendance due to family commitments.

Next executive committee meeting: Date TBD, 6:00 p.m.

Agenda and Items Discussed

1. General Info (Yang)

a. General meetings will continue to be quarterly, the third Monday of each quarter.

2. Upcoming Events (Juan)

a. Purple Tie Gala
   i. October 16, location TBD (Does anyone know of free or discounted event spaces available? If so, please email ASAP.)

ii. Chair: Elizabeth

iii. Fundraising goal: $30,000

iv. Attendee goal: 450

3. Membership and Social Committee (Sasha)

a. Next social event
   i. Noch's Pizza on July 27: Remember to bring $5 to help cover cost of food.

b. Roster updates: We welcomed 12 new members last month! A big thanks to Lisa for all her hard work!

4. Treasurer (Melissa)

a. No updates at this time.

5. Secretary (Noor)

a. Please e-mail Jason if you would like to be added to next meeting agenda.

Record keeping is important. For all major projects, keep an account of all contracts, invoices, detailed receipts, tasks, time lines, committee meeting agendas, and copies of every event-related e-mail sent. These records can serve as a blueprint the next time your group takes on a similar project.

Keep group records well organized in a central location. Develop a plan for leaders to pass down these records, this "institutional knowledge," to their successors. For more information on leadership transitions and institutional knowledge, see Chapter 37.

Engaging Your Audience

During meetings, be energetic and upbeat, feed off your team's reactions, encourage interaction, and allow the occasional departure from seriousness. Use 20 minutes before or after your meeting as a social time with refreshments.

Try these suggestions to make your meetings and communications more fun and interesting:

- Recognize birthdays, personal events for members (such as weddings or births), and special outside achievements.
- Add humorous or inspirational quotes to the meeting agendas or a cool factoid to the monthly newsletter.
- In meetings, have members give shout-outs to fellow teammates for accomplishments.
- Share inspirational or motivational videos or pictures before or after your meetings.

Create a Collaborative Environment

> **Tip** When it will be weeks between meetings, schedule e-mails to remind everyone of goals and deadlines while providing updates or other important news items.

After a meeting, it's critical to follow up and reinforce what was discussed to promote better understanding and reinforce people's memories. Immediately after, send out an e-mail thanking everyone for a good session and briefly remind them of what was covered. Later, take a moment to check in with individual members or committee leaders to see if assigned tasks are being completed and address any problems that may have surfaced.

Consider implementing some of the communications tools that follow to keep members engaged and informed about their individual responsibilities. Periodically, reexamine the communication effectiveness of your group and what could be improved to help your team reach its maximum potential.

Contact Lists

Make a list of all team members that includes each person's position, phone number, e-mail address, and birthday. E-mail the list to everyone. Save a copy that's easily accessible to your members (such as a members-only section of your website). This facilitates communication and socializing.

E-mail and Listservs

When used effectively, e-mail is one of the most powerful tools available to keep your team connected. It also allows you to maintain a permanent record of communication.

Keep the e-mail addresses of your members accurate and have them somewhere easily accessible, perhaps on a contact list. When leaders are communicating to the membership through e-mail, it is a good practice to have all messages flow through a primary source. Select one person on the leadership team to be responsible for any communications going out to the members.

If you have more than a handful of members or if your membership base changes regularly, consider an e-mail listserv. A listserv, also referred to as a distribution list, is a central e-mail address that distributes messages to every member of the listserv. This benefits not only you; your members can easily stay in touch with the entire group as well. By simply sending something to one e-mail address, you can easily communicate with all your members.

If your group becomes too social with the listserv, consider providing them with an online forum or separate social and official listservs. E-mail listservs are available from numerous free sources and are even included with some Web domains.

WARNING

Be responsible with e-mail communication!

- Remember that e-mail is text based, so vocal inflections or nonverbal communication may not always carry through, leading to a misinterpretation of your meaning.
- Always double-check to whom your e-mail is addressed and be careful when clicking "reply all".
- Never e-mail when you are frustrated or angry. Take a break, and e-mail later when you're calmer.
- Be careful not to overuse e-mail. Overwhelmed members may begin to ignore your messages.

Collaboration Tools

We've seen incredible advances in online group collaboration tools, such as Google Documents, Basecamp, and Asana. These resources are invaluable when working on a project with a team in multiple locations.

Collaborative resources can range from simple to complex. To store files for easy access by members, look for a cloud service. If your projects have many components, goals, and tracking requirements, consider a project management site that combines time lines, resource assignments, file storage, and task delegation.

If you find your team members, advisors, partners, and resources in different locations often, consider connecting them through collaborative resources so your team can share information and resources across the organization without being limited to when schedules happen to line up. This also allows the leadership to monitor the work of your group and provide feedback, updates, and resources in real time to your members.

Forums

A forum (or message board) is another effective way to encourage discussions outside meetings. If you have a website, many domain-hosting companies provide them at no additional charge.

Forums are great for seeking feedback. Encourage members to visit your forum to discuss items of interest there rather than clog inboxes with "reply all" e-mails. It's a cleaner and easier way to read opinions, keep up with debates, and look back-on previous discussions. Simply link the forum or message board to the members-only section of your group's website.

Calendars

By using resources such as Google Calendar or TimeBridge, you can keep members up-to-date on major events, meetings, or deadlines within the organization. Members can then easily integrate the team calendar with most major e-mail programs, collaboration programs, and phone calendar applications.

Include the following information:

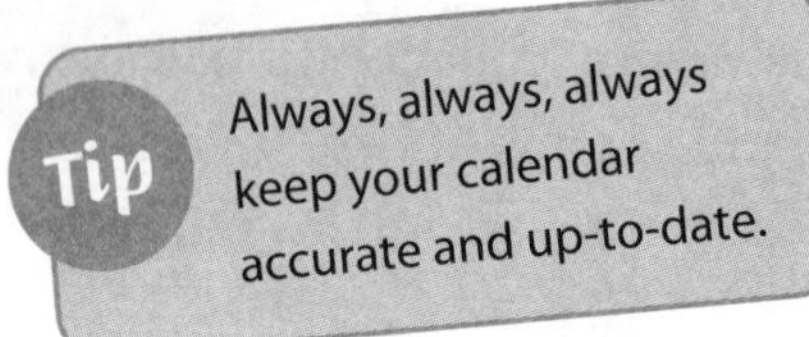

- Dates for team meetings, executive board meetings, and committee meetings
- Dates of important events
- Key deadlines for projects
- Notable dates for responsibilities the team has to other organizations
- Deadlines for including information for internal and external communication publications
- Major holidays or other events

Make sure your team's calendar is organized, neat, and easy to read.

Determine What's Effective

Each group is unique and dynamic. Work with your team to identify effective approaches for communication with your target groups.

Establish Your Communication Strategy

There are many factors to think about when determining your communications strategy. Different organizations have different needs based upon how your group is formed and how it operates. Consider the following questions when thinking about your communication needs:

- How big is the group? Different strategies and resources are effective for larger groups than smaller. For example, a listserv may not be needed for a group of eight people. Alternately, all 300 members of a larger group should not be utilizing a single collaborative website account.
- What is our structure? How will that affect our communication needs?
- How frequently do members communicate with one another?
- How often do we need to inform members of important items?
- What works best to communicate information to our leaders? Members? Advisory Board? Partners? Customers?
- Who on our team has excellent communication skills to help implement good practices and strategies?

Talk the Talk

Communication is central to success in every relationship. Spend the extra time to plan, evaluate, and improve both your oral and written communication. When a team and its leaders prioritize honest and frequent communication, all parties feel more informed, engaged, and empowered.

Trent B. Weaver is director of operations and logistics for curriculum and instruction at the Tennessee Department of Education. He studied performing arts at Baylor University, and communications and public administration at the University of Memphis. In addition, he works with NGOs in the areas of organization, communications, and fundraising.

Chapter 31

Create Partnerships

If everyone is moving forward together, then success takes care of itself.

—HENRY FORD

We are hard-wired for partnership. As individuals, schools, businesses, nonprofits, and governments, we are constantly looking to others to inform us. Innovation, creativity, and finding new answers to the world's oldest problems all depend on our ability to work together. Remarkable power comes from forming long-lasting relationships, one that has allowed us to build skyscrapers and iPhones, to sequence the human genome, and to topple the Berlin Wall.

At the root of any good partnership is collaboration: multiple parties working together toward a common goal, each bringing something to the table that the other does not. Complementary in nature, a good organizational partnership has the potential for greater, more sustainable impact than either organization alone. That's why working together works.

Why Partner?

Like everything else in the world, partnering has advantages and disadvantages:

Advantages

- *Access*: Increases your organization's access to target populations, personnel, volunteers, and information.

- *Opportunities*: Expands your organization's opportunities for funding and acquiring other resources.
- *Knowledge*: Diversifies your knowledge base, furthering your organization's commitment to collaborative learning and development.
- *Impact*: Broadens the impact of both organizations through pooled resources and expanded access. This benefits the shared goals of your partnership and the individual goals of each organization.
- *Status*: Boosts the status of your organization. This can mean your status in the communities you hope to have an impact on (how you are received within the communities) and your registered or exemption status (for example, a partner organization may be able to act as your umbrella 501(c)(3)).

Disadvantages

- *Expending resources*: While partnering may expand your resources, maintaining a partnership also requires that you expend limited resources of time, effort, ideas, and money.
- *Personality management*: The people who facilitate partnerships have diverse personalities. Some may be helpful, accommodating, and organized, and others not.
- *Compromise*: Establishing shared goals may mean compromising some of your individual organizational goals.

Many of the advantages of partnering can be grouped under one umbrella: sharing resources in order to widen your impact. Why form a partnership—where two or more organizations work together but remain distinct entities—instead of merging all resources into one superorganization?

First, maintaining organizational independence encourages innovation. By keeping your individual organizational goals separate from those of the partnership (although they should overlap), your goals are diversified instead of consolidated. Diverse ideas and strategies foster innovation.

Second, large-scale impact isn't always more profound than small-scale impact. While impact is about how many people you reach, it's also about the significance of that impact. If two small organizations working to eradicate poverty in one rural village in South Africa decide to form a superorganization with the goal of eradicating poverty in all of southern Africa, what happens to the rural village? The superorganization will likely have to generalize its approach, standardizing services or programs that were previously tailored to the specific needs of the rural village. Maybe poverty is compounded by access to clean water, an issue unique to the rural village that does not affect the other regions targeted by the superorganization. The rural village stands to lose not access to the superorganization's programs or services, but an optimization of approach in regards to the rural village's needs.

Organizations that have the potential to form strong partnerships are often reluctant to do so. They may be wary of sharing resources with their "competition," afraid of losing ownership over their work, or simply untrusting of other organizations. Yet countless studies have shown that collaboration enhances critical thinking, which in turn equips organizations with the tools to find shared solutions to shared problems.[1]

Is partnership always a good thing? In what circumstances might partnering not be beneficial?

Ingredients Necessary for a Good Partnership

There are numerous kinds of partnerships, some of which we'll detail later in this chapter. Any good partnership, however, consists of the following ingredients:

- Similar or overlapping organizational goals
- Two or more partners with unique skills and resources that support the shared goals of the partnership
- A common location and language or strategies for navigating these barriers
- Open, regular, and organized communication
- Mutual respect
- A power dynamic that is well defined and mutually agreeable

Find the Right Partner

Ask yourself this: Does my organization possess all the smarts, energy, resources, and skills to accomplish our goals? If the answer is no, you may want to consider forming an organizational partnership. An organizational partnership is an agreement between two organizations to collaborate in some capacity, working toward a goal that neither organization could accomplish if not for the partnership.

Follow these guidelines when searching for a good partner:

- *Determine what you need from a partner.* Are you looking for financial support? Access to a particular community? Help creating press and advertising materials? A certain skill set or particular expertise? Assistance navigating bureaucracy? Let's say you run an international literacy organization and want to partner with a local literacy organization to start a new chapter in a remote, underresourced area. If such an organization doesn't exist and what you really need from a partner is access to the local population, you may decide that your potential partner's physical location is more important than its specific organizational goals.
- *Do your research.* Survey the field. What enterprises already exist whose work is similar to yours? The Internet is a great place to start by using search terms like "literacy nonprofit" or "LGBTQ advocacy," or referring to nonprofit databases such as idealist.org. But you have plenty of other resources available. Ask friends, family, professors, and colleagues for suggestions, and scan relevant books and articles.
- *Refer to the "ingredients" checklist.* Do any of the organizations you've researched have the potential to be a good match for a partnership? You may not have answers about all the ingredients before contacting a potential partner, but keep the list in mind as you do your initial research. You may also find that some ingredients carry more weight than others.
- *Get in touch.* Contact your potential match and set up a time to talk in person, over the phone, or using Skype. If you have found an organization that has most or all of the ingredients for partnership, you're ready to set up a time to talk. Deciding on a time by e-mail is fine, but it is really critical that your first introductions are as personal as possible.

Note Partners should get out of the partnership what they put in. Partnering takes work! But the benefit should always outweigh the cost.

The Ideal Partner

An ideal organizational partner has certain characteristics. And don't forget: you are your partner's partner! Both you and your partner should strive to be:

- Motivated by the fundamental ideals of partnership—sharing, collaborating, expanding, changing, and evolving.
- Able to communicate individual organizational goals and interested in working to establish shared partnership goals.
- A good fit for each other in terms of size, scope, budget, and impact. What this means can vary greatly depending on the needs of each organization, but as a rule of thumb, a good fit is one where each partner's size, scope, budget, and impact contribute to the strength of the partnership.
- Willing to communicate openly and regularly and understand the importance of communication in sustaining a partnership.

Remember in your search for the right partner that when ideal partner organizations join forces to solve a problem, advance a cause, or create a product, they have the potential to maximize impact in the communities they serve. Once you decide you need a partner, you can use Exercise 31.1 to help you brainstorm which organizations might make a good fit.

Meg: Lexie and I cofounded Project Harmony Israel, a four-week English language summer camp for Arab and Jewish young people that aims to create a safe social space where they may interact personally in a peaceful, nonpolitical atmosphere. We partner with Hand in Hand, a network of integrated, bilingual Arab-Jewish schools in Israel. While we consider Hand in Hand to be our parent organization, the strength of our partnership rests on the fact that both organizations have something to gain from the relationship. A small operation, Project Harmony Israel acknowledged early on that to be successful, we would be dependent on resources (an institutional framework that would provide us with both facilities and access to the local population) from a local Israeli organization. Understanding the limitations of our organization helped us see how integral it was to our organization's future that we find a partner and to determine exactly what it was that we needed from that partner.

Exercise 31.1 Brainstorming Strategic Partnerships

To begin brainstorming potential partnerships, start by thinking broadly about the various sectors of society. The example below shows potential partners for a socially conscious technology start-up. Read through and discuss the advantages of each choice. Then apply the framework to your own group, by making a list of potential partners who represent the many sectors of society.

1. Local school district: Opportunity to run after-school club to engage students with technology in an informal educational setting
2. Local community center (Boys and Girls Club): Similar opportunity as the local school district and has a framework already in place for after-school programming
3. National business with a local branch (Cola-cola, Toyota): Can provide funding for us in exchange for advice on ways to make socially conscious investments
4. Local media outlet (NBC, NPR station, town newspaper): They can host segments or write articles about us in exchange for technology services and advertising on our website
5. Green technology nongovernmental organization (Hara, BrightSource Energy): We can work together on an environmentally conscious social media campaign
6. Environmental studies department of a university: Faculty or students from the department may wish to study the longitudinal environmental impact of our organization, providing useful data for us and the community
7. Local representatives to state legislature: Work together to institute tax incentives for other socially conscious businesses, appealing to voters and benefiting us financially
8. Local artists: They can design our logo and other graphic needs in exchange for technology services and advertising on our website
9. Local food bank (Feeding America, Greater Chicago Food Depository): Opportunity for our customers to contribute to the food bank by agreeing to an additional fee on their bill: we collect and deliver food

(continued)

10. Local religious institutions (churches, synagogues, mosques): We can provide technology education classes to adults, and they can host a fundraising event at their institution and donate the proceeds to our organization

Who are my potential partners? Why would they make good partners?

1.

2.

3.

4.

5.

6.

7.

8.

9.

10.

Proven Strategies for Good Partnerships

Management scholars Jennifer Alexander and Renee Nank have studied cross-sector partnership (for example, between the public and nonprofit sectors) and have shown that successful partnerships rely on mutual trust, which can be developed through "sharing information, integrated responsibilities and authority, and collaborative decision making."[2]

- *Share information*: Communicate to your partner all information, both negative and positive, that may be relevant to their organization's work or to your partnership.
- *Integrate responsibilities and authority*: One partner should never have all of the responsibility or authority. The purpose of a partnership is to share responsibility, such that each partner has authority over a portion of what must be accomplished.
- *Implement collaborative decision making*: When making decisions that affect the partnership, your partner should be included in the decision-making process. Individuals within each organization who are working in partnership should be chosen mindfully for their interpersonal skills and relevant experience in the field. A case study showed that these factors can be more important to the ultimate success of a partnership than economic benefits.[3]
- *Be mindful of personal experience and skills*: Consider your own experience and interpersonal skills when deciding whether to seek a partnership, and in recruiting individuals to work for your organization.

Is there a limit to the number of partners you should have? Thinking about your experience with partnerships, what strategies have you found effective? How can you apply them to your social change efforts?

Make the Connection and Build the Relationship

The primary goal of your first formal conversation should be to humanize the potential partnership. This is easiest if you meet in person, but in a global age, obstacles such as scheduling, distance, or finances may make that impossible. Video chatting is the most effective alternative, and talking on the phone is also a good option. Avoid communicating strictly by e-mail as much as possible.

> *Lexie*: A Hand in Hand principal e-mailed Project Harmony a month before camp was scheduled to begin saying: "The Ministry of Education decided there must be construction at the school all summer, so camp cannot happen." We sent many frantic e-mails over the next few harrowing days. Then we decided to call a senior administrator at Hand in Hand. Immediately we understood what the principal really meant was that camp couldn't happen on school property, not that camp couldn't happen at all! We were able to use a nearby community center, and camp went as planned. An immediate phone call to clarify the principal's e-mail would have avoided a lot of misunderstanding and panic.

You want to get to know your partner as best you can and as soon as you can. It will set a precedent for open, honest communication. Partners are more likely to uphold their end of the bargain when their investment in the partnership is not just organizational but personal. Whatever your position is within the organization, your first conversations should be about getting to know the people you hope to work with, the content of the work that they do, and sharing a bit about yourself and your aspirations.

If you and your prospective partner agree to establish an official partnership, the next step is to formally declare the terms of the partnership in a formalized partnership agreement. If you have the resources to do so, you may wish to consult a lawyer to oversee this process. Involving a lawyer is highly recommended if you expect a lot of financial profit or if you're working with valuable intellectual property. Otherwise, lawyers can be very expensive and not absolutely necessary—just set up a formal meeting with your partner (this can be on Skype) for the specific purpose of creating your partnership agreement and follow the steps below. Review the checklist together, carefully and thoroughly. Put into writing what you each hope to derive from and contribute to the partnership. The agreement should state:

- The shared goals of your partnership
- The roles, responsibilities, and expectations of each partner organization
- A plan for both how and how often you and your partner will communicate

- How you and your partner plan to split expenses (and profits, if applicable)
- Which specific staff persons are responsible for managing operations and mediating conflicts between partners
- A system for measuring and evaluating the partnership's success
- A contingency plan for how to dissolve the partnership

You may also want to establish a time line of short-term goals you hope to accomplish together (for example, organizing an event; launching a new project; raising $10,000). Short-term goals get the collaboration ball rolling.

Your partnership will grow and change over time. To maximize the likelihood of the partnership strengthening over the long term, do the following:

- *Be prepared to adapt.* You're probably a pretty ambitious person with big dreams. The terms you establish for your partnership may be too ambitious given your budget, time line, or resources. That's okay if you're prepared to adapt your goals or adjust your expectations to achieve your organization's goals.
- *Be prepared to disagree.* There is a huge amount to gain from disagreement! Disagreeing with your partner (about philosophy, methods, or logistics, for example), as long as you both communicate your opinions respectfully, helps you consider multiple possibilities and perspectives. This is at the heart of critical thinking.
- *Be prepared to make mistakes.* Maintaining an organizational partnership requires patience, diligence, and commitment. There's a good chance you'll drop the ball occasionally. You may make an undeliverable promise, encounter an unforeseen obstacle, or just overextend yourself. It happens. But if you're mentally prepared for the possibility, you'll recover.

Sustain the Partnership

Partnering is an ongoing process. Here are ways to help sustain a healthy, productive partnership:

- *Communicate*: Communicate regularly, openly, and honestly with your partner.

- *Evaluate*: Periodically evaluate your partnership. What's working? What's not?
- *Be aware of external changes*: Relevant fields and sectors may rapidly change in ways that could affect your partnership's operations or goals. Stay tuned to what's happening outside your organizations.
- *Adjust your goals as necessary*: Internal and external changes may force goal adjustments. Failing to adjust your goals can undermine the partnership.
- *Actively collaborate*: Your relationship will be strengthened if you collaborate in an active way. You may put on an event, host a workshop, or launch a fundraiser. Do something that focuses on doing together, not just thinking together.

Kinds of Partnerships

There are multiple kinds of organizational partnerships; some can be classified in several categories. Here are some of the more common kinds of partnerships and advice for working with specific sectors.

Parent-Project Partnership

In this partnership, one organization acts as host or parent to the other organization. Parent organizations are typically much larger operations than the project organization—with bigger budgets, more substantial facilities, a larger or more demonstrated impact, or more community recognition. The project organization may benefit from the institutionalization of the parent organization. The parent organization often looks to project organizations for innovation and expansion.

Product Partnership

A product partnership occurs when two organizations enter into partnership in order to create a specific product, such as a local business partnering with an arts organization to produce a city beautification mural. They may be short-term partnerships with the power to greatly enrich both organizations.

Generational Partnership

The actors of an organization are often diverse in age, sex, race, ethnicity, and religious, sexual, and political identities. Certain organizations attract a homogeneous staff and support base, particularly in regard to age. Members of university student groups are usually comprised of 18- to 22-year-olds, whereas law firms have a higher concentration of middle-aged adults. Generational partnerships are the collaboration of a younger organization and an older organization.

Figure 31.1. Types of Partnerships

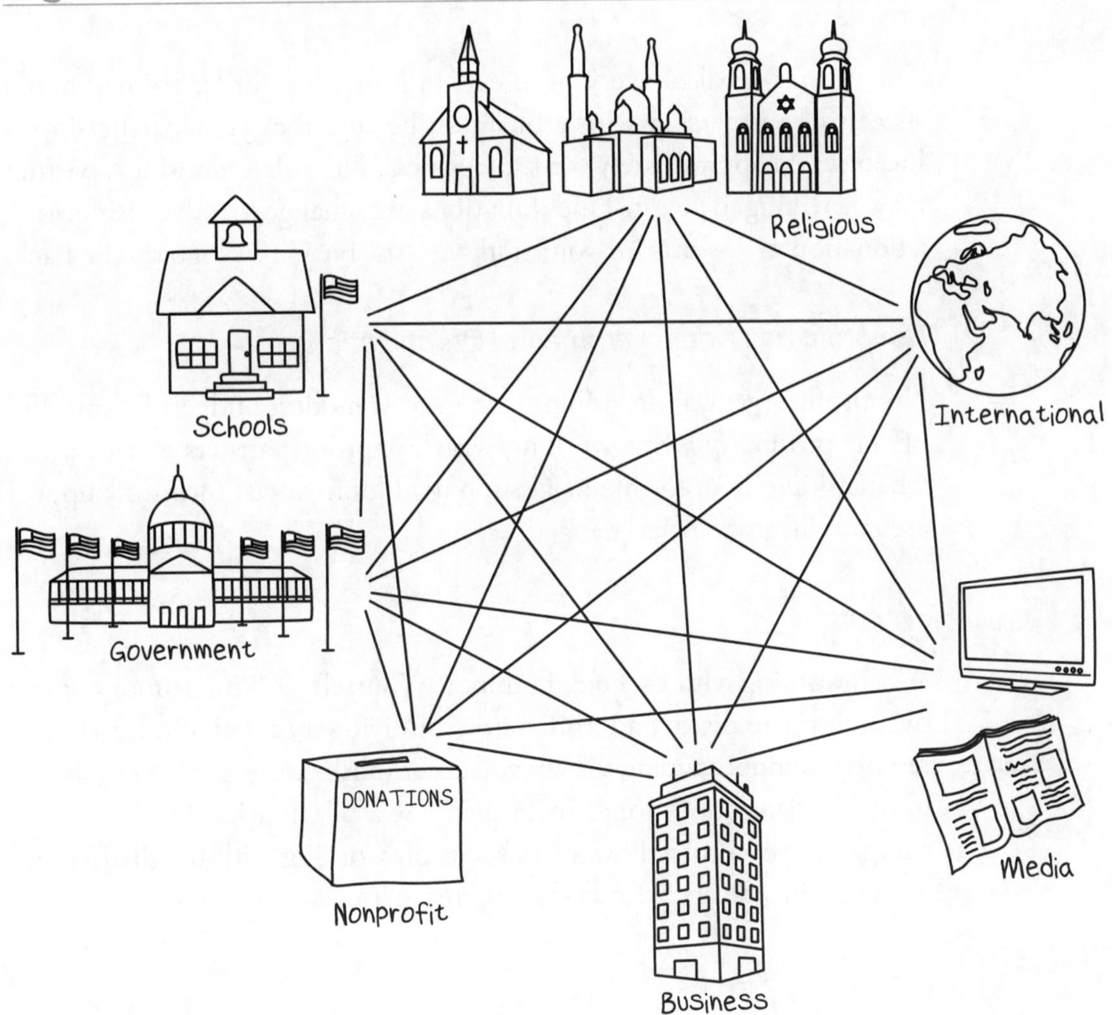

Advice for Working with Specific Sectors

Public/Government

If you are dealing with the public sector, you'll likely find yourself addressing many layers of bureaucracy. Improving a public park may require obtaining permits; pushing a recycling initiative may require collecting signatures; gathering basic information may involve dozens of phone calls around the country. Working with public and government sectors requires patience. When you find valuable information on the Internet, bookmark the page; when someone is particularly helpful over the phone, get his name and direct extension so you can reach this person again quickly.

Private/Business

The primary goal of every business is profit, so in order to maintain a successful partnership with a business, be sure that your partnership is incentivized appropriately for the business. Note that a business partner may be willing to give in-kind donations in exchange for advertising, as in a donation of T-shirts for your staff with the business's logo on the back.

Nonprofit and Nongovernmental Organizations

Nonprofit organizations often operate on a modest budget. Be mindful of this possibility when working with nonprofit partners and cautious when asking them for financial support. Nonfinancial forms of support are more likely to be exchanged.

Schools

When working with a school, familiarize yourself with the school's power dynamics. Are district administrators, individual school administrators, teachers, or donors going to help you accomplish your goals? For example, if your organization hopes to implement a districtwide healthy eating campaign, you probably want to focus on working with the district and local administrators before targeting teachers.

Media

When approaching media to promote your organization, study their format and audience and tailor your pitch to their needs. For example, a town paper may have a column featuring accomplishments of local young people; you could send them a short biography and some information about your organization.

Foundations

Your partnership with a large foundation will likely be financially based. Every foundation has different policies and requirements for grant recipients, so research! You may need to acquire 501(c)(3) status before applying for a foundation grant or find a 501(c)(3) to be your umbrella organization. Tailor your grant application to the mission of the foundation: play up those aspects of your organizational goals that are suited to the foundation's goals.

International

Partnering internationally can be a logistical headache, but it doesn't have to be. Invest in Skype credit; you can cheaply call your partner's office or cell phone through your computer. Speaking is more efficient and effective than e-mail. Make sure to become familiar with the business customs of your partner's country.

Religious Organizations

Working with religious organizations requires openness and sensitivity to the religion's particular traditions. Be aware of certain conversational topics or styles of dress that are taboo so as not to offend your partner. Be prepared to make cultural mistakes and to apologize even if you did not mean offense. Respect goes a long way.

Think through the various types of organizations and discuss the unique advantages each has to offer. What collaborations would most help your group right now?

Navigate Power Dynamics

While organizations that enter into a partnership should share common goals, individual partners may differ greatly in age, size, scope, funding, and impact. Understanding these differences—and seeing their potential benefit—is critical to a partnership's long-term success.

> *Meg*: On paper, Hand in Hand and Project Harmony appear to be a picture-perfect parent-project partnership. However, Hand in Hand has a huge bureaucratic structure that's cumbersome and extremely complicated. There's also a branch based in the United States, the American Friends of Hand in Hand. A community of educators, administrators, and activists creates and implements full-time, academic-year educational programming for over 800 young people. Where is Project Harmony meant to fit into all of this?

Here are some of the primary obstacles in navigating this complicated parent-project power dynamic.

Maintain Independence

If your organization is small in size or scope, you may be at risk of getting lost within your parent organization. To avoid this, make sure not to stray from the original terms that defined your partnership: a partnership that represents a long-term collaboration of two distinct organizations with both unique assets and shared goals.

> *Meg*: Project Harmony raises its own funds, creates its own curricula and programming, and recruits its volunteer staff; Hand in Hand provides us with facilities and access to their population. By adhering to the bargain, we reinforce the strength of our partnership.

What's the value of maintaining organizational independence?

> *Lexie:* For us, it means preserving creative control (over philosophical approach, programming content, and the choice to form additional partnerships); encouraging innovation (by providing an organizational framework that is distinct from Hand in Hand's); and diversifying resources that our parent-project partnership attracts (as a smaller operation, we have access to funding opportunities that Hand in Hand does not, and vice versa).

Establish Legitimacy

The key to establishing legitimacy is to get to know as many people within and connected to your parent organization as you possibly can. Take the time to communicate your vision and mission to others.

> *Meg*: In developing our partnership with Hand in Hand, we laid out the terms of our relationship but with only a handful of senior administrators. We missed the opportunity to communicate with a vast number of those in the field. We realized we couldn't claim to be partnering with a large organization when only a few people really understood the tenets of our partnership. We had to reach out to people in all levels of the organization.

Make your partnership agreement felt and heard throughout both organizations.

What strategies can you use to successfully navigate the power dynamics of your partnership?

Evaluate Your Partnership

Is My Partnership Working?

Periodically and methodically evaluate your partnership. Refer back to your ingredients checklist and ask yourself whether the tenets of your partnership still hold true. If your partnership no longer fulfills the majority of your organizational needs, it's time to make a change. This process is similar to romantic partnerships. Relationships are dynamic; sometimes partners must decide to go their separate ways or transform the relationship (for example, by revising expectations or proposing marriage).

Some of the original terms of your partnership are static, like whether you and your partner have a common location and language; others (your individual organizational goals or the acceptability of your partnership's power dynamic) are likely to evolve over time. It may or may not be possible to accommodate new goals within the existing framework of your partnership. Say you founded an organization originally committed to eradicating adult illiteracy, but experience showed that it will be more valuable to promote children's literacy instead. If you previously partnered with a retirement home to access their population, it's time to find a new partner.

Exercise 31.2 will help you decide whether a potential partnership will work for you.

Exercise 31.2 Is This Partnership Good for Me?

Use this table to help determine if a potential partnership is right for you. If the totals in the "Yes" and "Maybe" columns are higher than the total in the "No" column, go for it!

Ingredients	**Yes**	**No**	**Maybe**
Do our goals overlap?			
Do they have the resources I need?			
Are we located in the same city? Same country? If not, do I have a strategy for communicating?			
Do we speak the same language? If not, do I have a strategy for our communication?			
Are they the right size?			
Total			

Troubleshooting Partnerships

Sometimes partnerships just don't work, and there are many potential reasons. Here are a number of steps you can take to figure out what's gone wrong and how to fix it:

- *Take a deep breath. Sleep on it.* It is easy to get flustered and irritated when your partnership isn't going as planned. Try to distance yourself from your emotions in order to better assess what's really going on.
- *Identify the source of the problem.* It may not be easy to identify the source of your partnership's problem. Often it will force you to do serious introspection and analysis. For example, you may be overwhelmed by your own workload and assume that means your partner isn't doing their fair share. Is this really the case? Or are you just overwhelmed and looking to place blame? It's possible your partner will be willing to pick up more of your shared responsibilities if you communicate to them that you're overwhelmed.

Why might it be difficult to determine the original source of a problem in your partnership? What can you do to prevent future problems from arising?

- *Communicate with your partner.* In order to problem-solve, you must use your best communication skills. Speak only about your personal experience, withholding accusations. For example, you could say: "I've been doing a lot of work on X Project, and I'm really overwhelmed by what I still have left to do. How are you feeling about your workload? Could we reassess the division of responsibilities?" As opposed to: "I have been doing so much more than you for the X Project and that's why we're never going to accomplish our goals." Then listen to your partner. Your partner may wish to communicate a problem that you never knew existed, and if you expect to be heard, you must make an effort to listen.
- *Use the ingredients checklist.* If speaking with your partner hasn't solved the problem, refer back to the ingredients checklist. Have any of the main tenets of your partnership changed? Do you still have overlapping goals? Do you still have a mutually acceptable power dynamic?

What to Do When It's No Longer Working

Often your decision about what to do when things aren't working anymore won't be clear. For example, as your organization grows, a partner once considered a parent may no longer fulfill that role for you. But that parent has probably been a contributing factor to your success, so you don't want to burn any bridges or seem ungrateful for the support you have received from your partner. And perhaps you may find other ways to collaborate in the future. Regardless, when you know something has to change, here are suggestions for how to proceed with tact and grace.

Break Up

Just like a break-up at the end of a long-term relationship, have the conversation in person if possible and by phone or Skype if not. Breaking up with a text message or e-mail never ends well. Thank your partner for the impact they have had on your organization's development. Explain the reasons you feel it's time to end your partnership. Your partner may or may not be surprised by this news, so be prepared for a variety of reactions. Remember that if the partnership is no longer working, the best thing to do is break up even if it's awkward or difficult. An unsuccessful partnership can do more harm than good.

Transform

Transforming your relationship can mean a number of things, but at its core, it is about going back to the basics. This conversation will be similar to the first time you connected with your partner in that you'll need to establish new goals and needs. Use the ingredients checklist as a guideline for renegotiating the terms of your partnership.

While it is very important to talk to your partner about what's working and what's not working, make an extra effort not to play the blame game. The decision to transform your relationship means that you remain committed to the partnership, and you must uphold one of the most important tenets of good partnership: mutual respect. Transformation is about identifying the source of your issues and working through them together, not about finding fault in a particular person, program, decision, or circumstance.

Coming together is a beginning, staying together is a process, and working together is success.

HENRY FORD

Your partner may not be interested in transforming your partnership. Perhaps they'll propose alternatives to your proposition. Always be open to these suggestions. Voice your opinions, and ask lots of questions. When your organization is in partnership with another organization, it is easy to forget that there are real, live people masked by the bureaucratic structures in place. Respectful, effective, open, and honest communication with the people you're partnering with is the glue that holds your relationship together.

Meg Sullivan and **Lexie Tabachnick** cofounded Project Harmony Israel, an integrated summer camp for Arab and Jewish youth in Jerusalem, as University of Chicago students. Meg graduated in 2011 with a degree in interdisciplinary studies in the humanities and Lexie in 2012 with a degree in psychology. In three years, Project Harmony Israel served over 175 campers and raised over $30,000. They have partnered with the Hand in Hand schools in Israel, American Friends of Hand in Hand, ARTS! By the People, and the Amir Project in order to bring their campers the best shared experience possible.

Chapter 32

Organize a Conference

When you hear the word *conference,* your reaction may be something along the lines of "bor-ing," followed by an intense urge to catch some zzzs. Far too often, conferences mean little more than stale bagels and overrated speakers. But when a conference is designed well—when it understands its mission and objectives, who it's trying to benefit, and how to do so—it can be one of the most powerful tools for bringing people together to inspire individual and collective action. We present some standard elements necessary to produce a conference that inspires and excites, to which you will add your creative energy to organize a unique and powerful event.

Plan Your Conference

Audience

First, you'll need to identify the audience of your conference. This will influence your execution. Who is your audience, what are they looking for, and what special characteristics do they have that you should take into account?

Objectives

Good conferences have a set of objectives that reflect the interests of the people they're intended to benefit. Start by writing a list of objectives with your team. What should people take away from the conference? New information? Skills? Contacts? Something else?

Discuss this list with a larger group. Brainstorm. Have you left anything out? Is it too ambitious? Whittle it down to what can realistically be accomplished.

Conference Types

Most conferences fall into a few common types that reflect the overarching objectives of the event and use certain structures (panels, poster sessions) to achieve their objectives. Referring back to your list of objectives, you should be able to find one or more conference types that match your goals. These types aren't exhaustive; there are conferences that don't fall into any of these categories, just as there are conferences that fall into several of them.

Awareness Building

Awareness-building conferences teach participants about a new topic or introduce them to an issue or challenge to which they've likely had little exposure. They tend to use lectures and panel discussions by experts to educate participants.

Capacity Building

Capacity-building conferences teach participants various skills, functioning much like training sessions. They often employ interactive, hands-on content structures like workshops and small discussions.

Network Building

Whether it's within a community, like a national network of student groups, or between communities, like a set of nonprofits, the most fundamental component of any conference is bringing together a set of people. A network-building conference is an event that has this as its primary purpose. These conferences emphasize participant interaction (by hosting cocktail parties or scheduling networking hours, for example).

Information Sharing

In the professional and academic worlds, conferences that serve to share best practices and new information within a specific field are quite common, featuring short presentations by experts as well as poster sessions. For example, at an education research conference, scientists present their work in poster or lecture form or on panel discussions.

Content Structures

A conference is made up of different types of events, or content structures. Think about what content structures you could use to best achieve your objectives:

Keynotes
Description: Keynotes usually open or close conferences and allow people to learn from and be inspired by a leader in the field.
Where you'll find them: Almost every conference type.

Panel Discussions
Description: Panel discussions bring together a few experts to discuss a specific topic and answer questions.
Where you'll find them: Awareness-building or information-sharing conferences.

Workshops
Description: At a workshop, an expert instructs a group of participants in a skill or technique.
Where you'll find them: At many conferences, but especially capacity-building conferences.

Small Group Discussions
Description: Small group discussions allow participants to reflect on the presented material. Participants can share their experiences and perspectives with others.
Where you'll find them: At capacity-building conferences.

Poster Sessions
Description: Poster sessions are an efficient way to share a large volume of specialized information. Hundreds of posters can take up a relatively small space. Programs listing the poster titles with their location make it easy for attendees to find posters of interest.
Where you'll find them: At information-sharing conferences.

Networking Sessions

Description: Often organized around mealtimes, these sessions are explicitly set aside for participants to meet one another.

Where you'll find them: At most conferences, but always at network-building conferences.

Time

Consider the length of your conference. A day? A weekend? A week? How much time is needed to achieve your objectives? Don't forget practical limitations like financial constraints and your audience's attention span. Readjust your objectives if you can't fit everything in.

Figure 32.1. Different Types of Content Structures

Location

Your budget and the number of people you think will attend will influence your location. The content structures will also affect your venue selection. For example, if you're hosting a poster session, you'll need one or more large rooms. If there will be lectures, you need a facility that provides podiums, microphones, and speakers.

Build Support

With the basics ironed out, you need to build the critical support to make your conference happen.

Assemble a Staff

Your staff will consist of the members of your group as well as any other friends or colleagues you can recruit to the project. There are three specific principles to keep in mind when building and maintaining a successful conference staff.

Understand Motives

The people whose time you're asking for have commitments to other people and projects, so understand why they are getting involved in the conference. Knowing your staff's motives will help you keep them engaged, committed, and excited about the work you're doing together.

Assign Specific Jobs

It sounds odd, but you need structure to foster creativity. People need clear definitions of their positions and well-outlined objectives and goals. Once they're confident in their roles, they can start to take ownership of assigned tasks and implement their own ideas.

Invest in Relationships

Invest in the people who are planning the event with you. Invite your group to do something social together. Check in periodically and ask people how they're doing. Your staff will be more invested in the planning process and enjoy it more.

Build Administrative Support

Make a List of Possible Supporters

List likely sources of support and note ways they can help your organization, such as providing financial resources, offering their knowledge, and making connections. If you're putting on a conference at a university, you'll commonly find these allies on campus:

- *Office of the provost*: The chief academic officer of the university, the provost sets academic priorities, oversees and facilitates new initiatives, and sets university policy.
- *Community service offices*: This is the home base for service-based student organizations, as well as students who volunteer both on and off campus.
- *International or study-abroad offices*: These offices coordinate international fellowships and study-abroad opportunities.
- *Academic departments*: This includes professors, staff, and students with an interest in the topic of the conference.

Focus on Your Pitch

No matter how many great potential allies you have, you're operating in an environment in which people are usually already overcommitted, so you'll have to convince them to carve out additional time and resources for you. Follow these guidelines:

- *Align your request with the organization's mission.* How does your conference align with their goals and offerings? Have you gotten their leaders involved? How does the program meet the objectives stated in their strategic plans?
- *Leave written proposals.* By leaving a written proposal or summary of your work with the organization, your message, ideas, proposed event, and pitch will stay intact as your request is passed along to others.
- *Be clear about what you want.* Before meeting with relevant parties, determine the type of support you'll need and how much. You're more likely to garner support if you can clearly articulate how much support you really need. You might ask for:
  - Funding
  - Space
  - Advertising in organizational publications
  - Help recruiting famous keynote speakers

Make a Budget

Here are a few tips that you can use, no matter what your bottom line looks like.

Have a Budget

You need a detailed budget. Before approaching any funding source, you must have at least a rough idea of what you'll need, how much you'll need, where you'll purchase or obtain it, and how much it will cost:

- *Align your budget priorities with your objectives.* Keep in mind the objectives you've prioritized when allocating resources. This doesn't mean you should spend the majority of your money on your top objective, but it does mean you should consider relative priorities when making tough decisions.
- *Aim high but stay realistic.* Don't be afraid to include the big-budget items. Just be aware that you may not receive funding for them.
- *Align budget requests with funding priorities.* Frame your initiative in terms of potential funders' priorities. For example, universities fund curricular programs, student support programs, intellectual exchanges, and research. Showcase your activity in terms of the things your funder routinely supports.

> *Nathaniel*: When we were planning the first Global Engagement Summit, we knew that we could still hold the event without the $20,000 needed to fly in delegates from the developing world, but we included it in the budget anyway. Supporters appreciated our idealism and our realism, and we were able to raise the extra cash.

Diversify

Everyone who reviews your funding request will look for evidence that you're seeking financial support from other sources. Counterintuitively, often the more funding sources you list (especially sources who have already pledged support), the more money you're likely to receive from any one source.

Execute

Plan Tasks

This list is designed to help you categorize the elements of planning into a more manageable framework so you can delegate tasks. Keep in mind the topics discussed in "Common Lessons."

Common Lessons

There are three primary lessons to learn:

- *Lesson 1*: Budget time for conference components. Identify how much time to budget for each event (lecture, workshop, and so on). Consider the minimum time needed for the activity to be productive, the fact that speakers can arrive late, and that hot topics or popular speakers will run over the allotted time.
- *Lesson 2*: Create an event-planning time line. A time line will help you pace yourself, as well as realize when you're running behind schedule.
- *Lesson 3*: Meet regularly. Nothing can replace face-to-face meetings to ensure that everything is proceeding as planned.

Participants

At the core of your event are the people you're bringing together. You'll need to recruit, select (if using a competitive application process), and then bring together this group.

- *Make an application*: This won't apply for all events, but if space is limited, you'll need an application to narrow down the attendees.
- *Spread the word*: Recruit participants using e-mail, flyers, Facebook, and advertisements.

Logistics

What are the tasks that need to be accomplished? The logistics of a conference involve:

- Arranging transportation and accommodations for all participants
- Planning meals
- Finding, reserving, and preparing space for different events

Get the Word Out

Who needs to hear about your event? How will you reach your audience? How will you get your conference invitations into the hands of potential staff, delegates, keynote speakers, and sponsors? Consider the following:

- Create a distinctive logo or visual scheme for your project.
- Design brochures, flyers, a website, and any other materials you think will be useful.
- Disseminate publicity materials.
- Generate a list of press contacts in your local area (or, depending on the scope of your event, nationally, or globally).
- Write press releases and distribute them to these contacts.

Funding

You'll need to find money to pay for food, housing, transportation, honorariums, marketing materials, space, and more. To do this, you can employ a variety of strategies, ranging from charging attendees to grassroots fundraisers. To read more about various fundraising strategies, refer to Chapter 22.

Websites

Websites can do more than simply house static information.

> *Nathaniel*: At the Global Engagement Summit, we have two websites. The first is used when we're recruiting participants and need to share a lot of information quickly and easily. As the summit approaches, we switch to a user-driven site that incorporates Wiki technology and blog software. This allows us to interact with our participants before, during, and after the event, including posting notes from workshops and providing our delegates with space to create profiles.

Be Prepared

Anticipate Changing Roles

During this last phase of planning and implementation, your staff will undergo a few considerable changes. Some people will drop the ball when you expect them to come through, and others who haven't been as involved will pick up the slack. You'll also need to transition your planning staff into an implementation staff that will make sure that all the tasks of implementing the event, from walking speakers to the lecture hall to registering delegates who've just arrived, are completed.

Create a Master Event Guide

A good planning guide will include:

- Comprehensive event task lists, organized by time
- Location guide showing where each task is to be performed
- Hour-by-hour staff availability and task assignments

Follow-Up

The best conferences are those that plan ways to keep people engaged when they return home and put to use their new awareness, skills, or relationships. A few ways you can help ensure your event is one of these rare gems:

- *Distribute informational materials.* Give your attendees materials that help frame their experiences. Reiterate what you want them to gain from their participation in the conference. This helps your participants mentally summarize and relive their experience, decreasing the likelihood that memory will reframe the experience as just another event.
- *Network.* Make sure you've set up a structure to keep your participants in communication with you and each other. This could be a blog, a weekly online newsletter, Facebook, or a multitude of other social networking services.
- *Provide new opportunities.* Keep your past attendees engaged by providing them with new opportunities for funding, internships, volunteer opportunities, anything of potential value to them.

Symposia

Anna Offit graduated from Georgetown Law, where she served as editor in chief of the Georgetown Journal of Legal Ethics. She received an MPhil in social anthropology at Cambridge University and is currently pursuing a doctorate in anthropology at Princeton University. She draws upon her experience to share a few best practices regarding symposia.

Anna: In March 2012, law students at Georgetown had a question they wanted answered: Why do prosecutors feel compelled to uphold a conviction when evidence—even the DNA variety—later suggests a defendant is innocent? To grapple with possible explanations, we invited a filmmaker, a defense attorney, a professor, and a prosecutor to a conversation about an unlikely subject: the culture of prosecution—an exploration of how lawyers in our criminal justice system navigate the tension between what they know is right and what they feel professionally obliged to do.

In ancient Greece, *symposia* were occasions to drink wine and celebrate big ideas. Today it's not the scale, the budget, or even the wine that makes a symposium meaningful. It all hinges on a good question.

By definition, a symposium is a specific type of conference that poses a single, very focused question. In a series of lectures and panels, symposium speakers answer this question from perspectives informed by their own unique backgrounds and experiences.

In particular, two guiding principles made the event a success:

1. Use your symposium to create knowledge—not just to spread it. The real power of a symposium is its ability to carve out a new area in an academic field. With cross-disciplinary participants and an engaged audience, you can tackle complex issues—and get new voices into the mix. Our symposium was also motivated by questions that aren't usually discussed by legal academics: How do prosecutors understand their roles? And what social practices reinforce these understandings? The participants were forced to test their own assumptions against those formed by lawyers in different professions, and the dialectic illuminated why these lawyers act the way they do.

2. Invite participants to submit written reflections for publication. Law school symposia are typically accompanied by a journal issue. But blog items, short response papers, and web posts are other ways to expand the walls of your discussion room. We devoted an issue of our law journal to articles solicited from students and faculty from within and outside. This created a tangible take-away from the event, something that would live on in posterity for anyone with an interest in the question we posed. Similarly, the lecture and panel portions of the event itself were webcast as well as videotaped and posted online for instant global access.

Nathaniel Whittemore is the founder of the Global Engagement Summit (GES), which has provided training for global change leadership and project development to hundreds of young leaders from around the world. His success with GES paved the way for him to develop and lead the Center for Global Engagement at Northwestern University to improve young people's ability to cross borders and create change.

Chapter 33

Serve on a Board

Teamwork is the ability to work together toward a common vision. The ability to direct individual accomplishments toward organizational objectives. It is the fuel that allows common people to attain uncommon results.

—ANDREW CARNEGIE

Boards are the embodiment of Carnegie's words. Most boards strive to create a team that has a well-balanced group of individuals with diverse talents and experiences, who work together to advise it based on their collective wisdom. For instance, Teach For America's (TFA) board of directors consists of many different executives, including the CEOs of Sony, The Weather Channel, J. Crew, and Coach; the president of Spelman College; professors of economics and public service; multiple venture capitalists; and a recording artist. Each one has a specific expertise that is different from that of the organization's staff and executive leadership.[1] This group of leaders helps strategize and chart the larger trajectory of the organization, drawing on their unique combination of skills to add value and drive the mission forward.

Why Serve on a Board?

There are three core reasons to consider serving on a board:

1. Your ideas will guide the actions of an organization of interest to you, helping you make an impact on matters you value.

2. You will meet experts from many different fields, creating long-lasting relationships that could help your career or social change efforts in the future.
3. You'll gain insight into the inner workings of a successful organization, better preparing you to build your own group should you decide to do so in the future.

If you want to generate impact and be part of a larger movement, working together on a board of various experts in a field you care about is a smart move. You gain a valuable learning opportunity while the board gains your perspective and insights. If you are in a younger demographic than most board members, this can be especially useful to a board that seeks to better understand the perspective of your generation. Furthermore, serving on a board equips you with a network of professionals who can help you in future efforts. Building strong relationships with established leaders and learning from their expertise will enable you to successfully develop any projects you embark on.

> *Eunice*: As a teenager, I was thrilled to be invited to help Nestlé USA create an advisory board for its foundation. I decided to join the board because I saw it as a unique opportunity to help give grants to other young people who are working on community service initiatives. One of my favorite parts of my Nestlé experience was helping to write the foundation's bylaws because I felt that my work had a meaningful and long lasting impact on future boards.

Know Your Options

Boards can generally be classified into three main types: boards of directors, advisory boards, and councils. Table 33.1 shows the characteristics of each type.

Find a Compatible Match

Now that you're familiar with the types of boards out there, it's time to decide if you'd be interested in serving an organization in a board member capacity. Exercise 33.1 will help you determine if there's enough overlap between the expectations you and the board have for one another.

Table 33.1. Board Comparison

	Board of Directors	Advisory Board	Council
Who	• Professionals • Experts in the field • Government officials	• Members of a demographic group that the larger organization seeks to consult. • Recruited from outside the organization. • Some organizations have youth advisory boards that allow young adults to engage in nonprofit work via an established framework for involvement.	• Members of a particular demographic or those interested in a particular facet of the organization. • Recruited from inside the organization. • Some youth councils are used to serve fellow youth in the community
What	• The organization's "compass" • Also known as a board of trustees or a board of governance. Dictates the direction of the organization as a whole.	• Form follows function • Created to serve various functions, from graphics management to fiscal development and oversight. • Used primarily as a resource. • An organization might have a student advisory board to provide student perspectives on specific subjects.	• Form follows function • Same multipurpose nature as advisory boards. However, unlike advisory boards, councils have projects of their own to execute.
Roles and responsibilities	*Fiscal oversight:* Develop and analyze he budget. Resource acquisition: Ensure the receipt of appropriate resources. *Strategic planning:* Map out the organization's future. *Decision making:* Vote to decide policies and practices. *Recruitment:* Recruit other board members or individuals who may add value. *Public relations:* Represent the organization in public. *Legal:* Write and amend the corporation's bylaws.	*Program administration:* Responsible for implementing various programs within the organization. *Exploratory research:* Evaluate and report on how proposed projects would be implemented. *Gauging public opinion:* Consulted when evaluating perceptions or attitudes of a given demographic. *Publicity:* Convey the organization's mission to the public to generate interest.	*Program administration and development:* Lead and implement specific projects. *Spokesperson:* Serve as ambassadors of the organization to the community. *Nonprofit collaborations:* Collaborate with other nonprofit organizations with similar interests. *Publicity:* Convey the organization's mission to the public to generate interest.

Exercise 33.1 Is This Board "The One"?

Commitment Issues: Before Taking the Plunge

Issues	You	Board
1. *Time commitment.* In the You column, answer the question: How much time can you give? In the Board column, answer: How much time does the board require?		
2. *Travel and/or conference calls.* You column: Can you take part in a travel-intensive/call-intensive group? Board column: How much traveling or conference calling is estimated?		
3. *Financial costs.* You column: How much can you pitch in for extra costs (e.g., travel costs that might not be covered)? Board column: How much money does the board require?		
4. *Meeting times.* You column: What times (daily, weekly, seasonally) are you free? Board column: When are the board's regularly scheduled meetings?		
5. *Value.* You column: How important is the work of this board to you? Board column: How important is the work of this board to the cause and to the world?		

Mission Possible: Believing in Your Mission

Issues	You	Board
1. *Mission.* You column: What's your personal mission (check out Chapter 20 if you don't have one written down)? Board column: What is the board's mission statement?		
2. *Do the mission statements match?* Write yes or no. If "yes" continue with this worksheet. If "no," erase the answers, find another board, and come back and start again.		
3. *Why do I want to be on this board?* Get a head start on the interview, and articulate your reasons now.		
4. *What can I contribute?* Think not what the board can do for you but what you can do for the board. Then write it down.		

(continued)

Microscopia: Fine Print That Matters

Issues	You	Board
1. *Financial contribution.* Board column: Does the board require a contribution to join and if yes, how much? You column: Can you afford it?		
2. *Demographic requirement.* Board column: What requirements (e.g., age, geographic, citizenship) does the board have, if any? You column: Do you fit their requirements?		
3. *Teamwork.* Board column: Who would you be working with on the board? You column: Can you work well with these others (members, partnering organizations, businesses)?		
4. *Responsibilities.* Board column: What responsibilities will the board expect you to fulfill? You column: Can you fulfill those responsibilities well? Make a special note if there are any you may excel at or drop the ball on. These will be important to share with the board in your application, interview, and initial meetings.		
5. *Impact.* You column: How long do you want to stay in the position you would have on the board, and what specifically do you want to accomplish and change? Board column: Is the board able to make the specific changes you are interested in and would they give you that opportunity?		

Now, compare the "You" and "Board" columns. Are you and the board compatible?

Help Them Get to Know You

Now that you've got your eye on a certain board, the courting phase can begin. You know you're a catch, and we know you're a catch. So let's talk about first impressions.

The First Impression: The Application

When pursuing an opportunity to join a board, you may be asked to complete a written application. Just like the start of any other relationship, the people reviewing your application (generally current board members) are interested in you, not your titles. Here are some helpful tips.

Personal Impact

Your application should detail the contributions that you personally have made to the clubs, organizations, and companies you've been a part of.

Quantify

Always quantify your impact when possible. Numbers stand out and help reviewers gauge the scope of your work.

Scope

If you're describing a campus or small community organization, be sure to briefly describe the group. Reviewers may not be familiar with the fact that the College of Southeast Ohio Institute for Social Enterprise is the school's largest initiative or that you were the first student to be in charge of its rural outreach program.

Honesty

Include all the relevant, impressive things you've done, but don't make it look like a laundry list of everything in your trophy case since kindergarten. A good way to ensure you represent everything honestly and accurately is to run your résumé by the people you worked with on the respective projects to make sure they agree you have accurately described your contributions.

Most applications have short answer or essay questions. When answering these questions, keep your audience in mind. Print out a draft of your résumé and highlight activities or accomplishments your application reviewers would find interesting (or refer to your answers in Exercise 33.1). If you know that a board is looking for someone with strong skills in a specific area, emphasize activities that require those skills. For instance, if you're applying to a literacy-focused board, highlight projects you've been involved in that pertain to literacy. Write about the library you helped build or the children you tutored.

As you fill out the application, read the questions carefully and be sure you answer the questions. Keep your responses concise.

- Describe the work that you did within your group, not just the work that your group did as a whole.
- Make the scope of your accomplishments understandable.
- Omitting key information is as bad as falsifying information.

Note When you are talking about how amazing you are, never exaggerate or misrepresent yourself. In leadership there's really only one option and that's full transparency. Honesty is *always* the best policy.

The First Date: The Interview

Don't get us wrong: you're *amazing*. But while self-confidence is attractive, arrogance is not. To capture the heart of the right board, just follow these rules.

Step 1: Know Their Type

Google current board members, and learn about their background and expertise. This will give you a sense of the types of people they like to work with and will help you decide which of your qualities to emphasize. If you notice that the board is composed of people who lack a particular area of expertise that you have, you can explain to your interviewers how you can fill that void and make a significant contribution. While you'll probably recognize some of yourself in the current board members, your appeal might be that you offer a fresh perspective.

Step 2: Express Your Interest

Boards want members who want them. Show that you appreciate the work the board has done and that you understand its potential impact. Show you are interested by taking the time to do your homework. You can't do an effective job as a board member if you don't know the history behind the organization or the activities it has pursued. Know about past events, and even more critical, know the future plans of the organization. The more you understand the organization, its members, its mission, and its future direction, the better you'll be able to address it effectively.

Use this information in your interview to explain why you'd be a good fit for the board. For example, if the board is part of an organization that's making an effort to expand into rural areas, explain during your interview how you think this idea will contribute to the organization's growth, the experience you've had in rural outreach, and what you'd specifically like to do with this group to support the rural effort. Or if you think it's a potentially bad idea, don't be afraid to express disagreement with the board's work. As long as you do so politely and provide a potential solution, you'll earn respect.

Step 3: Match Your Profile

Reread your application right before the interview to refresh your memory of what you've submitted. Also, come prepared with multiple copies of your résumé (white or bright white paper in at least 20-pound bond), which should be updated with anything that's happened since you submitted the application.

Step 4: Be Friendly

There's nothing that a simple smile and eye contact can't help. It only takes a person three to seven seconds to make a judgment about you, and that judgment is based on your approachability.

Step 5: Ask Questions

When the interviewer asks if you have any questions, demonstrate your interest in the board and your knowledge of the organization by asking a few thoughtful prepared questions.

Divya: Here are a few questions I usually ask:

- What is your favorite part of serving on the board?
- What does the board do outside of meetings to network and improve relationships between board members?
- If there were one organizational problem you could fix with the help of the board, what would it be, and why?
- What do you think will be the board's most critical function one, three, and five years into the future?

Step 6: Get the Family Vote

Tip: Positive networking is your friend. Getting a position can sometimes be about who you know. Don't be ashamed to ask someone to send an e-mail or make a phone call on your behalf.

Some boards have a selection committee that functions like admissions committees. It's this board that will inform you at some point after the interview if you've been selected. Others have elections in which votes are cast by either the board members themselves or a larger body that elects representatives to the board. If you have to take part in an election, reach out to everyone who will be voting. Early on in the process, talk to them and listen to what they want to see in their leaders and what changes they envision for the group. Respond personally with your thoughts on what they've said, and add in any ideas you may have. If campaigning is part of the group's culture, ask them for their support, and if they are enthusiastic, try to see if they would help you secure more support by talking to other members. Prior to the election, make sure you've had a meaningful dialogue with everyone who will be voting. If the group size is too large to approach each person individually, at least try to e-mail everyone personally.

Step 7: Keep in Touch

Follow up immediately with an appropriately sized (longer than a text message, shorter than an essay) thank-you via e-mail. Provide your interviewer with updates of your activities by calling or e-mailing periodically. If the group takes a while to decide, this will help keep you fresh in their minds. Also, if you are given any advice during the interview (a book to read, a person to talk to), follow up on that advice.

The Proposal: Yes, No, Maybe So?

So you aced the interview, as we predicted. The board members would love to have you join their board. How do you respond?

You: YES! If this is your reaction, skip A and go directly to B.
You: Uhhh … [awkward silence]. If this is your reaction, go to A.

A. Occasionally you'll find you have to break some hearts. Maybe you don't have enough time, realize you're just not that into the board or their mission, can't make the type of commitment they're asking for, find there's a conflict of interest, or just aren't feeling it's the right place. It's okay to say "no, thank you." Decline graciously. Thank the board for the offer, tactfully explain why you can't join, and remember not to burn any bridges because you never know when your paths will cross again.
B. Congratulations! Say thank you and accept in a timely manner. Celebrate with others, share the joy. Live happily ever after.

Eunice Buhler is a graduate student at Stanford University. Former vice president and founding member of Nestlé's Very Best in Youth Foundation Advisory Board, she sat on the board of directors and the youth advisory council of Youth Service America, the State Farm Youth Advisory Board, and the board of directors of Always Ready Kids.

Divya Srinivasan is a senior at MIT. She helped establish the Washington, DC, chapter of Pratham International and has served on the Boston chapter's core team. In addition, she has served on advisory boards for the chancellor of MIT as well as executive committees for GlobeMed and Active Minds.

Chapter 34

Develop Community Ownership

Our true destiny... is a world built from the bottom up by competent citizens living in solid communities, engaged in and by their places.

—DAVID W. ORR

Community ownership is a problem-solving method that empowers people to identify major challenges in their communities, propose and test viable solutions, and sustain improvements over an extended period. Local leaders and outside experts may work with citizens to develop ideas that work, but the community as a whole takes responsibility for the problem. The result is often more effective, relevant, and sustainable because the problem-solving process itself causes the community to become invested (hence, "community ownership") in the solution.

Community Ownership = Participation + Empowerment

British anthropologist Robert Chambers writes that community participation is a process that "enables local people to do their own analysis, to take command, to gain in confidence, and to make their own decisions."[1] This process of promoting community participation might involve training sessions, town meetings, interviews, and fundraising drives; it takes time and resources. The community may not always agree with the outside experts or their local leaders, but the process allows problems to be identified and consensus to be built.

Let's look at an example.

The Scenario

Consider a community overrun with gang violence. A group of students from a nearby college are aware of the crime epidemic and want to do something. Let's say they decide to hire a security guard to patrol the streets at night. To pay him, they start a campus group that hosts periodic fundraisers. This doesn't help much because the guard can be in only one place at a time, and because he's from another town, the neighbors don't know or trust him. Eventually the campus group loses steam, and the funds to pay the security guard run out. Crime continues to grow, and the students' well-intentioned efforts have produced no lasting effect.

What do you think went wrong in the scenario? How could the initiative have been better implemented?

The Analysis

The students' efforts were neither successful nor sustainable because they didn't ask the local community to participate in identifying underlying causes of the problem, pulling together existing resources, and developing possible solutions. In addition, their efforts didn't bolster local leaders' skill sets so that they might better respond to such problems in the future.

The Community Ownership Solution

Had the students tried to devise a community-owned solution, they might have started by setting up meetings with local leaders like the police chief, the Boys and Girls Club director, and the high school principal. From these individuals they might have learned that the violence is fueled by gang rivalries and that the gang members are generally high school dropouts. Many of the gang members' parents work late into the night, and there aren't a lot of safe places in the community for young people to go after school. The Boys and Girls Club, an after-school haven for teens, is reducing its hours of operation due to budget cuts.

With a deeper understanding of the causes of the problem, the group might have devised a plan to keep the Boys and Girls Club open late into the evening, staffed by community volunteers. The basketball court could have been used to host regular tournaments, and the meeting rooms could have been used to provide tutoring.

After completing their research the team might have put together a plan to obtain sponsorships for the club's activities from successful business owners across town. They might have also worked with their school administrators to institutionalize a tutoring program, which would offer course credit to students who volunteered. Over time, this initiative might have attracted new generations of students, professors, mentors, and community members.

Who Has the Answers?

A community's greatest assets are its people and their concern for the well-being of their friends and family. However, while community participation stresses local involvement, it doesn't mean steering clear of external influences such as the students in the example. In fact, local community leaders often consult outside experts.

The example of a crime prevention initiative harnesses both internal and external assets and is driven by a solid and sustainable partnership. Had the students used their fundraisers to start this crime prevention program, their efforts would have met with greater success in the long run.

A Participatory Approach Is Key

In the past, projects of all kinds have failed to give communities a stake in their success, failed to leverage existing social capital, and ultimately failed to strengthen the fabric of the community and build the capacity of its members. Through participatory methods, community leaders, community members, and outside experts work together to devise solutions that the local population can implement and sustain. This sort of civic involvement is the lifeblood of high-functioning, healthy communities and a crucial component of any successful project.

Now that we've worked through an example of how you might implement a community ownership solution, let's break down the essential components needed to facilitate community ownership.

Exercise 34.1 will help you think more about a participatory approach.

Exercise 34.1 Think Critically about Community Ownership

1. Think of a situation in which community ownership would be critical, or select one of these options:
   - Improving lunchroom nutrition at local schools
   - Implementing a large-scale vaccination program in a poor rural community
   - Introducing a simple technology to clean household water supply in an urban slum
2. List specific stakeholders you would approach and your strategy to engage each one.
3. Design an action plan for how you would engage the community in the design, implementation, and evaluation of your initiative.
4. What would be your exit strategy?
5. What potential unintended consequences might arise from your initiative? How would you ensure that you did no harm?

Do Your Homework, Show Up, and Listen to the Community

If you can, find a way to live in the community for a while. At the very least, make frequent visits to meet with community members. As Woody Allen once said, "80% of life is showing up!" Talk to people who live in the community, and try to understand how they see the world. What are the prevailing perceptions, assumptions, and moral forces that guide decision making?

There are many ways to learn about communities. Prior to showing up, you can prepare yourself by doing some background research:

- Read novels, newspaper articles, and academic journal articles about the locale.
- Ask local leaders what sources they recommend, which restaurants serve typical foods, what basic phrases are useful (if working in a community that speaks another language), and what customs are unique to their community.
- Have a basic understanding of an area's socioeconomic background, general geography, and history.
- Learn about ongoing controversies or notable circumstances. And if you're working in an area that is not traditionally welcoming to outsiders, you'll need to be even more humble in your approach.
- Familiarize yourself with the prevailing religions and culture.

Tip When getting to know the community, consider shadowing someone affected by the problem you're trying to solve.

Other methods like surveys, focus groups, community meetings, and interviews can also be extremely helpful when getting to know a community. The nature, size, and scope of your project will dictate what methods can be used. For example, if your project is targeting a city of 100,000 people, consider collecting existing data from municipal authorities or surveying a representative sample of the population. If your project targets a single high school classroom, get to know the target population on a personal level.

Before doing your own research, look for existing information first, which can save substantial time and financial resources. You might also find it helpful to contact other groups working on similar issues in the area, as they can help uncover information. They'll also show you how to engage the community based on their past successes and failures. Get your information from many sources so you can compare similarities and differences.

How would you recommend a stranger get to know your community?

Seek Community-Driven Solutions

As you learn more about a community by showing up and listening, you'll be able to identify what is most likely to work. Be bold but realistic with your ideas. Identify and harness the most powerful forces at work in a community and try to redirect them toward your ultimate mission. Ask yourself, what are the conditions and incentives necessary to get people to do what I need done?

Daniel: I may not have paid much attention to a few telling encounters in the Middle East had my own grandmother not passed away from diabetes in Palestine. These experiences opened my eyes to the severity of the diabetes epidemic in the developing world. Through these and many other interactions, I learned that diabetes is a leading cause of death and disability in the region. As I ate meals with families, an older woman would mention that she was losing her eyesight, or I would hear that a husband nearly lost his foot because of diabetes complications.

From these conversations, I gained a deeper understanding of the problem and what the solution might look like. In the context of conflict and economic deterioration, social networks are an invaluable resource and an integral part of daily life for Palestinians. Friends and family visit with one another on a regular basis and often discuss ailments over a cup of coffee. When someone becomes ill, family members care for each other and share resources. I soon learned we could leverage this existing social infrastructure to encourage people to start improving one another's health and well-being. In short, we could use preexisting social networks to "spread health."

After talking with many other Palestinians suffering from diabetes and after consulting with local doctors and nurses, I decided to start what would become Microclinic International (MCI). My goal wasn't to start from scratch and set up a new health organization (reinventing the wheel can waste time and money and cause harm to other effective community efforts). Rather, I identified some modest objectives (for example, providing people with information). I recruited leaders already working in the community who were eager to get involved. Together we established a network of diabetes "microclinics"—small groups of friends, family, and neighbors who share access to education, technology (like a glucose monitor), and group support. The initial microclinics were set up with the cooperation of local leaders but aren't owned or affiliated with a government, a nongovernmental organization, or even a hospital. Ultimately the microclinics are groups of people brought together by shared feelings, challenges, and goals.

In what ways did Daniel take into account the community when designing a solution? How can you incorporate community ownership into your current efforts?

Build and Manage a Team

The process of recruiting a dedicated team is time-consuming and sometimes difficult, but a solid management system will ensure that the community remains invested in the project. Involving the community also means that local leadership must guide the day-to-day activities of the project after the startup phase.

Daniel: As we expanded our efforts to Jordan, our local and global teams decided that volunteer efforts alone wouldn't be sufficient to sustain our work, so we recruited managers who could oversee the daily execution of the project. The local leadership was able to respond with resources and ideas as unexpected management problems arose.

Plan and Implement Together

Tip As an outsider to a community, managing well is critical: you must invest the time to develop relationships with the local leaders and gain their trust.

At any level, project management is fundamentally about relating to people. An effective manager should be able to identify where the needs of staff and community members intersect with project goals in order to best match individuals and their interests with the tasks at hand. Effective managers know that personal motivations aren't just financial; they include intellectual stimulation, the feeling of being trusted with responsibility, recognition of a job well done, or the gratification obtained from helping others.

Leila: Managing teams of community members who implement MCI's projects in various communities around the world requires a careful balance of clear, concise direction together with enough flexibility to adapt to the needs and resources of each local community.

Engineer Self-Sustainability

If community ownership is the key to long-term sustainability, how will you ensure your project continues once you're gone? Any type of intervention in a community should plan for an exit strategy from the onset. Think back to the example at the beginning of this chapter about the students who raised money to hire a security guard. Even if the idea itself had worked, what would happen a few years down the line after the initial group of student leaders had graduated? What would the students do if the people donating money to their group decided to support a different cause? You must ensure that responsibilities are understood, that accountability mechanisms are in place, and that appropriate compensation is offered.

Evaluate Together

You might also need to put together a comprehensive evaluation plan that addresses all aspects of sustainability. Include your local partners in both the development and implementation of your evaluation plan so they are well-informed about the results of your project, what's working, and what needs to be improved.

Thinking about these issues means not only considering cultural sensitivities, ensuring that your work maintains interest and doesn't offend, but also thinking about political and economic sustainability. If you'll be working in a politically charged context, how will you ensure that you're not seen as challenging the government or other organizations working on similar projects?

Daniel: To address the sustainability question, MCI chooses its partners carefully. When we were first getting started, we worked directly with individual people—health care workers and local volunteers who have established humanitarian credentials within their communities. As our organization expanded, we selected partners like governments and other NGOs that have the capacity and infrastructure needed to scale our model in a much larger way.

In addition, to ensure economic stability, I purchased supplies locally so participants in the microclinics would have access to replacement items. This allowed me to negotiate lower prices for the participants while supporting the local economy.

Note Thinking this through with local partners is an important part of the process of community ownership. Make it your goal to create a program that can run without your help and can be sustained and owned by the members of the community.

How to Achieve Community Ownership

These steps can be iterative, in that you may need to do some of the earlier steps multiple times when you're working in a community and your goal is to ensure local ownership. While above we presented more descriptive philosophies for community ownership, below you will find the philosophies translated into concrete steps. Exercise 34.2 will also give you a chance to see how others are—or aren't—following these steps.

Exercise 34.2 How Does Community Ownership Work in the Real World?

Using academic sources or the media, look for a project implemented by a non-profit, NGO, or social entrepreneur that you find to be interesting. Contact as many community members as possible where the initiative took place (aim to get at least three), and ask them about each of the components of community ownership described above. Describe the initiative and its location below:

Initiative:

Interview Questions

1. Do you feel that the people leading this initiative were well informed about the community? Was it apparent if they had done their homework prior to launching the project? How did their preparation (or lack of it) affect the success of the project?
2. How much time did the leaders of the project spend in the community? What do local community members think about this?
3. Did the project managers meet with local leaders before they implemented the project? What about while they were (or are) implementing? Do you think local buy-in for the project was (or is) strong?
4. Did the project duplicate any preexisting services? Do you know of any competitors locally?
5. How were local community members involved in the planning of the project?

(continued)

6. Is there a local advisory board or other mechanism for community members to discuss the initiative and provide feedback or advice?
7. Was any training conducted to teach community members how to implement the project? If so, what did they think about this training?
8. What kind of evaluation was (or will be) carried out? Did any community members participate in designing or implementing the evaluation?
9. What does your community think of the project? What are your personal opinions of the project?
10. Would you say the project is "owned" by the local community or by the non-profit, NGO, or social entrepreneur who had the original idea?

Do Your Homework

- Read about the community before arriving, using both academic and news sources.
- Know the basic geography, history, and socioeconomic profile of the community
- Learn a few key phrases in the local language of the community.

Show Up

- Spend as much time as possible living in the community.
- Spend time doing the same day-to-day activities that people you'll be working with do: buying groceries, using local transportation systems, eating at local restaurants.

Listen

- Ask to meet with as many local leaders as you can, not to sell your idea but to learn about their perspectives, needs, challenges, and resources.

- Be prepared to hear and accept "no." Your ideas may not be welcomed for a variety of reasons. If you sense a general aversion to the project you want to implement, be respectful and accept that it's not the right time or place to implement your idea. Projects that don't have local buy-in are doomed.
- Make sure you're not duplicating or competing with preexisting services. If you find that people are already doing something similar, see if it makes sense to partner with them to add value.
- Be very culturally sensitive and show respect for local traditions, religious beliefs, language, and norms.

Plan Together and Seek Community-Driven Solutions

- Invest ample time in careful planning of your initiative, and include key local community members in the process.
- Be open to changing your plans if it means greater local buy-in.
- Develop an action plan that incorporates feedback from relevant community members.

Build a Team and Implement Together

- Set up a local advisory board with a diverse group of community members that meet regularly to discuss your initiative and provide advice and feedback.
- Remember that good management is about people, not about management tools. If you're managing a local team, ask at the start what type of management style works for them. Be willing to adjust your management techniques as needed.
- Invest time to train local community members and transfer knowledge. For example, if you need to teach someone about Excel in order for him or her to be able to manage the budget after you leave, make sure you allocate time to do so.

Engineer Self-Sustainability and Evaluate Together

- Make a conscious effort to turn over more and more of your responsibilities to local staff as the project progresses.
- Any initiative needs to be evaluated. Involving community members in the design and execution of the evaluation plan will help ensure they're more invested in the results.

Plant the Seeds of Change

It is not more bigness that should be our goal. We must attempt, rather, to bring people back to ... the warmth of community, to the worth of individual effort and responsibility ... and of individuals working together as a community, to better their lives and their children's future.

ROBERT F. KENNEDY

Throughout these steps, it's critical to remain humble. You may have the best of intentions and great skills and experiences to contribute, but ultimately you don't have all the answers. The solutions lie within the community itself and your job is to facilitate their success, not your own. The most rewarding experience is when your local partners have adapted your project or idea—or some version of it—as their own. That's when you know community ownership has really taken root.

Daniel Zoughbie is the founder, CEO, and president of Microclinic International. His research and community service activities combine the fields of international health, international relations, and higher education. He received a BA from the UC, Berkeley; an MSc from Oxford as a Marshall Scholar; and a DPhil (PhD) from Oxford as a Weidenfeld Scholar.

Leila Makarechi is the COO and executive vice president of Program Management at Microclinic International. She's also worked for the United Nations Development Program, covering more than 92 projects in 21 countries. She has a BA from UC Berkeley; an MPA from Columbia University; and an MPA from the Institut d'Études Politiques.

Make It Last:

Add Value and Sustain Success

Chapter 35

Apply Social Entrepreneurship

Social entrepreneurs are not content just to give a fish or teach how to fish. They will not rest until they have revolutionized the fishing industry.

—*BILL DRAYTON*

Social entrepreneurship begins with the radical notion that we can use the tools of business—markets, investors, growth plans, and even the profit motive—to solve the world's most pressing social problems.

This chapter explores how businesses can be thought of as drivers of social change. It will familiarize you with the basic tenets of social entrepreneurship as well as encourage you to embrace these principles as you think about making change in your own community.

Business as Part of the Solution

Many activists find it hard to believe that businesses could help solve social problems. After all, many of the problems that activists confront are related to the misdeeds of big corporations. Think about pollution, political corruption, and sweatshop labor. For activists who care about these issues, businesses aren't the solution—they're the problem. Others will argue that businesses shouldn't solve social problems because that's not their job. Their job is simply to make as much money as possible.

In this chapter, we explain that this way of dividing the world isn't right. If you take a step back and look at the big picture, business can and should a part of the solution.

Profit Can Drive Social Progress

Businesses succeed when they help people solve real problems. Think about the things we spend money on: food, education, housing, and health care. Businesses that can successfully address problems involving major needs like these will tend to thrive. As Adam Smith wrote, it's not the "benevolence of the butcher" that gets us our dinner; it's his own "self-interest." The community benefits because the butcher wants to make money. Likewise, dotcom companies that make search engines and e-mail services make it easier for us to answer questions, find things we need, and connect with important people. It's precisely because of their social benefits, not despite them, that these businesses succeed.

Taking the long view of history, we can see that our society is far healthier, more educated, and safer because we have an economy that allows people to freely build solutions to the problems that they encounter and then exchange those solutions with others at market. Business has been one of the greatest drivers of social good our world has ever known.

Social Entrepreneurs

Social entrepreneurs deliberately flip assumptions about money and business on their heads. Instead of thinking of businesses as building products in order to make profit, they think of profit as a tool to help build better products. The business is merely a vehicle—one of the most powerful vehicles ever created—for building products or processes that have positive effects on the world.

Meanwhile, social entrepreneurs challenge us to think beyond our typical conceptions of public service. For social entrepreneurs, public service is more than participation in public affairs; it's more than advocating for powerful people in government or corporations to change their decisions; and it's more than providing services directly to those in need. All these are worthwhile activities. But for social entrepreneurs, public service is supposed to be a fundamentally creative act. The goal is to propel humanity by building something new. None of our familiar models of businesses as profit-maximizing machines, or of public service as participation, activism, or community service, quite captures the creative promise of social entrepreneurship.

To help you understand these distinctions, consider these four ways of approaching a given public problem in Exercise 35.1.

Exercise 35.1 Four Approaches to the Same Problem

Imagine a town where over a hundred homeless men and women struggle to find food each night. Brainstorm some approaches to solving this problem. For each, list some obstacles you might encounter. We'll help get you started.

	Traditional Charity	**Traditional Business**	**Traditional Political Activism**
Approach	Start a soup kitchen. Ask people to donate food, and then find volunteers to staff the soup kitchen.	Start a restaurant that serves inexpensive food. Market your food to the low-income population.	Gather signatures in support of an initiative to increase funding for local food banks. Hold a rally in support of the homeless population to raise awareness.
Obstacles	How will you convince people to donate soup and volunteer their time? If your effort is successful, how will you expand the number of people donating and volunteering?	Will you be able to build a profitable business by selling to the poorest members of the community? If yes, then think about why it isn't already being done.	Will you be able to compete for the attention of politicians and community members when they have so many other issues on their plate?

(continued)

Social Entrepreneurship

After looking at these three models, you decide to take another approach, one in keeping with the spirit of social entrepreneurship. You devise a plan for a secondary market for healthy leftover food. Here's how it will work:

- You'll develop partnerships with local restaurants. They'll donate excess food that remains at the end of each night (which normally is thrown away), which you will sell at a low price. You'll recognize the business partners on your program's website and give them a plaque for "supporting our town's neediest."

Figure 35.1. Four Approaches to Solving a Problem

- You'll situate a food cart in an area where the homeless population congregates. You'll sell the excess food at a 90% reduced cost—a muffin for 25 cents, a sandwich for one dollar—to patrons who register their names at the local homeless shelter.
- The money you generate from the food sales will help pay for the gas required to transport the food as well as maintenance of the food cart.
- Your pilot succeeds in one neighborhood. Now you work to expand it to other neighborhoods.

Discuss how this solution is different from the traditional charity approach, the traditional business approach, and the traditional political activist approach using these prompts:

- Why sell food rather than give it away?
- How does the recipient value the food differently when it's charity versus something purchased?
- How does this plan use existing resources more efficiently than traditional businesses can?
- What are the benefits of working outside direct government support?
- What are the obstacles you might confront with this model?

Key Components of Social Entrepreneurship

We began this chapter by claiming that social entrepreneurs leverage the tools of business to solve the world's biggest social problems. But what are those tools? There are three primary ideas that social entrepreneurs take from the best of traditional entrepreneurship:

1. *Disruption*: a focus on thinking up radical new solutions
2. *Accountability*: an obsession with measuring results and improving impact
3. *Scaling*: a bias toward growth and the efficient use of existing resources in order to maximize impact

Disruption

Being an entrepreneur means more than just "starting a business." While many businesses will try to win by building slightly better features of a product or slightly cheaper models, the entrepreneur's goals are loftier—to find new ways to solve the same problem. In the words of business historian Peter Drucker, entrepreneurship is the process of "shifting economic resources" into "areas of higher productivity and great yield."[1] By this he means that entrepreneurs take an existing, relatively unproductive way of doing something and radically transform it so that it yields far greater results for far less money. They call this "disruption." Explore disruption in Exercise 35.2. Instead of competing in existing markets, according to existing rules, social entrepreneurs create new markets by changing the rules altogether.

Exercise 35.2 Disrupting Our World

Our world is full of disruptive inventions. Indeed, the economist Joseph Schumpeter said that the essence of capitalism was "creative destruction," or the victory of new ways of doing things over the old.

- Brainstorm a list of disruptive inventions. Think about areas like transportation, technology, food, and health care. What breakthroughs have fundamentally changed the way markets work?

- Are there problems in your life that might be solved with disruptive solutions? Think about areas like education, food, and jobs. Imagine what those disruptions might look like.

Like traditional entrepreneurs, social entrepreneurs think disruptively. They agree with Martin Luther King Jr. when he said that "true compassion is more than flinging a coin to a beggar." True compassion is "seeing that an edifice which produces beggars needs restructuring." In other words, instead of finding ways to provide more food, the social entrepreneur examines the systems of power that create food scarcity in the first place. The social entrepreneur attempts to "disrupt" the system that leaves people homeless and hungry.

Case Study: Using Social Entrepreneurship to Alleviate Poverty

In the 1970s, a Bangladeshi economist named Muhammad Yunus hatched a disruptive idea: the rural poor could pull themselves out of poverty if they could get access to funds needed to start their own businesses. To Yunus, poverty was a trap. The poor are in need of high-quality resources, but because profit-minded people see high risks and low rewards from working with them, the poor are least likely to access those resources. Lacking access, the poor get poorer, reducing their access further, making them poorer still. It's a vicious cycle.

Yunus began helping poor families escape this trap by giving them financial advice and small loans that they could invest in income-generating businesses. This microfinance model was a resounding success. Traditional businesses hadn't seen this opportunity because they assumed the poor wouldn't pay back their loans. (In fact, as the world found out from Yunus's efforts, the poor are remarkably good at paying back loans.) Traditional nonprofits didn't see this opportunity either, because they focus on addressing the outcomes of poverty, like hunger and lack of health care, rather than its roots.

Microfinance isn't a cure-all. Results have been mixed, especially as far less socially conscious firms have copied the model, charging higher interest rates and sometimes bankrupting the families they are attempting to help. But Grameen Bank continues to thrive and received, with Yunus, the Nobel Peace Prize in 2006.

Case Study: CommonPlace

The Social Good

Max: In his book *Bowling Alone: The Collapse and Revival of American Community*, Robert Putnam makes two remarkable arguments. First, he uses statistical evidence to show that when people trust each other and share information at the local level, nearly every aspect of the communities they live in starts to get safer, more productive, healthier, and happier. He calls this trust and information flow "social capital." Most of us simply call it "community."

Putnam explains how groups like the Masons, the Boy Scouts, the Rotary Club, and Little Leagues have all played a vital role in building up social capital in our communities. These humble organizations have helped make our democracy work.

The Problem

Max: Putnam's second argument is more alarming: nearly all of these traditional civic organizations are in a state of decline. People are joining fewer clubs, meeting fewer people, trusting their neighbors less, and disengaging from what's happening in the community around them. As a nation, we've disconnected from our communities.

Putnam suggests a few reasons for why. One reason is that people work longer hours, making it harder to start new hobbies or volunteer. Meanwhile, we have new forms of entertainment, like TVs and computer games, that keep us indoors, out of the public. And our culture has changed, with the baby boomer generation less likely to value things like civic engagement and community awareness than their parents did.[2]

Desire for Change

Max: Having watched President Obama elected to office with the help of a digitally plugged-in younger generation, among many others, and having watched the financial crisis expose how needy our neighborhoods really are, my roommate and I refused to believe that people no longer wanted to engage with their communities.

Disruption

Max: We had a different theory about the decline of local community. Perhaps it wasn't that people didn't want to engage, or didn't have enough time to engage; maybe the problem was that the tools of civic engagement had grown rusty, and no longer fit into lives. The "technology" of our local community had grown old. It needed to be updated. To reinspire civic engagement, we can't just create more community centers or Rotary Clubs. We need to build new models for our time.

Solution

Max: That's the problem we set out to tackle when we started CommonPlace, our civic technology venture. Our goal was to empower neighbors and local leaders to organize in their communities. Our solution is "disruptive," mostly because it's in the middle of two worlds: the high-tech world of Internet communications and the old-school world of community organizing. We challenge these communities to think differently: the technologists to think about the civic effects of the tools they build and the community engagement advocates to consider the potential of technology to revitalize local civic engagement.

Often a powerful way to come up with disruptive ideas is to bring two communities of knowledge together. What are two different areas that you're passionate about? How might you combine them to create something that no one has tried before?

Accountability

Social entrepreneurs are obsessive with making returns on their investments. For traditional businesses, returns are measured in dollars and cents. But for the social entrepreneurs the situation is necessarily more complex; they must devise metrics for measuring the impact their solutions are having on the world, in addition to the amount of money they bring in. This is often called their "double bottom line," both money and social good. Some refer to the "triple bottom line" of "people, planet, and profit," or helping people, staying eco-friendly, and making money.

Consider Esther Duflo, an MIT economist who's famous for her use of rigorous methods to test the effectiveness of poverty relief programs. Her research group, the Poverty Action Lab, has pioneered the use of randomized control trials, which involve the random selection of different groups within a given population and then the running of slightly varied tests, to measure the impact of different variables.

For example, one active debate in the aid community is how much anti-malaria mosquito nets should cost to people who need them. Mosquito nets are proven to be an extremely effective way to save lives in communities where malaria is endemic. But how should we get the nets to these communities? Should they be given away for free? Sold at discounted prices? Or sold at full market value?

Many believe intuitively that aid organizations should give malaria nets away for free. This way, they reason, everyone will be able to afford them, and the nets will be distributed as widely as possible. Others worry, however, that if malaria nets are given away for free, the recipients won't value them as much as if the community were educated about their importance and spent some of its own money buying them. If the nets are sold for even a small amount of money, they say, they'll be more likely to be used.

Others go even further than this. They argue malaria nets need to be sold at the full market price, because anything else will drive other malaria net suppliers out of the market. In other words, if wealthy foreign organizations discount the cost of malaria nets, no one from the community itself can compete in the market by selling malaria nets, so they won't sell them. The community would become completely dependent on the aid organization. And what happens when that aid ends?

What's interesting about the malaria net debate is that it's highly empirical; you can arrive at your answer through evidence.

- Describe how you might use Duflo's randomized control trials to test the effect of malaria net prices on three dependent variables: (1) people's access to malaria nets, (2) their willingness to use them, and (3) the presence of local people selling malaria nets. How would you vary the "treatment" (the delivery of malaria nets) to test those different variables?
- How would you measure outcomes? What would you be looking for in each case?
- What do you personally expect the results will be? What should malaria nets cost?

Scaling

A final hallmark of social entrepreneurial organizations is their bias toward growth, both within a given community and across multiple communities. This process of first improving your model and then sharing it around the world is known as "scaling," and it's a defining stage for social entrepreneurs.

Growth can create problems. There are basic operational problems, like the difficulty of delivering the same quality of service to many communities at once. And then there are potential culture problems. Since social entrepreneurs are often from outside the communities they serve, their solutions can feel imposed, at odds with the culture and traditions of a community that didn't necessarily ask for them.

To protect against this, social entrepreneurs often consider their goal to be empowering the creative energy of others rather than supplying a prebaked solution. Instead of providing "services" to communities directly, they provide "platforms" that amplify the hard work of those who engage. Microloans, for example, don't solve poverty directly. (The loans have to be paid back, after all.) Rather, they serve as an enabler of the initiative and skill of others, promoting the formation of businesses and services. Many social entrepreneurial ventures take on this form.

Max: Because the most successful local civic organizations tend to be run by people who live in the communities they're serving, we believed that the best ways to help local community engagement was to create a platform that empowered local residents to organize their own services more effectively. We wanted to lower the cost of engaging to help new leaders emerge from all different parts of the community.

Here's how CommonPlace works. Every day it sends an e-mail newsletter to everyone in the community, written by neighbors and local leaders. Because the newsletter is written by its readers, people can play the role of both helping and asking for help. In one post, you can help others resolve their problems, "Can I borrow a ladder?" to "Who's interested in creating a neighborhood watch?" As the days go by, residents realize that their own power in the community has expanded. They know more people and have immediate access to an information distribution channel in town, allowing them to organize whatever inspires them. Our hope is that through CommonPlace, this knowledge of their own power will inspire people to create social change in their communities.

We don't impose a service on a community. We enable leaders in their own communities to get their voices heard effectively. As we've grown, it's been gratifying watching how different communities with different needs use the tool in different ways. The tool has been used for everything from renting goats to organizing radical sustainability initiatives.

Why Now?

Why social entrepreneurship now? Why do we need to come up with new ways of understanding business and new ways of understanding public service after all this time? The answer seems rooted in two major worldwide trends: first, technology has helped to distribute the means of starting a business or organization into more people's hands than ever before; and at the same time, the traditional ways of addressing social problems no longer seem to work.

We are incredibly powerful, at least by historical standards. In the 20th century, life spans increased dramatically, basic education was extended to hundreds of millions, and the advance of civil rights has given far more people the power to act on their own initiative. Coupled with this, information technologies have made it drastically easier to build up skills, mobilize resources, coordinate the production of goods and services, and find people who want to engage with our work. We're wealthier, more educated, freer, and more connected than ever before.

At the same time, there's a sense in the US and around the world that the old solutions won't do. Information technology has connected the world, exposing us to the problems people in faraway places face, inspiring us to act. But how? Warranted or not, many look at decades of social initiatives at home and abroad and see a system that's not up to the challenge.

Social entrepreneurship is part of a wider emergence of a new global citizen sector. We live in a world where individuals are empowered to solve the problems they encounter. We act, knowing that if we don't, perhaps no one will.

Max Novendstern is CEO and cofounder of CommonPlace, a neighborhood networking start-up in Cambridge, Massachusetts. Max studied American history at Harvard College, where he was the editor-in-chief of the *Harvard Political Review*. Before college, he worked in the highlands of Peru, organizing a cooperative of indigenous artisans.

Chapter 36

Revitalize Your Efforts

The greatest accomplishment is not in never falling, but in rising again after you fall.

—*VINCE LOMBARDI*

Is your team suffering from a lack of energy? Maybe you've just assumed a leadership position of a group that's a bit dysfunctional. Or maybe you've led the group for some time and have observed a gradual decline in its vitality. The small changes you try to implement aren't working, and you're feeling frustrated. You need a jump-start, a refresh and reset. The challenge ahead isn't trivial.

Think of this chapter as your team doctor: it'll not only help you diagnose and treat the problem, but will also prescribe preventative measures to minimize the chance of future flare-ups.

Determine the Causes

There are five common reasons for organizational vitality declines:

1. *Team cultural issues*: The culture of a team may be off for a number of reasons, including a lack of ownership or transparency, failure to give credit where credit's due, or interpersonal conflict.

2. *External shifts*: Shifts in the external environment can make an organization or its mission irrelevant or outdated.
3. *Leadership changes*: Senior and midlevel leadership changes can be rocky, especially if there's no smooth transfer of information and best practices.
4. *Inadequate growth opportunities*: A lack of opportunities for team members to grow and lead can result in underwhelming group participation.
5. *Talent mismatch*: The pipeline of talent coming into the team may not be well suited to the team's existing culture and goals.

Let's break these down a bit further. . .

Team Cultural Issues

Team culture is strongly related to leadership style and often projects from the top down. Although it can be difficult to define, there are four key components of team culture, each of which can result in problems if the balance is thrown off.

Ownership

A culture of ownership means that all members feel personally invested in the team's work and success. Members who feel a sense of ownership accept accountability and continuously work to improve the team. This can be achieved only in a team that empowers everyone to speak up and take charge.

Transparency

A culture of transparency means that leaders continuously communicate with the team so that everyone understands the group's current actions and future direction.

Recognition

When a team acknowledges its member's contributions, either formally or informally, members feel valued and are more likely to take on greater responsibility and feel greater ownership. Lack of recognition can cause members to question the importance of their contributions. On the flip side, when things go wrong, there should be a process to provide critical feedback in a constructive way.

Interaction

The way members interact is a critical factor. A sense of camaraderie among team members promotes communication and a steady exchange of ideas—and makes everything more fun!.

External Shifts

The world changes quickly, and it can be difficult for a team to adapt. Perhaps the external culture is no longer excited about what your team has to offer in the face of new fads and preferences. Perhaps a new technology has made part of your offering obsolete. Do you actively strive to remain relevant? Are you keeping up with social media?

When a team loses relevance, the disconnect and disappointment are felt at all levels. As team members realize their work isn't making the impact they'd imagined and their potential is being wasted, motivation drops.

Leadership Changes

Look at any leadership changes your team has undergone in the last year. Have any of the departures left gaping holes in your team's culture or operations? Senior leadership changes can dramatically affect culture, especially if the leader who left was a strong influence. Midlevel management changes more often affect continuity of work because key information or skills may have left with the managers.

Inadequate Growth Opportunities

You need to provide your team with adequate opportunities for growth, both informal and formal. Informal opportunities include initiatives outside an individual's specific role, like leading recruiting or social events. Formal opportunities include promotions or raises commensurate with performance. Evaluate the opportunities you're providing to all members in your enterprise. Allowing members to take on new challenges leads to greater enthusiasm and personal investment in the team.

Talent Mismatch

The recruiting process should make every effort to ensure that the people you're bringing in fit the team culture and goals. If new members lack enthusiasm or cultural fit, the effects can be jarring. Determine what qualities and values are critical to the success of your team, and screen for them when recruiting.

Diagnose the Problem

Now that you're familiar with the common causes of organizational decline, you're ready to diagnose your team's specific problems. This process requires an honest assessment of the team's past and present weaknesses. An effective evaluation requires multiple perspectives and should take these actions:

1. Brainstorm with other leaders.
2. Review the recent history of your team.
3. Organize an executive retreat.
4. Create and implement a member or staff survey.
5. Summarize and compile your findings.

Make a list of the strengths and weaknesses of your team as well as some possible explanations. Begin your team's jump-start by thinking through the prompts in Exercise 36.1. Involve other leaders who have shown great dedication and share your revitalization vision. Brainstorm separately and then share your thoughts. Compare your assessments and revise accordingly. Seek outside advice and input at this stage to get fresh perspectives.

Exercise 36.1 Begin Your Team's Jump-Start

Perform this exercise to start thinking through how to jump-start your team:

1. List your team's five greatest weaknesses.

2. For each weakness, write the corresponding long-term goal you'd like to accomplish.

3. For each long-term goal, write down three short-term changes you'll make to get the ball rolling.

Next, look at your team's history, and try to find the point when the team began to lose energy and focus. What other factors were changing at the time? What was happening externally? What factors were shifting internally? This will help restore institutional memory and identify which factors contributed most strongly to the decline.

> *Om*: When trying to revitalize my school's Interfaith Council, I found that it was very helpful to hold a retreat that would give the board of directors and executive leaders an opportunity to voice their concerns, articulate new ideas, and commit to ways in which they wanted to contribute. A formal retreat allows a team to set aside time away from day-to-day tasks and step back and assess where an organization is going and how much progress has been made on overarching goals. It's important to ensure that the retreat fosters honest dialogue without any negative repercussions for voicing concerns and opinions. Instead of communicating exclusively in a large group setting, interactive exercises and smaller breakout sessions are often more effective at spurring innovation and generating enthusiasm. If your group has budgetary or time constraints, think simple—set aside a few hours in a library conference room and have a potluck-style meal. The enthusiasm our retreat generated among the leaders led to a stronger sense of commitment and increased our eventual impact.

> **Tip** Be sure to have a scribe appointed to record all of the thoughts that come out of the retreat.

Next, gather feedback from all other members on the state of the team. Using the brainstorming that has occurred thus far, design a detailed survey of the salient points. Include room for additional suggestions because the most important changes usually come from the bottom up.

Finally, take stock of all of the work you've done. Review your brainstorming notes, findings from the retreat, and survey results. Identify common themes in strengths and weaknesses, and compile the ideas for change.

Follow the Treatment Plan

Although each team is unique, there are common strategies you can use to spearhead a successful revitalization. Your success depends on effective strategy, communication, and execution.

Ten-Step Plan to Revitalization

1. *Develop a new vision*: This new vision looks to the future for the team.
2. *Engage in a functional tune-up*: Adopt new protocols, communication tools, positions, and committees that allow the group to function more efficiently based on your assessment.
3. *Communicate the new strategy internally*: Make sure that the entire team is committed to the changes.
4. *Communicate the new strategy externally*: Discuss the new strategy with partners, funders, and all other relevant outside stakeholders.
5. *Transform your image*: Consider changing your logo, pamphlets, website, and other images to reflect the qualities you want your team to have and attract publicity to cover the changes.
6. *Hold a kick-off*: Unveil your new image, initiatives, and long-term plan with a celebratory event that will attract many current and potential members and supporters.
7. *Hit the ground running*: Take advantage of the excitement by immediately beginning to implement all the new initiatives planned.
8. *Track your progress*: Continuously track progress in a transparent manner to make sure everyone knows where the team stands on each goal.
9. *Adjust your own role as leader*: Move on from any micromanaging that might have been necessary to shape the broader revitalization, letting the newly revitalized membership become more invested.
10. *Continuously improve*: Hold regular reviews to make sure that your team is continuing to make progress and continuing to improve.

Form a Strategy

You're now in an ideal place to form a new vision and set specific goals. To get started, ask yourself, "What should the future version of my team look like?" The answer should address the most essential dimensions you explored in your assessment. Make a table that contrasts the current version of your team with the version you'd like to see exist when you eventually step down as leader and begin thinking about the short-term and long-term actions necessary to get there. Table 36.1 provides an example.

Table 36.1. Example of a Revitalization Vision

Organization: Student Health Policy Society

Purpose: To provide a means for members to explore and discuss their interests in health care policy.

CURRENT SITUATION	VISION OF REVITALIZED ORGANIZATION
Weaknesses	**Strengths**
• Lack of enthusiasm	• Lots of spirit and enthusiasm
• Dwindling membership (20 students)	• Large, diverse membership (100+)
• Inadequate funds	• Triple budget with surplus
• Reputation for Inefficiency	• Reputation for energy, improvement, and efficiency
• Small, hypercentralized leadership	• Ample opportunities for members to get involved and lead
• Outdated website	• Brand new website for membership, with additional administrative tools
• Social disunity	• Strong sense of community, with individual members recognized for their efforts
Activities	**Activities**
• Inner discussions on different topics	• Traditional dinner discussions
• Occasional contributions by guest speakers	• Campuswide debates on health care issues cosponsored with other organizations
• Academic newsletter with dwindling distribution and deadlines that are rarely met.	• Academic publication in health policy, with regional distribution
	• Annual national conference on an important health care issue
	• Petitions for specific health policy changes on the state and national levels
	• Forums with policy experts, academics, and politicians
	• Career fair with resources for summer internship and employment opportunities in health care policy
	• Social events for members

(continued)

Table 36.1. *(continued)*

Officers	Officers
• President, vice president, treasurer, secretary	• President, vice president, treasurer, secretary, publicity/public relations chair, editor-in-chief of new academic journal, debates/discussion chair, social chair, political advocacy chair, historian
Administrative Functions	**Administrative Functions**
• One to two board meetings per month, date and time decided with each new meeting • Meetings are disorganized and vary in length	• One board meeting every week, with regular date and time decided for the whole semester or year. • Meetings last one hour, and printed agendas with time limits for each talking point are distributed to each board member. Board members are responsible for e-mailing the president 48 hours before the meeting to add necessary talking points.
• Minimal communication between meetings	• Several e-mails sent daily over an executive board e-mail list, with updates on progress.

Before you can begin implementing your vision, be sure your team has the basic machinery to handle it. Start by giving your team a functional tune-up. Adopt new protocols, communication tools, positions, and committees that improve communication, clarify responsibility, increase accountability, and allow the leadership to function as a well-oiled machine, without unnecessary layers of bureaucracy.

Communicate Your Strategy

Now that your team has the tools in place, you must present the new strategy and get buy-in from key internal and external constituents.

Internal Communications

Communicating the new strategy and vision internally is essential to your success. You want all members to feel included in the process and excited for the changes and challenges ahead. Host a kick-off event that includes a town hall employee-wide meeting to commemorate the launch, generate enthusiasm, and gather momentum. Make sure to explain how you arrived at this new strategy, the anticipated results, your own enthusiasm, and what everyone can expect in the coming weeks.

Ask other team leaders who understand this new vision to speak about your plans for the future as well so as to present a united front. Unveil the upcoming events and new initiatives planned for the next year.

External Communications

Think through which other key stakeholders need to be updated about the new strategy and vision for the team. For specific stakeholders, hold meetings soon after the internal kick-off to explain the strategy. More broadly, logos, websites, and brochures can serve as strong and broad signals of change. Consider updating your logo with a fresh design or new colors. Make sure your website is current and has all relevant information on the revitalization. Consider reaching out to the local press to cover the new strategy for the team and generate publicity.

Execute on Your Strategy

Now it's time to get going! Your launch event has built up excitement, so take advantage of that momentum to hit the ground running. Distribute your action plan so everyone on the team knows what to expect. Identify which groups are responsible for which actions. Identifying a leader for each group may be helpful so that one person is accountable for progress against the action plan.

Be transparent about progress toward all objectives, and don't be afraid to go into detail. Track each action item weekly. A useful system may be to color-code progress against each item: green if on schedule, red if off schedule, and yellow if questionable. This "stoplight tracking" system will allow everyone to quickly see where progress is being made, and identify which areas are more difficult to advance. Be sure to celebrate the wins as you continue to push on.

As initiatives succeed, adjusting your own role as leader will be critical. Remember that execution is a dynamic process; your approach has to be responsive to the many changes happening in your team. At the start, centralized leadership may be necessary to get the team started. Then step aside as the team comes back to life and members express more interest and enthusiasm. Providing flexibility and freedom to lead initiatives is a crucial part of making your team feel invested. Gradually shift your focus to the larger picture, concentrating on directing long-term growth, increasing resources, managing people, and leading new areas of expansion.

Prevent Future Recurrence

Yasmin: In my experience, the best revitalization plan is implemented with the intention of safeguarding the future vitality of the team. Once your team has regained its vitality, it is helpful to create a system that will allow leadership and employees alike to take stock of progress, challenges, and potential improvements.

The process of taking stock and making corresponding modifications is best achieved through a system made famous by Toyota called *kaizen*, meaning "continuous improvement." This is a four-step process: Plan, Do, Check, Adjust.[1]

The cycle keeps repeating. Seek to foster a culture in which all levels of members and staff are always looking for improvement in their area of work and are empowered to make those improvements.

Finally, take steps to ensure that the culture remains intact yet dynamic. Ensure ongoing training of all members in the team's values and strategic vision. Encourage leadership at all levels so that realizing the vision is not entirely dependent on you.

After all your hard work, you'll be rewarded with a group infused with new and lasting energy, from top to bottom and bottom to top.

Sample Time Line for a Revitalization Project

Weeks 1–3: Assessment

- Assess the strengths and weaknesses of your team.
- Hold a retreat with the executive leadership team to flesh out ideas.
- Implement a survey to get thoughts from all team members.
- Compile findings to get a comprehensive view of the current state of the team.

Weeks 4–6: Strategy

- Develop a detailed new vision for the future version of the team with specific goals and action items.
- Prime your team for change by adopting new protocols, communication tools, and committees to function more efficiently.

Weeks 7–9: Communicate

- Communicate the changes to the entire team, and hold a celebratory launch event.
- Communicate the changes to all external stakeholders.
- Transform your logo, website, and other visuals for the new look.

Weeks 10–12: Hit the Ground Running

- Begin implementing the new initiatives.
- Track progress against goals, and review progress periodically to make sure everyone knows what is going well and what needs more focus.
- Adjust your own role as leader to allow members to become more invested, and allow yourself to take a broader view.

From Week 12: Continual Improvement

- Continue to hold regular reviews to make sure the team is on track.
- Work for continuous improvement: assess weaknesses, plan a strategy, implement the strategy, evaluate the result, and repeat from the start.
- Periodically review your mission statement and goals to keep them fresh and relevant.

Yasmin Mandviwala graduated in economics and Spanish from Dartmouth College, where she served as chair of the Special Programs Committee. Yasmin worked as an analyst at McKinsey & Co. in New York, and as an energy portfolio consultant at Acumen Fund in India. She is pursuing an MBA from Harvard Business School.

Om Lala graduated in government from Harvard College, where he founded the Harvard Interfaith Council. He worked for Senator Edward Kennedy and was special assistant to the Assistant Surgeon General. He earned his MPH from Cambridge University, and MD/MBA from Harvard. He is an associate at McKinsey & Co. in New York.

Chapter 37

Transition Leadership

At this point, you've identified a problem, designed a solution, built a team, and implemented your goals. Your enterprise is functioning just as you envisioned. Congratulations! But now your group is about to undergo a major leadership transition. What do you do?

Leadership transitions can encompass many types of organizational changes: perhaps the primary leader is leaving the group; perhaps the entire team is turning over at once; or perhaps you're moving from one position to another within the same organization. In order for your impact to be sustainable and enduring, you must ensure that you lead the transition of the group into the hands of a capable, competent, and passionate new leader or team. Many companies and initiatives suffer—or even fail—because second-line leadership was not selected appropriately or trained sufficiently. For everyone involved in the project, it's crucial that leaders take transitions seriously. You need to thoroughly consider the person you're selecting, how to provide the necessary tools to lead effectively, and what role you'll play after the transition takes place.

Transitions can encompass many types of changes with respect to your involvement with a project or group. But the most obvious—and perhaps most critical—type of leadership transition occurs when a leader leaves an organization and hands over control to a successor. As the original leader, you must recognize your contribution to the team and figure out a systematic and comprehensive way to institutionalize that impact while not overstaying your welcome. Although this chapter focuses on transitions that involve the primary leader of a group, the lessons contained are applicable to any transition.

Whatever your reasons for leaving, you have a responsibility to yourself, your idea, your team, and your beneficiaries to ensure a smooth and comprehensive transition from you to your successor. Particularly when you've founded a group or enterprise and feel a strong sense of ownership over the project, this leadership transition can be more difficult than you might expect. In order to ensure your project is sustainable and can survive after you leave, pay close attention to each of the following three steps:

Step 1: Select your successor.
Step 2: Transfer knowledge and relationships.
Step 3: Move on.

Select Your Successor

Once you've decided it's your time to go and informed your team of your plans in a timely and sensitive manner, the first step in the leadership transition process is selecting your successor (and there may be more than one person).

Identify the Core Characteristics of Your Ideal Successor

Consider what your ideal successor would look like. Start abstractly and think strategically about the role you're trying to fill and the characteristics that would make an individual suited to fill that role. You may not want your successor to be exactly like you. Think about using the transition period as an opportunity to consider improvements to the role itself and thus to the ideal candidate. If you don't already have one, work up a job description (see "Components of a Position Description" in Chapter 29), and use it to guide how you evaluate candidates.

Know Where to Look for Your Successor

When the time comes to begin looking for the ideal candidate to fill your undoubtedly large shoes, start with the people you know, and work your way out from there. Start within your own organization. Do you have a managing director, a "right-hand-man/woman," or someone who has been by your side since the beginning? If so, don't overlook this person. Particularly in young social ventures, understanding an organization's ethos and having institutional memory are even more valuable than having a specific set of technical skills or experiences. If you look beyond your group's existing walls, start by consulting your mentors, allies, and partners. Seek their guidance and use their networks to identify passionate, capable potential successors.

Formalize the Selection Process

Regardless of whether you're going to select a successor from inside or outside your organization, formalize the selection process. Outline a schedule for reviewing applications and undergoing an interview process, and consider involving your board of directors or a selection committee in the process. By decentralizing decision-making authority in a group, you benefit from the informed opinions of other stakeholders, and you are able to let people down more easily (in a small business or club, some of the candidates may be friends or allies, and you want to try to avoid burning bridges if possible).

Be Flexible

You'll need to balance expediency concerns (how long until you actually leave) with concerns about how close your "next you" is to an ideal fit for the position. This is where you'll have to be flexible, keeping in mind that there are rarely, if ever, perfect candidates. Try to find a successor who brings as many of the desired skills and characteristics as possible, but remember that much of what your successor needs to know in order to do the work can be taught and learned.

Transfer Knowledge and Relationships

Perhaps the most important aspect of leadership transitions is the process of transferring institutional know-how from one individual or team to the next. Institutional knowledge comprises the substance of your group's work, or the collective information carried by members of your team about relationships, facts, events, procedures, and lessons learned related to your group's work. Effectively transferring institutional knowledge from person to person and from year to year is key to your group's success. There are three areas to focus on in order to ensure that your successor has a sturdy foundation to work from once you leave.

Integrate Internal Management

Leadership transitions require attention to integrating the new person into the rest of the group. It's your responsibility to introduce your successor to the team and ensure that the group feels comfortable and confident around their new leader. Your successor will struggle unless the team trusts, respects, and legitimizes her authority.

> *Sarah*: When I transitioned my organization to the next executive director, she spent three weeks shadowing me, which gave her an opportunity to get to know everyone's personal and professional styles. It also gave everyone else an opportunity to get used to having her involved in key organizational decisions and processes.

Maintain External Relationships

You've probably interacted with a number of external stakeholders along the way, including mentors, donors, institutional gatekeepers, members of partner organizations, and beneficiaries. All the time you invested into building those relationships will be for naught if you do not effectively weave your successor into those relationships. No one will ever have the same relationships you had and everyone's personality is different, but you must make an effort to integrate the new leader into the broader network of individuals involved in your organization's growth and progress.

> *Sarah*: I arranged a series of informal meetings with external stakeholders, with both myself and my successor present, before I left my team.

Build Institutional Memory

Managing organizational memory is perhaps the most challenging aspect of leadership transition; outgoing leaders must pay close attention to transferring information about both what your group does, as well as how you do it. According to research on institutional memory published by Morten Hansen, Nitin Nohria, and Thomas Tierney, in many large companies, institutional knowledge is codified using computer-based resources, but for many small social ventures, institutional knowledge may be "closely tied to the person who developed it and is shared mainly through direct person-to-person contacts."[1] Especially if your group relies on this personalization strategy for knowledge management, it is critical that you take the time to train your successor and explain the ins and outs of your operation.

As you prepare to leave, you may choose any one of the following strategies for effectively transferring institutional knowledge, but you must choose at least one (if not some combination) in order for your successor to have the tools necessary to lead the organization well.

Codification

Make explicit your operations and lessons learned by writing them down and disseminating them using high-quality, reliable technology. Whether you decide to use advanced software resources or simply train your team on how to use online services like Google Docs and Dropbox to write down any information that could be reused in the future, the key to the codification method's success is the extent to which everyone participates. If your group elects to use this method, be sure to fully indoctrinate your successor in the process so that she can both share and learn from previous experiences and lessons.

Personalization

Use individual expertise to solve problems; consult one another frequently to share experiences, ideas, and lessons learned. It's perfectly acceptable for your group to use this personalized method of knowledge transfer, particularly when the group is small and lean.

However, when it comes time for a leadership transition, you must pay close attention to ensuring that you walk your successor through everything you have learned in a careful and complete manner. If you haven't codified your expertise, then all that knowledge will be lost when you leave. Figure out a method that works for both of you, and stick to it.

Sarah: In the case of my transition out of the executive director role at my former NGO, the new leader and I would lock ourselves in a room for hours at a time, and I would walk her through different conceptual areas one by one—from external relationships, to internal management practices, to personality types, to programming strategies, to reoccurring challenges, and everything in between. This process was critical to my successor's ability to hit the ground running when I left.

Share and Discuss

Periodically transfer knowledge to new and old members of your team through group sharing and discussion. Many groups choose to meet frequently as a team to keep all players abreast of each other's experiences, successes, and challenges. A typical strategy is to have each person on the leadership team share her progress from the preceding period (say, the past week), seek advice on challenges faced, and share any information that may be relevant to others in the future. The upside of the sharing method is that institutional knowledge is disseminated among a number of individuals who can help each other (and your successor) when necessary. The downside is that you spend a lot of time in meetings when you could be implementing.

Note Want more information? There are countless resources available on the subject of managing and transferring institutional knowledge and memory. In fact, there is an entire knowledge management subdiscipline within organization studies. Search "knowledge management" for more insight.

Move On

This critical step may be challenging for both you and your organization. Personally, you need to stay engaged in your cause in a way that doesn't become a burden for you or your team. You should strive to be a resource for your successor: work with her to figure out what she may need you

Figure 37.1. Strategies for Transferring Institutional Memory

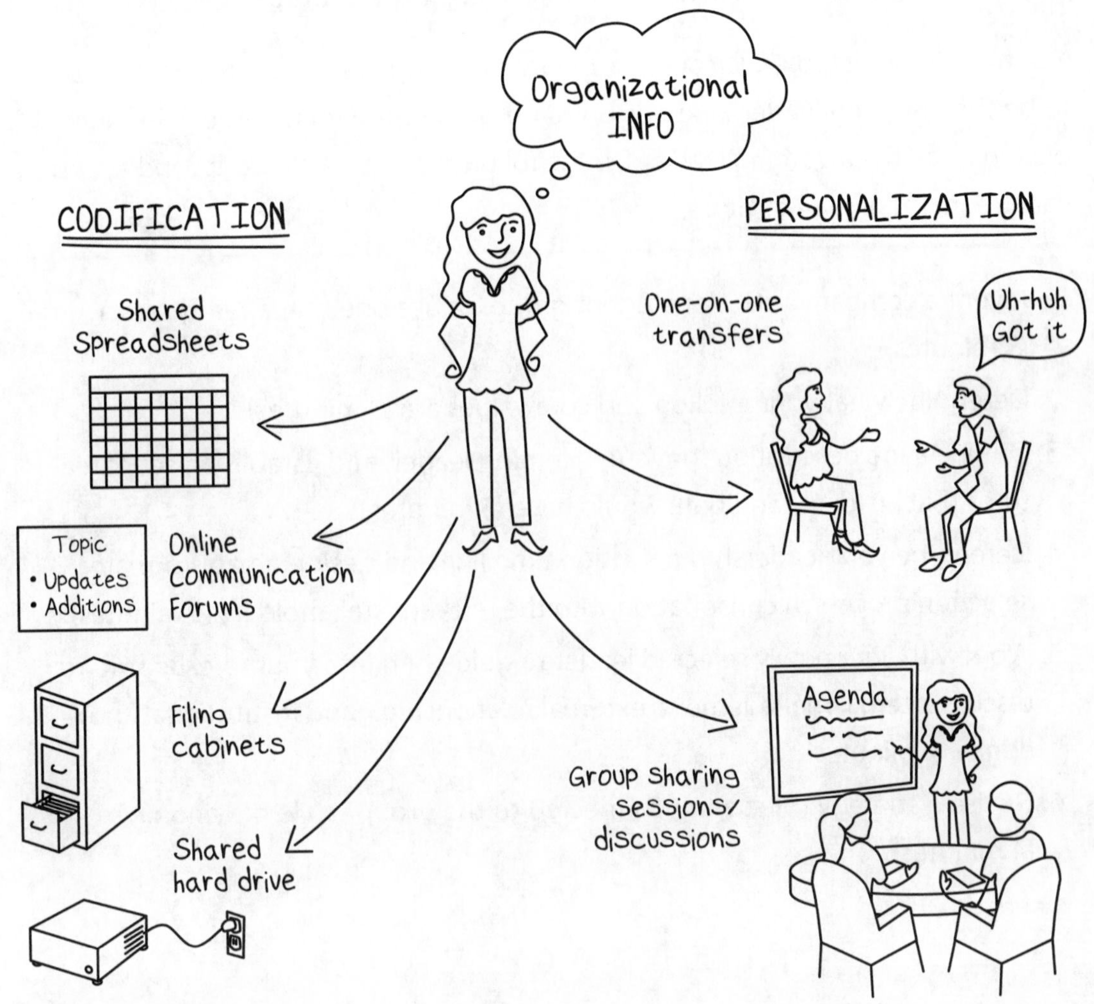

for most, and then determine a strategy for keeping in touch on these issues when necessary. Perhaps you want to have monthly meetings for the first six months after you leave, or maybe you decide that weekly e-mail updates are a better option. Whatever you decide, make sure the policy is driven by your successor and her needs. And whatever you do, don't stifle your new leader. You've just empowered her with the tools to run the organization, and now you have to let her do just that.

In order for your team and all of the stakeholders involved to trust and respect the "new you," you'll have to do the same.

Exercises 37.1 and 37.2 offer role-play exercises for leadership transitions.

Exercise 37.1 Devise a Leadership Transition Strategy

For this 30-minute role-play activity, get into a group of three. Select one person to be the outgoing leader, one person to be a current team member, and one person to be the incoming leader. Do the following steps as a group, and act out each segment of the activity:

1. Invent a company, NGO, or student group, or use one that already exists (3 minutes).
2. Determine what your mission and core values are (3 minutes).
3. Outline a job description for your incoming leader, and establish a set of features that an ideal candidate would have (5 minutes).
4. Determine your leadership transition time line and design an appropriate selection process in consultation with the relevant stakeholders (5 minutes).
5. Work with your newly selected leader to guide him into your role. Be sure to discuss internal management, external relationships, and institutional knowledge (10 minutes).
6. Devise a strategy for staying connected to the group while moving on (4 minutes).

Exercise 37.2 Work Through a Difficult Transition Process

For this 20-minute activity, consider the following scenario and answer the accompanying questions. This activity can be done alone or in a group.

Scenario: It is your senior year, and the community service organization that you founded during your sophomore year is struggling to survive. Your group has been having trouble getting funding from your school, and members are becoming less active as the year winds down. You are graduating in three months and worried about how you can ensure that your club survives once you leave.

(continued)

1. Will you try to transition leadership of the group to a new leader, encourage the group to merge with another existing organization, or encourage the group to fold?

2. If you decide to transition leadership of the group to a new leader, how will you identify and select this person?

3. What steps will you take to transfer knowledge to the successor and what does your time line look like?

4. How will you involve different stakeholders (e.g., other group members, former funders) in the process?

5. How will you stay involved with the group once you graduate?

Sarah: From my research on management and culture in international organizations, I've learned that one of the biggest challenges facing many socially oriented groups is dependence on a founder-leader who just won't go away. Their enduring presence means that they can cripple the organization's ability to mature and become sustainable.

You've done your job in transitioning leadership to the next generation, and now you have to let go. If you've done your job successfully, your legacy will not be forgotten, and what everyone will remember is that you were able to help ensure that your venture was sustainable beyond your leadership. You were able to make it last.

A New Beginning

As you think through how to make a leadership transition of a group effectively and thoroughly from one person or team to the next, keep the three core tenets of this book in mind:

Do what works: By laying out a time line for your own departure, formalizing a process to recruit and select a successor, and being strategic about transferring institutional knowledge, you are providing objective benchmarks for yourself, which will facilitate the most effective transition possible.

Work together: As you move away from your current role, you should be constantly engaging stakeholders in your process. Whether they are mentors, donors, partner organizations, or team members, use your networks and relationships to enable a smooth transition process.

Make it last: In order to ensure that your organization is self-sustaining, create the circumstances to guarantee that your successor or successors are passionate, capable, and have access to the tools they need to do the work effectively. If you want your idea to have real impact, then it will have to outlast your leadership.

In closing, remember that effectively transitioning from one position to another or from one team to another is critical to your group's ability to have a long-term, sustainable impact, as well as your own.

Sarah Kleinman is completing a PhD in international relations at Oxford University as a Rhodes Scholar. She earned a BA in history and MA in sociology from Stanford University. Sarah was the executive director of an HIV/AIDS youth activist NGO called FACE AIDS. Before leaving for Oxford, she successfully led the transition to a new executive director. Sarah has also worked as an associate for McKinsey & Company.

Chapter 38

Incorporate as a Business

For-profit businesses and nonprofits have a lot in common. Both provide goods or services to society, both need revenue to spend on operations, and both are managed and run by individuals striving to achieve the goals of the organization.

What sets the for-profit apart from the nonprofit is—as you may have guessed—profit. Both for-profit businesses and nonprofits may reinvest profits in the organization, but in a for-profit, additional profits are distributed among owners—the founders, partners, and investors. In a nonprofit, additional profits are reinvested into furthering the organization's mission.

Incorporating as a for-profit business has important implications for taxation and fundraising. Whereas a 501(c)(3) nonprofit corporation is exempt from federal and state taxes, a for-profit corporation pays taxes on all income. Funding for a for-profit typically comes from investors rather than donors. Investors exchange their funds for partial ownership of a company they expect to expand profitably; when the company eventually is sold, the investors leave with more funds than they originally contributed. Review the advantages and disadvantages of becoming a 501(c)(3) in Chapter 39 for a quick list of salient differences between for-profit and nonprofit corporations.

Is It Harder to Launch a Socially Conscious For-Profit Than a Nonprofit?

Not necessarily. The assumption is that investors may be hesitant to fund companies focused on a social mission, and potential donors won't want to give money to a for-profit enterprise. That said, there are a lot of funding options available for socially conscious for-profits. Profit-motivated venture capital and angel funds are major funding sources for for-profits, and venture philanthropy is emerging to help for-profits achieve philanthropic goals. Funding may also come from strategic investors—the CEOs who mentor you and your team, for example—and from family and friends. Business plan and social enterprise competitions (common on university campuses); leadership, community, and project grants (be creative); and online fundraising platforms (e.g., Kickstarter and Indiegogo) are great ways to get some no-strings-attached cash. For more on sources of funding, see Chapter 22.

A for-profit organization need not be all about profit. Social entrepreneurship is on the rise, and more and more companies are adopting social missions. Examples abound. Runa is a for-profit company that sells guayusa tea and thus supports small farmers—first, by helping them build infrastructure, and second, by purchasing their guayusa leaves, providing a major, reliable source of income. Runa further promotes sustainable development through its nonprofit partner, Fundación Runa, which supports social empowerment and environmental protection programs.

The founders of companies like Runa were bothered by the social and environmental problems they saw around them and decided to build for-profit companies to sell the products they loved. In the specific for-profit models such companies have adopted, financial success is integrally connected with success in achieving the social mission: more product sold equates to more producers employed and paid or to lower waste and environmental pollution.

If you're still hesitant to adopt a for-profit model to support your cause, remember that you can form a nonprofit partner organization later, if needed. To better define your organization's purposes and needs, complete Exercise 38.1.

Annie: I initially planned to make my organization, Global Village Fruits, a nonprofit or establish a nonprofit partner organization. Today Global Village Fruits, Inc. is a stand-alone for-profit company. What would have been the focus of the nonprofit—advising and providing seed funding to small farmer groups so they could develop processing infrastructure to get themselves out of poverty—is aligned not only with the profit aim of the company but also with the interests of investors, since these farmer groups then become new suppliers. The for-profit model has turned out to be the most straightforward and effective way to pursue Global Village Fruits' social mission.

Exercise 38.1 Clarify Your Organization's Purposes and Needs

Prioritize your purposes: What do you want your organization to do?

Example: To get rural fruit farmers out of poverty.

1.
2.
3.
4.
5.

Whose help do you need, and what do they seek? Try to be as specific as possible: different types of workers, advisors, and institutions will have different motives.

Example: Whole Foods: seeks a delicious, healthy, ethical food product delivered at a reasonable price.

1.
2.
3.
4.
5.

If making money is one of your top three priorities or is a priority for one of the top three people whose help you need, consider becoming a for-profit business.

Plan for Incorporation

Incorporating comes with upfront costs as well as annual required taxes and filings, so think carefully before you incorporate. First, make sure that your idea for generating profit is solid. Do your research and bounce your ideas and supporting evidence off people who know the market.

Hundreds of nonprofit organizations can operate in the same way to address the same problem, but if you want to make money, you have to do something unique or do something ordinary in a unique way. You need a strong answer to the question "Why will your company succeed where other companies haven't?" This is where business planning comes in: figure out why your team and your business are destined for success in the current market. If your argument isn't cogent, you should probably head back to the drawing board before incorporating.

Once you have a clear plan for making a profit, there are quite a few different scenarios in which you should incorporate:

- You have a cofounder or cofounders and need to form an agreement about how profits will be divided. Seek legal advice when writing a founder's agreement to make sure that it has the flexibility needed to give rewards according to contributions (and not simply who was there first) as the company develops.
- You're launching a new product or service and need liability protection. To launch a new food product, for instance, you must have a legal structure to protect your personal assets in case someone thinks your product made him ill and sues your company.
- You need to hire employees. Although you could write personal checks to individuals for their help prior to incorporating, it's advisable to get set up for official hiring if you repeatedly need outside help.
- You need to fundraise or issue shares. You need an entity in order to accept investments, and you issue shares of that entity—your company—in exchange for these funds.

The Labyrinth of Legal Structures

Now that you've committed to incorporating a for-profit business, it's time to enter the labyrinth of legal structures. You'll need to choose between the C corporation (C corps), S corporation (S corps), and limited liability company (LLC). Each has limited liability protection, which protects your personal assets in case of lawsuit. Seek (free, if possible) advice from an attorney or an accountant when choosing your company's legal structure.

Here's a brief rundown of the major features of C corps, S corps, and LLCs.

- *C corporation:* This is the traditional and most common type of corporation:
  + May have an unlimited number of shareholders
  + May offer stock publicly
  + Strongly preferred structure for venture capital investment
  – Subject to double taxation: first at the corporate level and second at the shareholder level

Why Venture Capitalists Prefer Investing in C Corporations

1. A company typically distributes common stock to shareholders, but venture capitalists usually require preferred stock in return for investment. C corps can have two (or more) classes of stock.
2. Your funders want your company to have the funding it needs to succeed. In a C corp, you can issue shares to funders as you encounter them without worrying about hitting a maximum shareholder limit.
3. Venture capitalists don't want the company's accounting and tax matters passed down to them, as happens with flow-through tax treatment in S corps and LLCs.
4. Ownership of a corporation is freely transferrable. This transferability is crucial for the initial public offering of the company, a typical venture capital exit strategy.

An S corp or LLC will likely need to convert to a C corp in order to secure venture capital funding.

Note The S corp is formed by filing articles of incorporation to become a C corp and then filing an S election using IRS Form 2553 by March 15 for the current fiscal year.

- *S corporation:* This is increasingly the preferred form for small businesses:
  + Flow-through tax treatment (income is not taxed at the corporate level)

+ Easy to convert to C corp for fundraising
– May not have more than 100 shareholders

- *LLC:* This is a newer, hybrid entity with features from corporations and partnerships:
  + Flow-through tax treatment
  + May have an unlimited number of shareholders
  + Less stringent formation and ownership requirements than a corporation
  – Difficult to convert to C corp

Select Your State of Incorporation

Most companies incorporate in the state in which they do business, but some opt to incorporate in another state with more favorable corporate laws. Over half of public companies are incorporated in Delaware, mainly because of tax advantages. These advantages are typically less significant for smaller companies and may be outweighed by the additional paperwork obligations and the need to pay for a registered agent in that state. The registered agent provides a legal address for the corporation within the state of incorporation, as required by the state government.

Incorporate as a For-Profit

Once you've decided when and where to incorporate, incorporating as a for-profit is pretty straightforward. The filing fees and requirements vary by state, so check with your secretary of state for state-specific information. You may incorporate by yourself or pay for help from an incorporation service provider or attorney.

Step 1: Register a Name

Search name databases online to make sure that your preferred corporate name is available in your state and is not too similar to any others already in use. Trademark law prohibits companies from operating under names that could be mistaken for the name of a trademarked company. For instance, don't try naming your high-tech furniture company—or any other type of company, for that matter—Microsofty. The same rule applies for names taken by small companies little known to the public. Don't assume a name is up for grabs just because you don't know of a company with a similar name. If you later decide you'd like to change the name of your company, you can file a doing-business-as (DBA) form to do business under a different name than the legally registered name. Once you are set on a name, you can trademark it to ensure that no other company adopts the same name or a similar one.

Step 2: Apply for an Employer Identification Number

Get an employer/taxpayer identification number (EIN/TIN) and any additional licenses or permits required by your state. The EIN/TIN enables the IRS to track your business's payments back to you. The EIN/TIN is used in place of your social security number to establish a bank account separate from your personal account.

Step 3: File Articles of Incorporation

When filing articles of incorporation, remember to include your company's name and address, the nature of the business, the name and address of the registered agent, and the names and positions of company directors or managers. Pay the filing fees specific to your legal structure in your state of incorporation. For a corporation, you will need to name individuals to be president, secretary, and treasurer. These titles will be relevant for legal paperwork, but you can give other titles (such as CEO and director) in your operating organization. Use broad but clear language when describing the nature of your business to give yourself room for future expansion.

Step 4: Write Bylaws

Corporate bylaws or an LLC operating agreement are "internal documents," meaning they're not filed with any agency but are kept as part of your corporation's business records.

Corporate bylaws typically include the corporation's identifying information, names of officers, number and types of shares and stock classes, and the procedures for meetings of directors and shareholders, record keeping, and amending the articles of incorporation and bylaws.

Tip Open a bank account. Be sure to keep your personal and corporate payments and accounts separate. In addition, establish a record-keeping system (on paper, online, or both) for your business's finances.

LLC operating agreements usually include each owner's percentage of ownership, share of profits and losses, and rights and responsibilities, as well as what happens if an owner leaves the business.

Step 5: Perfect Your Business Plan

> **Tip** Satisfy insurance requirements. Insurance requirements vary according to the goods or services you provide. Browse through the insurance pages of the Small Business Administration's website (www.sba.gov) to find out what insurance your business needs.

If you haven't done so already, get your business plan in order. A business plan is vital for securing funding: investors and even no-strings-attached supporters will want to ensure that you've done your homework before they hand over the cash. Use this chapter as a reference as you continue to plan your company. Planning will be crucial to achieving your company's goals—financial and social. For more guidance on writing a business plan, check out the Small Business Administration's online tutorials at www.sba.gov.

Incorporate as a Hybrid

New legal structures are emerging for organizations that seek both profit and social benefits. The main types are the low-profit limited liability company, the benefit corporation, and the flexible-purpose corporation. Each of these legal structures is available in a limited number of states, and availability is increasing as more and more states recognize the enormous positive potential of social entrepreneurship. Check with your secretary of state for updates.

Annie Ryu is a serial social entrepreneur and a senior at Harvard College. She cofounded and codirects Remindavax, an mHealth initiative that leverages text-message reminders to decrease treatment nonadherence and improve health outcomes globally. She has launched Global Village Fruits, a for-profit company importing healthy and innovative jackfruit products from Indian farmers' cooperatives for sale in US specialty food stores.

Chapter 39

Incorporate as a Nonprofit

Your team is growing, and some of your new efforts require funding. A member suggests applying for a grant. A potential donor asks if you're a legally recognized nonprofit organization. Should you seek 501(c)(3) status?

To Be or Not to Be a 501(c)(3)

By incorporating, you become a legally recognized organization: a corporation. There are essentially two types of corporations: for-profit and nonprofit. For-profit corporations sell goods or services to make money for owners and shareholders, while nonprofit corporations are primarily dedicated to furthering a particular social mission. When a nonprofit finds itself with extra funds, those funds are reinvested in a way that promotes or advances the group's mission.

501(c)(3) is the designation assigned by the Internal Revenue Service (IRS). It refers to the part of the tax code that says nonprofit corporations are exempt from paying some federal and state income taxes. Many colleges, religious groups, hospitals, and humanitarian groups are 501(c)(3) organizations. These organizations do not have to pay taxes; they are tax exempt. In addition, their donors are allowed to claim charitable deductions on their income tax returns, a policy instituted by the government to incentivize donations to organizations working for the public good.

Note If your team intends to engage in political work such as substantial lobbying or campaigning, think about forming a 504(c)(4) corporation, since many 501(c)(3)'s are not permitted to participate in substantial political work. Note that donations made to 501(c)(4) organizations are not tax deductible since they tend to be for political campaigning.

There are advantages and disadvantages to both of these forms of governance:

Advantages

- Eligible to receive grants from the government and private foundations.
- Exempt from federal and state income and sales taxes and may also be exempt from property taxes.
- Individuals who make donations to your group may claim charitable tax deductions on their tax returns as long as they receive no goods or services in return for their donations.
- Qualify for discounted postal rates.
- Many newspapers, radio stations, and periodicals have reduced rates for nonprofits looking to advertise, and some public service announcements are free.
- Individuals involved as directors, members, and officers are protected from personal liability for any claims against the corporation.

Disadvantages

- Prohibited from paying any profits or offering private benefits to directors, officers, or members.
- All income and work must be related to the organization and its mission.
- If the organization disbands, all assets must be awarded to another 501(c)(3) organization rather than divided among members.
- All assets must be used for tax-exempt purposes.

- Group's finances are open to public inspection.
- Tax returns must be filed annually and your finances properly documented and maintained.

If you're not sure if you want to be a for-profit or nonprofit organization, a third option is to team up with a fiscal agent, an already established 501(c)(3) that would be in charge of receiving and administering your donations. If you choose this option, you must have complete confidence in the fiscal agent's management and ethics. Donors make checks payable to the fiscal agent, and the agent grants this money to your organization, sometimes taking a percentage as a fee. With this arrangement, it's more difficult to receive grants from foundations. In addition, the IRS looks at this arrangement carefully to ensure that all funds are used for the purposes designated by 501(c)(3) status. That said, the arrangement is not uncommon: every officially registered student organization can funnel funds through its tax-exempt university.

Exercise 39.1 Should We Become a 501(c)(3): A Checklist

Is Your Organization ...	**Yes**	**No**
1. Interested in receiving grants?		
2. Seeking donations of amounts of $100 or more?		
3. Receiving enough income that exemption from taxes is attractive?		
4. Sending out mass mailings?		
5. Offering events that will benefit from large-scale publicity and marketing?		
6. More concerned with solving social problems than accumulating profit?		
7. Thinking about forming chapters?		

If you have checked yes more than three times, you should consider becoming a 501(c)(3).

Incorporate as a 501(c)(3)

Achieving 501(c)(3) status is time-consuming and requires patience, attention to detail, and self-motivation. You'll work closely with the Office of Secretary of the State (SOS) in the state in which your corporation will be registered and the IRS. All forms discussed in this chapter can be found at your secretary of state's website or office or the IRS, and all must be filed with these same respective offices.

> **Tip** Before you begin, budget $250 to $600 for filing fees and mailing expenses. Fees vary slightly from state to state.

Step 1: Register a Name

After choosing a name for your organization (brilliantly created with the help of Chapter 19), register it with the SOS using the Trade Name Registration form. While you wait for official approval, which can take a few weeks, temporarily reserve your name with the SOS's Name Registration form.

Step 2: Apply for an Employer Identification Number

The nine-digit Employer Identification Number (EIN) is like a corporate social security number; the IRS uses it to identify your organization. To get your EIN, complete IRS Form SS-4. Allow approximately 10 days for the application to be processed if submitted online and up to 30 days if sent by mail.

The EIN enables you to open a bank account. This is a good time to set up an accounting system and entrust your finances to a person or finance committee within your organization. Generally the group secretary or treasurer fulfills these responsibilities. Before obtaining a bank account, pass a corporate resolution that gives the appropriate member the authority to draw and sign checks and to transact any other business with the bank on behalf of the organization. One caveat is that at least one of the authorized signatories on the account must be a legal adult (either age 18 or 21, varies by state).

Step 3: File Articles of Incorporation

To be classified legally as a corporation, your team needs articles of incorporation. These define the rules that determine the management of your corporation. Requirements vary slightly by state, so obtain the appropriate Articles of Incorporation form from the SOS. The filing fee is usually under $100. Like your mission statement, the Articles of Incorporation should be clear but general because they can be difficult to amend.

Typically the following information is included:

- The name of your organization and address of its registered office. These should match the information you provided on the Name Registration form.
- Names and addresses of your board of directors and their liability. Most states require a minimum of three initial directors.
- Purpose of the organization. Here you prove that you are a charitable organization. The language should be simple but strong. Make sure your purpose is well explained.

Phebe: I cofounded a 501(c)(3) organization called Change the World Kids. Our purpose statement read, "The Corporation's purpose shall be to act for the benefit of the public by establishing, maintaining, and operating a volunteer organization of teenagers who are dedicated to making the world a better place through fostering awareness in people of all ages, identifying and undertaking projects selected by the members, and educating the public about issues identified as important to the welfare of the earth and to the people who inhabit it." Following this was text clarifying that all profit will benefit the public good and that no activities will be undertaken that are outside the requirements of a 501(c)(3) corporation.

- Provisions for the dissolution of the corporation. This identifies the process by which your corporation would be dissolved and its assets distributed. 501(c)(3) organizations must leave all remaining assets to another 501(c)(3) organization.
- Start and end dates of your incorporation. Unless otherwise specified, the start date is when the state approves your Articles of Incorporation. The end date refers to the length of time the corporation will exist, so it should be listed as "perpetual," unless you have a specific ending date.

- Name of registered agent. This is the person organizing the corporation by filing the legal papers. The registered agent must be a resident of the state.
- How you will handle the management of your corporation's affairs. Include the following sentence: "The management of the affairs of the Corporation shall be vested in its Board of Directors."

Do I Need a Lawyer?

A lawyer's expertise is valuable, and like most other valuable things, lawyers cost money. You may be able to find a lawyer to help you for free because many lawyers dedicate a percentage of their time to charity, or pro bono, work. Try to find a local lawyer for whom your idea might resonate or who already knows about your efforts. Ask other small nonprofits about socially conscious lawyers.

When you find a lawyer, set up a meeting to explain your mission statement and reasons for becoming an 501(c)(3) organization. Practice your pitch before the meeting, making sure you can show passion, plans, and goals. If you can get only a few minutes, prioritize asking a lawyer to check your Articles of Incorporation and bylaws before you submit them.

Step 4: Write Bylaws

Bylaws provide the legal framework for the organization, describing its structure and governing how it moves forward. They answer the questions "How?" and "What if?" The SOS may have examples that you can adapt. This should be a team effort and requires close attention to a number of issues:

- What is your organization's membership and process of meeting? What are the criteria for membership? What are the basic responsibilities of the members? How many members must there be? When and where do you meet? How are members notified of a meeting? How are special meetings planned? What is the process for making decisions or voting? It's important to define the powers of the members and list the reasons and process for dismissing a member.
- How is your board of directors constituted, and how does it operate? The directors should be chosen carefully and be well informed

about their position's responsibilities. The board should have the collective skills, expertise, passion, time, and connections to advance the mission. You'll need to decide how the board operates, including how often it meets; length of term; how it deals with vacancies, removals, officers, and standing committees; and how it makes decisions.

> *Phebe*: Change the World Kids benefited from having a diverse group of board members from various professional backgrounds: a lawyer, fundraiser, educational leader, religious leader, previous town official, and nonprofit executive.

- How will you provide for sound fiscal management? The success of an organization is influenced in large part by the management of its finances. Bylaws should include the rules for writing checks, making deposits, issuing loans, and making contracts on behalf of the organization. Determine your fiscal year, which is usually one of two options: the calendar year or the year from July 1 through June 30.

Do I Need an Accountant?

An accountant can provide advice that ensures you are keeping the proper records to file necessary tax returns and prepare budgets helpful for both the short- and long-term operation of your organization and procuring grants.

Setting up the bookkeeping for your corporation may involve learning to use a software program designed for financial management, such as Quicken or QuickBooks. When filling out Forms 1023 and 8718 (forms for tax-exempt status), consult with an accountant who has expertise in financial estimates. As with a lawyer, an accountant may be willing to help you at a discounted rate or for free.

- As your corporation matures, you may need to make changes to the bylaws. In your original bylaws, provide for that circumstance by including language like this: "These bylaws may be altered, amended, or repealed and new bylaws may be adopted by a vote of two-thirds of the members present and voting at any annual or special meeting provided that the notice of such meeting shall set forth the text of any proposed alliterations, amendments, or new bylaws."

- Are there any other issues that you can foresee becoming part of the operation of your organization? If you have a long-term plan, you may be able to include such rules in the original bylaws.

Phebe: Change the World Kids is considering expanding the organization to include chapters in other states, so we included criteria and guidelines for that in our original bylaws. Consider including a nondiscrimination policy or an indemnity clause that protects the members and directors from personal liability: "Members or directors—when acting in good faith and with the best interests of this corporation—cannot be personally charged or responsible for expenses in conjunction with any legal action against the corporation."

Compared to the Articles of Incorporation, bylaws do not have to be perfect because they are registered internally with your corporation (not the state) and can be easily amended with a resolution by the board.

How to Get Your Organization's Finances in Order

1. Choose a bookkeeping system.
2. Vote to decide who will be responsible for banking. (Pass a corporate resolution.)
3. Research banks to determine which one will serve you best. Pay attention to fees, interest rates, checking costs, minimum balance requirements, availability, and locations around town.
4. Open a checking account. Make sure signatories bring to the bank all the necessary information (social security numbers, EIN, two forms of identification, nature of your group's business). Make an initial deposit that covers the minimum balance, plus any charge for checks (at least $500).
5. Develop a budget and stick to it.

Step 5: Apply for Tax-Exempt Status

The IRS is a complicated government agency, and it's well worth reading its booklet "Applying for 501(c)(3) Tax-Exempt Status" before undertaking the application process. After incorporating in your state and securing an EIN, it's time to fill out IRS Form 1023, Application for Recognition of Exemption under 501(c)(3) of the Internal Revenue Code, which officially grants tax-exempt status from the IRS. A filing fee of $250 or $500 is required depending on your expected budget. You will also need to complete Form 8718, User Fee for Exempt Organization Determination Letter Request, and Publication 557, Tax-Exempt Status for Your Organization.

You must apply for 501(c)(3) status within 15 months of incorporation. The average processing time is typically 2 to 12 months. Note that close to half of all applications are not approved either because they are flatly rejected or abandoned by filers. The IRS may ask for additional information during this period of review. Respond quickly to any requests, and if you are confused or daunted by the questions, call the contact person listed on your letter.

Include a thorough description of all the activities of the corporation. Where will the funds for your activities and efforts originate: donations, grants, fundraisers, or something else? Will you have private or public support? You'll need to include a budget that shows your past and future projected income and expenses, as well as a balance sheet. If you are completely new, then estimate expenses by creating an action plan.

What's the next step after receiving 501(c)(3) status from the IRS? Celebrate! You're now part of an extensive network of organizations dedicated to bettering our world. The paperwork isn't over yet; you'll be filing annual tax returns and reports with the SOS and IRS. If you sell goods regularly (such as organization apparel or handmade products from your group), you may need to apply to your state for a sales tax exemption certificate. If a bank account was opened previously, amend your application to reflect the new nonprofit status. You are a recognized legal entity, ready to take the next steps into the world!

Phebe Meyers graduated from Middlebury College, where she studied geography and environmental studies. At age 13, she cofounded a 501(c)(3) corporation called Change the World Kids, a teen-run community service organization. She has helped raise over $250,000 to conserve and reforest habitat in Costa Rica and cowrote a $55,000 matching grant from the US Fish and Wildlife Foundation.

Chapter 40

Incorporate Reflection

Life can only be understood backward, but must be lived forward.

—*SOREN KIERKEGAARD*

Wake up. Throw on clothes from the top of the pile. Step out into the world with a small laptop and big ideas. Skim Twitter feeds, Facebook updates, and a few favorite blogs. Lead a team meeting. Check in with family while running to an event. E-mail yourself ideas as they come. Find a few minutes to exercise. Squeeze in time with friends. Head back home early to deliver on promises made. Pass out exhausted. Repeat daily.

For many young leaders, this is the circle of life. Unfortunately, such perpetual motion can squeeze out space for reflection, the crucial factor that drives innovative and sustained impact. In this chapter, you'll learn why and how to take a time-out.

Jonathan: In college, I participated in a group that made breakfast weekly for residents of a homeless shelter. Halfway through our first year, we had a reflection conversation that focused on a resident who frequently came early for breakfast to give us tips (and criticisms) while we worked. We realized his advice was always spot-on so decided to invite him to join us in cooking.

He was happy to help, and we learned that he had been a sous chef. Later, another resident with restaurant experience volunteered. With their help, we worked in shifts and ate breakfast with the shelter's residents instead of only cooking and serving. During the meals we heard stories of painful mental illness, battles with drug addiction, family disputes, and simple bad luck.

As the weeks progressed, our service gradually turned into a weekly discussion group between students and homeless individuals in which our assumptions about the causes of homelessness were tested. For example, we became particularly close to a male resident who had been abandoned by his family for being gay and needed a place to stay during a job search. Over time, shared interests emerged among us, jokes were told, and cooking skills significantly improved.

The process of reflecting on our service completely transformed the experience from an isolated and somewhat run-of-the-mill volunteer project to a mutual process of empowerment and learning.

Reflection as Learning

Reflection is a part of the larger theory of experiential learning, which is widely used in management and leadership studies. Broadly speaking, experiential learning theory views organizations as organic systems that, like human beings, must continuously adapt and improve based upon conclusions drawn from new data and experience.[1]

Incorporate Reflection in Your Life

Whenever we fly, the flight attendant reminds us to put our own breathing masks on before assisting others in case of an emergency. Although seemingly selfish on the surface, this advice is fundamentally centered on others. The stronger we remain, the more we have to offer our neighbors. The same is true for reflection. Remaining centered in our own vision, values, and curiosities frees us to lead and—most importantly—to listen. Here are three suggestions for integrating regular reflection into your life.

Hide Out

Find a local spot near where you normally wouldn't go, and give yourself thirty minutes of solitude there every week. During this time, ask yourself:

- What was the best thing about the past week?
- What would I change and why?
- What can I do better next week?
- What are the larger goals that I aspire to reach? What's the next immediate step to take to get closer to them?

Journaling 2.0

Despite the surprising emotional depth that can be conveyed in Twitter's 140 characters, an old-fashioned journal is still the best tool for individual reflection. But journaling should be much more than the simple writing of thoughts. Try these approaches:

- *Journal in questions.* After writing a journal entry, summarize it in the form of an essential question it seems to address. Over time these questions will form a theme. These themes may identify passions or form new project ideas.
- *Journal with art.* Art is a powerful way to convey meaning. Try sketching or designing a collage rather than writing ideas.
- *Journal with technology.* New technologies can increase the intellectual and visual appeal of your writing. Use WordPress or Tumblr to blog. Create visual reflections that combine voice, art, and writing using cloud-based applications like Prezi or Skitch. Keep all of your thoughts and notes together across multiple devices using Evernote.

Create a Wordle

The people you care about or work with are in the best position to give you feedback. Periodically ask friends or colleagues to send you three words in response to a prompt such as, "What are three things I could work on improving?" or "What are three strengths you think I bring

Figure 40.1. Wordle

to this project?" Ideally you can solicit responses anonymously using Google Forms or SurveyMonkey.com. Take the responses and submit them into a Wordle at Wordle.net to identify themes and patterns.

Wordle.net is a great tool for many reflection activities. You can submit your personal journal entries or your team's project plans into a Wordle to see patterns in the language you're using. Figure 40.1 shows a Wordle of this chapter.

Incorporate Reflection in Your Team

Reflecting in your team should begin by identifying your reflection goals and planning activities around them. Here are activities for three common reflection goals groups have:

Goal 1. Figure out what works by reflecting on data.
Goal 2. Improve relationships among team members.
Goal 3. Make impact last by building team knowledge.

Do What Works: Reflect on Data

Data allow teams to demonstrate the impact of their projects. However, quantitative data on their own don't tell you why things turn out the way they do or how to react as a team. Reflecting on data allows you to understand the causes and implications of your results. Here are some ways to reflect on data from your projects:

- *What? So what? Now what?* At any point, a group can reflect on three fundamental questions: *What* happened? *So what* is the meaning, and what is the impact of this? *Now what* do we feel should be done in response?
- *Poster session.* Groups usually sit around a table when examining impact charts and graphs. Break this monotony by making your charts and graphs on large pieces of paper and posting them around the meeting room. Encourage honest sharing by handing out markers and asking everyone to mill around the room and write their observations on the data. Then review the comments as a group.
- *Keep or change.* Follow up each project with a team discussion about what aspects to keep for future years and what to change. If team members have difficulty discussing the change recommendations openly, have everyone write their ideas anonymously on slips of paper. Then have team members pick at random and read aloud.

Work Together: Improve Relationships Between Team Members

To keep people invested, they need to feel connected and inspired. Consider these team-building activities:

- *Build in short talks.* The popularity of TED and NPR's "This I Believe" segments demonstrate the power of sharing ideas through storytelling. Build opportunities for team members to share their own reflections for five or ten minutes during regular team meetings and events.
- *Map assets.* Dynamic, productive teams work hard to find, recognize, and mobilize the gifts, passions, and capabilities held by members. Asset maps can have a variety of forms but are united in their attempt to catalogue assets present in the group and cluster them in order to surface synergies and strategic opportunities for group work. See Exercise 40.1 for asset mapping activities.

Note Jody Kretzmann and John McKnight, codirectors of the Asset-Based Community Development Institute at Northwestern University, pioneered the asset mapping methodology and have produced a host of useful guides and tools. Many of these are available for free download at abcdinstitute.org.

Exercise 40.1 Asset Mapping

Title Your Life Story

Break into groups of a few people each. Ask them to think about and then share what they would title their autobiography. What would they title the chapter that covers their involvement with this group?

Value Values

Honor the deeply held values of individuals in the group while building a sense of shared values across the whole. At an early meeting of your team, bring a piece of butcher paper or poster board with you. Draw a large circle in the center with lines stemming off for each of your team members. Then draw a second circle around the perimeter so the diagram looks like a wheel with spokes. On the outermost circle, ask team members to write the values most important to them in the context of the team's work. If the group is large (over 10 people), listing three each should suffice. Smaller groups should list five to seven. As a group, put the values listed most frequently in the center circle. Facilitate a discussion around the values shared as a group, and the values that particular individuals hold deeply. Discuss strategies for how your collective work can be grounded in shared values while being respectful of individual priorities. Refer back to the diagram throughout the life of your group. Make amendments or remind yourselves of commitments made.

(continued)

Figure 40.2. Shared Values

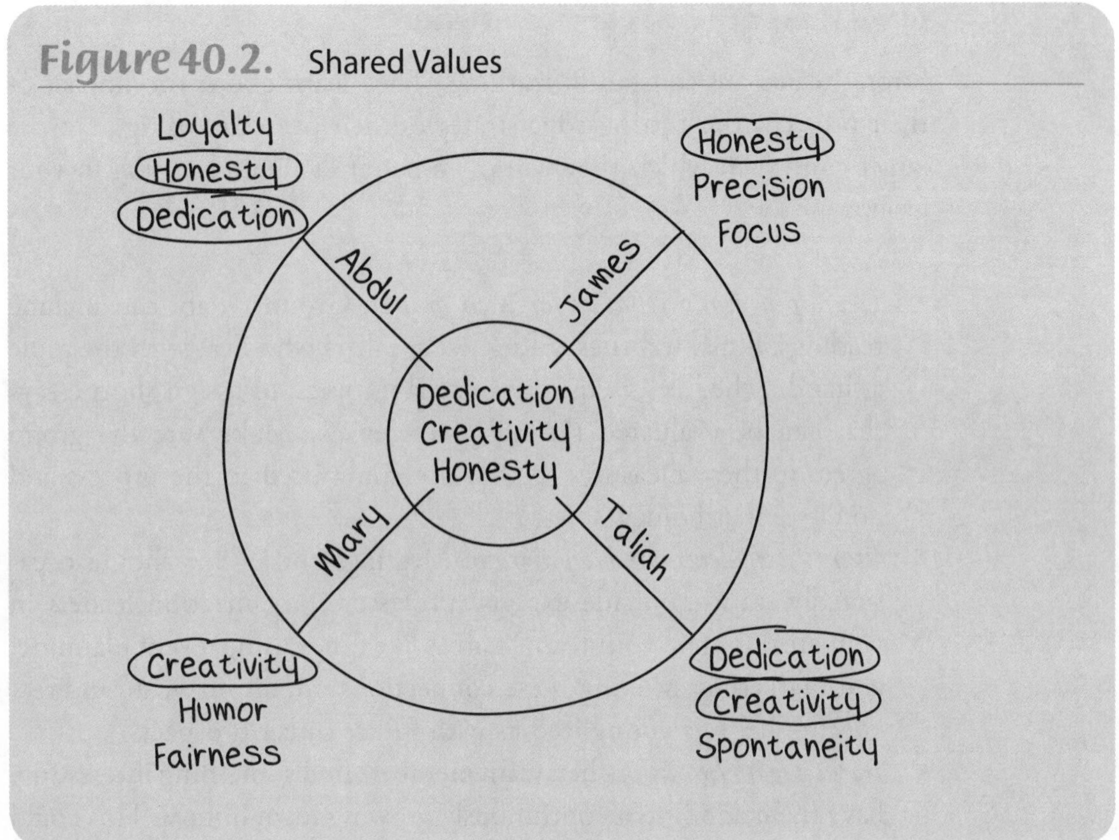

Tips for Facilitating Good Group Reflection

- *Be upfront about the activity.* Most people are leery of reflection activities. Avoid the eye-rolling and skepticism by clearly explaining activities and intended outcomes before they begin.
- *Don't be afraid of silence.* The most common mistake facilitators make is answering their own question or posing another to break the silence. The best comments come after 30 seconds of thought. Wait out the awkward silence.
- *Come prepared, but be flexible.* Beforehand, think about where the discussion is likely to go. Prepare a few questions that you want raised. If conversation lags, you'll be ready to keep it moving.

Make It Last: Build Team Knowledge

Strong teams are constantly learning. They learn about the impact of their projects, the cutting-edge strategies their peers are using, and the larger context in which they work. To better facilitate learning in your group:

- *Develop a group syllabus for each project.* Group syllabi can include readings, films, websites, and guest speakers who deal with the topic at hand. Schedule discussions of syllabi topics, or assign short essays that can be evaluated through peer review. Make sure the group agrees to these measures so they are committed to the process and don't see it as homework.
- *Run a staff development program.* Meetings and events should occasionally feature outside experts (professors, organization leaders in your area) to train your team in areas like fundraising, event planning, and marketing. Making these connections can also have an indirect effect of helping young leaders with future career prospects.
- *Build a team library.* When team members find something interesting, have them add it to a continuously growing team library. This could take a physical form or be housed online using cloud-based tools like box.net. Team libraries help to build institutional knowledge that can be transferred when team members change from year to year.
- *Track ideas.* Web-based tools like Ashoka Changeshops, OpenIDEO, IdeaShare, and Yammer provide amazing (and often free) platforms for generating, developing, and tracking ideas within your group and exposing them to global networks.

Incorporate Reflection in Your Collaboration

Collaborative reflection happens between your team and other teams such as clients, partners, advisors, and community stakeholders. This can be a difficult undertaking. The other group is likely different from yours in a number of ways (cultural, socioeconomic, professional, etc.). Here are three suggestions to get started:

- *Eat meals together.* Food is the ultimate equalizer and a great excuse for reflection. Schedule a shared meal.

- *Solicit written evaluations.* Allowing your target audience to evaluate your work gives valuable insight into yourself and empowers the evaluator.
- *Create opportunities to be taught.* Look for interesting skills or perspectives members of the collaborating group might be able to teach you and your group. Ask them to host a workshop, develop a guide, or lead a brief lecture that can help your team develop these skills.

Reflection for Innovation

Innovating for the public good is a messy process. Leaders must be ready for and open to trial and error amid constantly evolving needs, constraints, and opportunities. Success in these environments is *partly* determined by the creativity of an idea, of course. But the best ideas also can emerge when we least expect them, often while our sights are set in a different direction entirely. It is only through continuously reflecting on our action that we can appreciate these epiphanies and allow them to push us to deeper levels of impact than we ever imagined.

The unexamined life is not worth living.

SOCRATES

Jonathan Marino is director of content and strategy at the MapStory Foundation, a nonprofit organization that helps the public share observations of change in place over time, primarily through www.mapstory.org. He was a 2008 Fulbright Scholar and cofounder of the Global Engagement Summit and Center for Global Engagement at Northwestern University.

Chapter 41

Make Social Responsibility a Career

Never doubt that a small group of thoughtful, concerned citizens can change world. Indeed it is the only thing that ever has.

—MARGARET MEAD

What words come to mind when you think about a career as a social innovator? *Inspiring*? *Idealistic*? How about *practical*? Maybe *practical* doesn't come to mind immediately, but you can make a life (and living) out of fighting for social change and the greater good. And you won't have to live off instant noodles either! This chapter reveals the tips, tricks, and trade secrets to help you lock down that career of service you've long dreamed of but never thought was practical—until now.

Do Your Self-Reflection Homework

Chances are that if you're reading this chapter, you've already identified a cause you're passionate about and have dared to think (even fleetingly) of working at it full time. If not, it might be a bit premature to begin thinking about careers. Instead, focus more on identifying what really moves you, what stirs you to action (turn to Chapter 2 for help with this). You should also have thought about your talents and skills—the things you excel at and enjoy doing. If not, turn to Chapter 1 for some exercises to help you identify your strengths. Once you've identified the area you're most passionate about, as well as the things you're best at, you'll be armed with the self-knowledge necessary to move forward in your search for a fulfilling career advancing your ideals.

Know Your Opportunities

Begin by talking with your mentors, teachers, career counselors, and school advisors about your skills and passions, asking questions about possible resources, future directions, or relevant opportunities and career paths. You should also do the following:

Search the Web

Visit the websites of organizations related to your cause of interest to view the range of positions and the bios of current employees. This will give you a good idea of the types of skills, activities, and accomplishments that organizations are looking for, as well as previous jobs and experiences of current employees. Often you'll learn about a cool opportunity just by reading about what these people have done in the past.

> **Tip** Choose a position that aligns with your interests, and contact the individual to request a short meeting. Use this opportunity to learn more about his professional and educational background as well as what he actually does at work.

Network

Request meetings with professionals in fields that interest you. Learn more about what they do and whether they have any professional involvement in the causes you're interested in. If not, ask if they know others who are involved in a related subspecialty or niche.

You can also use these meetings to map out what others have done to get to where they are today. You can ask about the path that led them to their current position. Here are some open-ended questions to ask that are related to your interests:

- What made you decide to get involved in this field?
- What do you most enjoy about your work?

- What are the biggest challenges you face in your work?
- What do you see as the upcoming trends and directions for this field in the next ten years?
- If you could redo anything, what would you do differently?

You'll begin to get a better idea about the experiences and educational background needed to achieve your goals.

> *Lyric*: Don't be shy about contacting someone you don't know. A note demonstrating sincere interest in learning from someone can go a long way. I've been amazed by how generous high-achieving, busy people are with their time, whether they're in academia, government, an NGO, or business.

It's beneficial to manage these contacts because your network will become a valuable resource for you. Use programs like Microsoft Excel to manage your meetings and contacts. Table 41.1 is an example.

- Create a short elevator pitch: a prepared sound bite about yourself and your professional goals that you could deliver in the span of a short elevator ride. This will help you present yourself with confidence in a range of networking environments. It can also be used for informal meeting introductions, e-mail introductions, and cover letters.
- Social-networking sites (LinkedIn, Twitter) can offer dynamic ways to develop your own professional profile, view others' profiles, link with forums, and expand your network with people around the world.

Table 41.1. Meetings and Contacts Log

Name	Contact Information	Brief Bio	Date of Meeting	What We Discussed/ What I Learned	Things to Follow Up On

- Everyone likes to be thanked for their time. Follow up with a "thank-you" to everyone who meets with you. Stay in contact with them every so often, even if it's just a short e-mail, note in the mail, or phone call.

Kelly: Talk with everyone. You never know when a good piece of advice will surface. In college, I met with professionals in fields related to childhood cancer. I learned that if I wanted to make a difference on a broad policy level, a background in law would provide me with the best tools to do so. Interestingly, one of the most influential meetings I had was with someone in a field I had already eliminated as a personal career direction. A pediatric oncology nurse revealed that if she could relive her life, she would have gone to law school so that she could influence national public policy affecting children with cancer.

WARNING

Be mindful when posting any information about yourself online. Before posting, ask yourself if the information or photos are appropriate for viewing by future employers.

Gain Valuable Experience

Acquiring real-world experience in the form of internships, volunteer work, and paid employment can help you gain a better understanding of whether a career is right for you. But before you delve into the wide world of work, take a step back and look at the big picture (Exercise 41.1).

Exercise 41.1 The Big Picture Tutorial

Three things I want to accomplish as a social innovator:

1.
2.
3.

What my current education may eventually help me do (for example, a career that it will help me pursue or a position it will help me attain):

1.
2.
3.

My learning goals and personal objectives for this internship or work experience:

1.
2.
3.

How the skills and challenges of this work experience will contribute to the long-term goals I've outlined already:

1.
2.
3.

Now that you've better defined what you hope to get out of a work experience, you're ready to get out there and start searching for one. To help guide your search, follow these four steps.

Narrow Your Area of Interest to a Specific Issue

You should have a clear idea of the general area you're interested in now, but you may not have committed to a specific issue yet. And that's okay in the long run, but when you're searching for a work experience, at least for the short term, pick just one issue to work on. For example, if your area of interest is the environment, you might choose as a specific issue overfishing, air pollution, or eutrophication of lakes, to name just a few.

Choose an Enterprise

Every issue can be addressed by a variety of organizations. Take health care. If you want to address health systems issues in lower-income countries, you could work for McKinsey and Company (private), the Clinton Foundation (nonprofit), the Boston University Center for Global Health and Development (academic research center), the Rockefeller Foundation (philanthropic foundation), or the US Agency for International Development (government). Each type of organization plays a unique role in strengthening health systems in lower-income countries. For example, with the Clinton Foundation, you might be working with local partners in sub-Saharan Africa to conduct resource planning and allocation for its HIV treatment delivery project. With the Boston University Center for Global Health and Development, you might be a Boston-based program manager who coordinates a research project that assesses the technical and logistical needs for the Zambian health system to adopt a program to prevent mother-to-child transmission of HIV.

If you want to work for the government, it's helpful to understand the realities of bureaucracy. You won't be able to tear down the walls of an agency or completely revamp its operations over the course of a summer or even a year. In any case, setting clear goals for your position will ensure that you make the most of your opportunity while also creating realistic expectations about the skills and experience you will gain from your position.

Choose Your Location: Domestic or International?

Do you want to work in the United States or abroad? Much of this decision will depend on the specifics of the issue that most concerns you. Here are the pros and cons of domestic versus international work:

Domestic Work

Pro

- Familiarity with cultural setting
- Fewer costs (less travel, immunization, travel insurance costs)
- Better able to deal with emergency (family, friend, personal injury or illness)
- Mentorship opportunities may be more available given resources
- In general, do not have to deal without modern amenities

Con

- May have less responsibility and be doing mundane, repetitive work
- If you wish to do international work, you may not be getting the experience you need to have the type of impact you want
- If work is internationally focused, may not always see the fruits of your labor
- US work ethic sometimes leads to lack of work/life balance

International Work

Pro

- Possibility of increased responsibility
- Gain invaluable insight and job experience
- Learn how to work in a multicultural environment
- Gain hands-on experience on how to create effective change, opposed to what foreign donors believe is right
- Learn how to function efficiently in a high-stress environment and learn to creatively problem-solve

Con

- Increased costs (travel, immunizations)
- Possible exposure to infectious diseases
- Safety risks related to political unrest and crime
- Resource-constrained living conditions
- Feelings of isolation, home sickness
- Challenging to effect change as an outsider
- Providing only short-term change
- Mentorship may be not as structured
- Frustration from slower pace of work
- Diet may lack necessary nutrients

A Note about Working in Lower-Income Countries

In general, there are two types of jobs in lower-income countries: the field (think rural area, isolated, inconsistent electricity, no running water, hours away from any major city) and what we'll call the office (think urban area, modern amenities, with periodic trips to the field). If you plan to work in international health or development, most employers require that you have some work in the field before even considering you for the office (about two years is standard), so try to find opportunities that will give you a great fieldwork foundation. While the work may not be exactly what you want to do (there's a high likelihood you won't be personally responsible for saving babies, but you may assist those who are), you'll still get a much better idea of the lifestyle and daily activities of the job, while also gaining valuable insight, skills, and knowledge to guide you in your future decisions. Most important, you'll also discover your limits and preferences for working abroad.

Shin: Living and working in the rural part of the Leribe District of the Kingdom of Lesotho, I learned that I loved working with local health care workers; I also learned that there is a slower pace of work and life in Lesotho, and trying to rush colleagues to meet deadlines only delays project success further. I learned that I didn't always need electricity or a hot shower, but I did need a consistent supply of protein and vitamins in order not to pass out. Finally, I learned that seven months is a long time away from family and friends but that living your passions every day is a fulfilling way to stay in contact.

Find an Opportunity

Most people identify employment positions by first identifying prominent organizations they'd love to work for, then contacting them to see if they're hiring. But the smaller and less established the organization, the more significant a role you can usually play. Don't get hung up on names or status; instead pick an organization because it works on your issue, matches your personal learning goals, and can take you on. Seek out opportunities, not big names.

Jennifer: I happened to go to a college that didn't send too many students into the nonprofit sector. I knew what I wanted to do (health and infectious disease work in Nepal), so I spent a few days poring through study-abroad books, contacting Nepali physicians in my area, and searching online. Sure enough, I found an NGO that accepted undergraduate volunteers to work in its clinics in Nepal and had a fabulous two months in the Himalayas. A little ingenuity coupled with a strong interest will generally get you where you want to go.

Work Your Connections

Tip If you're interested in the nonprofit world, Charity Navigator (charitynavigator.org) is an invaluable resource. Along with a company's 990s (tax forms), Charity Navigator also provides a score to assess an organization's overall effectiveness.

See if those around you—your peers, professors, mentors, friends, or Facebook friends—might know people connected with the types of organizations you'd like to intern for. They may even be willing to forward your resume. But if you don't have any such connections, don't worry. Persistence and resourcefulness go a long way. And once you have a job, you'll have ample opportunity to cultivate connections for further opportunities.

Run a Background Check

Once you've identified an organization you might want to join, check the group's finances, leadership, and impact. It's a sad but true fact that some nonprofits don't really deserve the name "charity"—some exist as tax havens for their founders, some are so chronically underfunded or poorly run that they don't do a bit of good, and others are mixed up with the wrong characters.

Figure 41.1. Gain Valuable Experience

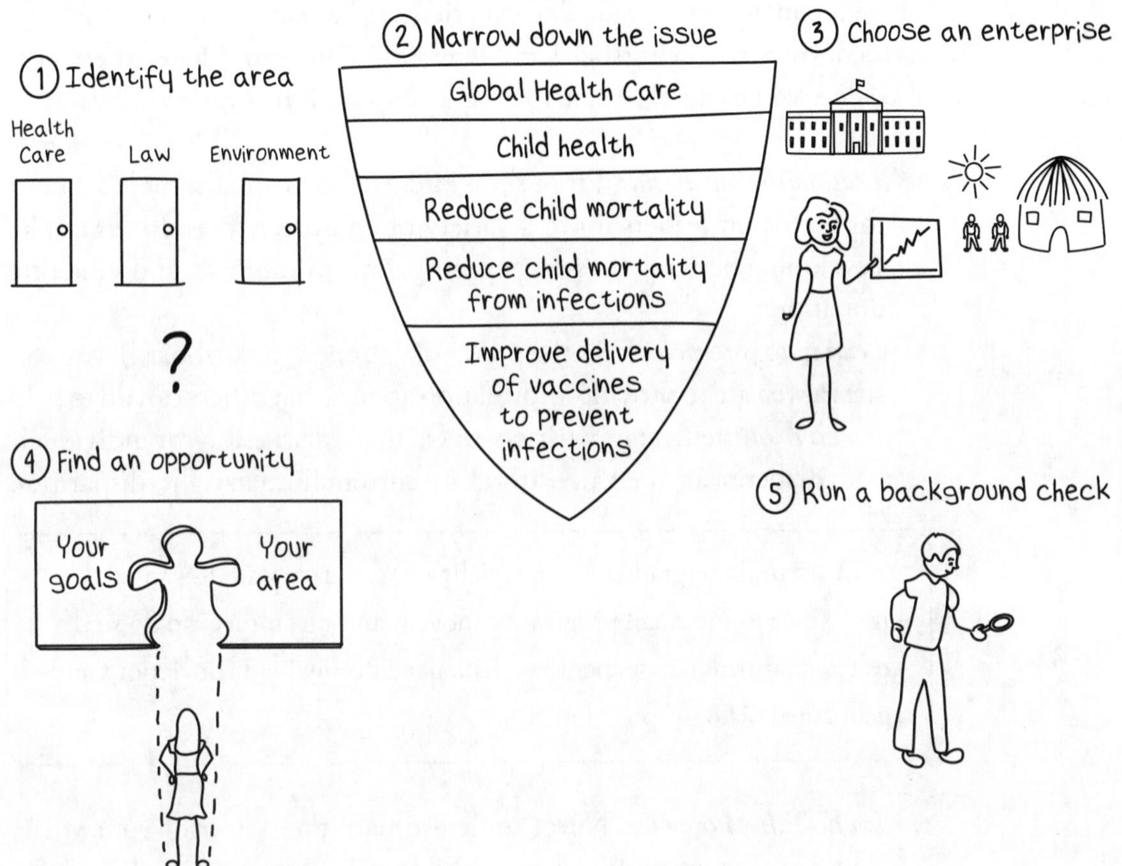

A Note about Funding

If you're a student and the opportunity you're interested in is unpaid (and assuming you lack the time and the energy to solicit family, friends, Forbes 100 Wealthiest People, and others for donations), start your search for funding at your school. Many schools offer grants of some kind to students interested in doing service work. If you can add a research component to your work, you'll almost certainly be eligible for some institutional support. And your research may also benefit the community!

Develop Your Leadership Skills

There are many, many valuable experiences that can help you decide if a career devoted to solving social problems is right for you. These experiences also allow you to develop valuable leadership skills in a variety of ways:

- *Lead with your hands.* From soup kitchens to hospitals, there's a need for hands-on leadership in a variety of volunteer roles; for example, developing better processes, engaging other volunteers, and soliciting donations.
- *Lead with your pen.* With the power of your pen (or keyboard), you can start a website to provide information about what others can do to help the environment, start a listserv to facilitate discussion for individuals with diabetes, and pen an editorial on current human rights disparities.

> *Yuriy*: As an undergraduate in a socially conservative state, I wanted to give a voice to the small progressive movement on campus. To do so, I created a satirical newspaper that challenged deeply held convictions and encouraged dialogue on campus.

- *Lead with your voice.* Never underestimate the power of your voice. You can, for example, educate children in your community about the dangers of drugs, influence local policy issues by attending town hall meetings, or even meet with your legislators.
- *Lead by example.* Contributing to the development of future leaders is one of the most noble—and perhaps most important—leadership activities possible. You can provide a positive influence and encourage leadership development for children in your community through a variety of activities: coach a youth sports team, tutor elementary students at a local school, or lead a Boy or Girl Scout troop.

> *Yuriy*: When I started a satirical newspaper in college, the first of its kind at my university, I had zero managerial experience. After scaring several potential scribes away with my heavy-handed micromanagement, I learned a lesson about leadership. Successful leadership involves, among other things, recruiting talented people, working harder than everyone you're managing, and respecting the effort of those working under you,

even when you disagree with their vision. When your staff don't believe their work is being taken seriously, they will simply stop producing solid work. A successful leader maintains meritocratic order while respecting the work of every cog in the machine.

Enjoy the Journey

A great work experience can lead you to seek out a career in that same field. In other cases, you may think that a field is right for you and dive right in, only to find it wasn't actually a good fit. And that's okay. Few journeys are straight lines. If your path meanders a bit, that's quite normal, and it will make for some wonderful adventures, so enjoy the ride. Just stay true to your guiding principles, and you're sure to stay on the right path.

Kelly: My own leadership experience has been and continues to be a constant evolution, starting with a "stomp-a-thon" fundraiser in middle school (a dance raising money to "stomp" out leukemia), to visiting kids in the hospital, volunteering at camp, planning hospital events, writing a book, developing a national online resource, and lobbying Congress.

Figure 41.2. Many Roads Lead to the Same Goal so Enjoy the Journey

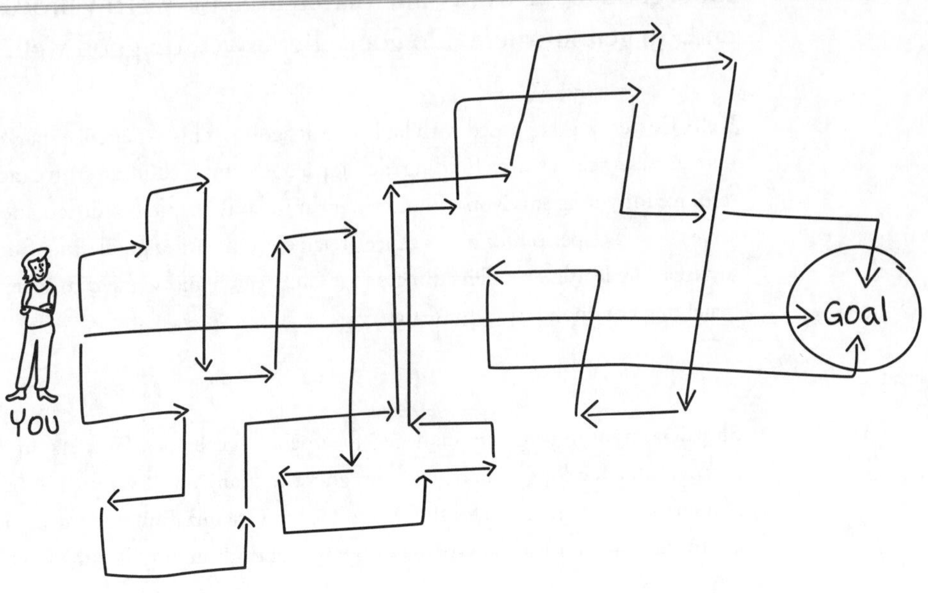

As you grow, learn, and encounter new experiences, you may also find new inspirations, causes, and issues that compel you. Explore all the options that interest you along the way. And if you remain focused on one cause, you may find that over time, your involvement in that cause changes as you learn more and discover new ways to become involved.

Jennifer: Prior to medical school, I thought my career would look something like this: I'd train in field epidemiology, learn everything I could about tropical infectious diseases, then nab a great job at a well-respected NGO. I thought I should probably go to medical school just to get that final credential, tick that last box I might need for my work with the NGO. What I didn't plan on was how much I'd love clinical medicine. Instead of joining an NGO after graduating, I decided to train as a general surgeon. And while my career path has changed, global health remains of great concern to me. Now, however, my focus has shifted to the global burden of surgical disease, a cause that allows me to make positive change in the world while engaging a skill set I find fulfilling in its own right.

Your journey will be filled with incredible successes and spectacular failures, moments of absolute clarity and head-scratching ambiguity, lifelong friends and less-than-ideal colleagues. Nonetheless, every experience and person holds a key lesson in your journey as a leader and social change agent. Embrace these lessons wholeheartedly and accept that, good or bad, these experiences and people will move you closer to your ultimate goals. Recognize that no matter what the experience, you're adding a bit more good to the world, and that in itself is a worthy process and a worthy end. So get out there. Do good. Better yet, do good well.

Kelly Cotter was diagnosed with leukemia at age 11. This experience sparked her involvement to increase cancer research funding, develop a book about children with cancer, create an online resource for young survivors, volunteer at camps and hospitals, educate medical students, and serve as a spokesperson for many cancer-related events. After graduating from law school, Kelly served as the legislative affairs director for CureSearch and worked to increase federal funding benefiting childhood cancer research.

Shin Daimyo is program manager for mental health at Partners in Health, where he manages and develops mental health programs in Haiti and Rwanda. His background includes conducting policy research for the World Health Organization, serving as Florida health policy committee director for the Obama campaign, and improving health systems in the Kingdom of Lesotho.

Jennifer Kasten graduated summa cum laude from the University of Kentucky. As a Marshall Scholar, she earned an M.Sc. in the control of infectious disease from the London School of Hygiene and Tropical Medicine and an M.Sc. in the history of science and medicine from Oxford. She earned her MD from Columbia University College of Physicians and Surgeons and is a general surgical resident at the University of Washington.

Yuriy Bronshteyn graduated summa cum laude from the University of Kentucky. He was then awarded a Jack Kent Cooke Scholarship to attend Vanderbilt University School of Medicine. Since graduating from medical school in 2010, he has been training as a resident physician in the Department of Anesthesia and Critical Care at Massachusetts General Hospital in Boston.

Lyric Chen, an attorney in Washington, DC, is interested and active in access to justice, women's rights, and development of the rule of law. She holds degrees from Harvard Law School, Oxford University, and the University of Michigan, Ann Arbor, and is a Truman, Fulbright, and Marshall Scholar.

Chapter 42

Make Social Responsibility a Lifestyle

I think of a hero as someone who understands the degree of responsibility that comes with his freedom.

—BOB DYLAN

Most of this book is dedicated to organized action, a planned solution to fixing a social problem. But strengthening or starting a business or nonprofit is not the only way to promote positive change. In fact, for sustained change to occur on a broader level, it needs to become integrated into everyday life. The message we want to leave you with is that as we enter this new era of social responsibility, the way we conceptualize social responsibility has changed. It is neither something isolated you think about from 7:00 to 8:00 p.m. on Tuesday evenings at your volunteer meetings nor an all-encompassing commitment requiring a blood oath or vow. Socially responsible values guide the way you live your life. Social responsibility is a lifestyle.

Embrace Grounded Idealism

Social responsibility as a lifestyle is based on a guiding philosophy of grounded idealism. You are idealistic and will fight for the best in the world; however, you don't approach things out of blind passion alone.

You are smart about your passion and take time to understand the context of social issues, researching what can be done to make effective, sustainable change.

It isn't enough to explain your decisions and actions with a justification such as "I'm helping people" or "I'm trying to make the world a better place." You do a disservice to your cause when you approach social change from such a perspective. Do your homework and strive for quality and sustainability. Understand the reality of the current situation and what has the greatest likelihood of succeeding and resonating with your audience or target population. Find a happy medium that benefits from your excitement for innovation and the logic of evidence.

Find a Balance

Too often we're presented with two options:

- *Drive-thru do-gooding*: Texting HELPNOW to donate five dollars to the latest disaster relief effort, dropping canned food in barrels during the holidays, or any other single-serving quick-fix

  or

- *Epic humanitarianism*: Emulating the social justice titans who are our heroes and have called us to action. These leaders brilliantly solved serious social problems, but in order to do so, they had to abandon much of their regular lives, leaving home, family, and friends behind.

> **Tip** No matter what your talents and interests are, there is a way to use them to fulfill your social responsibility.

These options are limited to the extremes: either autopilot or a life sentence. If you want to donate five dollars per year or relocate to a rural village without running water or Wi-Fi, go for it: these actions are valuable and create a foundation for meaningful social progress. But we want you to engage in the full spectrum of actions between (and including) these extremes. We want you to have the freedom to define social responsibility for yourself—to customize the actions you take in your daily life.

We advocate a balance, defining social responsibility as neither an errand on the to-do list nor a day job, but as a way to think about yourself and your world—a way to approach goals, choices, and actions by defining social responsibility as a lifestyle.

Act with Purpose

I hear and I forget. I see and I remember. I do and I understand.

CONFUCIUS

Turn values into action. You can incorporate positive change into your daily life in any number of ways. Embracing social responsibility as a lifestyle is about integrating your values into your everyday choices: your decisions on personal style, relationships, career, finances, health, community, entertainment, food, and more. It can be something major like your career choice, something trendy like your spring break trip, or something as simple as the clothing you wear or the coffee you drink. Exercises 42.1 and 42.2 will help you do this.

Note Having trouble brainstorming simple changes? Visit WeAreWhatWeDo.org, a London-based nonprofit focusing on simple behavior changes you can make to do good on a daily basis.

Exercise 42.1 Improve Your Daily Schedule

Plan out your daily schedule with three simple things you can do that will lead to living a more socially responsible lifestyle.

Figure 42.1. Every Action Can Be More Socially Responsible

The Usual Way	The Socially Responsible Way
Morning	
Afternoon	
Evening	

Exercise 42.2 Self-Assessment of Current Lifestyle and Goals

Think about how you currently function in the 15 categories listed on the next page ("What I do now"). Then think about what changes—large, small, in between—you can make in each ("What I'd like to do"). Then develop your action plan.

Here's an example in the Finance category:

What I do now: Use checking services of large bank with many convenient ATMs around town, but known to invest customers' savings in companies that use child labor or are anti-unions.

What I'd like to do: Put my checking or savings account in a community development financial institution, which promotes economic development in underserved communities and whose recent investments include renovating a local school and giving loans to a small business trying to bring fresh produce to the inner city.

Action plan: (1) Find a community development financial institution near me. (2) Open a new account, talk to branch manager about the current development work the bank is doing, and make sure it aligns with my values. (3) Pay my remaining bills and close out my current account, making sure that all my automatic bill pays are notified of the change. (4) Transfer my money to new bank.

(continued)

	What I do now	What I'd like to do	Action plan
Health			
Career			
Education			
Finances			
Home			
Habits			
Hobbies			
Relationships			
Family			
Community			
Food			
Entertainment			
Style			
Travel			
Technology			

Act with Purpose

Tip Frequent shopper? Sign up with SocialVest, an organization helping "purchase on purpose" by giving you a percentage of your online purchases to donate to the causes of your choice.

Social responsibility can be part of anything and everything you do. Volunteering, starting an organization, or driving change from within a company are all ways to be socially responsible. At the same time, what you do in the rest of your life still matters. Realizing that every action can be made more socially responsible can feel overwhelming at first, but you don't have to do it all at once, and you don't have to do it all perfectly.

Almost nothing is purely, perfectly, or objectively good. We all get to weigh our own evidence and opinions, or the evidence of people we trust, and make our decision from there. There is no one right way to live. There is only the right way *for you*, right now, and that may change as your circumstances change, as new evidence comes to light, or as the world changes.

Note Check out *The Better World Handbook* for a great list of ideas and explanations for why your changes will matter.

My Values

Janet Frishberg is a writer, and social innovator who lives in San Francisco. She is the cofounder of the community-based workshop FemSexComm. Three things she values are urban gardens, used bookstores, and English peas.

Janet: A socially responsible lifestyle is one where we match our values to the way we spend the three things we have: time, money, and energy. The things you read, what you do with friends or family, who you talk to, where you exercise: these all can reflect your values. The energy you put into social responsibility as a lifestyle can range from the very small (changing your brand of toothpaste to buy one that doesn't contain toxic detergents) to the very large (getting your entire housing association to source 50% of its food locally). Where do you put your energy? Is there anything you're angry about or that frustrates you? Could you turn that into action to try to make things better?

Start Where You Are

Janet: Go with what you're already passionate about. Not sure what that is? Try this thought experiment: if you were granted one wish to change something about the world and it had to be an altruistic one that drove social innovation, what would you ask for? I would ask for a just and sustainable food system. The next question I need to ask myself is, How can I live in a way that helps create a better food system?

Do What Works

Janet: It's your social responsibility to learn about what's happening in the world and then take action that reflects what you've learned. When I was 19, I went to the Sahara desert in Morocco. As we drove in a 4x4 to a camp in the desert, I was struck by all the plastic bags that were caught on little shrubs near the ground. Everywhere I looked, for miles and miles of flat desert, were plastic bags. It was one of the most physical manifestations I've ever seen of the way we're trashing the planet. Because of that experience, I can't look at a plastic bag the same way, and I'll do anything I can to avoid using them.

You cannot avoid the reality that everything you do has an impact on the world and other people in some way. You can begin asking questions and learning about how to do things better and then taking actions to create a lifestyle that mirrors your values.

Make It Last

Janet: One part of making it last is about creating structural changes. I saw my friend Sarah do this beautifully. She started a new job at a community health clinic and realized that all the cleaning products they were buying were totally unsustainable and toxic. She found out who was responsible for ordering their products each month, researched alternatives that would be affordable and safe for the planet and their employees, and then sat down with that person to explain to them her perspective and the positive alternative she was suggesting. The result? Better cleaning products for multiple local branches of this clinic, all because she cared and put her time and energy into changing something.

What can you do to make it more fun to do the things you know are more socially responsible? Is there a way to create a more structural or systemic change that will make it easier for other people to live in a socially responsible way too? Once you've made a change and it feels normal and easy for you, ask yourself what the next step up would be.

Start with What You Care About

Janet: Sometimes social responsibility is framed with a lot of don'ts or shouldn'ts: you shouldn't leave the tap on while you're brushing your teeth; don't fly on airplanes. Turn it around from "shouldn't" or "don't" and instead ask, What do I value? What is beautiful or even sacred to me? What brings me joy? What do I care about?

Now go out and create a life that mirrors those things. What you do and the way you live matters, and no one else can do it for you.

Exercise 42.3 Articulate Your Values

It's important to start by trying to understand what you care about. What matters to you? What do you value? How are you going to use your time, money, and energy toward those things? Take time to reflect on what you value and make a list (or get creative and illustrate your values!) below:

Leave a Legacy

Be the change that you wish to see in the world.

MAHATMA GANDHI

You matter. Your actions matter. When addressing such large, deeply seeded social issues, it's easy to get overwhelmed. But realize that every change that's happened, all the progress that we've made as a society, can be traced back to one individual with a vision and a purpose. You have great ideas. Some will work, and others won't. But your example can create a legacy of good. Even simple changes you make can inspire others to change for the better. Every day is an opportunity. Ask yourself: What can I do to make today matter?

Notes

Introduction

1. Corporation for National and Community Service. (2010, June 15). Federal report shows greatest spike in volunteers since 2003. Washington, D.C.: The Corporation for National and Community Service.
2. Corporation for National and Community Service, Office of Research and Policy Development. (2010, June). Volunteering in America 2010: National, state, and city information. Washington, D.C.
3. Office of Social Innovation and Civic Participation.(2012). About SICP: The community solutions agenda. Retrieved July 2012 from www.whitehouse .gov/administration/eop/sicp/about.

Chapter 2

1. American Humane Association. (2011). Animal shelter euthanasia. Retrieved from http://www.americanhumane.org/animals/stop-animal-abuse/fact-sheets/animal-shelter-euthanasia.html
2. U.S. Equal Employment Opportunity Commission. Disability discrimination. Retrieved October 12, 2012, from U.S. Equal Employment Opportunity Commission: http://www1.eeoc.gov/laws/types/disability.cfm?renderforprint=1
3. United Nations High Commissioner for Human Rights. (2011). *Discriminatory laws and practices and acts of violence against individuals based on their sexual orientation and gender identity*. United Nations General Assembly Human Rights Council.
4. Same-sex marriage. (2012). Retrieved from *Encyclopaedia Britannica*: http://www.britannica.com/EBchecked/topic/753687/same-sex-marriage
5. U.S. Bureau of Labor Statistics. (2012, October 5). The employment situation—September 2012. Retrieved October 12, 2012, from United States Department of Labor Bureau of Labor Statistics: http://www.bls.gov/news.release/pdf/empsit.pdf

6. Schevitz, T. (2012, November 26). FBI sees leap in anti-Muslim hate crimes—9/11 attacks blamed for bias. *San Francisco Chronicle.*
7. The World Bank. (2011). World development report 2012: Gender equality and development. Washington, D.C. : The International Bank for Reconstruction and Development/The World Bank.
8. The World Bank. (2011). World development report 2012: Gender equality and development. Washington, D.C. : The International Bank for Reconstruction and Development/The World Bank.
9. The World Bank. (2011). World development report 2012: Gender equality and development. Washington, D.C. : The International Bank for Reconstruction and Development/The World Bank.
10. United Nations General Assembly. (1948, December 10). The universal declaration of human rights. Retrieved October 2012, from United Nations: http://www.un.org/en/documents/udhr/index.shtml
11. Ogden, C. L., et al. (2010). Prevalence of high body mass index in US children and adolescents, 2007–2008. *Journal of the American Medical Association, 303*(3), 242–249.
12. School Health Policies and Programs Study. (2007, October). SHPPS 2006—Pregnancy prevention. Retrieved October 2012, from Centers for Disease Control and Prevention: http://www.cdc.gov/healthyyouth/shpps/2006/factsheets/pdf/FS_PregnancyPrevention_SHPPS2006.pdf
13. Kirby, D. (2007). *Emerging answers 2007: Research findings on programs to reduce teen pregnancy and sexually transmitted diseases.* Washington, D.C.: The National Campaign to Prevent Teen Pregnancy.
14. Jalongo, M. R., & Heider, K. (2006). Teacher attrition: An issue of national concern. *Early Childhood Education Journal, 33*(6), 379–380; Ingersoll, R. M. (2002). The teacher shortage: A case of wrong diagnosis and wrong prescription. *NASSP Bulletin*, 16–31.
15. OECD. (2010). PISA 2009 results: Executive summary.
16. National Association of Secondary School Principles. (2011, January). Breaking down the PISA results. *News Leader, 58*(5).
17. Makin, J. (2011, December). Implications of climate change for skin cancer prevention in Australia. *Health Promotion Journal of Australia, 22*, S39-41.
18. Liou, J.C., & Johnson, N.L. (2006, January 20). Risks in space from orbiting debris. *Science, 311*, 340–341; Law, K., et al. (2010, August). Plastic accumulation in the North Atlantic subtropical gyre. *Science Express;* Pichel, W., et al. (2007). Marine debris collects within the North Pacific subtropical convergence zone. Marine *Pollution Bulletin, 54*, 1207–1211.
19. Gottret, P., & Schieber, G. (2006). *Health financing revisited: A practitioner's guide.* Washington, D.C.: The International Bank for Reconstruction and Development/The World Bank.
20. Kessler, R. C., et al. (2005, June). Prevalence, severity, and comorbidity of twelve-month DSM-IV disorders in the national comorbidity survey replication (NCS-R). *Archives of General Psychiatry, 62*(6), 617–27.

21. Office of Statistics and Programming, National Center for Injury Prevention and Control, CDC Using WISQARS. (2011). 10 leading causes of death by age group, United States—2010. Retrieved October 2012, from Centers for Disease Control and Prevention: http://www.cdc.gov/injury/wisqars/pdf/10LCID_All_Deaths_By_Age_Group_2010-a.pdf
22. U.S. Cancer Statistics Working Group. (2012). *United States cancer statistics: 1999–2008 incidence and mortality web-based report.* Atlanta: U.S. Department of Health and Human Services, Centers for Disease Control and Prevention and National Cancer Institute.
23. Hoyert, D. L., & Xu, J. (2012). *National vital statistics reports—Deaths: Preliminary data for 2011.* Atlanta: U.S. Department of Health and Human Services, Centers for Disease Control and Prevention.
24. Centers for Disease Control and Prevention. (2004). *The health consequences of smoking: A report of the surgeon general.* Atlanta: Department of Health and Human Services, Centers for Disease Control and Prevention, National Center for Chronic Disease Prevention and Health Promotion, Office on Smoking and Health.
25. The World Bank. (2012, February). An update to the World Bank's estimates of consumption poverty in the developing world. Retrieved October 2012, from The World Bank: http://siteresources.worldbank.org/INTPOVCALNET/Resources/Global_Poverty_Update_2012_02-29-12.pdf
26. The World Bank. (2012, February). An update to the World Bank's estimates of consumption poverty in the developing world. Retrieved October 2012, from The World Bank: http://siteresources.worldbank.org/INTPOVCALNET/Resources/Global_Poverty_Update_2012_02-29-12.pdf
27. R.A. (2011, May 3). Rich and poor, growing apart. Retrieved October 2012, from The Economist: http://www.economist.com/blogs/freeexchange/2011/05/income_inequality
28. Food and Agriculture Organization of the United Nations. (2010, September). Global hunger declining, but still unacceptably high. Retrieved October 2012, from Food and Agriculture Organization of the United Nations: http://www.fao.org/docrep/012/al390e/al390e00.pdf
29. Food and Agriculture Organization of the United Nations. (2010, September). Global hunger declining, but still unacceptably high. Retrieved October 2012, from Food and Agriculture Organization of the United Nations: http://www.fao.org/docrep/012/al390e/al390e00.pdf
30. U.S. Census Bureau. (2011). *Income, poverty, and health insurance coverage in the United States: 2010.* Washington, D.C. : U.S. Government Printing Office.
31. Coleman-Jensen, A. (2011). *Household food security in the United States in 2010.* Washington, D.C. : U.S. Department of Agriculture, Economic Research Service.
32. U.S. Bureau of Labor Statistics. Labor force statistics from the current population survey. Retrieved October 2012, from United States Department of Labor Bureau of Labor Statistics: http://data.bls.gov/cgi-bin/surveymost

33. United Nations Office on Drugs and Crime. (2009). *Global report on trafficking in persons.* United Nations Office on Drugs and Crime, Global Initiative to Fight Human Trafficking.
34. The World Bank. (2011). *World development report 2012: Gender equality and development.* Washington, D.C. : The International Bank for Reconstruction and Development/The World Bank; Wong, E. (2012, July 22). Reports of forced abortions fuel push to end Chinese law. *The New York Times.*
35. Savage, D. (2012, May 20). Registry tallies over 2000 wrongful convictions since 1989. The Los Angeles Times.
36. Woodward, B. (2009, January 14). Guantanamo detainee was tortured, says official overseeing military trials. *The Washington Post.*
37. Negrin, M. (2012, July 3). Guantanamo Bay: Still open, despite promises. ABC News; *The New York Times.* (2012, October 17). Guantanamo Bay Naval Base (Cuba). Retrieved October 2012, from The New York Times: http://topics.nytimes.com/top/news/national/usstatesterritoriesandpossessions/guantanamobaynavalbasecuba/index.html

Chapter 3

1. Itaborahy, L. P. (2012). *State-sponsored homophobia: A world survey of laws criminalising same-sex sexual acts between consenting adults.* The International Lesbian, Gay, Bisexual, Trans and Intersex Association. http://old.ilga.org/Statehomophobia/ILGA_State_Sponsored_Homophobia_2012.pdf

Chapter 5

1. Osbourn, A. F. (1953). *Applied imagination.* New York: Charles Scribner's & Sons.

Chapter 6

1. National Coalition for the Homeless. (July 2009). Mental health and homelessness. Nationalhomeless.org/factsheets/Mental_Illness.pdf
2. Folsom D. P., Hawthorne, W., Lindamer, L., Gilmer, T., Bailey, A., Golshan, S., Garcia, P., Unulzer, J., Hough, R., & Jeste, D. V. (2005). Prevalence and risk factors for homelessness and utilization of mental health services among 10,340 patients with serious mental illness in a large public mental health system. *American Journal of Psychiatry, 162*(2), 370–376. (As referenced on nationalhomeless.org)

Chapter 7

1. U.S. Preventive Services Task Force. (2002). Screening for breast cancer: recommendations and rationale. *Annals of Internal Medicine, 137*(5 part 1), 344–346; Yankaskas, B. e. (2010). Performance of first mammography examination in women younger than 40 years. *Journal of the National Cancer Institute, 102*(10), 692–701.

2. International Campaign to Ban Landmines. (October 2005). *Landmine monitor report 2005: Toward a mine-free world.* New York: Human Rights Watch.
3. Bruschini, C., & Gros, B. (1998). A survey of research on sensor technology for landmine detection. *Journal of Humanitarian Demining, 2.*
4. Sabatier, J. M., & Korman, M. S. (2003). Nonlinear tuning curve vibration response of a buried landmine. In R. S. Harmon, J. H. Holloway Jr., & J. T. Broach (Eds.), *Detection and remediation technologies for mines and minelike targets VIII.* Bellingham, WA: SPIE; Sabatier, J. M., & Korman, M. S., & Fenneman, D. J. (2003). Nonlinear acoustic techniques for landmine detection: Tuning curves and two-tone tests (A). *Journal of the Acoustical Society of America, 114,* 2456; Sabatier, J. M., & Korman, M. S. (2001). Nonlinear acoustic techniques for landmine detection: Experiments and theory (A). *Journal of the Acoustical Society of America, 110,* 2757.

Chapter 8

1. Office of the Surgeon General. (2001). *Youth violence: A report of the surgeon general.* Washington, D.C.: Office of the Surgeon General.
2. Drug Abuse Resistance Education America. (2012). *The new D.A.R.E. program.* Retrieved October 2012, from The Official D.A.R.E. Web Site: http://www.dare.com/home/newdareprogram.asp
3. Hecht, M. e. (2006). The dissemination of keepin' it REAL through D.A.R.E. America: A lesson in disseminating health messages. *Health Communication,* 267–276.
4. Zernike, K. (2001, February 15). Antidrug program says it will adopt a new strategy. *The New York Times.*
5. Miller, T. &. (2008). *Substance abuse prevention dollars and cents: A cost-benefit analysis.* Rockville, MD: Center for Substance Abuse Prevention, Substance Abuse and Mental Health Services Administration.
6. Ries, E. (2011). *The lean startup: How today's entrepreneurs use continuous innovation to create radically successful businesses.* New York: Crown.
7. Rogers, E. M., & Singhal, A. (1999). *Entertainment-education: A communication strategy for social change.* Mahwah, NJ: Erlbaum.

Chapter 9

1. Dyer, J., Gregersen, H., & Christensen, C. M. (2011). *The innovator's DNA: Mastering the five skills of disruptive innovators.* Boston: Harvard Business School Press.
2. Ries, E. (2011). *The lean startup: How today's entrepreneurs use continuous innovation to create radically successful businesses.* New York: Crown.

Chapter 11

1. Partners In Health. (2010). *Partners In Health: A model for delivering health and social justice for the poor.* Retrieved December 26, 2012, from Partners In Health: http://model.pih.org/files/PIH-overview-and-model.pdf

2. Levinson, M. (2012). *No citizen left behind.* Cambridge, MA: Harvard University Press.
3. Levine, P. (2007). *The future of democracy: Developing the next generation of American citizens.* Boston: Tufts University Press.
4. American Political Science Association. (2004). *American democracy in an age of rising inequality.* Retrieved from: http://www.apsanet.org/imgtest/taskforcereport.pdf

Chapter 12

1. McMillian, D. W., & Chavis, D. M. (1986). Sense of community: A definition and theory. *Journal of Community Psychology, 14*, 6–23.
2. Pentland, A. (2012). The new science of building great teams. *Harvard Business Review, 90*(4), 60–70.
3. Achor, S. (2010). *The happiness advantage: The seven principles of positive psychology that fuel success and performance at work.* New York: Crown.
4. Achor, S. (2011, June 23). The happiness dividend. *Harvard Business Review Blog Network.* Retrieved from http://blogs.hbr.org/cs/2011/06/the_happiness_dividend.html
5. Ibid.

Chapter 13

1. World Health Organization (2012, June). *Prevention of blindness and visual impairment.* Retrieved December 1, 2012, from World Health Organization: http://www.who.int/blindness/causes/magnitude/en/index.html
2. Rani, D. P. (2010, July). Consultant, International Center for Advancement of Rural Care, LV Prasad. (S. Tyle, Interviewer).
3. Kloth, C., & Applegate, B. (2004). Inter-Organization collaboration and partnerships: A critical analysis. 2004 OD Network Annual Conference. http://www.applegateonline.com/storage/pdf/InterorgCollabArticle.pdf
4. Human Rights Campaign. (June 2012). Buyer's guide. hrc.org/apps/buyersguide/index.php.

Chapter 14

1. Dees, G., Anderson, B. B., & Wei-skillern, J. (2004). Scaling social impact: Strategies for spreading social innovations. *Stanford Social Innovation Review*, Spring 2004.
2. GSANetwork. (2012). History and accomplishments. www.gsanetwork.org/about-us/history.
3. Dees, Anderson, & Wei-skillern.
4. Ibid.
5. Ibid.

Chapter 16

1. Bornstein, D. (2007). *How to change the world: Social entrepreneurs and the power of new ideas.* New York: Oxford University Press.

2. Interview with Bill Drayton. (May 25, 2007). NOW on the news with Maria Hinojosa, accessed October 2, 2012. www.pbs.org/now/news/321.html.
3. Ibid.
4. Bornstein.

Chapter 17

1. Opencontent.org. *Defining the "open" in open content.* Retrieved December 2012, from Opencontent: http://opencontent.org/definition/

Chapter 18

1. Barnes, J. E., Noll, J. G., Putman, F. W., & Trickett, P. K. (2009). Sexual and physical revictimization among victims of severe childhood sexual abuse. *Child Abuse & Neglect, 33*(7), 412–420.
2. United Nations, Economic and Social Council, Commission on Human Rights (1996). Report of the Special Rapporteur on Violence Against Women, Its Causes and Consequences, Ms. Radhika Coomaraswamy, Submitted in accordance with Commission on Human Rights Resolution 1995/85, E/CN.4/1996/53,50.
3. World Health Organization/London School of Hygiene and Tropical Medicine. (2010). Preventing intimate partner and sexual violence in women: Taking action and generating evidence. Geneva: World Health Organization; Centers for Disease Control and Prevention. (2004). Sexual violence prevention: Beginning the dialogue. Atlanta, GA: Centers for Disease Control and Prevention.
4. Centers for Disease Control and Prevention.
5. World Health Organization/London School of Hygiene and Tropical Medicine.

Chapter 19

1. Hochschild, A. (2005). *Bury the chains: The British struggle to abolish slavery.* New York: Houghton Mifflin Harcourt.

Chapter 22

1. Flexible Purpose Corporation, California Corporations Code, SB 201, U.S. § 2500–3503 (2011); Benefit Corporation, California Corporations Code, AB 361, U.S. § 14600–14631 (2011)

Chapter 23

1. Chance, J. Is it more effective to touch 100 potential customers once or 25 potential customers four times? Retrieved January 7, 2013, from http://www.businessknowhow.com/directmail/response/reach.htm; Thanks are also due to Hal Hofman, former radio executive, for his insight into marketing strategy.
2. American Lung Association. *American Lung Association homepage.* Retrieved January 7, 2013, from American Lung Association Web Site: http://www.lung.org/

3. Meeker, M. (June 7, 2010). Internet trends. [CM Summit videotaped presentation]. Retrieved from http://paidcontent.org/2010/06/07/419-mary-meekers-internet-trends-cm-summit-edition/
4. Concept Marketing Group. (2013). *Press release example and template.* Retrieved January 7, 2013, from Concept Marketing Group: http://www.marketingsource.com/pressrelease/releaseformat/
5. Polland, J. (2012, August 29). *The ultimate guide to exploring Paris in style.* Retrieved January 7, 2013, from Business Insider: http://www.businessinsider.com/paris-for-design-lovers-2012-8?op=1

Chapter 24

1. Riesberg, D. (2007). *Cognition: Exploring the science of the mind.* New York: W. W. Norton, p. 150.
2. Andresen, K. (2006). *Robin Hood marketing: Stealing corporate savvy to sell just causes.* San Francisco: Jossey-Bass.
3. Gerber, A. S., & Rogers, T. (2007). The effect of descriptive social norms on voter turnout: the importance of accentuating the positive. *The Journal of Politics.*
4. Goldstein, N. J., Martin, S. J., & Cialdini, R. B. (2008). *Yes! 50 scientifically proven ways to be persuasive.* New York: Free Press.
5. Ibid.
6. Center for Information and Research on Civic Learning and Engagement. (2008). Youth voting: Why youth voting matters. http://www.civicyouth.org/quick-facts/youth-voting/. Accessed May 28, 2012.
7. Klem, K. (2010). *Louisville-Courier* letter to the editor.

Chapter 25

1. National Education Association. Research spotlight on best practices in education. http://www.nea.org/tools/17073.htm, accessed June 1, 2012.
2. Gardner, H. (1993). *Multiple intelligences: The theory in practice.* New York: Basic Books.
3. Ives, B., & Obenchain, K. (2006). Experiential education in the classroom and academic outcomes: for those who want it all. *Journal of Experiential Education, 29,* 61–77.
4. Kuh, G. D. (2008). High-impact educational practices: What they are, who has access to them, and why they matter. Washington, DC: Association of American Colleges and Universities. http://www.neasc.org/downloads/aacu_high_impact_2008_final.pdf
5. Kuh, "High-Impact Educational Practices."
6. Glatthord, A., Boschee, F., Whitehead, B., & Boschee, B. (Eds.). (2012). Curriculum evaluation. In *Curriculum leadership: Strategies for development and implementation* (3rd ed.). Thousand Oaks, CA: Sage.

Chapter 27

1. Darley, J., & Batson, C. D. (1993). From Jerusalem to Jericho: A study of situational and dispositional variables in helping behavior. *Journal of Personality and Social Psychology, 27*, 100–108.
2. Haney, C., Banks, W. C., & Zimbardo, P. G. (1973). Interpersonal dynamics in a simulated prison. *International Journal of Criminology and Penology, 1*, 69–97.

Chapter 28

1. Ensher, E. A., & Murphy, S. E. (2005). *Power mentoring: How successful mentors and protégés get the most out of their relationships.* San Francisco: Jossey-Bass.
2. George, B. (2007). *True north: Discover your authentic leadership.* San Francisco: Jossey-Bass.
3. Zachary, L. J., & Fischler, L. A. (2009). *The mentee's guide: Making mentoring work for you.* San Francisco: Jossey-Bass.

Chapter 29

1. Gladwell, M. (2000). *The tipping point.* New York: Little Brown.
2. Dyer, W., Dyer, W. G., & Dyer, J. H. (2007). *Team building: Proven strategies for improving team performance.* San Francisco. Jossey- Bass.
3. Weitzel, S. R. (2000). *Feedback that works: How to build and deliver your message.* Greensboro, NC: Center for Creative Leadership.
4. Gottman, J., & Silver, N. (1999). *The seven principles for making marriage work.* New York: Three Rivers Press.
5. Kouzes, J. M., & Posner, B. Z. (2008). *The student leadership challenge: Five practices for exemplary leaders.* San Francisco: Jossey-Bass.

Chapter 30

1. Corvette, B. A. (2007). *Conflict management: A practical guide to developing negotiation strategies.* Upper Saddle River, NJ: Pearson.
2. Frey, L. R. (1999). *The handbook of group communication theory and research.* Thousand Oaks, CA: Sage.

Chapter 31

1. Bruner, J. (1985). Vygotsky: An historical and conceptual perspective. In J. Wertsch (Ed.), *Culture, communication, and cognition: Vygotskian perspectives.* Cambridge: Cambridge University Press; Gokhale, A. (1995). Collaborative learning enhances critical thinking. *Journal of Technology Education, 7*(1); Rau, W., & Heyl, B. (1990). Humanizing the college classroom: Collaborative learning and social organization among students. *Teaching Sociology, 18*(2), 141–155.
2. Alexander, J., & Nank, R. (2009). Public-nonprofit partnership: Realizing the new public service. *Administration and Society, 41*(3), 364–386.
3. Shaw, M. M. (2003). Successful collaboration between the nonprofit and public sectors. *Nonprofit Management and Leadership, 14*(1), 107–120.

Chapter 33

1. Lublin, N. (April 23 2012). Get the most out of your board. *Harvard Business Review*, <blogs.hbr.org/cs/2012/04/geting_the_most_out_of_your_bo.html>.

Chapter 34

1. Chambers, R. (1995). Paradigm shifts and the practice of participatory research and development. In *Power and participatory development: Theory and practice*, N. Nelson & S. Wright (Eds.). London: Intermediate Technology Publications.

Chapter 35

1. Drucker, P. F. (1993). *Innovation and entrepreneurship*. New York: Harper Business, p. 21.
2. Putnam, R. D. (2000). *Bowling alone: The collapse and revival of american community*. New York: Simon & Schuster.

Chapter 36

1. Deming, W. E. (1986). *Out of the crisis*. Cambridge, MA: MIT Center for Advanced Engineering Study.

Chapter 37

1. Hansen, M. T., Nohria, N., & Tierney, T. (March-April 1999). What's your strategy for managing knowledge? *Harvard Business Review*, P1.

Chapter 40

1. Kolb D., & Kolb, A. (2009). Experiential learning theory: A dynamic, holistic approach to management learning, education and development. In *Sage Handbook of Management Learning, Education and Development*, S. J Armstrong & C. V. Fukami (Eds.). Thousand Oaks, CA: Sage, 2009.

INDEX

Page references followed by *fig* indicate an illustrated figure; followed by *t* indicate at table.

A

Abdul-Jabbar, Kareem, 350
Abortion (sex-selective), 33
Abstract of grant, 253–254
Access to health care, 37–38
Accountability: social entrepreneurship and social good, 452–453; traditional business, 452. *See also* Social responsibility
Achor, Shawn, 139
Acronyms as names, 205
Acting with purpose, 522, 525
Action plans: accomplishing your goal through, 222–223; activism, 298; budget extra time to accommodate mistakes, 223; using data to guide your, 223; deadlines and calendars incorporated into your, 223–224; example of a sample, 227–228; identifying special skills of your team members for, 225; Potential Scheduling Conflicts, 223, 224–225; program description, 256; scheduling your, 225; Self-Assessment of Current Lifestyle and Goals exercise, 524–525; ten-step revitalization, 462; when falling short of goal adjust your, 226*fig*. *See also* Collective action
Active listening, 329
Active Minds, 428
Activism: "act" component of, 298; amplifying your voice, 296–298; description and focus of, 280–281; "1100: zero" campaign against Iraq War, 291; going into politics to promote your, 295; influence people with power, 285–286; making your pitch for, 281–288; Measure, Evaluate, Improve, Repeat application to, 293; petitions to further your, 288–290; problem solving approach by traditional political, 445–447*fig*; taking it to the streets, 291–293; testifying to promote, 285–288; voting component of, 294; voting with your wallet, 296. *See also* Collective action
Activism pitch: avoid common mistakes in, 283; boil down your message, 281–282; focus on the positive, 283–284; include call to action in your, 284–285; sample testimony used as part of, 287–288; tell a story, 282–283
Activism voice: letters to the editor to amplify your, 297; making the news to amplify your, 296–297; social media used to amplify your, 298
Adams, Christina L., 325
Adapting and evolving, 161, 163–164
Add social value principle, 166, 167, 172
Addictions, 39
Admiration. *See* Role models
Adobe Creative Suite, 324
Advertising: Internet, 265; political campaigning, 322–325
Affiliation spread, 153
African Americans, unemployment rates of, 32
Age discrimination, 31
Agendas: benefits of preparing a team meeting, 377–379; sample of effective meeting, 378
Agriculture Organization report (2010), 40
Alexander, Jennifer, 393
Allen, Woody, 433
Alsop Louis Partners, 244
Amazon Instant Video, 65
American Friends of Hand in Hand, 405
American Productivity and Quality Center, 174
Americans for Informed Democracy (AID), 211
Americans with Disability Act, 31
Amir Project, 405
Andressen, Katya, 283
Animals: cruelty to, 30; endangered species, 30, 59–61; factory farms, 30; habitat destruction and impact on, 37; homelessness of, 28, 30; pollution and health of, 30; puppy mills, 31
Anti-malaria net debate, 453
Apple, 146
Applied Imagination (Osborn), 69
Appropriate Infrastructure Development Group (AIDG), 211–212
Articles of Incorporation: 501(c)(3) incorporation, 491–492; for-profit incorporation, 486
Articulate Your Values exercise, 527

ARTS!, 405
Asana, 383
Ashoka: Innovators for the Public, 2, 167
Ashoka Changeshops, 504
Asset-Based Community Development Institute (Northwestern University), 502
Asset Mapping exercise, 502
Astrum Solar, 76
Audience: educational curricula designed for specific, 304–305; engaging during team meetings, 380–381; identify your conference, 406; identify your media, 262–263; know your media, 262; making an activism pitch to your, 281–288

B

Back-of-the-napkin brainstorming, 69–70, 77
Background checks, 514
Bad press, 272
Balance Strengthening and Starting strategy: advantages and disadvantages of starting, 123–124, 125*fig*; advantages and disadvantages of strengthening, 122–123, 125*fig*; description of, 119–120, 121; the Method in action using the, 187–188; starting your own group, 124–126; striking a balance, 127; warning about wanting to be the boss, 126
Balanced social responsibility, 521
Basecamp, 383
Batson, Daniel, 333
The Beads-to-Business Workbook (Emerge Global), 184–185
Begin Your Team's Jump-Start exercise, 460
Best, Charles, 133
Best practices information, 173–174
The Better World Handbook, 526
Big-picture brainstorming, 310
The Big Picture Tutorial exercise, 510
Bill & Melinda Gates Foundation, 76, 202
Bing, 62
Bisexuals. *See* LGBT/LGBTQ community
Blair, Tony, 225
Blake, William, 365
"Bleeding hearts," 5
Blogs: marketing your cause through, 279; reflection through, 499
Board member selection: the interview process, 424–427*fig*; making first impression through the application, 423–424; responding to the proposal to join board, 427–428
Board member service: step 1: know your options, 419, 420*t*; step 2: find a compatible match, 419–422; step 3: help them get to know you, 423–427*fig*
Boards: Is This Board "The One" exercise on serving on a, 421–422; reasons to consider serving on a, 418–419; teamwork of effective, 418; three types and characteristics of, 419, 420*t*. *See also* Teams
Boettcher, Richard, 145
Books research source, 64
Bornstein, David, 169
Bosnian War, 41
Boston University Center for Global Health and Development, 511
Bowling Alone: The Collapse and Revival of American Community (Putnam), 451
Brainstorming: back-of-the-napkin, 69–70, 77; beginning process of, 68–69; Brainstorming My Strategic Partnerships exercise, 391–392; developing educational curriculum using big-picture, 310; Disrupting Our World exercise use of, 449; Drylands Natural Resource Center (PMC) case study on, 76–79; Ethics Activity exercise using, 332; for execution of goal, 222; ideas that may serve voters, 320; narrowing down the options, 73–75; origins of the term, 69; revitalization ideas, 459–461; see what sticks process of, 74*fig*; self-sustainable solutions through, 158*fig*; town hall, 73, 78; WeAreWhatWeDo.org for behavior changing, 522; whiteboard, 70, 78; Whiteboard Brainstorming exercise on, 71–72. *See also* Ideas
Brainstorming My Strategic Partnerships exercise, 391–392
Branching spread, 153
Breast cancer problem, 96
Breast self-examination, 96
Brigham Young University, 176
Bronshteyn, Yurly, 516, 519–520
Budgets: conference, 412; cost per mille (CMP), 265; grant application statement on, 258; planning your media, 264–265
Buhler, Eunice, 419, 428
Build on What Works strategy: define what works for, 95–96; description of the, 94–95; improve on what works, 98, 100; Land Mine Detection case study on, 99–100; learn what has worked in other places, 96–98, 99; the Method in action using the, 182–183; using others' experiences to lay foundation for your own work, 95*fig*
Bullying: against LGBT/LGBTQ youth, 32; cyberbullying form of, 43–44; violence associated with, 43–44
Bureau of Labor Statistics, 32
Burns, Ken, 375
Bush, George H. W., 4
Bush, George W., 4
Bush, Lauren, 3
Business model: Emerge Global's, 193–194; Integrate Social Entrepreneurship strategy using principles of, 166, 168–169, 172; nonprofit incorporation as a for-profit, 479–487; problem solving approach by traditional, 445–447*fig*; social entrepreneurship approach to solutions through, 443–447*fig*. *See also* For-profit businesses
Business/private partnerships, 398
"Buycott," 296
"Buying for Workplace Equality Guide" app, 146
By the People, 405
Bylaws: 501(c)(3) corporation, 493–494; for-profit corporation, 486

C

C corporation (C corps), 483–484
Calendars: action plan incorporation into your, 223–224; creating collaborative environment using, 383–384
California Student Safety and Violence Prevention Act, 153
Call to action, 284–285
Campaigning. *See* Political campaigning
Cancer treatment, 92
Carbon dioxide, 37
Carnegie, Andrew, 418
Carter, Jimmy, 4

Case studies: Change.org, 106; Drylands Natural Resource Center, 76–79; Gay-Straight Alliance Network, 153; Generation Citizen, 131–132; Global Village Fruits, 50; Health Leads (formerly Project Health), 91; Home Water Filtration System, 171–172; Land Mine Detection, 99–100; Muhammad Yunus, 450; Population Media Center (PMC), 108–109; ReSight, 144; University of Pennsylvania's Engineers Without Borders, 162–164. *See also* Exercises; Social problems
Case studies. *See* Problem case studies
Catalog of Federal Domestic Assistance (CFDA), 246
Cause. *See* Problem cause
Center for Disease Control and Prevention, 38
Center for Global Engagement (Northwestern University), 207, 214, 218, 505
Center for Reproductive Rights (Northwestern University), 203
Center on Wrongful Convictions (Northwestern University), 43
Centers for Disease Control and Prevention, 181
Challenge What Works strategy: how to use the, 110–111*fig*; identifying deficits, 112–113; innovation element of, 110–116; the Method in action using the, 186–187
Chambers, Robert, 429
Chance. *See* Opportunity
Chanel, Coco, 269
Change. *See* Organizational change; Social change
Change the World Kids, 491–492, 493, 494, 496
Change.org: assessing the effectiveness of the name of, 201; case study on tracking and evaluating data collected, 106; online petitions through, 289; social change work by, 3
Charity Navigator, 514
Chase Community Giving, 233
Chavis, David, 136
Chemical waste, 37
Chen, Lyric, 508, 519
Choosing a name: avoid overused words and phrases, 204; avoid trying-to-hard (or inadvertent) acronyms, 205; avoid words that may be misleading, 205; considering your structure, cause, and activities when, 202–203; examples of name styles, 201; importance of, 200; last-minute checks before finalizing name, 206*fig*–207; tone and function of a name, 200–201
Christensen, Clayton, 114
Chronic disease, 38
Churchill, Winston, 527
CityYear, 2
Clarify your Organization's Purposes and Needs exercise, 482
Clarkson, Thomas, 207
Climate change, 36
Clinton, Bill, 4
Clinton Foundation, 511
Coal mining, 37
Coca-Cola, 200
Code of ethics, 328*fig*
Cohen, Alison, 131–132
"Collaborative capital," 183–184
Collaborative environment: calendars to facilitate, 383–384; collaborative tools to create, 383; contact lists to facilitate, 381; e-mail and listservs to facilitate, 382; how effective communication can create, 381; how forums can build a, 383
Collaborative tools, 383
Collect Role Models exercise, 343
Collective action: choosing your vehicle for, 124–126; cultivating community ownership of, 128–134; deciding on how to frame your, 121; fostering partnerships for, 140–146; fostering team unity for, 135–139; incorporating reflection in your, 504–505; software tools for facilitating, 363; starting your own group for, 123–124, 125*fig*; strengthening by joining an established group for, 122–123, 125*fig*. *See also* Action plans; Activism; Partnerships; Teams
College of Southeast Ohio Institute for Social Enterprise, 423
Commensal relationships, 140
CommonPlace, 452, 454
Communication: active listening required for effective, 329; characteristics of the most beneficial modes of, 138; creating collaborative environment through good, 381–384; damage of mixed messages during, 374; determining what's effective, 384–385; Emerge Global's strategies for using, 192; essentials of team, 374–377; facilitating quality, 137–138; as foundation of functioning team, 137; importance of good, 373; managing team friendships through effective, 370; partnership, 403; regarding the development of your educational curricula, 304; revitalization plan, 462, 464–465; team meeting, 377–381. *See also* E-mail communication; Online communication
Community: assessing supply and demand needs of the, 154–155; cultivating social change ownership by the, 128–134; defined as social capital, 451; developing relationships with local leaders of, 435; do your homework and listen to the, 433; educational curricula and resources available through, 305; engaging in problem solving, 66; learn about the, 129–130; nurturing a sense of, 135–137; Putnam's argument on decline of, 451; scale deep versus scale out to increase your impact in the, 152–153; town hall brainstorming with the, 73, 78; understanding the problem as perceived by the, 132–133. *See also* LGBT/LGBTQ community; Stakeholders
Community ownership: build and manage a team for, 435–436; description of, 429; do your homework, show up, and listen to the community for, 433; engineer self-sustainability, 436–437; Generation Citizen case study on promoting, 131–132; get the community perspective to cultivate, 132–133; How Does Community Ownership Work in the Real World? exercise on, 438–439; how to achieve, 437–440; importance of cultivating, 128–129*fig*; integrating social entrepreneurship by cultivating, 169; learn about the community for cultivating, 129–130; the Method in action cultivating, 188–189; participation and empowerment through, 429–431; plant the seeds of change for, 441; promote shared responsibility for, 133–134; seek community-driven solutions and, 434–435; Thinking Critically about Community Ownership exercise on, 432
Community participation: community ownership solution to empowering, 430–431; description of, 429–430; as key to finding community solutions, 431; scenario and analysis of, 430

Competition: constructive versus constrictive, 142; Girl Scout cooperation versus, 141; Seeing Competitors as Partners exercise, 143
Conference content structures: keynote address, 408; networking sessions, 409; panel/plenary discussions, 408; poster sessions, 408; small group discussions, 408; workshops, 408
Conference execution: be prepared for anything, 415; common lessons learned on, 413; conference website, 414; follow up to conference, 415; funding, 414; logistical issues, 413; nonmonetary donations, 414; participant issues, 413; publicity, 414
Conference planning: deciding on content structure, 408–409*fig*; deciding on location, 410; deciding on the length, time, dates, 409; establishing objectives and type of conference, 407–408; identifying your audience, 406
Conference support: administration, 411; assemble a staff, 410; making a budget, 412
Conferences: follow up to, 415; master event guide for, 415; paying for expenses of attending, 175; sharing your results through, 174–175; successful organization of a, 406–417
Conferences types: awareness building, 407; capacity building, 407; information sharing, 408; network building, 407; symposia, 416–417
Confucius, 226, 522
Contact lists, 381
Cooperation: Girl Scout competition versus, 141; Microsoft Office for the Mac example of, 146; Working Together: A Continuum approach to, 145*fig*–146
Cost per mile (CMP), 265
Cotter, Kelly, 509, 517, 518
Council for Education of People with Visual Impairment, 144
Criminal justice system: racial and ethnic discrimination in the, 32; wrongful convictions of the, 43
Crisis management: correcting marketing mistakes, 272–273; dealing with difficult or confrontational interviewers, 271–272; mitigating bad press, 272
Crowd funding, 233
CureSearch, 518
Curiosity: cultivating a problem identification mind-set through your, 49; Global Village Fruits case study on using your, 50
Curriki (Curriculum Wiki), 177
Cyberbullying, 43–44
Cylons for Equality, 204

D

Daimyo, Shin, 513, 518–519
D.A.R.E. (Drug Abuse Resistance Education) program, 101–102
Darfur genocide, 41, 131
Darfur peacekeepers, 205
Darley, John, 333
Data: evaluating evidence from the, 105–106; guiding your action plan through, 223; measuring what matters, 103–105; reflection on the, 500, 501; "vanity metrics" used as, 104
Data collection: considerations for methods of, 104; online surveys for, 105. *See also* Metrics
Data evaluation: Change.org case study on, 106; improving your approach based on the, 106–107; process of, 103–105. *See also* Evaluation
De Bono, Edward, 110
De Gaulle, Charles, 280
Dees, Gregory, 152
Deforestation, 37
Delaware incorporation, 485
Design a systemic solution steps: consideration of the entire system, 87–88; creating multiple efforts to solve the problem, 86–87; Draft a Game Plan exercise, 89; identifying factors/root causes responsible for problem, 85–86, 90
Design a Systemic Solution strategy: as all about expanding your thinking, 85; Challenge What Works by using the, 112–113; Draft a Game Plan exercise on, 89; for the problem of sexual violence, 181–182; for the problem of homelessness, 85–90
Developing countries: access to education in, 33–34; female genital mutilation and honor killings in, 33; global poverty found in the, 39–40; hunger found in, 40
Devise a Leadership Transition Strategy exercise, 476
Dimon, Jamie, 149
Dinh, Amy, 330, 334
Disability rights, 31
Discrimination: age, 31; disability rights, 31; LGBT/LGBTQ rights, 31–32; racial and ethnic, 32; religious, 32–33; women's rights and, 33
Disrupting Our World exercise, 449
Disruption: building a better community center through, 451–452; description of, 447; Disrupting Our World exercise on, 449; as social entrepreneurship component, 447, 448, 450
Dissemination spread, 153
Do Good Well method: in action, 179–195; Do Good Well Network role in applying the, 9; introduction to the three steps of, 8, 81; overview of the, 7–8, 81–82; the toolbox strategy for change used with, 9; watching the method in action, 179–195. *See also* Do What Works step; Make It Last step; Work Together step
Do Good Well method in action: first, the problem, 179–180; second, the opportunity, 180; third, considerations for the, 180–181; step 1: Do What Works, 181–187; step 2: Work Together, 187–190; step 3: Make It Last, 190–195
Do What Works step: Build on What Works strategy, 94–100, 182–184; Challenge What Works, Innovate, and Keep What Works strategy, 110–118; Design a Systemic Solution strategy, 85–93, 181–182; Measure, Evaluate, Improve, Repeat strategy, 101–109, 184–187, 293; the Method in action using the, 181–187; overview of the, 8, 81, 83–84; reflect on data using the, 500, 501; as transitional leadership tenet, 478. *See also* Do Good Well method
Do What Works strategies: activism, 280–298; choosing a name, 200–207; do what's right, 326–334; educational curricula, 299–316; fundraising, 231–260; goals and planning, 219–230; media and marketing, 261–279; running for office, 317–325; writing a mission statement, 208–218
Do What's Right strategy: conducting an ongoing dialogue on, 333–334; Ethics Activity exercise for, 332; formulating a code of ethics, 328*fig*; right action principle

of the, 326, 328–330; right attitude principle of the, 326, 327–328; right reaction principle of the, 326, 330–331; studies on ethics, 333
Doctors Without Borders (Médecins Sans Frontierès), 204
Doing-business-as (DBA) name, 485–486
Domain names, 275
Domestic internships/volunteer work, 512
Donation solicitation: hosting fundraiser event for, 241–242; issues to consider for, 238–239; writing an effective fundraising letter for, 239–241
Donations: conference nonmonetary, 414; crowd funding of small, 233; description of funding through, 234; measuring media strategy success through, 263; soliciting, 238–245; website section for, 275
Donors: asking them for donations, 237; expressing gratitude to your, 237; A Primer on Venture Capital, 242–245
DonorsChoose.org, 133, 203, 233
DoSomething.org, 3, 171, 175
"Double bottom line," 452
Downstream causes/effects, 87–88
Draft a Game Plan exercise, 89
Drayton, Bill, 2, 165, 167, 168, 443
Dropbox, 363
Drucker, Peter, 326, 448
Drylands Natural Resource Center case study, 76–79
Duflo, Esther, 453
Duke University's Center for Advancement of Social Entrepreneurship, 152
Dyer, Jeffrey, 114, 360
Dyer, W. G., 360
Dyer, William, 360
Dylan, Bob, 520

E

E-mail communication: be responsible when using, 382; CommonPlace use of, 454; send out goal reminders between meetings, 381; send out team meeting agendas using, 378. *See also* Communication
The Earth Partners LP, 76
Echoing Green, 167
Education: curricular cuts and exclusions impacting, 34–35; debate over sex, 34–35; How Can I Use Education to Further My Cause exercise, 301–302; inequalities of, 35; lifetime impact of, 315–316; problem category of, 54–55; reform of, 35; UN's Universal Declaration of Human Rights (1948) on access to, 33–34. *See also* Learning
Educational curricula: communicating about the development of, 304; cuts and exclusions in, 34–35; determine how it can help your cause, 300–302; development of, 307–314; evaluation framework for, 314; implementation objectives for, 315; importance of designing effective, 299; know your audience when designing, 304–305; legal policies and guidelines for, 307; multiple intelligences approach to, 305–306*fig*; Planning Your Curriculum exercise on, 311; understand how people learn and the purpose of, 303
Educational curricula development: step 1: requirements analysis, 307, 308*fig*; step 2: establishment of goals, 307, 308*fig*; step 3: basic structure selection, 308*fig*–310; step 4: big-picture brainstorming, 308*fig*, 310; step 5: content development, 308*fig*, 310, 312; step 6: testing and refinement, 308*fig*, 312–313; step 7: implementation, 308*fig*, 313–314, 315; step 8: evaluation and continuous improvement, 313–314
Edward M. Kennedy Serve America Act, 4
Einstein, Albert, 85
Elected office. *See* Political office
"1100: zero" campaign, 291
Emerge Global: The Beads-to-Business Workbook used by, 184–185; "collaborative capital" foundation of, 183–184; communication strategies used by, 192; description and mission of, 179; Example of a Beads-to-Business Programmatic Goal and Indicators of, 185–186; key steps to designing business model of, 194; the Method in action through, 180–195; the social entrepreneurship business model used by, 193–194
Emerge Lanka foundation, 188
Emotion: Five Incidents That Affected Me Emotionally exercise on, 22–23; identifying what moves you to, 21; problem identification and, 52; sense of community through shared emotional connection, 136
Employer/taxpayer identification number (EIN/TIN), 486, 490–491
Employment: The Big Picture Tutorial exercise on, 510; choosing specific issue and enterprise for, 511; domestic or international, 512–513; finding an opportunity for, 513–514; gaining valuable experience through, 509, 515*fig*; leadership skills development through, 516–517; a note about working in lower-income countries, 513. *See also* Unemployment
Endangered species: description of, 30; Kemp's Ridley species problem, 59–61
Energy conservation, 36
Engineer Self-sustainable Solutions strategy: adapt and evolve, 161; build institutional knowledge, 159–160; description of, 147–148, 156–157; the Method in action using, 192; planning for tomorrow, 157–159, 162; secure financial stability, 160–161; University of Pennsylvania's Engineers Without Borders case study, 162–164
Engineers Without Borders (Canada), 195
Engineers Without Borders (University of Pennsylvania) case study, 162–164
Ensher, Ellen, 337
Entrepreneurship. *See* Social entrepreneurship
Environment: climate change, 36; creating a collaborative, 381–384; energy conservation and recycling, 36; pollution, 36–37; resource depletion and habitat destruction, 37; safe for whistle-blowers, 331
Environmental Defense Fund, 203
Ethical behavior: conducting an ongoing dialogue on, 333–334; decision-making studies on, 333; Ethics Activity exercise, 332; formulating a code of ethics for, 328*fig*; having the right attitude for, 326, 327–328; having the right reaction for, 326, 330–331; taking the right action for, 326, 328–330. *See also* Values
Ethics Activity exercise, 332
Ethnic discrimination, 32
Evaluation: of community ownership self-sustainability, 436; educational curricula, 313–314; grant application

information on planned program, 257–258; partnership, 401–405. *See also* Data evaluation; Measure, Evaluate, Improve, Repeat strategy
Evernote, 499
Evidence-based goals, 220–221
Evolving and adapting, 161, 163–164
Executive summary of grant, 253–254
Exercises: Articulate Your Values, 527; Asset Mapping, 502; Begin Your Team's Jump-Start, 460; The Big Picture Tutorial, 510; Brainstorming My Strategic Partnerships, 391–392; Clarify your Organization's Purposes and Needs, 482; Collect Role Models, 343; Devise a Leadership Transition Strategy, 476; Disrupting Our World, 449; Draft a Game Plan, 89; Ethics Activity, 332; Five Incidents That Affected Me Emotionally, 22–23; Four Approaches to the Same Problem, 445–447*fig*; Get Started Innovating, 115–116; How Can I Use Education to Further My Cause, 301–302; How Does Community Ownership Work in the Real World?, 438–439; How to Evaluate Working Styles, 352; Improve Your Daily Schedule, 523; Improve Your Pitch, 236; Is This Board "The One," 421–422; Is This Partnership Good for Me?, 401; Leading Questions: Improving Your Leadership Skills, 368; Map Mentors, 340; Mission Development Tutorial, 216–217; My Strengths and Weaknesses, 26–27; Planning Your Curriculum, 311; Problems and Causes Worksheet, 56; Seeing Competitors as Partners, 143; Self-Assessment of Current Lifestyle and Goals, 524–525; Set Team Goals, 229–230; Should We Become a 501(c)(3): A Checklist, 496; Team Toxins, 363; Ten People I Admire, 24–25; Ten Things I Value, 20–21; Ten Things I'm Grateful For, 18–19; Ten Words That Describe Me, 15–16; Thinking Critically about Community Ownership, 432; Whiteboard Brainstorming, 71–72; Work through a Difficult Transition Process, 476–477. *See also* Case studies
Experience: gaining internship, volunteer work, or employment, 509–517; making a lifestyle out of social responsibility, 520–530; researching through first-hand, 65; sea turtle research, 66
Experiential learning, 312

F

FACE AIDS, 478
Facebook: activism through, 298; bottom-up approach to growth by, 150; Emerge Global's use of, 192; online branding through, 276*fig*–277; political campaigning through, 322; tracking and evaluating your idea through, 117. *See also* Social-networking sites
Factory farms, 30
"Failure Report" (Engineers Without Borders) [Canada], 195
Farmer, Paul, 2
Federal grants, 246
Feed America, 203
FEED bag, 3
Feedback: how to receive, 364–365; issues to consider when giving, 363–364; providing your team member friends with honest, 369; on revitalization from team members, 461; "team toxins" forms of, 364; tips for giving effective, 364
Feedback That Works: How to Build and Deliver Your Message (Weitzel), 363
Fellowships, 233
Female genital mutilation, 33
FemSexComm, 530
50 Cent (Curtis James Jackson, III), 200
Financial stability, 160–161, 163
First Amendment (US): free speech guaranteed in the, 41; freedom of religion guaranteed in the, 32–33
Fischler, Lori, 348
Five Incidents That Affected Me Emotionally exercise, 22–23
501(c)(3) corporation: using an accountant to help set up your, 494; advantages and disadvantages of incorporating as, 488–490; applying for tax-exempt status, 495–496; comparing for-profit corporation to, 479; foundation grants requiring status of, 399; getting finances in order, 495; keeping records on your status as, 237; using a lawyer to set up your, 492; partner organization acting as your umbrella, 387; Should We Become a 501(c)(3): A Checklist exercise on, 496; steps required for incorporating as, 490–496. *See also* Internal Revenue Service
501(c)(3) incorporation steps: step 1: register a name, 490; step 2: apply for Employer Identification Number (EIN), 490–491; step 3: file Articles of Incorporation, 491–492; step 4: write bylaws, 493–494; step 5: apply for tax-exempt status, 495–496
501(c)(4) corporation, 489
Flannery, Matt, 3
Flickr, 192
For-profit businesses: challenge of launching socially conscious program as a, 480–481; Clarify your Organization's Purposes and Needs exercise to consider status as, 482; comparing nonprofit organization and, 165–166; incorporating a nonprofit organization as a, 479–487. *See also* Business model; Organizations
For-profit incorporation: challenges of launching socially conscious programs with, 480; Clarify your Organization's Purposes and Needs exercise to consider, 482; different legal structures used for, 483–484; as a hybrid, 487; insurance requirements of, 487; issues to consider when deciding on, 479–481; planning for your, 482–485; record-keeping system required for, 486; selecting your state of incorporation, 485; steps required for, 485–487; why venture capitalists prefer investing in C corporations, 484
For-profit incorporation steps: step 1: register a doing-business-as (DBA) name, 485–486; step 2: apply for employer/taxpayer identification number (EIN/TIN), 486; step 3: file Articles of Incorporation, 486; step 4: write corporate bylaws (or LLC operating agreement), 486; step 5: perfect your business plan, 487
Ford, Henry, 140, 386, 405
Forge Partnerships strategy: considering range of opportunities for, 145–146; the Method in Action using, 190; ReSight case study on using, 144; Seeing Competitors as Partners exercise on, 143; turning competition into collaboration through, 141–142; types and ideal of partnerships for, 140–141; Working Together: A Continuum for, 145*fig*
Forum (or message board), 383
Foster Team Unity strategy: bring out the best in others, 138–139; description of, 120; encourage ownership

of the solution, 137; facilitate quality communication, 137–138; the Method in action using, 189; nurture a sense of community, 135–137; promote happiness, 139
The Foundation Center, 246
Foundations partnership strategy, 399
Four Approaches to the Same Problem exercise, 445–447*fig*
4Rs Framework of open content, 176–177
Francis of Assisi, St., 167
Friendster, 150
Frishberg, Janet, 528, 530, 531
Fulbright, J. William, 317
Funding sources: crowd funding, 233; donations, 232; fellowships, 233; grants, 233, 245–259; for internships and volunteer work, 515; investors, 233–234; student- or university-based, 234; venture capital, 242–245, 484
Fundraising: applying for grants, 245–260; Improve Your Pitch exercise on, 236; preparing for, 232–235, 237; soliciting donations, 238–245; as two-way street, 231–232. *See also* Social entrepreneurship
Fundraising events: soliciting donations at, 241; suggestions for types of, 241–242
Fundraising pitch: description and elements of, 234–235; examples used to illustrate your, 237; Improve Your Pitch exercise on, 236; A Primer on Venture Capital, 242–245; "60-second elevator pitch," 245
Fundraising preparation: gathering your paperwork, 237; identify your financial needs, 232; identifying potential sources of funding, 232–234; illustrating with examples, 237; perfecting your pitch, 234–236; planning, asking, expressing gratitude, 237

G

Gandhi, Mahatma, 529
Gang violence, 44
Gardner, Howard, 305
Gay & Lesbian Leadership Institute, 202
Gay-Straight Alliance Network (GSA) case study, 153
Gays. *See* LGBT/LGBTQ community
Gender inequality, 33
Generation Citizen, 203
Generation Citizen case study, 131–132
Generational partnership, 397
Genis, Sean, 99–100
Genocide: Darfur, 41, 131; description and impact of, 41; STAND's work against, 131. *See also* Holocaust
Genocide Intervention Network: how their vision is leveraged by their mission, 212–213; mission statement of, 208–209; significance of name, 205
George, Bill, 347
George Washington University School of Public Health and Health Services, 108
Georgetown Journal of Legal Ethics, 417
Gerber, Alan, 283
Get Started Innovating exercise, 115–116
Giamatti, A. Bartlett, 299
Gini index, 39–40
Girl Scout competition, 141
Girls Helping Girls, 260
GirlTank, 203, 260
Gladwell, Malcolm, 351
Global Engagement Summit, 412, 414, 417, 505
Global Giving, 233
Global health patterns, 38
Global poverty: description and significance of, 39–40; UN's Millennium Development Goal to reduce, 39, 40
Global Village Fruits: as case study on identifying a problem, 50; Global Village Fruits' for-profit status, 481
GlobeMed, 428
Goal setting: step 1: design goals, 220–222; step 2: prioritize goals, 222; step 3: brainstorm execution, 222; step 4: develop an action plan, 222–225, 227–228; step 5: evaluate, 226*fig*
Goals: connecting your name to your, 201; driven by mission statements, 220; educational curricula establishment of, 307, 308*fig*; Emerge Global's Example of a Beads-to-Business Programmatic Goal and Indicators, 185–186; evidence-based, 220–221; identifying your media audience and, 261–263; for incorporating reflection in your team, 500–504; know when to say no to a, 225; mentor search facilitated by identifying your, 339; with MERITS, 220; mission statement as defining social change, 210; nonprofit incorporation as a for-profit in order to achieve mission-driven, 479–487; prioritizing, 222; program description of objectives and, 255–256; Self-Assessment of Current Lifestyle and Goals exercise on, 524; send out between meeting e-mail reminders on, 381; Set Team Goals exercise, 229–230; setting specific, 222; social responsibility as social progress, 5; understanding that many roads lead to the same, 517*fig*; UN's Millennium Development Goal to reduce global poverty, 39, 40; what works in planning and, 219–230
Goethe, 298
GOOD.is, 175
Google, 62
Google Calendar, 383
Google Documents, 383
Google Forms, 500
Google Scholar, 65
Google+, 276
Google's AdSense, 265
GoToMeeting, 363
Gottman, John, 364
Government: grants from the, 246–247; partnership strategies for working with, 398. *See also* Political office
Grameen Bank, 2
Grant application steps: step 1: identify appropriate grants, 245–247; step 2: learn about the grant makers, 247; step 3: understand the application process, 247; step 4: make sure you meet eligibility criteria, 248; step 5: complete the application, 248; step 6: review the application, 248; step 7: stay optimistic, 248
Grant applications: abstract or executive summary, 253–254; budget, 258; conclusion, 259; Letter of Inquiry (LOI), 250–253; need statement, 254–255; organizational description, 254; program description, 255–258; statement of purpose, 254; title page, 253; what to do after your submit the, 259
Grants: applying for, 245–248; checklist for, 249; description and types of, 233, 245, 246; websites to find sources of, 246
Grants.gov, 246
The Grantsmanship Center, 246
Gratitude: identifying what you are grateful for, 16; Ten Things I'm Grateful For exercise on, 18–19

Great Pacific Garbage Patch, 37
Gregersen, Hal, 114
Grounded idealism, 1, 520–521
Group assessments, 221
Group syllabi, 504
Groups. *See* Teams
Guantanamo Bay facility, 43
Gun control debate, 44

H

Habitat destruction, 37
Haiti aide, 156
Half the Sky (WuDunn and Kristof), 3
Hamlet (Shakespeare), 13
Hammons, John Tyler, 295
Hand in Hand, 390, 394, 400, 405
The Happiness Advantage (Achor), 139
Harris, Sydney, 316
Harvard Business School's Social Enterprise Conference, 174
Harvard College Global Health Review, 345
Harvard Interfaith Council, 461, 468
Hate crimes, 44–45
Hathi, Sejal, 239, 241, 260
Health: access to care, 37; addictions, 39; chronic disease, 38; global, 38; mental, 38, 90. *See also* Public health system
Health Leads (formerly Project Health) case study, 91
Helen Keller International, 203
Hepatitis C, 39
Hiring team members: components of an offer letter, 359; issues to consider when, 358
HIV infection: addictions and risk of, 39; sex education to reduce rates of, 35; women's rights and relationship to rates of, 33
Holmes, Oliver Wendell, 117
Holocaust, 41. *See also* Genocide
Home Water Filtration System case study, 171–172
Homelessness problem: of animals, 28, 30; designing a systemic solution for the, 85–90; poverty relationship to, 40; reflections of provided services to homeless, 497–498; relationship between mental health and, 90
Homelessness systemic solution: designing multiple efforts as part of the, 86–87; Draft a Game Plan exercise on, 89; for the entire system, 87–88; identifying multiple reasons/root causes for problem, 85–86, 90
Homer, 336
Honor killings, 33
Housing discrimination, 32
How Can I Use Education to Further My Cause exercise, 301–302
How Does Community Ownership Work in the Real World? exercise, 438–439
How To Change the World: Social Entrepreneurs and the Power of New Ideas (Bornstein), 167
How to Evaluate Working Styles exercise, 352
Human rights: access to education as, 33–34; free speech, 41; reproductive rights, 42
Human Rights Campaign (HRC), 146, 201
Human rights violations: genocide, 41; human trafficking violation of, 41–42; labor rights and sweatshops, 42; wrongful imprisonment and torture, 42–43
Human trafficking: impact and effects of, 41–42; Polaris Project's work against, 127
Humes, James, 373
Hunger, 40
Hwang, William, 309–310, 312, 316
Hybrid incorporation, 487

I

Ice-breakers, 360
IdeaEncore, 177
Ideal partners, 390
Idealism, 1, 520–521
Ideas: *The Better World Handbook* for social change, 526; distinguishing a solution from an, 68; Drylands Natural Resource Center case study on brainstorming, 76–79; keep a list of all of your, 74; narrowing down the, 73–75; power of sharing, 501; test driving your, 116; tracking, 504. *See also* Brainstorming; Innovate strategy; Knowledge
IdeaShare, 504
Improve strategy. *See* Measure, Evaluate, Improve, Repeat strategy
Improve Your Daily Schedule exercise, 523
Improve Your Pitch exercise, 236
Income inequality index, 39–40
Incorporation: as 501(c)(3) nonprofit organization, 237, 387, 399, 479, 488–496; as for-profit organization, 479–487; as a hybrid organization, 487
Indicorps, 203
Infectious diseases, 38
Innovate strategy: actions to take for, 113–114; Challenge What Works and, 110–113; Get Started Innovating exercise, 115–116; illustration on, 111*fig*; test driving your idea, 116. *See also* Ideas; Keep What Works strategy; Social innovation
The Innovator's DNA (Dyer, Gregersen, and Christensen), 114
InnoWorks, 312
Institutional knowledge: resources on subject of, 474; self-sustainable solutions by building, 159–160; Transitional Leadership for building, 159–160; University of Pennsylvania's Engineers Without Borders, 162–163
Institutional memory transfer: illustration of strategies for, 475*fig*; resources on subject of, 474; transitional leadership task of, 472–474
Insurance requirements, 487
Integrate Social Entrepreneurship strategy: add social value principle of, 166, 167, 172; comparing nonprofits and for-profit organizations, 165–166; cultivate community ownership principle of, 166, 169, 172; description of, 147–148; Home Water Filtration System case study on, 171–172; innovate to turn problem into an opportunity principle of, 166, 167–168, 171–172; making a profit and a difference with, 170*fig*; the Method in action using, 193–194; solve problems with business principles for, 166, 168–169, 172. *See also* Social entrepreneurship
Intel, 171
Interfaith Youth Core (IFYC), 213
Internal Revenue Service: 501(c)(3) tax-exempt status granted by, 237, 488, 495–496; IRS Form 2553 for S election filing, 484; IRS Form SS-4 for EIN number, 491. *See also* 501(c)(3) corporation
International internships/volunteer work: a note about working in lower-income countries, 513; pros and cons of, 512

International partnership strategy, 399
Internet: be responsible with e-mail communication on the, 382; finding opportunities for social action by searching the, 507; researching by watching content on the, 65; search engines for the, 62–63; warning on credibility and accountability issues of, 63. *See also* Websites
Internet advertising, 265
Internships: The Big Picture Tutorial exercise on, 510; domestic versus international, 512–513; gaining experience through, 509, 515*fig*; how to select issue and enterprise for your, 511; leadership skills development through, 516–517; a note about funding your, 515
Interview crisis management: correcting marketing mistakes, 272–273; dealing with difficult or confrontational interviewers, 271–272; mitigating bad press, 272
Interviews: board member selection, 424–427*fig*; crisis management for, 271–273; print, 270; radio, 270–271; television, 267–268
Investor funding, 233–234
Iraq War activism, 291
IRS Form 2553, 484
Is This Board "The One" exercise, 421–422
Is This Partnership Good for Me? exercise, 401
It Gets Better Project, 44

J

Jackfruit story, 50
Jackley, Jessica, 3
Jackson, Curtis James, III (50 Cent), 200
Jewelry program. *See* Emerge Global
Jobs, Paul, 339
Jobs, Steve, 339
Jones-Romansic, Mona, 350, 355, 372
Journaling, 499
Jumo, 177
Just Naive Enough, 201

K

Kasten, Jennifer, 514, 518, 519
Kaur, Ravneet, 260
Keep America Beautiful, 203
Keep What Works strategy: Challenge What Works element of, 110–113; innovation element of, 110–116; testing your ideas and, 117–118
Keller, Helen, 203
Kemp's Ridley species problem, 59–61
Kennedy, Robert F., 441
Kenya's Drylands Natural Resource Center case study, 76–79
Khazei, Alan, 2
Kierkegaard, Soren, 497
Kim, Jim, 2
King, Martin Luther, Jr., 450
Kiva.org, 3
Kleinman, Sarah, 472, 474, 477, 478
Klem, Katherine, 281, 282, 283, 288, 291, 292, 293, 297, 298
Kloth, Chris, 145
Knowing your world: animals, 28, 30–31; discrimination, 31–33; education, 33–35; environment, 36–37; health, 37–39; human rights, 41–43; importance of, 28; poverty, 39–41; understanding interconnection of world's problems, 29*fig*; violence, 43–45
Knowing yourself: cultivating problem identification mind-set by, 49; Global Village Fruits case study on value of, 50; importance of getting to, 13; information required for, 17*fig*; understanding what you care about to, 16–25; understanding your strengths and weaknesses, 25–27; Who Are You? questions to, 14
Knowing yourself exercises: Five Incidents That Affected Me Emotionally, 22–23; My Strengths and Weaknesses, 26–27; Ten People I Admire, 24–25; Ten Things I Value, 20–21; Ten Things I'm Grateful For, 18–19; Ten Words That Describe Me, 15–16
Knowing yourself questions: How Do Others See You?, 14, 15; How Do You See Yourself?, 14, 15
Knowledge: identifying the gap in, 58–61; leadership transition of relationships and, 471–474; prior, 303, 305; reflection used to build team learning and, 500, 504; subdiscipline on management of, 474; sustainability solutions by building institutional, 159–160, 162–163; transition of institutional memory and, 471–474, 475*fig*; understanding how people learn and acquire, 303; using your symposium to create, 416. *See also* Ideas; Learning
Knowledge gap: defining the problem and identifying your, 58–61; questions to help identify, 59–60
Kopp, Wendy, 2
Korman, Murray S., 99, 100
Kretzmann, Jody, 502
Kristof, Nick, 3

L

Labor rights, 42
Lala, Om, 461
Land Mine Detection case study, 99–100
Laub, Carolyn, 153
Leadership: declining organization vitality due to change in, 458; employment, internship, and volunteer work to develop, 516–517; succession planning, 470–471; transitional, 159–160, 469–478. *See also* Team leaders; Transitional leadership
Leading Questions: Improving Your Leadership Skills exercise, 368
The Lean Startup (Ries), 104, 116
Learning: determining how it can help your cause, 300–302; experiential, 312; prior knowledge role in, 303, 305; reflection as part of, 498; reflection used to build team knowledge and, 500, 504; understanding the process of, 303. *See also* Education; Knowledge
Legacy of social responsibility, 529–530
Legal curricular issues, 307
Legislation. *See* United States legislation
Legitimacy of organization, 401
Lesbians. *See* LGBT/LGBTQ community
Letter of inquiry (LOI): components of, 251; description of, 250; sample of, 252–253
Letters to the editor, 297
Leventhal, Howard, 284
LGBT/LGBTQ community: "Buying for Workplace Equality Guide" app support of, 146; discrimination against, 31–32; It Gets Better Project for teens of the, 44; problem category of discrimination against, 55; rights of the, 31. *See also* Community
Lifestyle: Self-Assessment of Current Lifestyle and Goals exercise on, 524; social responsibility lifestyle, 520–530

Limited liability company (LLC), 384, 483
LinkedIn, 508
Listservs, 382
Local government grants, 247
Logos, 273
Lombardi, Vince, 456
Lonsdorf, Richard, 325
Lowry, Mackenzie, 267–268, 279
Lublin, Nancy, 3
Lung cancers, 39

M

Magazines research source, 64
Makarechi, Leila, 436, 441
Make It Last step: Engineer Self-sustainable Solutions, 147–148, 156–164, 192; Integrate Social Entrepreneurship, 147–148, 165–172, 193; the Method in action using the, 190–195; overview of the, 8, 81, 147–148; reflection: build team knowledge using, 500, 504; Share What Works strategy, 148, 173–178, 194–195; Start Small, Then Scale What Works strategy, 147, 149–155, 190–191; as transitional leadership tenet, 478. *See also* Do Good Well method
Make Our Food Safe Coalition, 202
Malaria net debate, 453
Male television fashion, 269
Mammograms, 96
Mandviwala, Yasmin, 466, 468
Map Mentors exercise, 340
MapStoryFoundation, 505
Marino, Jonathan, 497–498, 505
Massachi, Dalya, 247, 260
Mathew, Sheba, 339, 344, 345, 346, 348, 349
McDonald's, 150
McKinsey & Co., 76, 478
McKinsey and Company, 511
McKnight, John, 502
McMillian, David, 136
Mead, Margaret, 506
Measure, Evaluate, Improve, Repeat strategy: applied to activism, 293; Change.org case study on, 106; D.A.R.E. program's successful, 101–102; evaluate the evidence, 105–106; illustration of the, 102*fig*; improve your approach, 106–107; measure what matters, 103–105; the Method in action using the, 184–187; Population Media Center (PMC) case study on, 108–109; repeat, repeat, repeat, 107. *See also* Evaluation
Médecins Sans Frontierès (Doctors Without Borders), 204
Media personality: alert the media and submit press releases, 265–267; crisis management, 271–273; radio interviews, 270–271; television interviews, 267–270
Media strategy: budget for your campaign, 264–265; creating a successful message, 263–264; identifying your audience and goals, 261–263; letters to the editor, 297; for partnerships with media, 399; for promoting activism, 296–298; for traditional and social media, 264. *See also* Social media
Meeting minutes, 379–380
Meetings and Contacts Log, 508*t*
Mental health: global state of, 38; relationship between homelessness and, 90
The Mentee's Guide (Zachary and Fischler), 348
Mentor (*The Odyssey* character), 336
Mentoring team: considering who to approach to be on the, 339; providing multiple mentors as part of your, 338
Mentors: building a mentoring team using multiple, 338–339; characteristics of an ideal, 337–338*fig*; Collect Role Models exercise to find a, 343; as essential to new organizations, 336; forging a strong relationship with your, 346–348; how to approach new, 344–346; identify new, 342–344; identifying your goals and needs for a, 339; Map Mentors exercise on, 340; pay it forward by becoming a, 348–349; sample introductory e-mail to a potential, 346; tie projects to people for securing a, 341–342
Mentorship search: step 1: considering characteristics of ideal mentor, 337–338*fig*; step 2: build a mentoring team, 338–339; step 3: identify your goals and needs, 339–340; step 4: tie projects to people, 341–342; step 5: identify new mentors, 342–344; step 6: approach new mentors, 344–346
Mercado Global, 183
MERITS goals, 220
Meteorologists Against Global Warming, 204
Metrics: activism, 293; measuring what matters, 103–105; setting goals that are trackable using, 221; "vanity," 104. *See also* Data collection
Meyers, Phebe, 491–492, 493, 494, 496
Microclinic International (MCI), 434, 436, 437, 441
Microfinancing (microloans), 450, 454
Microsoft, 146
Microsoft Office for the Mac, 146
Millennium Development Goal (UN), 39, 40, 42
Mind-set: cultivating the problem identification, 48–49; problem identification, 48
Mission Development Tutorial exercise, 216–217
Mission-driven goals: description of, 220; nonprofit incorporation as a for-profit in order to achieve, 479–487
Mission statements: characteristics of a great, 209–210; as defining organization goals for change, 210; description and function of, 208; examples of, 210–212; figure out what your group cares about most for writing, 215*fig*; Genocide Intervention Network's, 208–209; as guiding the organization, 209; Mission Development Tutorial exercise, 216–217; setting goals that are driven by, 220; vision versus, 212–213; why the words matter, 218; writing your, 213–214. *See also* Vision
MIT Media Lab Entrepreneurship Program, 137
MIT Mobility Lab (M-Lab), 178
Morse, Alex, 295
Motivation: cultivating problem identification mind-set by knowing your, 49; identifying what makes you emotional factor of, 21–23; identifying what you are grateful factor of, 16, 18–19; identifying what you value factor of, 19–21; identifying who you admire factor of, 23–25; problem identification questions on, 51–54; starting your own group, 126; understanding what you care about to understand your, 16–25; Who Are You? illustration on understanding your, 17
Multiple intelligences, 305–306*fig*
Murphy, Susan, 337
Muslim Americans, 33
Mutualistic relationships, 140

MVP (minimal viable product), 116
My Strengths and Weaknesses exercise, 26–27
MySpace, 150

N

Nambudiri, Vinod, 366, 372
Names: connecting your goals and style to your, 201; factors to consider when choosing your, 202–203; register a doing-business-as (DBA), 485–486; registering a 501(c)(3) corporation, 490; tone and function of, 200–202; Trade Name Registration with the SOS (Office of Secretary of the State), 490
Nank, Renee, 393
National Coalition for the Homeless, 90
National Education Association, 304
National Institutes of Health, 285
National Society to Prevent Blindness, 203
Need statement, 254–255
Nestlé USA, 419
Nestlé Very Best in Youth Foundation Advisory Board, 428
Networking: finding opportunities for social action through, 507–509; privacy warning for, 509; tips for effective, 508*t*–509. *See also* Social-networking sites
New Enterprise Associates, 144
Newsletters research source, 64
Newspaper research source, 64
Newton, Sir Isaac, 94
Nightingale, Florence, 167
9/11 terrorists, 33
Nonprofit/nongovernmental organizations (NGOs): adapt and evolve for longevity of, 161; background checks on, 514; balancing strengthening existing group versus starting a new, 122–127; building institutional knowledge, 159–160, 162–163; Charity Navigator and 990s (tax forms) to assess effectiveness of, 514; choosing quality good work over quantity, 155; Clarify your Organization's Purposes and Needs exercise for your, 482; comparing for-profit and, 165–166; engineering self-sustainable solutions, 147–148, 156–164; 501(c)(3) incorporation of, 237, 387, 399, 479, 488–496; 501(c)(4) incorporation by, 489; for-profit incorporation of, 479–487; forging partnerships within, 140–146; fostering team unity in, 135–139; hybrid incorporation of, 487; incorporated as a for-profit business, 479–487; partnership strategies for working with, 398; partnerships between government and, 6; planning for tomorrow, 157–159, 162; revitalizing efforts of, 456–468; securing financial stability, 160–161, 163; social entrepreneurship by, 165–172, 443–450; top-down versus bottom-up approach taken by, 150; transitional leadership during change, 159–160, 469–478; types of spread by, 153–154. *See also* Organizational strategies; Organizations
Northwestern University: Asset-Based Community Development Institute at, 502; Center for Global Engagement at, 207, 214, 218, 505; Center on Wrongful Convictions at, 43
Novendstern, Max, 454, 455
NPR's "This I Believe" segments, 501
Nuclear power accidents, 37
"Numbers campaign," 291

O

Obama campaign (2008), 4, 451
Obesity rates, 38
Observation: cultivating a problem identification mind-set through your, 49; Global Village Fruits case study on, 50
The Odyssey (Homer), 336
Offit, Anna, 416, 417
Ohio State University School of Social Work, 145
Oil drilling, 37
Onie, Rebecca, 91
Online branding: blogs for, 279; Facebook for, 276*fig*–277; managing your media, supporters, and going viral for, 279; Twitter for, 277–278; websites for, 273–275; YouTube for, 278
Online communication: Emerge Global's strategies for, 192; media strategy for traditional and, 261–265; the Method in action sharing outcomes through, 194–195; organizations engaged in sharing outcomes through, 175; sharing through open content, 176–177; warning on permanence of comments made in, 329. *See also* Communication
Online surveys: collecting data through, 105; petitions through, 288–290; SurveyMonkey.com for conducting, 500
Open content sharing, 176–177
Open-minded: cultivating problem identification mind-set by staying, 49; Global Village Fruits case study on remaining, 50
OpenIDEO, 504
Opportunity: building a social responsibility career by identifying, 507–509; for forging partnerships, 145–146; innovate to turn problems into an, 166, 167–168, 171–172; for internships, employment, and volunteer work, 513–515*fig*; the Method in action, 180; role of chance in problem identification and, 51; team member friendships and new learning, 370–371; Web searches and networking to identify and find, 507–509
Oprah Magazine, 171
Organizational change: Devise a Leadership Transition Strategy exercise for, 476; envisioned as new beginning, 478; importance of transitional leadership during, 469–470; revitalization process for, 456–486; succession planning and implementation during, 471–475*fig*; three tenets of leadership transitions during, 478; Work through a Difficult Transition Process exercise for, 476–477. *See also* Social change
Organizational decline: diagnosing the problem of, 459–461; examining the causes of, 456–459; preventing future recurrence of, 466. *See also* Revitalization
Organizational strategies: activism, 280–298; choosing a name, 200–207; do what's right, 326–334; educational curricula, 299–316; establishing legitimacy, 401; fundraising, 231–260; goals and planning, 219–230; media and marketing, 261–279; writing a mission statement, 208–218. *See also* Nonprofit/nongovernmental organizations (NGOs)
Organizations: comparing nonprofit and for-profit, 165–166; offering great support to social entrepreneurs, 167; solving social problems using business principles of for-profit, 168–169, 172; transitional leadership during change, 159–160, 469–478. *See also*

For-profit businesses; Nonprofit/nongovernmental organizations (NGOs)
Orman, Suze, 339
Orr, David W., 429
Osborn, Alex, 69
Ottawa Mine Ban Treat (1997), 99
Otto, Courtney, 287

P

Pammal, Shalini, 312, 314, 315, 316
Parasitic relationships, 140
Parent-project partnerships: description and characteristics of, 396; navigating power dynamics of, 399–401
Parent-project power dynamics: establishing project legitimacy, 401; Hand in Hand as Project Harmony Israel's, 390, 394, 400, 405; maintaining independence from, 400; strategies for navigating, 399–401
Partners: Brainstorming My Strategic Partnerships exercise to assess possible, 391–392; communicating with your, 403; getting out of partnership what they put in, 389; the ideal, 390
Partners In Health (PIH), 2, 128, 156, 518
Partnership development: step 1: find the right partner, 388–393; step 2: make the connection and build the relationship, 393–395; step 3: sustain the partnership, 395–401
Partnership evaluation: Is This Partnership Good for Me? exercise on, 401; issues to consider for, 401–403; troubleshooting partnerships, 403; when to end or transform partnership, 404–405
Partnership ingredients: listed, 388; troubleshooting partnerships by checking the, 403
Partnership power dynamics: establish legitimacy strategy for, 401; maintain independence strategy for, 400; navigating, 399–401
Partnership relationships: making connection to build the, 393–395; proven strategies for building, 393; sustaining the, 395–401
Partnership strategies: for building relationship, 393; navigate power dynamics, 399–401; for working with specific sectors, 398–399
Partnerships: advantages and disadvantages of, 386–388; Brainstorming My Strategic Partnerships exercise on, 391–392; considering range of opportunities for, 145–146; different types of symbiotic relationships and, 140; evaluate your, 401–405; the ideal type of, 140–141; ingredients necessary for a good, 388, 403; the Method in Action using, 190; parent-project, 396, 399–401; ReSight case study on fostering, 144; Seeing Competitors as Partners exercise, 143; seeking out unique partners for fostering, 146; steps for developing an effective, 388–401; troubleshooting, 403; turning competition into collaboration through, 141–142; types of, 396–397*fig*; when to end or transform the, 404–405; Working Together: A Continuum for, 145*fig*. *See also* Collective action
Pasteur, Louis, 46
Pay it forward: by becoming a mentor, 348–349; sharing what works through, 177–178
Peer 2 Peer University, 203
Peer-reviewed journal articles, 64–65
Penn State University, 101
Pentland, Alex, 137–138
Pepsi Refresh, 233
Performance of International Student Achievement study (2009), 35
The PETA-Vegan Single Dads Fund for Saving the Whales, 202
Petitions: activism promoted through, 288–289; online or in person collection of, 289; sample of HIV prevention, 290
Pike, Daniel, 76–79
Plan for tomorrow strategy, 157–159, 162
Planned Parenthood, 203
Planning Your Curriculum exercise, 311
Polaris Project, 127
Political campaign platform: craft the message of your, 321; identify potential solutions, 320
Political campaign posters: components of, 323–324; illustration of an effective, 325*fig*
Political campaigning: advertise, 322–325; caution against sending too many emails during, 322; creating a poster, 323–325*fig*; design a platform for, 320–321; know the position element of, 318–319; know the voters element of, 319–320; share your message, 321–322
Political office: eligibility of, 318; extending your activism to holding, 295; job description of, 318; mission alignment of your organization and, 318; shadowing a current holder of, 319; as vehicle for making change, 317. *See also* Government
Pollution: animal health and, 30; chemical waste and carbon dioxide, 37; environment effects of, 36–37; Great Pacific Garbage Patch, 37
Population Media Center (PMC) case study, 108–109
Potential Scheduling Conflicts, 223, 224–225
Poverty: global, 39–40; homelessness due to, 40; hunger and, 40; unemployment and, 40–41; UN's Millennium Development Goal to reduce global, 39, 40, 42
Poverty Action Lab, 453
Power Mentoring (Ensher and Murphy), 337
Pratham International, 428
Prevention solutions, 91–92
Prezi, 499
Primary prevention, 91
Print interviews, 270
Prior knowledge, 303, 305
Prioritizing goals, 222
Private grants, 233, 247
Private/business partnerships, 398
Problem cause: considering upstream and downstream causes and effects, 87–88; designing systemic solution by first identifying, 85–86, 90; digging deep to understand the root, 62*fig*; identifying the, 54–55; moving from identifying the problem to, 54–55; Problems and Causes Worksheet exercise on, 56
Problem identification: Drylands Natural Resource Center case study on, 76–79; Global Village Fruits case study on, 50; importance of, 46–47; process of, 47–49, 51; questions to ask during, 51–54, 60*fig*
Problem identification process: action for, 47–48; illustration of the, 48*fig*; mind-set for, 48–49; role of chance in the, 51
Problem identification questions: Can I contribute meaningfully?, 53; Do I have a strong emotional reaction to it?, 52; Does it reinforce my personal values?, 52–53;

how to use the, 53–54; Is it something I'm interested in?, 51–52; Is it something I'm passionate about?, 52
Problem research: experience as part of, 65–66; Internet and television content used for, 65; reading and reading sources used for, 61–65; talking to community stakeholders as part of, 66; value of, 57–58
Problem research sources: books, newspapers, newsletters and magazines, 64; peer-reviewed journal articles, 64–65; search engines, 62–63; warning on, 63; Wikipedia, 62
Problem solving: brainstorming for, 68–72; using business principles for, 166, 168–169, 172; define the problem and identify knowledge gaps for, 58–61; designing a systemic solution component of, 85–93; Drylands Natural Resource Center case study on, 76–79; Four Approaches to the Same Problem exercise on, 445–447*fig*; importance of measuring progress of, 61; narrowing down the possible options, 73–75; the value of research for, 57–58; Whac-a-Mole school of, 90. *See also* Solutions
Problems: categories of, 54–55; Four Approaches to the Same Problem exercise on, 445–447*fig*; identifying, 46–54; identifying the cause of the, 54–56; the Method in action, 179–180; process of understanding the, 57–66; researching the, 57–58, 61–66; social innovation to create opportunity from a, 166, 167–168, 171–172; troubleshooting partnership, 403. *See also* Social problems; *specific case study*
Problems and Causes Worksheet exercise, 56
Product partnership, 396
Program description: evaluation plan, 257–258; goals and objectives, 255–256; methodology or plan of action, 256; staffing, 256–257
Project Harmony Israel, 390, 394, 400, 405
Promoting happiness, 139
Prostitution and human trafficking, 41–42
Prudential Spirit of Community Awards, 171
Public grants, 233, 246
Public health system: addressing prevention and treatment issues of the, 91–92; combining strategies to create the best solutions, 92–93; Health Leads (formerly Project Health) case study on, 91. *See also* Health
Publications, 175
Public/government partnerships, 398
PubMed, 65
Puppy mills, 31
"Purchase on purpose," 526
Putnam, Robert, 451
Pythagoras, 371

Q

Questions: assessing supply and demand, 154–155; definition of problem and identifying knowledge gaps, 58–60*fig*; effective solutions found by asking a, 96; problem identification, 51–54
Qwhisper, 244

R

Racial discrimination, 32
Radio interviews, 270–271
Rattray, Ben, 3
Ravenstahl, Luke, 295
Recognition, declining vitality due to lack of, 457
Records: 501(c)(3) nonprofit organization status, 237; for-profit incorporation, 486; Meetings and Contacts Log, 508*t*; team meeting minutes, 379–380; of what didn't work while scaling, 154
Recycling, 36
Red Cross, 221, 225
Reflection: Asset Mapping exercise on, 502; incorporating in your collaboration, 504–505; incorporating in your team, 500–504; incorporating into your life, 498–500; for innovation, 505; learning through, 498; on service provided to homeless, 497–498; your self-reflection homework, 506–507
Reflection strategies: create a wordle, 499–500*fig*; Do What Works: reflect on data, 500, 501; hide out, 499; journaling, 499; Make It Last: build team knowledge, 500, 504; shared values, 503*fig*; tips for facilitating good group reflection, 503; Work Together: improve relationships between team members, 500, 501
Reichel, Tova, 108–109
Relationships: commensal, 140; developing community leader, 435; forging strong mentor, 346–348; leadership transition of knowledge and, 471–474; mutualistic, 140; parasitic, 140; partnership, 393–401; reflection used to improve team, 500, 501–503*fig*. *See also* Team member friendships
Religious discrimination, 32–33
Religious organization partnering, 399
Remindavax, 50
Remote team management, 363
Renuka: the Do Good Well Method in action helping, 180–195; sexual violence against, 179–180
Repeat strategy. *See* Measure, Evaluate, Improve, Repeat strategy
Reproductive rights, 42
Research. *See* Problem research
ReSight case study, 144
Resources: copyright issues of sharing, 177; for creating collaborative environment, 383; depletion of, 37; educational curricula and community, 305; institutional knowledge and memory, 474; maximizing your media, 261–262; online sharing of, 176–177; setting realistic goals based on, 221; tracking who is using your materials and, 177
Revitalization: Begin Your Team's Jump-Start exercise on, 460; brainstorming ideas for, 459–461; causes leading to need for, 456–459; example of a vision for, 463*t*–464*t*; sample three-month time line for, 467–468; Ten-Step Plan to Revitalization for, 462–486; transparency during process of, 465. *See also* Organizational decline
Revitalization plan: communicate your strategy, 462, 464–465; example of a revitalization vision, 463*t*–464*t*; execute on your strategy, 462, 465–466; form a strategy, 462
Revitalizing efforts: step 1: determine the causes of lack of energy, 456–459; step 2: diagnose the problem, 459–461; step 3: follow the treatment plan, 461–466; step 4: prevent future recurrence, 466
Revolving Fund Pharmacy, 203
Ries, Eric, 104, 116
Right action principle: be self-aware, 330; be transparent, 329; communicate, 329; description of, 326, 328–329; Ethics Activity exercise on practicing the, 332

Right attitude principle: consolidate and clarify, 327; description of, 326, 327; Ethics Activity exercise on practicing the, 332; formulate a code of ethics, 328*fig*; get consensus, 328; learn what drives your team, 327
Right reaction principle: address the problem situation, 331; assess the situation, 330–331; creating a safe environment for whistle-blowers, 331; description of, 326, 330; Ethics Activity exercise on practicing the, 332; learn from your mistakes, 331
Robin Hood Marketing: Stealing Corporate Savvy to Sell Just Causes (Andersen), 283
Rockefeller Foundation, 511
Rogers, Todd, 283
Role models: identifying your, 23; Ten People I Admire exercise on, 24–25
Ruth, Babe, 135, 359
Rwandan genocide, 41
Ryu, Annie, 50, 481, 487

S

S corporation (S corps), 483, 484–485
S2 Capital, 144
Sabatier, James, 99
Saint-Exupéry, Antoine de, 219
Sample Action Plan, 227–228
Save the Whales, 201–202
Scaling: choosing quality good work over quantity when, 155; Facebook's bottom-up approach through, 150; Gay-Straight Alliance Network case study on, 153; keep a written record of what didn't work, 154; the Method in action using, 190–191; scale deep versus scale out types of, 152–153; as social entrepreneurial component, 447, 454–455; think big by starting small and then, 150–151*fig*
School partnership strategies, 398
School Yourself, 203
Scopus, 65
Search engines, 62–63
Second Amendment (US), 44
Secondary prevention, 81
Securing financial stability, 160–161, 163
Seeing Competitors as Partners exercise, 143
Self-Assessment of Current Lifestyle and Goals exercise, 524–525
Self-awareness, 330
Self-reflection homework, 506–507
Self-sustainable solutions: adapt and evolve for, 161; brainstorming to create, 158*fig*; build institutional knowledge for, 159–160; community ownership by engineering, 436–437; description of, 147–148, 156–157; Engineers Without Borders case study on, 162–164; the Method in action using, 192; plan for tomorrow to create, 157–159; secure financial stability for, 160–161
Selfridge, H. Gordon, 371
Seneca, 117
Sense of community, 135–137
Set Team Goals exercise, 229–230
SEVA, 144
The Seven Principles for Making Marriage Work (Gottman and Silver), 364
Sex education debate, 34–35
Sex-selective abortions, 33
Sex trafficking: impact and effects of, 41–42; Polaris Project's work against, 127
Sexual violence: against women, 33; designing a systemic solution for the problem of, 181–182; factors contributing to, 181; the Method in action helping victim of, 180–195
Shah, Sonal, 3
Shakespeare, William, 13
Share What Works strategy: copyright issues of, 177; description of, 148, 173; Engineers Without Borders' "Failure Reports" example of, 195; illustration of different formats for, 176*fig*; the Method in action using, 194–195; pay it forward, 177–178, 348–349; share outcomes, 173–176*fig*; share resources, 176–177
Shared responsibility, 133–134
Shared values, 503*fig*
Should We Become a 501(c)(3): A Checklist exercise, 496
Sight Savers, 144
Silver, Nan, 364
"60-second elevator pitch," 245
Skitch, 499
Skoll Foundation, 167
Skype: international partnering and use of, 399; keeping in touch with partner through, 389, 394; as tool for remote teams, 363
Smith, Adam, 444
Smoking addiction, 38, 39
Social change: act with purpose to create, 522, 526; balancing the strengthening and starting strategy for, 122–127; *The Better World Handbook* for ideas on, 526; community ownership by planting the seeds for, 441; cultivating community ownership of, 128–134; do what's right to make about, 326–334; for-profit business launching programs for, 480–481; mission statement as defining goals for, 210; promoting shared responsibility for, 133–134; social entrepreneurship driving progress in, 444; united action driving, 119; value-driven, 527–529; the vision for, 11–12. *See also* Organizational change; Social responsibility career
Social entrepreneurs: business model approach used by, 443–447*fig*; Four Approaches to the Same Problem exercise on, 445–447*fig*; public service approach by, 444–445. *See also* Social innovation
Social entrepreneurship: add social value principle of, 166, 167, 172; building a better community center through, 451–452; business as part of the solution approach by, 443–447*fig*; comparing for-profit and nonprofit, 165–166; cultivate community ownership principle of, 166, 169, 172; description of, 147–148; Four Approaches to the Same Problem exercise on, 445–447*fig*; Home Water Filtration System case study on, 171–172; innovate to turn problem into an opportunity principle of, 166, 167–168; key components of, 447–450, 452–455; making a profit and a difference with, 170*fig*; the Method in action using, 193–194; modern emergence and importance of, 455; Muhammad Yunus case study of, 450; solve problems with business principles for, 166, 168–169, 172. *See also* Fundraising
Social entrepreneurship components: accountability, 447; disruption, 447, 448, 449–452; scaling, 150–155, 190–191, 447, 454–455
Social good accountability, 452–453

Social innovation: The Big Picture Tutorial exercise on, 510; characteristics of, 110–111; defining, 112; description and force of, 6; gaining valuable experience in, 509–517; Mohammad Yunus' microcredit, 2, 167–169; reflection used for, 505; setting goals with impact and, 221; three causes of failed, 117; turning a problem into an opportunity with, 166, 167–168, 171–172; typical image of, 110; Understanding the Problem required for, 112–113. *See also* Innovate strategy; Social entrepreneurs; Social responsibility

Social media: activism promoted through, 298; Facebook, 117, 150, 192, 276*fig*–277, 298, 322; online branding through, 273–279; Twitter, 192, 277–278, 508. *See also* Media strategy

Social-networking sites: LinkedIn, 508; networking through the, 508; privacy warning when using, 509; YouTube, 65, 278, 279, 298. *See also* Facebook; Networking; Twitter

Social problems: access to health care system, 91–93; activism to solve, 280–298; designing a systemic solution for homelessness, 85–90; do what's right to help solve, 326–334; using partnerships to address complex nature of, 93. *See also* Case studies; Problems

Social progress: Do Good Well method of achieving, 7–8; Do Good Well Network role in, 9; examining the toolbox for achieving, 9; how the individual drives, 6–7; social innovation vehicle for, 6; as social responsibility goal, 5

Social responsibility: step 1: do your self-reflection homework, 506–507; step 2: know your opportunities, 507–509; step 3: gain valuable experience, 509–517; step 4: enjoy the journal, 417*fig*–518. *See also* Accountability; Social innovation

Social responsibility career: finding opportunities for action, 507–509; gaining valuable employment, internship, or volunteer experience in, 509–517; making a lifestyle out of a, 520–530; self-reflection required for, 506–507. *See also* Social change

Social responsibility era: catalysts of the, 1; grounded idealism of, 1; origins and development of the, 2–5; paradigm of the, 1–2; social innovation of the, 6; social progress of the, 5–9

Social responsibility experience: The Big Picture Tutorial exercise on gaining, 510; employment, internship, or volunteer work for, 509–517; exploring options for gaining, 509; making it a lifestyle, 520–530

Social responsibility lifestyle: act with purpose, 522, 526; Articulate Your Values exercise on, 527; embrace grounded idealism for, 1, 520–521; find a balance, 521; Improve Your Daily Schedule exercise on, 523; leave a legacy of your, 529–530; Self-Assessment of Current Lifestyle and Goals exercise on, 524–525; values driving your, 527–529

Social value principle, 166, 167, 172

SocialVest, 526

Socrates, 505

Solutions: asking a question to find effective, 96; beginning to brainstorm possible, 68–70; combining strategies to create the most effective, 92–93; community participatory approach to, 431; using data to guide your actions toward a, 223; define what works, 95–96; designing a systemic, 85–93, 181–182; distinguishing an idea from a, 68; do what's right to find, 326–334; Drylands Natural Resource Center case study on finding a, 76–79; encouraging ownership of the, 137; engineering self-sustainable, 147–148, 156–164, 192, 436–437; get the community perspective on the, 132–133; improve on what works, 98; learn what works, 96–98; narrowing down the options, 73–75; political campaign platform that identifies potential, 320; social entrepreneurship use of business as part of the, 443–447; Whiteboard Brainstorming exercise to find a, 71–72. *See also* Problem solving

SOS (Office of Secretary of the State), 490, 496

South Asian Community Health Project, 260

Spielberg, Steven, 339

Sri Lanka: the Method in action helping women to be financially independent in, 181–195; sexual violence against women problem in, 180–181

Srinivasan, Divya, 428

Staff development program, 504

Stakeholders: activism pitch to powerful, 285–286; developing relationships with local community, 435; engaging in problem solving, 66; leadership transition of relationships with, 472; town hall brainstorming with, 73, 78. *See also* Community

STAND, 131

Stanford Social Innovation Review, 175

Stanford University's prisoner/guards study, 333

Starbucks, 150

Start Small, Then Scale What Works strategy: assessing supply and demand, 154–155; choosing quality good work over quantity, 155; description of, 147, 149–150; Gay-Straight Alliance Network case study on, 153; keep a written record of what didn't work, 154; the Method in action using, 190–191; scale deep versus scale out, 152–153; scaling what works, 150–151*fig*

Starting (your own group): advantages of, 123–124; balancing strengthening by joining a group against, 125*fig*; caution regarding your motivation for, 126; disadvantages of, 124; striking a balance between strengthening and, 127

State grants, 247

Statement of purpose, 254

Story/storytelling, 282–283

"Street activism," 291–293

Strengthening (joining established group): advantages of, 122–123; balancing starting your own group against, 125*fig*; disadvantages of, 123; striking a balance between starting and, 127

Strengths and weaknesses: knowing your own, 25; My Strengths and Weaknesses exercise on, 26–27

Student-based funding, 234

Students for Choose, 204

Succession: being a resource while allowing successor to move on, 474–475; planning and recruiting your successor, 470–471; transfer of knowledge and relationships to successor, 471–474, 475*fig*

SugarSync, 363

Suicide: bullying associated with, 44; as common cause of death in the US, 38

Sullivan, Meg, 390, 399, 400, 401, 405

Supply and demand: Do they want what they have? for assessing, 154–155; Do we have what they need? for assessing, 155

SurveyMonkey.com, 500

Sustainability. *See* Self-sustainable solutions
Sweatshops, 42
Syano, Nicholas, 77, 79
Symposia, 416–417
Synergy (Harvard College), 349
Systemic solutions. *See* Design a Systemic Solution strategy

T

Tabachnick, Lexie, 390, 394, 400, 405
TakingITglobal.org, 175, 177
Tax status. *See* 501(c)(3) nonprofit organization
Taylor, Chas, 76–79
Teach for America (TFA), 2, 150, 201, 418
Team building: step 1: identify your needs, 350–351, 353; step 2: start with who you already have, 353; step 3: select a team structure, 353–354; step 4: recruit team members, 354–357; step 5: interview, 357–358; step 6: hire, 358–359
Team Building: Proven Strategies for Improving Team Performance (Dyer, Dyer, and Dyer), 360
Team communication: be a leader rather than dictator during, 375–377; creating a collaborative environment through, 381–384; damage of mixed messages in, 374; determining what's effective, 384–385; identifying key points of, 374–375; maintaining a unified front during, 374; during team meetings, 377–381; two-way, 376
Team leaders: identifying team needs, 350–353; interviewing candidates, 357–358; issues when working with friends, 365–371; Leading Questions: Improving Your Leadership Skills exercise for, 368; leading team communication tips for, 375–377; making leaders of others trait of great, 354; recruiting team members, 354–357; succession planning by, 470–471. *See also* Leadership; Transitional leadership
Team library, 504
Team management: build team synergy, 359–360; community ownership by building and, 435–436; create safe environment, 360; provide opportunities and reward achievements, 360–361; providing productive feedback, 363–365; recalibrating team when necessary, 371–372; of a remote team, 363; set ground rules and expect growing pains, 361; Team Toxins exercise for, 363; when working with friends, 365–371
Team meetings: agendas for effective, 377–379; engaging your audience during, 380–381; keeping accurate records of, 379–380; sample meeting minutes, 379–380
Team member friendships: authority issue of, 369; bring out the best in others, 366; build on the strengths of your, 369–370; communication component of, 370; issues to consider in case of, 365–366; Leading Questions: Improving Your Leadership Skills exercise for, 368; navigating friendships as team leader, 366, 367*fig*; opportunity for learning and building on your, 370–371; providing honest feedback regardless of, 369; recognize boundaries, 366; reflection: improve relationships and, 500, 501–503*fig*; treat all team members equally regardless of, 366. *See also* Relationships
Team members: assessing work styles of individual, 351–352; hiring new, 358–359; interviewing potential, 357–358; leadership transition of relationships with, 471–474; providing position description to, 356–357; recruitment of, 354–357; talent mismatch of, 458–459; Team Toxins exercise to prevent problems among, 362; when to add or remove, 371–372; working with friends who are, 365–371
Team Toxins exercise, 362
"Team toxins" feedback, 363–364
Team unity: bring out the best in others for, 138–139; encourage ownership of the solution for, 137; facilitate quality communication for, 137–138; increasing team efficacy through, 136*fig*; nurture a sense of community for, 135–137
Teams: building a, 350–359; building knowledge and learning of, 500, 504; building mentoring, 338–339; causes of declining vitality of, 456–459; incorporating reflection in your, 500–504; leadership transition of relationships and knowledge of, 471–474; providing productive feedback to members of, 363–365; recalibrating your, 371–372; structures of, 353–354, 355*fig*; sustaining a, 359–363; Team Toxins exercise, 363; working with friends who are on the, 365–371. *See also* Boards; Collective action
TED: Technology, Entertainment, Design, 201
TED talks, 501
Television: fashion for women and men on, 268–269; giving interviews on, 267–268
Television watching, 65
Ten People I Admire exercise, 24–25
Ten-Step Plan to Revitalization, 462–486
Ten Things I Value exercise, 20–21
Ten Things I'm Grateful For exercise, 18–19
Ten Words That Describe Me exercise, 15–16
Tertiary prevention, 91
Test driving ideas, 116
Testifying: activism promoted through, 285–288; forums for, 285–286; sample testimony, 287–288
Thinking: designing a systemic solution by expanding your, 85; as one of the five skills of innovators, 114; Thinking Critically about Community Ownership exercise on, 432
TimeBridge, 383
The Tipping Point (Gladwell), 351
Tobacco addiction, 38, 39
Today Show (TV morning news), 267–268
Torture, 42–43
Town hall brainstorming, 73, 78
Trackable goals, 221
Tracking ideas, 504
Trade Name Registration form, 490
Transforming partnerships, 404–405
Transgender Law Center, 203
Transgendered population. *See* LGBT community
Transitional leadership: bringing in a new beginning through, 478; Do What Works; Work Together; Make It Last tenets of, 478; three steps of, 470–477. *See also* Leadership; Team leaders
Transitional leadership steps: step 1: select your successor, 470–471; step 2: transfer knowledge and relationships, 471–474; step 3: move on, 474–477
Transitional Leadership strategy: building institutional knowledge through, 159–160; Devise a Leadership Transition Strategy exercise, 476; importance during organization change, 469–470; for transferring institutional

memory, 475*fig*; Work through a Difficult Transition Process exercise, 476–477
Transparency: organizational vitality decline due to lack of, 457; revitalization efforts, 465; Right action principle of, 329
Treatment: combined strategies available for cancer, 92; designing systematic solutions that address, 91–92
Troubleshooting partnerships, 403
True North (George), 347
Tumblr, 499
Twitter: activism through, 298; maintaining an active presence through, 192; online branding using, 277–278; tips for using, 508. *See also* Social-networking sites
Two-way communication, 376
Tyle, Sheel, 144
Tyle, Sujay, 337, 347, 349

U

Understanding the Problem: get the community perspective on, 132–133; process of, 57–66; required for innovation, 112–113. *See also specific case study*
Unemployment: increasing rates of U.S., 40–41; poverty relationship to, 40–41; racial and ethnic disparity in rates of, 32. *See also* Employment
Unite for Sight's Global Health and Innovation Conference, 174
United Nations: Agriculture Organization report (2010) on hunger by, 40; Millennium Development Goal of, 39, 40, 42; Universal Declaration of Human Rights (1948) of the, 33; US Guantanamo Bay facility condemned by the, 43
United Negro College Fund, 202
United States: diagnosable mental disorders in population of the, 38; disability rights in the, 31; educational issues in the, 33–35; food insecurity experienced in, 40; Guantanamo Bay facility of the, 43; increasing rates of unemployment in the, 40–41; LGBT rights in the, 31–32; suicide rates in the, 38
United States legislation: Americans with Disability Act, 31; California Student Safety and Violence Prevention Act, 153; First Amendment, 32–33, 41; on hate crimes, 44–45; Second Amendment, 44
United Way, 225
Universal Declaration of Human Rights (1948), 33
University-based funding, 234
University of Michigan Law School, 43
University of Mississippi's National Center for Physical Acoustics, 99
University of Pennsylvania's Engineers Without Borders case study, 162–164
University of Virginia, 76
Upstream causes/effects, 87–88
US Agency for International Development, 511
US Campaign Against Commercial Sexual Exploration of Children, 127
U.S. Department of Agriculture's Economic Research Service report (2010), 40
US Equal Employment Opportunity Commission, 31
US Fish and Wildlife Foundation, 496
US Naval Academy, 99, 100
US Substance Abuse and Mental Health Services Administration, 101
USASpending.gov, 246
USS Jimmy Carter, 99

V

Values: act with purpose based on your, 522; Articulate Your Values exercise on, 527; identifying what you, 19; social change driven by, 527–529; Ten Things I Value exercise on, 20. *See also* Ethical behavior
"Vanity metrics," 104
Venture capital funding: preference for C corporations by, 484; A Primer on Venture Capital for, 242–245
Vineyard, Sue, 231
Violence: abuse form of, 43; against women, 33; bullying, 32, 43–44; debate over gun control and, 44; gang, 44; hate crimes, 44–45
Vision: example of revitalization, 463*t*–464*t*; figure out your group, 215*fig*; mission statement versus, 212–213. *See also* Mission statements
Volunteer work: The Big Picture Tutorial exercise on, 510; domestic versus international, 512–513; gaining experience through, 509, 515*fig*; how to select issue and enterprise for your, 511; leadership skills development through, 516–517; a note about funding your, 515
Voters: brainstorming ideas that serve the need of, 320; learning about priorities and problems of, 319
Voting: activism through, 294; with your wallet, 296

W

Warren, Scott, 131–132
Watching television/computer screen, 65
Weaknesses and strengths: knowing your own, 25; My Strengths and Weaknesses exercise on, 26–27
WeAreWhatWeDo.org, 522
Weaver, Trent B., 374, 385
Web of Knowledge, 65
Websites: basic components that belong on your, 273–275; conference, 414; creating a, 273–275; donation section of your, 275; logo on your, 273. *See also* Internet
Weitzel, Sloan, 363
Welcker, Kelydra, 171–172
Whac-a-Mole school of problem solving, 90
Wheatley, Margaret, 134
Whistle-blowers, 331
White House Office of Social Innovation and Civic Participation, 4
Whiteboard brainstorming, 70, 78
Whiteboard Brainstorming exercise, 71–72
Whitney-Johnson, Alia: Emerge Global founded by, 179; the Method in action by, 179–185; personal and professional background of, 195
Whittemore, Nathaniel, 207, 218, 412, 414, 417
Whiz Kids (documentary), 171
Wikipedia, 62
Wiley, David, 176
Winter, Amos, 178
Women: fashion for television, 268–269; female genital mutilation of, 33; honor killing of, 33; the Method in action helping sexual abuse victim, 180–195; reproductive rights of, 42; rights of, 33
Wordle, 499–500*fig*
WordPress, 499

Work styles: "connector" (bringing in the right players), 351; How to Evaluate Working Styles exercise on, 352; "maven" (gathering and sharing information), 351; "salesperson" (building shared vision), 351
Work through a Difficult Transition Process exercise, 476–477
Work Together step: Balance Strengthening and Starting strategy, 119–120, 121–127, 187–188; Cultivate Community Ownership strategy, 120, 128–134, 188–189; Forge Partnerships strategy, 120, 140–146, 190; Foster Team Unity strategy, 120, 135–139, 189; the Method in action using the, 187–190; overview of the, 8, 81, 119–120; reflection: improve relationships between team members using the, 500, 501–503*fig*; as transitional leadership tenet, 478. *See also* Do Good Well method
Working Together: A Continuum, 145*fig*
World Bank report (2012), 39
World Economic downturn (late 2000s–present), 4
World Health Organization, 181, 285, 518
Writing for Community Success, 260
Wrongful imprisonment, 42–43
WuDunn, Sheryl, 3

Y

Yammer, 504
YouTube: activism through, 298; creating an online brand through, 278; gaining supporters through, 279; informative content found on, 65
Yunus, Mohammad, 2, 167–169, 450

Z

Zachary, Lois, 348
Zimbardo, Philip, 333
Zoughbie, Daniel, 434–435, 435, 437, 441